BROTHER XII

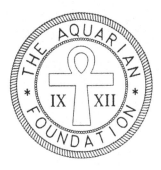

BROTHER XII

The Strange Odyssey of a 20th-Century Prophet

John Oliphant

Twelfth House Press
Halifax, Nova Scotia

Library and Archives Canada Cataloguing in Publication

Oliphant, John (date)
Brother XII: the strange odyssey of a 20th-century prophet
John Oliphant
Includes index
ISBN 0-9780972-0-3

Previously published under title
Brother Twelve: the incredible story of Canada's false prophet

1. Brother XII, 1878-1934. 2. Cults—British Columbia—Vancouver Island—
History. 3. Theosophists—British Columbia—Vancouver Island—Biography.
4. Imposters and imposture—British Columbia—
Vancouver Island—Biography. 1. Title.

CT9981.B76O45   2006 229'.934092   C2006-902882-6

Book Design by Brian Charles & John Oliphant
Maps by James Loates
Printed and bound in Canada
The text of this book has been printed on acid-free paper

Twelfth House Press
Box 27055
5595 Fenwick Street
Halifax, Nova Scotia
Canada B3H 4M8

This book is dedicated to
Margery Ellen Bell
with gratitude

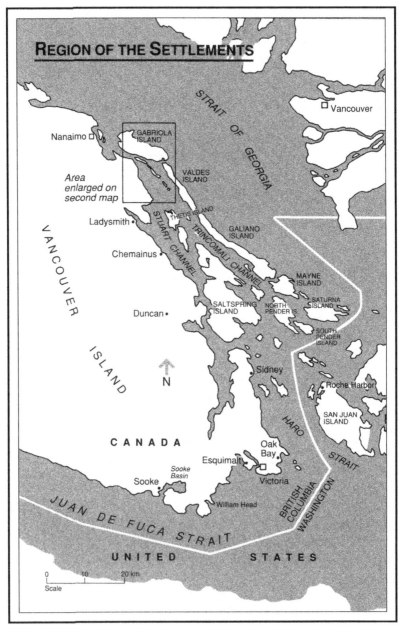

REGION OF THE SETTLEMENTS

Vancouver Island, British Columbia: the geographic region that Brother XII predicted would become "THE Center of spiritual energy and knowledge for the whole continent of North America—for the whole world in the not distant future."

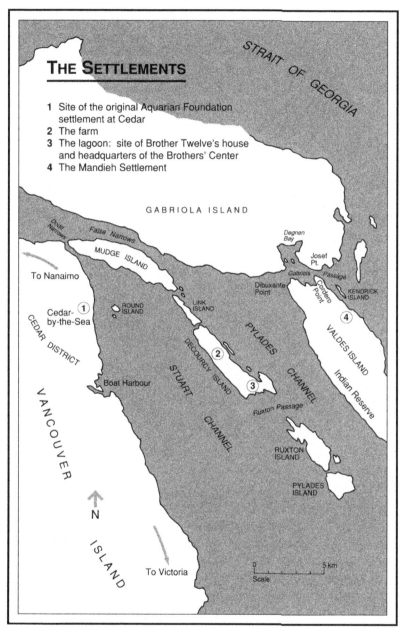

THE SETTLEMENTS

1 Site of the original Aquarian Foundation
  settlement at Cedar
2 The farm
3 The lagoon: site of Brother Twelve's house
  and headquarters of the Brothers' Center
4 The Mandieh Settlement

STRAIT OF GEORGIA

GABRIOLA ISLAND

Dodd Narrows

False Narrows

MUDGE ISLAND

Degnen Bay

Josef Pt.

To Nanaimo

Gabriola Passage

Dibuxante Point

Cordero Point

KENDRICK ISLAND

Cedar-by-the-Sea   ①

CEDAR DISTRICT

ROUND ISLAND

LINK ISLAND

④

VALDES ISLAND

DECOURCY ISLAND

PYLADES

②

Indian Reserve

Boat Harbour

STUART CHANNEL

③

CHANNEL

VANCOUVER

Ruxton Passage

RUXTON ISLAND

ISLAND

N

PYLADES ISLAND

To Victoria

0   5 km
Scale

Brother XII's domain comprised over 1,200 acres in the picturesque
Gulf Islands of British Columbia.

Contents

Once more I stand upon the Earth,
Upright, in human form, and upon my own feet,
I give you greeting, O Earth,
Even as before—many times before –
I have greeted you.
How firm thou art, how solid!
It is good to know thee again,
Linked to a body made of thy body,
Articulate, breathing,
Responding to thy pulsings,
Interlinked, interleaved, interwoven;
Ordained to serve the needs of men. . .

Foundation Letters and Teachings

Acknowledgments

This book would not have been possible without the assistance of many individuals who contributed to its creation. I would especially like to thank Edward Arthur Wilson's daughter, Margery Ellen Bell, for graciously sharing childhood memories of her father, and for the spirit in which she was willing to accept both the deeds and misdeeds of a man she never really knew. Her friendship and encouragement have been deeply gratifying.

I would also like to thank those former adherents and associates of Brother XII who kindly shared details of their experiences at the settlement; in particular, Eric Davenport, Frances Lucas, Herbert Jefferson, Alice Rudy, Dion Sepulveda, Valea Sepulveda, and the numerous others whose accounts of events were so essential to the narrative.

In Nanaimo, Stan Wardill was a cheerful source of information, as were the residents of Cedar-by-the-Sea, especially George and Dolly Hygh, and John and Phyllis Murdoch. Donald M. Cunliffe generously provided material from his father's legal files, including the Robert England letter that is quoted in Chapter Five.

I owe a debt of gratitude to Katherine McKelvie, widow of Bruce McKelvie, for sharing the Brother XII material that her husband had collected over the years. Harry Olsen and Cecil Clark also provided valuable information. Ted Davy, former General Secretary of the Theosophical Society in Canada and editor of *The Canadian Theosophist*, read the manuscript and offered important suggestions. In addition, the members of *The Secret Doctrine* class at Hermes Lodge in Vancouver made me welcome and helped me in my study of Theosophy, so vital to an understanding of Brother XII's beliefs and activities. The Lodge library was a rich source of information and a sanctuary at times from the outside world.

For both advice and assistance during the course of the project, I would particularly like to acknowledge Laura Anderson, Rick Baker, Vaughn Barclay, Morris Berman, Christopher Fortune, Neil Gilchrist, Erich Hoyt, Mark Laughlin, Adelle LaRouche, Esther Luk, Elliott McLaughlin, Corrine Nishi, Margaret Prang, James Santucci, Marion Van Berckel, Peter Vatcher, David Watmough, and George Woodcock. I would also like to thank Sheila Smyth, who played a critical role in shaping the manuscript in its early stages, and Pohsuan Zaide, whose perceptive editing contributed significantly to the final draft of the book.

To Douglas Gibson of McClelland & Stewart, I express my appreciation and respect. He believed in the book from its inception and guided it through its successive incarnations. Lynn Schellenberg was a skillful and insightful editor whose sense of humour and positive attitude made her a pleasure to work with. Literary agent Daniel Strone recognized the potential of the project and was an invaluable ally throughout. I'm also grateful to the Canada Council for its generous support, particularly to Richard Holden, and to the Ontario Arts Council for some timely funding.

And finally, I would like to thank my parents, Alice and Colin Oliphant, for their steadfast support throughout the duration of this project, although I'm sure they must have often despaired of losing their son to Brother XII. To all who had a part in the making of this book, my sincere thanks.

Preface

British Columbia's Gulf Islands, nestled along the eastern coastline of Vancouver Island, are renowned for their rugged natural beauty and Mediterranean climate, yet they're noteworthy for another reason as well—their lonely shores and secluded inlets are haunted by the spirit of a notorious cult leader known as Brother XII. The tales of gold, sex and black magic associated with his dictatorial reign over his island kingdom have gripped people's imaginations for years, though when I first learned of the story little was known about the man beyond the outlines of the legend that had sprung up around him and his flamboyant mistress, a whip-wielding devotee of ritual magic with the pulp-fiction name of Madame Z.

Intrigued by the tale, I set out to learn all that I could about Brother XII. In the years that followed, I tracked down and interviewed surviving disciples, located rare documents that shed unprecedented light on the events that transpired at his Aquarian Foundation, and investigated the mystery surrounding his death in Switzerland. In one case, an important cache of material in the possession of his former lawyer was destroyed in a fire only six months after I had photocopied it;

otherwise, key elements of the story would have been lost forever. I also travelled to New Zealand to meet with his daughter, our encounter being one of the highlights of my research. Eventually, I assembled the scattered pieces of an elaborate jigsaw puzzle, discovering in the process that the inscrutable figure at the heart of the mystery was far more fascinating, complex and significant than anyone had ever realized.

Brother XII: The Strange Odyssey of a 20th-century Prophet chronicles the life and exploits of Edward Arthur Wilson, an individual who has largely fallen through the cracks of history. In a sense, Brother XII, as Wilson called himself, was slighted by history, for though the lives of other occult figures have been extensively documented, his was not. He shunned the spotlight, seldom allowing himself to be photographed and resisting any cult of personality from forming around him. His relative obscurity may also be attributed to the remote location where he established his self-sufficient community, a locale that he believed would survive the coming conflagration so graphically depicted in his apocalyptic writings. Still, Brother XII cast a long shadow across the occult world in his time, bursting into prominence in the mid-to-late-1920s and becoming a controversial figure for his incendiary diatribes and his claim to be the Messenger of an ancient mystical Brotherhood known as the Great White Lodge. The grandiose nature of his mission and the bizarre and sensational events that characterized his career were such that if his life were to be a movie, it would be a *Gone With the Wind* of the occult, a sweeping saga featuring both the sacred and profane. Though other occult figures may be better known, for sheer drama, nothing rivals the story of Brother XII.

Wilson was a born mystic in touch with the spirit world from an early age. He was raised in a deeply religious atmosphere, delved deeply into the occult sciences, and traveled the world as a mariner while in search of esoteric knowledge. He had a profound understanding of metaphysics and prepared himself assiduously for a spiritual Work that he believed would alter the course of history. In 1924, he experienced an Egyptian initiation in the south of France followed by a period of inspirational writing, during which the teachings of the new spiritual movement were transmitted to him. Adopting the name Brother XII, he rapidly recruited thousands to his cause. Intensely charismatic, he was regarded as an Initiate by his adherents and was undoubtedly a megalomaniac driven to pursue a destiny of which few men would dare to dream.

Brother XII possessed genuine occult power, perhaps more than anyone in modern history, with the possible exception of Rasputin. In the fall of 1928, hauled into court in Nanaimo, British Columbia, by disaffected members of his organization, he unleashed a potent and withering psychic assault against his adversaries, knocking out a key witness and an opposing attorney, even toppling innocent bystanders, collateral damage in the onslaught. The powers that he demonstrated in this instance and on other occasions are the sine qua non of every bona fide occult leader, and though others claim to have such abilities or grandiloquently posture their prowess in these realms, Brother XII possessed this power in spades. For this reason alone, he deserves to be regarded as one of the most important occult figures of the past century.

Brother XII had a knack for extracting large sums of money from his disciples. In 1928, after only a three-hour meeting in a Toronto hotel, a North Carolina socialite named Mary Connally wrote a cheque to him for $23,000, a sum equivalent to $320,000 today, while a year later, Roger Painter, the "Poultry King of Florida" handed over $90,000 when he arrived at Brother XII's City of Refuge, over $1,250,000 in today's currency. The guru who urged his followers to renounce their personal possessions eventually fled with at least $400,000, equivalent to over seven million dollars today. By comparison, Bonnie and Clyde, ambushed on a dusty back road in Louisiana in 1934, died with $500 on their bullet-ridden bodies, whereas Brother XII and Madame Z, outlaws of a different order and inclination, escaped unscathed with almost a thousand times that amount.

A former sea-captain, Brother XII was a pirate at heart, for he raided rival groups for members and brought a swashbuckling swagger to the staid world of the occult. He proclaimed a doctrine of universal brotherhood, yet could be cruel and vindictive, making all those who opposed him walk the plank. He was both a forerunner of the New Age and a prototypical cult leader, the classic rogue messiah, a Nietzschean figure who sought to single-handedly reshape the world according to his vision and reclaim an absolute spiritual and temporal power that he believed he'd wielded in a previous lifetime. He had a meteoric career, burning out before his ambitions could be realized, leaving considerable human wreckage in his wake; even so, he can be reckoned among those 20th-century occultists who have exerted a profound though often unacknowledged influence in shaping the culture and beliefs of our time.

Since the publication of the original edition of this book, *Brother Twelve: The Incredible Story of Canada's False Prophet,* the number of Internet sites, blog entries, articles, commentaries, books and other materials devoted to various aspects of Brother XII's life has steadily increased. In addition, his writings are starting to reappear in print. *Foundation Letters and Teachings* has been republished by Teitan Press, while a collection of letters that Wilson wrote as a young man was published in the January, 2012 edition of *Theosophical History.* The former presents Brother XII in his own words as both inspired mystic and implacable critic of Western civilization, while the latter reveal a self-doubt and vulnerability that is in striking contrast to the armored invincibility of Brother XII, and indicate that Wilson indeed underwent a profound transformation at a critical juncture in his life.

Brother XII's career stands as a sobering reminder that one must beware of false prophets and fraudulent spiritual teachers, though the eternal truths that lie at the heart of his teachings still resonate today. "My work will live," he defiantly declared while being attacked by his enemies. His prediction may well come true, though it seems more likely that the myth that has grown up around him is what will endure. For all that is known about him, Brother XII remains an enigma, the ultimate man of mystery, an elusive figure who will never be fully understood, but who deserves his own special place in history.

John Oliphant
January 5, 2016

Foreword
by Colin Wilson

When John Oliphant first told me about Brother
XII—in Seattle in 1988—I was amused and greatly
intrigued. One of my favourite books has always
been Martin Gardner's *Fads and Fallacies in the Name of Science*,
full of uproarious accounts of cranks who believe the earth is
flat or hollow, or that God encoded his secrets in the Great
Pyramid. It sounded as if Brother XII deserved a distinguished
place in this gallery of monomaniacs and self-deceivers. Which
is why I immediately agreed to write a foreword to this book,
sight unseen.

A few weeks later, when I was back in Cornwall, John sent me
a copy of Brother XII's *Unsigned Letters from an Elder Brother*,
reprinted in 1979 by Aura Press of Montreal. Its first page re-
inforced my impression that Edward Wilson was a religious
nut with an exalted sense of his own importance. He begins
by demanding that his disciples should renounce all other
teachers and schools while under his guidance—another way
of demanding that they should cease to think for themselves—
then goes on to stake his own claim to uniqueness: "Most
of you have learned from past experience something of this

1

business of seeking knowledge; you have sought much and gained little; have found platitudes and moralisings, the out-worn and the threadbare, under a slightly differing form of words. The world is filled with make-believe teachers and the various cults they represent. Having sampled them, you should know their worth or their worthlessness." He then goes on to describe himself as an initiate and one of the Illuminati. . .

Yet within the next few pages, the Elder Brother began to hold my attention with assertions that made good sense. He begins by emphasizing the importance of the will in achieving "true knowledge"; this immediately distinguishes him from the religious cranks who ramble on about man's hopeless wickedness, and the need for surrender to the will of God. He then asserts that the beginning of "the work" depends on the transference of the center of consciousness from "the visible to the invisible, from the phenomenal to the real." Having said which, he makes it clear that he is not speaking about the need to believe a dozen impossible things before breakfast, but about the need to escape our restricted human viewpoint, and to take a broader and more scientific view, like that of someone who recognizes that, in spite of all appearances, the earth is not flat. He emphasizes, rightly, that this process calls for courage and perseverance. And when he goes on to speak about love, he shows the same oddly down-to-earth approach, emphasizing that it should be recognized as the fundamental creative force of the universe. He even quotes Ouspensky's early masterpiece *Tertium Organum*, which made such an impact in the 1920s because of its scientific approach to prob-lems of "the mystical."

Quite clearly, then, this man was no imposter, no "religious caterpillar," setting out to deceive the gullible with the usual vaporous generalizations. He possessed some degree of real knowledge. Then how had he turned into the vindictive and homicidal messiah that John Oliphant had described to me?

I had to wait another year to find out. And when, at last, the bulky typescript arrived in the post, I was at first intimidated by its sheer size—like most writers, I have only a limited time for reading. (Middleton Murry once said he couldn't afford to read a book unless he wrote one.) But when I finally settled down to it, I found myself totally absorbed. Long before I was halfway through, I was convinced that John Oliphant has written a book that will become a classic of its kind. I know of no more fascinating or better researched study of a "false messiah."

In fact, it was all so readable and informative that I found myself wondering what I could possibly say in a foreword that would not spoil the reader's pleasure by "giving away the plot." And it was not until I came to the very final pages (after a non-stop session of about six hours) that I saw the answer. John Oliphant has learned all the important facts about the "religious mission" of Brother XII. But he is unable to tell us some of the things that we would most like to know—things we could only learn if Edward Wilson had written an autobiographical work like the journals of George Fox. James Wilkie, the contemporary psychic who has the last word in the book, drops a hint of the kind of thing I would love to know. "In his youth, he was a restless soul. He had terrible depressions. He was in contact with forces he had to obey; he knew he couldn't lead a normal life. There was a time when he lived alone, completely isolated—he wanted no contact with a human being, I feel that when he was young he was more pure, more ordained psychically and spiritually."

This, of course, is why I found Wilson so fascinating—I had immediately recognized him as one of those curious, anomalous figures to whom I had devoted my first book, *The Outsider.* "Outsiders" are anomalous because it is so easy to jump to obvious conclusions about them, and dismiss them simply as cranks or psychotics. Nietzsche and Nijinsky went insane; van Gogh had a nervous breakdown and committed suicide; Dostoyevsky's most distinguished contemporaries dismissed him as hopelessly morbid (Tolstoy called him "the hospital muse"). But George Fox, the founder of the Quakers, went to the heart of the matter when he wrote: "I saw Professors and priests and people who were whole and at ease in that condition that was my misery, and they loved that which I would have been rid of. . ." Such men are "outsiders" because they are tormented by an urge to "self surmounting" that most people see as a kind of neurotic egoism. The young Fox describes how "I went to another ancient priest at Mancetter in Warwickshire, and reasoned with him about the ground of despair and temptations, but he was ignorant of my condition and bade me take tobacco and sing psalms. . ."

It seems obvious that Edward Wilson was one of the same type as George Fox, and that his restless travels around the world were an attempt to find something that eluded him. One of the most important clues to his career as a "messiah" is the fact that his parents were "Irvingites." Edward Irving was a Scottish minister, born in 1792, who was appointed to the Caledonian Church in Hatton Garden in 1822. He was convinced that the Second Coming was imminent, and his congregation experienced violent transports of religious emotion comparable to the behaviour of teenage fans at modern pop concerts. In 1830, he began to offer up prayers for some miracle to attest the truth of his visions, and in the following year members of his congregation began "speaking in tongues"— in languages other than their own, sometimes gobbledegook, but not infrequently foreign languages with which they were unfamiliar. The "voices" told Irving that he had been chosen to be a new Isaiah, and that at the end of forty days, he would have the power to work miracles; but it failed to happen. In 1833 he was dismissed, and a year later died of tuberculosis.

Now in this, and in dozens of other such cases, the "rationalist" explanation of hysteria and delusions of grandeur simply fails to cover the facts. There can be no doubt that many of Irving's followers spoke in foreign languages they had never learned. What we are now dealing with is a phenomenon known to everyone who has taken the slightest interest in "Spiritualism." To those who find it vaguely repellent, Spiritualism sounds like a fabric of self-deception; yet there can be no doubt whatever that many of its phenomena are genuine, and that mediums very frequently contact "the dead"—or at least some disembodied entities other than themselves. Yet it is equally certain that a large number of these "communications" are simply not to be trusted; as G. K. Chesterton complained, "they tell lies."

Worse still, they can lead fairly sensible people into a morass of self-aggrandizement. I can cite one example from personal knowledge. A friend of mine—let us call him "L"— proved to be an exceptional "dowser." Not only was he able to detect underground water, but he could even detect faults in underground electric cables—thus saving Electricity Board engineers a great deal of wasted effort. He often came to stay with us, and spent a great deal of time with a pendulum in his hand, for example, testing food to find out whether it would be good for him. (The pendulum may swing in a circle for yes, and back and forth for no.) He also found that the pendulum could "answer" all kinds of other questions, such as the age of "standing stones," of which we have many in the southwest of England. But as the years went by, he became increasingly cranky. He finally died quite suddenly, and I learned the truth about those final years from his friend (and mine) Jan de Hartog, the Dutch novelist. Jan told me that, through his pendulum, "L" had become convinced that he was in touch with some great primeval goddess, and that she had chosen him as her representative on earth; he would perform miracles, and go down in history as the saviour of the human race. This sounds like straightforward delusions of grandeur; but Jan knew better. He himself had learned to use a pendulum at a dowsers' conference, and begun to obtain incredible information, all of it objectively verifiable. But one night, living alone in a cabin in a remote area, his pendulum told him that he was in contact with the Earth Goddess, and that she had selected him as her messenger. This went on for several days, and Jan was staggered at the information that was pouring into his head. One night, the goddess offered to give him definite proof of her reality. The next day, she said, when he was out riding with a group of other people, a girl's horse would stumble near a waterfall, and she would break her leg. The following day, the horses passed the waterfall without incident. That night, Jan asked the goddess, "What happened?" and she explained that, at the crucial moment, her mind had been distracted, so she had failed to make the horse stumble. Jan was appalled. "Do you mean to say you were going to make that girl break her leg, just to convince me?" The goddess replied that that was precisely her intention. Whereupon Jan announced that he had no desire to hear from her again; a goddess with such deficient notions of morality was clearly a liability. . . And this was more or less what had happened to our friend "L," except that he had remained convinced of his divine mission.

It has happened to many others, and caused varying degrees of havoc. In Cairo in March 1904, a student of "magick" named Aleister Crowley heard a voice speaking out of the air and dictating a "message for mankind." The result was a strange Swinburnian compilation called *The Book of the Law*, and to the end of his life, Crowley believed it was dictated by Aiwass, his Holy Guardian Angel. On the basis of this work, Crowley believed that he was the Christ of a new age, and that the era of Crowleyanity would soon replace Christianity throughout the world. But his "Guardian Angel" failed to live up to his promises; there were humiliations, defeats, scandals, court cases (which he lost), and finally a period of poverty and neglect, ending in his death in Hastings. Readers of this life of Brother XII will recognize the pattern.

The career of Rudolf Steiner also provides some interesting parallels. When Steiner delivered a series of lectures to the Berlin Theosophical Society in 1900, he was already well known as a Goethe scholar and the author of a number of books on philosophy. Like Brother XII, he admired Madame Blavatsky, and had already demonstrated that he possessed certain "paranormal" powers. Like Wilson, he deeply impressed the Theosophists, and soon became head of the German section. His own brand of Theosophy was rooted in Christian mysticism. His success was tremendous, and he soon became—what Wilson failed to become—a deeply influential force throughout pre-war Europe. He broke with the Society when British Theosophists tried to foist a boy called Jiddu Krishnamurti on them as the new messiah. Steiner went on to found a "spiritual centre" in Switzerland, around an impressive building called the Goetheanum, founded successful schools and clinics, and for a while looked set to become the most influential spiritual teacher of the twentieth century. He even set out—like Wilson—to exert political influence. But he was hated by Nazis and Communists alike, and after the Goetheanum was burned to the ground in 1922, he wore himself out with lectures and interviews with "disciples" needing advice. In 1924, exhausted and discouraged, he died of a stomach ailment, possibly cancer.

So there is, it seems, a certain risk attached to becoming a prophet and spiritual leader. Steiner was better able to cope with it than Crowley, because he seems to have been a genuinely decent and saintly man. Yet all these "avatars" seem to find themselves drawn into the same web of difficulty and compromise. The writer and the artist work alone, and try to project their vision through words or music or paint on canvas. "Teachers" who try to exert a direct influence on other people, to become gurus and messiahs, seem prone to "entanglement," to involvement with fools and timewasters, which often brings out the worst in them. Even when, like Steiner, they are too decent as human beings to succumb to power-mania or paranoia, they seem to find themselves in a trap that defies all attempts to escape.

So this, in a nutshell, is the tragedy of Edward Wilson. John Oliphant's account makes it clear that, at the beginning of his "mission," he was balanced, clear-sighted, and self controlled. My own guess is that he was a genuine "outsider" figure who had spent his life in a tortured quest for personal evolution. His stay in the village in the south of France brought some kind of "revelation." (Jung has described in his *Memories, Dreams, Reflections* how he had many "visions" like the one described in the first chapter.) He was obviously an intelligent and widely-read man, and I suspect that his dire prophecies of the end of civilization may have been inspired by Spengler's best-selling *The Decline of the West.* The story of how, in the face of all obstacles, he founded the colony on Vancouver Island forms one of the most remarkable chapters in this book.

What then went wrong? Was Wilson, like Crowley and so many other messiahs, something of a sex maniac? The evidence points in that direction. Yet I think the true answer is that, like my friend "L," he lacked the psychological stability to remain balanced and normal while leading the highly abnormal life of a "spiritual leader" and guru. Some readers may prefer Wilkie's explanation that "he worked with angels—spirits of all kinds—sometimes of a lower order. He drew radical earthbound souls to him." The strange episodes of "black magic" in the courtroom seem to support this view. But in the last analysis, the reader must make his own judgement. What is so fascinating about this book is that the author has provided all the necessary materials in abundance.

CHAPTER
I
Messenger of the Masters

O n a crisp autumn day in 1924, a forty-six-year-old retired English sea-captain named Edward Arthur Wilson arrived in a small village in the south of France. A slender man with delicate features, iron-grey hair, and a neatly trimmed Van Dyke beard, he had little money and was in poor health. He rented a room in a small *pension* and unpacked his bags. He planned to spend the winter in the village living as quietly and cheaply as possible.

Wilson's travels as a mariner had taken him to nearly every country in the world, allowing him to mix with people of all nationalities at every level of society. According to his own account, these outward travels corresponded to an inner journey—a long and arduous search for knowledge. During his pilgrimage, Wilson visited temples, shrines, and sacred sites in many countries, including Egypt, India, China, and Mexico. He studied the religions of the world, investigated numerous occult doctrines, and immersed himself in the teachings of Theosophy. He also practised various spiritual disciplines by which he achieved higher states of consciousness. Throughout these difficult, often lonely years, Wilson sustained himself by his belief that he had a mission to serve mankind, and that his studies and travels were preparing him for a unique spiritual destiny.

In October, shortly after arriving in the village, Wilson had a number of remarkable experiences which signalled the beginning of his career as a spiritual leader. He described these experiences in a letter, which was later published in his book *Foundation Letters and Teachings:*

> October 19, 1924, I was not feeling well, and had gone to bed early. At this time, I wanted to get some milk to drink, so I lit the candle which stood on a small table at the side of my bed. Immediately after lighting it, I saw the Tau suspended in mid-air just beyond the end of my bed, and at a height of eight or nine feet. I thought, "That is strange; it must be some curious impression upon the retina of the eye which I got by lighting the candle. I will close my eyes and it will then stand out more clearly."
>
> I shut my eyes at once, and *there was nothing there.* I opened them and saw the Tau in the same place, but much more distinctly; it was like soft golden fire, and it glowed with a beautiful radiance. This time, in addition to the Tau, there was a five-pointed Star very slightly below it, and a little to the right. Again I closed my eyes and there was nothing on the retina. Again I opened them and the vision was still there, but now it seemed to radiate fire. I watched it for some time, then it gradually dimmed and faded slowly from my sight.

The next day, Wilson recorded his interpretation of the vision: the Tau cross, more commonly known as the *ankh,* or Egyptian ansate cross, confirmed to him that his path to initiation was Egyptian. It also signified that the Mysteries of that ancient spiritual tradition were about to be restored to the modern world. The five-pointed star symbolized adeptship, that state of profound knowledge and insight towards which he'd been striving.

The next day, Wilson was walking in meditation, when he heard certain words repeated in his mind with startling force and insistence. He realized that these "passwords" were related to his vision of the night before, and he immediately returned to his room to write them down.

On October 22, Wilson had again gone to bed early, as he was not feeling well:

> Lying in the darkness and thinking of nothing in particular, I was suddenly aware of a most extraordinary stillness. My window was wide open, but all the usual night noises were silenced; there was not a rustle of a leaf, nor any movement of the air. Then I became aware, in some interior manner, that I was to hear a Voice, so I lay still and listened. Immediately, I had the sensation of looking down an immense vista of Time, a roofless corridor flanked with thousands and thousands of pillars. I seemed to be looking into both Time and Space at once.
>
> Then, from an immeasurable distance, came the Voice, faint but very clear and wonderfully sweet; it conveyed a sense of unutterable majesty and power. The bed shook, the room wherein I lay was shaken, and the very air throbbed and vibrated. I listened to the Voice, filled with a sense of its immense and awful distance. It said—

> "THOU WHO HAST WORN THE DOUBLE CROWN OF UPPER AND LOWER EGYPT, OF THE HIGH KNOWLEDGE AND THE LOW, HUMBLE THYSELF, PREPARE THY HEART, FOR THE MIGHTY ONES HAVE NEED OF THEE. THOU SHALT REBUILD, THOU SHALT RESTORE. THEREFORE, PREPARE THY MIND FOR THAT WHICH SHALL ILLUMINE THEE."

A cold wind blew down that enormous aisle of pillars; somewhere in the endless distance, lights seemed to move; then from above my head, the light flooded me so that the distance and the vistas were dissolved. Then the light faded and I lay still, filled with a sense of wonder and a great reverence.

Wilson realized that the Voice belonged to one of the Dhyanis, a group of powerful Egyptian dieties. "I knew that the time was near," he wrote.

The following year, Wilson had resumed his travels. In the lounges of ocean liners, in railway carriages, and in cheap boarding houses, he wrote feverishly as the vision of his destiny burned before him.

In September, 1925, he arrived in Genoa, Italy. In the eleven months since his visions in the south of France, he'd experienced a marked widening of his normal consciousness. Automatic writing, which he had practised only intermittently before, had now become a faculty he could activate at will. He began to go into a trance regularly in order to receive a book of spiritual teachings.

The book was dictated to him by a "Master of Wisdom," one of those highly evolved spiritual Beings who, according to Theosophical teaching, form an occult Brotherhood known as the Great White Lodge, said to guide the destiny of the human race.

Daily, throughout the fall and winter, Wilson received the pages of the manuscript, often in an out-of-body state. "During the writing of some parts of it," he later explained, "I was taken in the subtle body to a certain place, and there given some of the sentences word by word by the Master as in quiet conversation between two individuals—the whole of Part Three was given in that way."

Wilson finished the manuscript on February 13, 1926, and immediately wrote to one of his associates (the identity of his correspondents during this period has never been determined), telling him about the book:

"Three or four months ago, I commenced writing something quite out of the ordinary, a statement of the fundamental philosophy of life. When I commenced it, I did not at all realize its deep significance, though I was kept continually amazed at the wonderful beauty and the deep truths that were given to me. Every line is written from the higher mental plane. For hours at a time and for days in succession, I was rapt right out of the body—the mere writing of it is something I shall never forget. It is to be called *The Three Truths*."

The Three Truths was a commentary upon three truths basic to Theosophical teaching: namely, the unity of all life; the immortality of the soul; and the law of karma. Wilson stated that the failure of the human race to recognize these truths and to incorporate them into its scheme of life was responsible for the appalling conditions of the modern world:

"The 'civilized' nations of the world are now entering upon an era of destruction and chaos, but it is to be followed none the less surely by an era of reconstruction and progress. These three truths are, in themselves, that spiritual basis upon which the new order shall be built."

The Master who had dictated *The Three Truths* now revealed to Wilson that he'd chosen him to be his personal *chela* or disciple. Since the Master was the twelfth "Brother" in the Great White Lodge, he gave Wilson, as his disciple, the name "Brother XII." This relationship between Master and disciple was poetically expressed in the foreword to *The Three Truths*:

THE WORD OF THE MESSENGER

As Mercury dwelleth near the Sun, so I abide in the heart of my Lord. My feet run upon His errands, and by my mouth are His words spoken. Many are my journeys; I have sojourned in far countries and have crossed wide rivers. Many houses have I built and afterwards demolished, and now I have builded me yet another house in your midst, O ye sons of men.

I speak the words of Him Who hath sent me forth; He is the Guide, the Instructor, the Keeper of the Mysteries. His words are sure and fail not. He is the Lighter of Lamps in the Temple of the Most High. Ye are the Temples, and the lamp is the light of Truth within you. . .

I am the Messenger of the Fire, the Messenger of the Whirlwind, the Messenger of the Day of Adjustment. By the Wind ye shall mount to the heavens—if ye be the children of discernment. . . But as for the stubborn, and the deaf, and the blind; the Wind of Destruction shall carry them away.

For the next several weeks, Wilson remained in continuous contact with his Master. He learned that he'd been chosen to carry forward the work of that earlier Messenger of the Great White Lodge, Madame Helena Petrovna Blavatsky, a remarkable Russian mystic and seer who'd founded the Theosophical Society in 1875, and whose works *Isis Unveiled* and *The Secret Doctrine* are regarded as occult classics. The Society was now in crisis: it had split into warring factions and its leaders were thought by many to have betrayed the ideals of its founders. Wilson's Master explained that the same Masters who had inspired Madame Blavatsky to found the Theosophical Society now wished to do a further Work in the world, and had chosen him to be their agent. His role in their multifaceted plan was to revive the original teachings so that Universal Brotherhood would become a living spiritual reality in the world.

On March 6, 1926, Wilson emerged from isolation to write: "At last I permit myself the luxury of a personal letter; I can relax. For twenty days, I have simply been the mouthpiece of the Master, and have rigorously excluded every personal thought or expression. Even as I write these words, you cannot yet know anything of the great Work which has been committed to us, save it be by intuition. You can as yet know nothing of the far-reaching plans for the future, and the wonderful rapidity with which they have developed. . ."

For the next three months, Wilson continued to receive detailed information about this new spiritual work. It would be organized around a group of "Brothers" who would serve as the nucleus for attracting like-minded people to the cause. The constitution of this inner group was of vital importance:

"Those who compose it will form collectively the Chalice into which the life of the Master will be poured. The Water of Life will take its colour from the vessel which contains it. That vessel must be clean, utterly free from the stain of selfishness or of ambition. Its purity must be most jealously guarded."

The Work would mark the advent of a new Age in the history of mankind:

In the great cycle of precession, the Pisces Age has ended, the sign of water and blood has set, and AQUARIUS RISES—the mighty triangle of Air is once more in the ascendant. In January of 1928, our work commences on the physical plane—the special work of restoration. Jupiter, lord of the great religions of the world, passes *out of Pisces* and comes to the conjunction of Uranus in the sign of Aries. That which seems immovable shall be destroyed, so that no vestige of it shall remain. The Star of Jehovah, the god of Israel and Christendom sets—and it sets in a sea of blood. Rejoice my Brothers, for the Great Gods, the Mighty Ones, shall be made manifest before the eyes of all men.

Wilson was aware that people might be skeptical of his claims, but this didn't concern him:

"The world will say, 'This man is mad,' but it has always said so of all who departed from its miserable conventionalities. Moses, Gideon, the Baptist—all were mad. Jesus was mad; of Him they said, 'He hath a devil.' Savonarola, Galileo, H. P. Blavatsky—all were mad in the opinion of the mediocre; mad or inspired. I also am mad—or inspired—but I am not mediocre. That within me has overcome sickness, and bonds, and a weak body. Make no mistake, Brothers, I am not a person filled with power, but *a Power* using a personality."

And again: "The hour has struck for this Earth to be plowed and harrowed. I have been called to drive the plow, to break the crust and to harrow the surface. You must choose whether you will be the plowshare or the clod which is broken, for the ground must be prepared that the seed may be sown."

Wilson saw himself as "a voice crying in the wilderness." He didn't care if others echoed him or cried him down, so long as he could give his message:

"While none amongst us may claim the title of leader, yet in time of crisis, one must spring to the front and thrust his body into the breach. Let that sacrifice be mine. . . I will declare the Truth, and will carry out exactly and precisely the Master's word. Neither now nor at any time, will I swerve a hair's-breadth from the course laid down. What He commands, that will I do."

During this period, Wilson received what would become the manifesto of the new spiritual movement. It was a 4,000 word "blueprint" of the Work, and was simply titled *A Message from the Masters of the Wisdom in* 1926. His Master assured him that the response to it would be overwhelming and that it would "sweep across the world like a prairie fire."

The intensive work, however, was taxing Wilson's already frail health. In one of his letters, he explained that he had to "live almost constantly in the pure and immensely powerful vibrations of His [the Master's] immediate aura. This is a great strain upon the lower vehicles, for they have to be attuned to those vibrations, and the result is that outwardly it makes me hyper-sensitive."

Although Wilson was in bed every other day with heart trouble, his Master told him he must leave Genoa and go to England to organize the Work there. He had qualms about the mission, since he would only have about five pounds left after paying his train fare. He also had few contacts in England who he felt would be sympathetic to the cause. On the eve of his departure, he wrote a final letter:

"Now I am to go to England almost at once. Beyond that, all is unknown. I have been told that I shall find those whom the Master has chosen; they will be brought to me when the time comes. I hope that it may be soon for the actual work of organizing is not in my line. I have little worldly wisdom or business ability. In the meantime, I live from day to day and cross no bridges until I come to them. I have Master's word for it that I shall find such help as I need, and that is sufficient."

On May 20, Wilson packed his few belongings into two suitcases, and boarded the train for England.

△   △   △

Who was this itinerant mariner and mystic who would become the leader of one of the most remarkable religious colonies in North America?

Edward Arthur Wilson was born on July 25, 1878, in Birmingham, England, the son of Thomas Wilson and Sarah Ellen Pearsall. His father was a master craftsman in the city's thriving metallic and brass bedstead trade, and eventually formed his own company, becoming a prosperous manufacturer. The family lived in the district of Ladywood, then moved to Edgbaston, where Thomas and Sarah raised their son and two daughters in an atmosphere of strict religious devotion.

Wilson's parents were "Irvingites," and their membership in the Catholic Apostolic Church was undoubtedly the most important influence in Wilson's development. This peculiar religious sect was founded in 1830 by a charismatic Scottish minister named Edward Irving. Thomas Wilson was a deacon in the Church—there was a small but fervent congregation in Birmingham—and the life of the family revolved entirely around religion. There were daily prayers in the home— morning and evening—and on Sundays the family worshipped in the brick and terracotta church in Summer Hill Road. The ecstatic outbursts and speaking in tongues that punctuated the services were believed to be direct outpourings of the

Holy Spirit. The Church's central teaching was the Second Advent, which was expected to occur within the lifetimes of the twelve "Apostles" around whom the Church was organized. Members prayed daily for this miracle: the dead would rise from their graves, and the faithful —"those with the seal of the living God on their foreheads"— would be caught up to meet the Lord in the air. Church members studied the Book of Revelation in minute detail, had an intricate interpretation of the chief numerical symbols in the Bible, and believed that Archangels, Seraphim, and Cherubim were living spiritual Beings. "Irvingites" were often persecuted for their strange beliefs.

In *Foundation Letters and Teachings*, Wilson writes: "From early childhood, I have been in touch with super-physical things, and have often received visitations from highly developed Beings, and these always brought me help or comfort or instruction. At first, I thought that these were 'Angels,' but as I grew older and received teaching, I learned of the Masters and Their work for humanity. This direct contact continued all through my life from time to time, but it was not until much later that I learned the reason for these experiences and the teaching that was given me."

The other great influence in Wilson's life was the sea. When he was a boy, his father apprenticed him on a Royal Navy windjammer training ship, where he acquired the skills by which he would earn his living for most of his life. On his early voyages, he had many adventures; he purportedly worked for a time on "blackbirders," transporting kidnapped Africans to Turkey, where they were sold as slaves.

In 1902, at the age of twenty-four, Wilson arrived in New Zealand. There he met Margery Clark, the daughter of an Australian grazier. The couple was married on Christmas Eve in Wellington, at the Catholic Apostolic Church in Webb Street. They soon had two children, a son and a daughter. Wilson supported the young family by working as a draftsman, surveyor, electrician, and farmer. Becoming restless, he uprooted the family and moved to Canada.

In 1907, Wilson arrived in British Columbia, where he worked as a baggage clerk for the Dominion Express Company. He was promoted several times, but quit to work as a pilot on lumber schooners and coastal steamers plying the waters between San Francisco and Alaska. He was away from home a great deal.

"I remember that I was in the hospital in Victoria for several months with diphtheria, and he only visited me once," his daughter Margery Bell recalls. "He brought me strawberries. Since then, whenever I have strawberries, I think of him."

The memory is a poignant one, since it was one of the last times the eight-year-old girl saw her father. Soon afterwards, sometime in 1912, Wilson deserted his wife and children and signed on board a ship bound for the Orient. His destitute wife, with the assistance of relatives, returned with the children to New Zealand.

Wilson makes few references to his past. In *Foundation Letters and Teachings*, he writes that in 1912 he passed through a "Ceremony of Dedication":

"It was then I understood that I had a work to do, but I did not know anything of its nature or when it was to be. This was followed by twelve chaotic years of testing and wandering in all parts of the world. Outwardly, I was unsuccessful in everything I did, but the inner work of preparation must have been going quietly on."

Wilson also refers to these years of wandering in *The Three Truths*: "Thou wast stripped and despised of kindred./Long years didst thou follow the Quest,/Ever seeking. . ."

Very little is known about the period between the "Ceremony of Dedication" in 1912 and Wilson's visions in the south of France in 1924, except that he travelled widely. He sailed around Cape Horn, up and down the coasts of Africa and South America, and throughout the islands of the Pacific. He served as a navigator during World War I, taking supplies from Norfolk, Virginia, across the Atlantic to England. At about the same time as he received his captain's papers, he joined the American section of the Theosophical Society. Membership records identify him as a resident of California, living in San Diego, Ocean Beach, and San Francisco, care of Maxwell & Company, Papeete, Tahiti. While in the South Seas, Wilson fell seriously ill, but was nursed back to health by a Scottish woman named Elma, who became his constant companion. He also spent time in an Italian monastery, became a brilliant astrologer, and contributed numerous articles to scholarly magazines. He is said to have known the South African statesman Jan Smuts, as well as such illustrious British figures as Sir Oliver Lodge, Sir Arthur Eddington, Sir Herbert Austin, Sir Neville Chamberlain, and the secret service agent Captain H. L. Stringer.

"He was one of the most fascinating personalities and conversationalists I ever met," Victoria businessman Walter Miles recalls. "His knowledge of world religions was stupendous. He corresponded with spiritual and political leaders all over the world. He knew all kinds of prominent people."

Wilson undoubtedly believed that the experiences of these years had inexorably led him to the most important stage of his life's work. In Genoa, he had received the *imprimatur* of the Masters. He was now the chosen instrument of the Great White Lodge, consecrated and sent forth to carry out its work for humanity.

△   △   △

Wilson arrived in England the third week of May 1926, shortly after the end of the General Strike, which had paralyzed the country for nine days. London was alive again with activity. In Piccadilly Circus, the traffic roared around the statue of Eros, newsboys called out the latest government scandal, and cinema-goers queued up to see Gloria Swanson's newest picture at the Plaza. Wilson made his way through the crowds to Paternoster Square, near the dome of St. Paul's Cathedral, to the address of *The Occult Review.*

In the offices of the world's leading occult periodical, Wilson learned from the editor, Harry J. Strutton, that far from being unknown in England, he was already being hailed as a gifted psychic and major prophet. Strutton informed him that an article Wilson had written in Genoa and mailed to the magazine had been printed in the May issue and caused a sensation. Letters had poured in from all over the world, and the article had become the focus for a heated debate over the value of prophecy.

"The Shadow," which appeared under the pseudonym "E. A. Chaylor" (Was the name "Chaylor" perhaps an allusion to *"chela"*?) took for its theme the adage "Whom the gods would destroy, they first make mad." The article was based upon information his Master had given him while staying in Genoa. As he wrote at the time:

> While it is true that we are still in the Kali Yuga ["The Black Age"], yet the cycle which will commence about 1975 will be more favourable on the whole. In it, the balance of power will be on the side of righteousness and progress. But between that time and the present, there stretches a veritable gulf of horror through which poor humanity must struggle as best as it can. The forces of Evil, knowing that their time is short, are making a supreme effort to engulf as many as possible. Soon they are to be "bound for a thousand years." That expression is scriptural and allegorical, but it well describes the conditions that will prevail.
>
> My Brothers, before they are bound, *they shall be loosed.* The flood of evil which is even now so unmistakably rising will be manifested on three planes. Physically, it will take the shape of national wars, anarchy, bloodshed, and Bolshevism. All restraints being removed, the passions of men will be loosed; private murder will be a common-place and go unavenged; every kind of foul excess will flourish unchecked. On the mental plane, the thoughts and inventions of men

will be placed at the service of demons, and will be used for the wholesale destruction of humanity. Those who perish will be more fortunate than those who remain.

Psychically, the prospect is more terrible even than this. There will shortly come about what I can only describe as the breaking of a dam. All the evil forces and powers of the lower astral worlds will burst the barriers which have hitherto restrained them. They will shortly flood this physical world in such a tidal-wave of horror as no living generation has seen. To find its parallel, one must go back to the closing periods of the great Atlantean epoch. . .

In "The Shadow," Wilson gave the reasons why this disaster was inevitable. He explained that the unceasing warfare on inner planes between the forces of Evil and the forces of Light had now reached a crisis. The situation had been made worse by the efforts of misguided Spiritualists trying to contact deceased relatives: by weakening the barrier which separated the two worlds, they made it easier for evil astral entities to invade the physical plane, thus helping to precipitate the horror which was soon to overwhelm mankind. Wilson's article concluded with a prophetic vision that he claimed to have received in full waking consciousness:

I saw the land (Europe) spread out below me. At the four corners stood four Men, holding each the corner of a black cloth. Now a wind came from the East, causing the cloth to billow and shake. Then I asked one of the Men, "What is the meaning of the cloth?" And he said, "*It is the Shadow of those things about to come upon the Earth.*" Then the four Men lowered the cloth, and it covered all the land.

The wind now blew with violence, and there was a great shaking, with clamour and confusion, and the cloth became soaked with blood. Then I asked the Man, "Why are these things done?" And he answered me, "*Because those things which hinder are about to be removed.*" And I said, "What are the things which are to be removed?" And again he answered me, "*They are three: the first two shall be destroyed by the third, and the third, when its work is accomplished, shall be changed.*"

Yet again, I asked him, "How soon shall these things be?" And he said, "*The lands which you see have passed the Cycle of Hate; they are now in the Cycle of Madness. The next Cycle is the Cycle of Destruction.*" And I said, "How long until this Cycle shall end?" And he answered me, "*In about two years it shall end, and destruction shall commence. Then, in nine years, the times of nine nations shall be accomplished.*"

Now the cloth dissolved away, and the land was seen to be desolate. The lines which had divided it were removed, and over all there was silence. Then, out of the silence, was heard a Trumpet, and a Voice speaking Wisdom. And because of the silence, the people heard the Voice, and thereafter, for a space, there was Peace in the land.

Harry J. Strutton, editor of *The Occult Review*, was deeply affected by the prophecy in "The Shadow." His several meetings with Wilson confirmed his belief that he was "a gifted natural seer." Wilson told Strutton that the "way of escape" referred to in the article was the Work of the Masters described in *A Message from the Masters of the Wisdom*. He gave Strutton a typescript copy to read, and explained that although most people would perish, a few individuals would be saved from the horrors that were about to overwhelm European civilization. These few would be spared by virtue of the saving grace within them: they would be the ones to carry forward this new Work of the Masters. Strutton was impressed by *The Message*. He immediately telephoned a small firm of printers, Edward and Charles Straker Limited, and arranged for them to print it for the very reasonable sum of twelve pounds. Grateful for Strutton's assistance, Wilson thanked him and left the office. He did not tell the editor that although the cost of printing *The Message* was modest, he'd arrived in London with only a few pounds to his name. Fortunately, events again conspired on his behalf:

"About this time, I received an offer of four pounds to help with the cost; this was from a poor man, dependent upon a salary, and he gave all he had. To this, I added four pounds from what was left over from my travelling expenses and incidentals. It was not enough, and I did not know what to do. Then, he who had given the four pounds received an unexpected present of money just at that time—this also was four pounds; he gave it at once and *The Message* was put in the press."

A Message from the Masters of the Wisdom announced the fact that the Masters were about to do a further Work in the world, that their plans were complete, and that the Work had commenced upon the physical plane. The basic teaching of *The Message* was Universal Brotherhood, but delivered in the context of a world crisis—the imminent destruction of the present social and political order—it possessed a compelling force and urgency:

"In the near future, existing institutions will be overturned, and practically all religious and philosophical teaching will be blotted out. Therefore, the Masters, foreseeing these things which are soon to come upon the Earth, have prepared the present Work. It is an Ark of Refuge wherein will be preserved all that is true in existing teachings, and into which a new measure of Knowledge and Power will be poured."

The immediate purpose of the Work was to provide individuals with the training and encouragement necessary for them to achieve spiritual enlightenment. The second part of the Work was the training of succeeding generations:

The children who by their karma will be drawn to parents who are linked up with this present Work belong to a group of highly evolved egos [souls] who are now beginning to come into incarnation. They must be kept free from karmic ties or links connecting them with the old and dying order. They will be the Thinkers and the Leaders in that new order which shall arise from the ashes of the old. . .

There will be a constant influx of these egos from the present time until approximately 1975. Those who are now children, or who are born within the next few years, will be the parents of that army which will be in its very early prime in 1975. It is these, the grandchildren of our present day, who will have the chief part in the great Work that ushers in the year Two thousand. The work we have to accomplish is spiritual and hidden; that of 1975 will be manifest and largely concerned with the affairs of the outer world. Our present task is to prepare those who will be the Rulers and Governors of that period, which will be an era of righteous government, when the people of the Earth will be justly ruled. We have to train these children in just Principles and in true Ideals.

The Message explained that the Work was one of preparation for the founding of a more evolved race of humanity:

The leading nations of Europe, together with their off-shoots and colonies, form collectively a distinct group or class with its special characteristics and destiny; these are known to students of world history as the fifth sub-race. Already these have reached their apex (as respects the parent or European nations), and have entered a period of rapid decline. This decline is rooted in moral and spiritual degeneracy. Knowledge and inventive genius is placed at the disposition of governments for purposes of mutual destruction; science is already invading forbidden ground and penetrating secrets which are the heritage of the succeeding (sixth) race. A halt must therefore be called, and the necessary re-adjustments made.

Those souls linked with the new race, *The Message* explained, were incarnating in increasing numbers. Many of these were adepts who would bring with them vast stores of knowledge supposed to have been lost with the earlier races of humanity:

> "These, the more advanced egos, will respond to the present call: they will be coordinated and linked together by means of this Work, and finally, under the direct guidance of the Masters Themselves, will form on the physical plane the nucleus of the coming sixth sub-race. The plans of the Masters involve the formation of Centers of Safety where, at a later stage, actual colonies will be founded and the coming type evolved. There will be more than one Center, but in each case, they will be in places secure from outside interference of any kind, and safe from surrounding chaos and disaster."

The Message also stated that the Work was a form of preparation for "HIM WHO IS TO COME," an Avatar or divine Being who would appear on Earth in the closing years of the century to found and stabilize the sixth sub-race.

The Work announced by *The Message* was directly concerned with the coming Age of Aquarius, a period that would last for approximately two thousand years: "*The Message* given is the first Trumpet-blast of the New Age, and the Standard we set up is the Standard of the new Order." *The Message* itself would act as a touchstone: those persons who had an affinity with the Work would be drawn to it by a process of "spiritual self-selection." *The Message* concluded:

> This is the Message of the Masters, the Message of Brotherhood. It is simple and easy to understand; the issue is perfectly clear. By every man to whom this Message comes, it must be either accepted or rejected. No neutral position is possible, for this Message shall divide the Wheat from the Chaff; it is a sword that shall pierce to the heart of every earnest man—the sword of Truth.

The declaration of the truth of Universal Brotherhood is the Messenger's guarantee and surest credential from the Masters Whom he represents. This and no other.

THE MESSAGE IS EVERYTHING, THE PERSONALITY OF THE MESSENGER IS NOTHING. ON THE ACCEPTANCE OF THE MESSAGE ITSELF, ALL MUST STAND OR FALL.

Peace be to all Beings.

△

After publishing *The Message*, Wilson visited his parents in Bournemouth, staying at their home at 4 Queens Park South. Thomas Wilson had retired, a wealthy man, to the south of England. In the lovely garden behind "Ontario," Wilson was able to relax and to reply to his growing volume of correspondence. In a letter dated July 17, 1926, he explained that he'd published "The Shadow" under the pseudonym "E. A. Chaylor" because "it is necessary that I personally remain unrecognized and unknown—it is an essential working condition, otherwise I should be pestered with phenomena hunters." In the August issue of *The Occult Review*, Wilson published a sequel to "The Shadow," also under the name Chaylor. This too created a tremendous stir.

In relentlessly grim language, "The Tocsin" painted the picture of Europe poised upon the brink of destruction. Wilson used the image of a bell tolling to vivid effect:

For centuries, it has rung out the triumphs of Might and sounded the dictates of Intolerance. It has heralded conquering armies and rung the Assembly for execution, the fire, and the stake. It has been the last sound to beat upon the ears of the dying, it has drowned the anguished cries of countless millions.

This Bell was shaped by human hands, fashioned in the hearts and minds of men. It was melted and moulded by fierce passions, and beaten by the hammers of selfishness upon the anvils of hardened hearts. Men made it, and men toll it.

Today, it sounds for Consummation, for the dissolution of the Old Order and for the uprising of the New. The chemist, brewing wholesale death in new and horrible forms, pauses in his work to listen to it. The feet of millions, armed and drilled for murder, keep time to its tolling. The politician, the publisher, the preacher—all hear it, but none give it heed. Only the people do not hear, or if they hear, they fail to understand; they are busied with their own concerns—affairs of the market, or of marriage, or of sport.

The article's ruthless criticism of modern civilization prompted a flood of letters to *The Occult Review*. Some readers accused Wilson/Chaylor of scare-mongering: "Mr. Chaylor loves to make our flesh creep, but does he really and honestly believe that 'in Europe today, all are morally and spiritually decadent'?" Numerous others wrote in to support him with astrology, numerology ("1928 reduces to 2, a number of selfishness, contention, and enmity"), Biblical scripture, Pyramidology, and their own premonitions of impending doom. One correspondent even suggested that "The Shadow" and "The Tocsin" be published together in a pamphlet and distributed countrywide: "There is as yet no *spiritual* Moscow to finance such a propaganda, but surely the financial difficulty should not be so great, seeing that even *A Message from the Masters of Wisdom* is offered to a troubled and discordant world for threepence!"

Sir Arthur Conan Doyle, the creator of Sherlock Holmes and a champion of Spiritualism, entered the fray. He wrote to the editor of *The Occult Review*, accusing Wilson of attacking Spiritualism: "Your contributor speaks as if Spiritualism itself, by thinning the walls which divide us from the unseen, may admit a flood of evil. Such a supposition would presuppose that in the Borderland, there was more evil than good, which cannot be said of God's realm. On the contrary, such a thinning of the barrier would give wider entrance to all the angelic forces which may save and redeem the world."

Wilson replied to Conan Doyle: "In the 'Borderland' of the Spiritualist, there *is* more evil than good, for while it is 'God's realm,' in the sense that all realms are subject to divine oversight, it is also a realm inimical to humanity, and man incurs great evil and danger by forcing an entrance thereto. Experimental, and therefore uninstructed tampering with the forces and powers of the astral world will result in widespread evil and disaster. I do not say that it may, but that it certainly will; it is not a supposition, but an unqualified statement based upon exact knowledge."

He concluded his letter by saying: "'The proof of the pudding is in the eating,' and I think that the issue will be decided beyond any possibility of dispute between this present time of writing and the close of 1928."

Wilson was less concerned now with answering his critics than he was with replying to those individuals who'd responded to *The Message*. It had been advertised in *The Occult Review*, and many people had written to him, wanting to know more about the Work.

He replied to these queries with a mimeographed letter which stated that the Masters were accepting as disciples those individuals who were prepared to serve unselfishly in the Cause. The letter claimed that the Work was the inauguration of a new era of righteousness and truth: it embodied the ideals of the New Age and worked for their practical realization. For the first time, the name of the new spiritual movement was given:

"We are called to serve as the Pioneers of a new Race and a new Ideal, and pioneering calls for vision, for courage, and for the strength of self-sacrifice. We are called to the mighty task of laying the foundations of the new Order, and a better civilization, the Aquarian. For this reason, the Masters have decided that Their Work shall be known in the world as THE AQUARIAN FOUNDATION.' "

Harry Strutton, editor of *The Occult Review,* gave Wilson his enthusiastic support. In an article written for *The Manchester Sunday Chronicle,* dramatically headlined, "DEVILS MOBILIZING FOR ATTACK, PERIL OF NEW ARMAGEDDON IN 1928," Strutton warned that Armageddon was approaching with relentless strides. Fortunately, a new movement had been initiated whose members were enlisting "on the side of the angels in this inner and outer warfare against the powers of hell." Strutton declared that no living soul would be exempt from the coming conflict, but reassured the public that in the end the forces of light would prevail.

Strutton also discussed the Aquarian Foundation in several editorials in *The Occult Review.* He wished the new movement every success. "It may be safely predicted, however," he observed, "that its progress will be in direct proportion to the fidelity of its adherents to the lofty ideals which seem to inspire it. 'By their fruits ye shall know them.' "

△   △   △

One of the most prominent individuals to respond to *The Message* was a famous English astrologer named Alfred Henry Barley. The former sub-editor of the magazine *Modern Astrology,* Barley had worked for many years with Alan Leo, the so-called "father of modern astrology." The bearded and kindly Barley was an outstanding scholar whose book *The Drayson Problem* was an intricate mathematical proof of a controversial theory linking the Ice Ages to the earth's rotation. Barley's wife, Annie, had been a teacher with the London County Council for twenty-eight years, working with handicapped children. She'd also served on the staff of *Modern Astrology,* and had been the Secretary of the London Astrological Society.

The Barleys lived in Hertford on the River Lea, twenty-five miles north of London. Although not wealthy, they were comfortable. Their home, "Leppington House," had a fine library—Alfred's prized possession—and the couple spent much of their time in astrological research and study. They were highly respected by their peers and had even been presented to King George V.

On September 6, 1926, Barley read *A Message from the Masters of the Wisdom*. He and Annie were Theosophists, but, like many members of the Society, were dissatisfied with the conduct and teachings of the current leaders. *The Message* struck a responsive chord, and Alfred wrote at once, requesting more information about the Work.

Brother XII sent the Barleys a paper that explained the reason why they'd been so curiously moved by *The Message*: it possessed a "peculiar and magical quality"—it had the power of arousing the Intuition:

"In the world today are many who in former lives have formed a link with the Masters, but who have no memory of the fact. These, through past effort or devotion, have earned the right to serve again; they do not know this themselves, and we, without personal contact, cannot recognize them. To these *The Message* comes, arousing the memory of the Ego, so that it can directly influence the personality; they feel *The Message* to be true, though perhaps they do not yet realize why it is so. These, the former disciples and servants of the Lodge, will respond—these and none other."

The explanation made sense to the Barleys, increasing their desire to find out more about the Work. They read Wilson's articles in *The Occult Review*, and at the end of September joined the Aquarian Foundation. In December, they purchased a copy of *The Three Truths*, which had just been published, and followed Brother XII's injunction to the Foundation members: "It should be read and *studied* by all."

Barley and Wilson corresponded at length about the Work,

discussing a variety of occult topics of mutual interest. Barley was impressed by Wilson's extensive knowledge and by the authority with which he expressed himself. He realized that Wilson was a man of formidable intellect, with an absolute mastery of esoteric matters. Wilson stressed in his letters that the nature of the Work was such that no attempt would be made to proselytize: "It is not a question of belief or of personal inclinations, but of spiritual affinity, and to which dispensation the individual is karmically linked."

Wilson emphasized that the Work had no connection with any of the "thousand-and-one sects or isms or neo-theosophical schools. In short, IT HAS NOTHING IN COMMON WITH THE EXISTING ORDER, nor with any of its component parts or institutions. It is part and parcel of THE NEW ORDER, of that which has yet to be revealed.

"Those who have a part in it belong spiritually and psychically to a future day and generation; they have been chosen in past Ages, and are dedicated to a definite end and aim. They are the nucleus of nations yet unborn, a little band chosen and selected by the Great Ones, the hope and seed of the future—they form collectively THE AQUARIAN FOUNDATION."

Wilson had now moved to Southampton, where he'd rented rooms in a house at 10 Westwood Road. The Barleys wrote to him there, requesting a personal meeting. To this suggestion, he readily agreed.

On January 5, 1927, Alfred and Annie Barley took a bus from London to Southampton, arriving at Wilson's lodgings at about two-thirty in the afternoon. "He himself admitted us at the door," Barley recalled, "and said that our coming was very important—more important than we realized." Wilson introduced the Barleys to Elma, the same woman who'd nursed him in the South Seas. She was gracious and well-spoken and shared Wilson's interest in Theosophy. Her devotion to him was obvious.

The two couples sat around the fire and Wilson talked

about *The Message* and the ruin which was shortly to fall upon England. He advised the Barleys to liquidate their securities and re-invest in Canadian securities, since they would depreciate less than any others in the coming financial debacle. Wilson told the Barleys he intended to go to British Columbia in a few months to establish the "Center of Safety" referred to in *The Message*. He spoke as if he took it for granted that the Barleys would join him there later.

"The conversation flowed on in such a way," Barley recalled, "that references to the subject of our own personal emigration were not direct and specific as they would have been in a shipping agent's office, but were more or less casual and incidental, as they would have been at a friend's supper table."

During supper, Wilson read the Barleys a "Special Urgent Letter" that he was sending to all the members of the Foundation:

> This Letter is not concerned with moral or spiritual issues, but is entirely practical. This people is shortly to pass through great tribulation, and warning is given, so that those who heed it may remove to a place of safety. To do so is not "selfish": those who personally avoid the trouble may be able later to help a Brother less fortunately placed. If you remain, all may be lost—even the chance of helping others. . .
>
> A small settlement is to be prepared in British Columbia. There are others, but this is the nearest and most suited to English people. It will be the first to be developed. Instructions as to ways and means will be given to those who are prepared to act. . . You should ACT now, and save what you can. If to sell now means considerable loss, not to sell means total loss in the near future. Every pound saved from destruction is one more pound available for the work of reconstruction later. . . If you feel that such action is too drastic, remember that the existing order is about to disappear. You and yours, and all that you have, will almost

certainly disappear with it. . .

The letter charged every member to observe complete silence in the matter: "Should you wish to warn friends, you must do so as if expressing your personal views and opinions only. Any departure from this course would be a betrayal of the confidence placed in you. By creating the tendency to general panic, it would jeopardize the opportunity of all. . ."

After the supper was cleared away, Wilson produced a map of Canada. He spread it out on the table and they all gathered around. Barley asked where the settlement would be located and Elma pointed to the district of Hope, about one hundred miles east of Vancouver, and said to Wilson, "That's the place, isn't it, dear?"

"He told us he himself was going out during February," Barley recalled, "and that Mrs. Wilson was to follow him about a month later, and that he thought a few others would be going out with her, partly as company and partly in order that by travelling together, economies might be effected, especially in the matter of baggage and freight. He recommended us to stock up with clothing and bedding as these things were dear in Canada."

Later that evening, a young man named Frederick Pope came in and was introduced to the Barleys as a member of the group that would be going out to Canada.

The Barleys stayed the night, and had breakfast with Wilson the following morning. They'd been very much impressed by his "earnestness," and by the Work he'd described to them, which was very much in accord with their own ideals.

Annie Barley later recalled: "Before we left, we had almost made up our minds to go to Canada. We left him, saying that we would think the matter over and let him know. I remember when he saw us to the bus and said goodbye, we were again greatly impressed with his words on parting, which were: 'Goodbye—forget everything but the Work.'"

△   △   △

On January 25, 1927, Brother XII issued a General Letter to the Foundation's members, announcing that the Master had directed him to go at once to North America to inaugurate the work of the White Lodge there. He would visit both the United States and Canada, but the work in Canada came first on his schedule:

"Commencing in the East, I have to cross Canada, establishing this Work and linking all together as I go. At certain predetermined points, I hope to meet gatherings of the many Brothers who are already looking towards the present Work. At each of these points, I want to leave behind me a strong, virile, united body, a center through which the power of the Master can radiate. Remember, my Brothers, that these will be magnetic centers—one of the reasons why I must come in person is because they can be formed in no other way."

He then addressed the question foremost in the minds of many members, one which had prompted considerable speculation and debate—the location of the Center for the nucleus of the new race:

You are all familiar with the idea that North America is the place chosen for the beginnings of the sixth sub-race. There have been many guesses as to what part of North America would be chosen—it has even been given out by certain people that California, or lower California, would be selected. North America is a big place, and guesses sometimes go wide of the mark—also the secrets of the White Lodge are well kept, especially in matters relating to racial cycles and development. I may now tell you that there will be more than one Center; one of these *will* be in California, and yet another in Mexico, but these come later.

The Center chosen by the Manu (Vaivasvata) to be the cradle of the coming sixth sub-race is neither Mexico nor California, but Southern British Columbia. Why? There are many reasons, one of these being that one of the chief objects to be attained is body-building, and there we have the ideal conditions needed for all-round development. This is to be THE Center—the first actually to be formed upon the continent for this particular purpose, and from which the material for the nucleus of other Centers will later go forth.

This locality has been actually and definitely selected—it is HIS choice alone, and while it is already known to me, I have not seen it in the physical body as yet. It is in the securing of this chosen site that I shall need your help, and the help of our Brothers in the United States—in that and in other matters. You have to bear in mind that the place now chosen by the Manu will be not only the Center of the present Work, it will be THE center of spiritual energy and knowledge for the whole continent of North America—for the whole world in the not distant future.

Brother XII told the members that much of the Masters' work had already been accomplished on inner planes, and that it was now their privilege and responsibility to give it expression in the outer world. They would each become channels for the power and knowledge of the Masters, working with them for the aid and blessing of mankind:

My Brothers, I do not have to tell you that this is a great vision; it is the greatest vision in the world today—the vision of the new Age. Already others have caught glimpses of it and are trying to give expression to it through ideas and devices of their own. But that is not our way because to us it has been given to follow and to work with Those Who are the Originators and the true Executors of the Plan. That is the vision as it has been shown to me; make it your own, consecrate your lives to it: then shall we see its form and fruit upon the physical Earth—the counterpart of that pattern eternal in the Heavens.

Your Brother in Service,
XII

The Barleys, meanwhile, had decided to go to Canada and become members of the new community. They liquidated their assets, selling their house and Alfred's library. They were disconcerted when they realized that after all their expenses had been paid, they only had fifteen-hundred pounds left.

The Barleys wrote to Wilson, advising him of their preparations and asking him how they should address their luggage. They were surprised when he wrote back and informed them, without further explanation, that their destination was, not Hope, but a small coal-mining town on Vancouver Island called Nanaimo.

"It is significant of the ascendancy he had gained," Barley later commented, "that we accepted the alteration without demur, assuming that plans had to be changed owing to circumstances beyond our control."

The Barleys had been led to expect that a fairly large contingent would be going out to Canada. They were surprised, again, to learn that only two other individuals besides themselves and Elma would be making the trip: Frederick Pope and an eccentric ex-British Army captain named Sidney Sprey-Smith. Wilson, however, didn't seem dismayed by the size of the group, nor by the fact that there hadn't been a wider general response to *The Message*:

As was foreseen, very few responded, for people as a whole in Great Britain must pass through 'great tribulation'—the harvest of individual and national karma. The work in Great Britain has been the throwing of a life-belt to a few. Also, we must remember that this Work is primarily concerned with North America, not with Europe, for it is in America that the new sixth sub-race type is to be developed. Already, and before I have as yet set foot in North America on the business of the Lodge, there has been a great response there. In the United States and Canada, *no less than seven organizations have aligned themselves with this Work.*

Wilson also didn't hesitate to make some bold claims for the spiritual agents who stood behind the Work: "The Masters M. and K.H., who founded the early Theosophical Society, are actively engaged in it, as is also that Master Whom the Western world knows and venerates as the Christ."

In the third week of February, 1927, Wilson boarded the Cunard liner *Montroyal* at the Southampton docks. Propellors churning, the great ship cast off her moorings and eased out of her berth. Excited passengers crowded the railings to wave farewell as the liner turned to face the English Channel. Brother XII was on his way to bring the Work of the Masters and the Great White Lodge to America.

CHAPTER
II
The Aquarian Foundation

I n Canada's capital city of Ottawa, the Peace Tower pierced
the icy vault of the heavens and the frosty air echoed with
the cries of skaters on the Rideau Canal. To the south of
the Parliament Buildings, streetcars glided down the frozen
streets, stopping to let off groups of muffled passengers. On
this typical evening in March 1927, the city was bathed in
mauve light. A little band of pilgrims—well-educated, cultured,
and respected members of the community—converged on
the Ottawa Lodge of the Theosophical Society to attend a
special event. Tonight, they would hear a talk by a mysterious
Englishman who had recently arrived in Canada—Brother
XII.

Ten days earlier, the *Montroyal* had sailed up the ice-choked
Saint Lawrence River and docked in Montreal. Brother XII
had been enthusiastically received by Theosophical Society
members there, since his arrival in Canada had been heralded
several months earlier when *The Message* had been printed in

The Canadian Theosophist, the official organ of the Society in Canada. In Montreal, Brother XII quickly recruited some of the first Canadian members to the Aquarian Foundation.

Inside the Ottawa Lodge, the air was filled with anticipation as the members packed the assembly hall to capacity. They sensed that Brother XII's talk would be something of great importance. On one wall, a wooden plaque bore the Society's motto: "There is no religion higher than truth." On the other, a portrait of Madame Blavatsky hung, her solemn gaze lending an air of purposefulness and credibility to the proceedings. Rows of wooden chairs faced the front of the hall, where Brother XII sat on a raised platform with the executive of the Lodge. All eyes in the hall focused upon the figure of the slight Englishman. The president struck a small brass gong to start the meeting. At the awaited moment, Brother XII rose to speak:

"Friends, this evening, I shall try to give you a vision, to make you see something of what this Work is to be in the future. In the first place, if you are to see this vision clearly, you must try not to see me. Into my mind, there comes a verse which was spoken of St. John: 'What came ye out to see; a reed shaken by the wind?' That is a very good simile, for the reed, as you know, denotes weakness, but it is shaken by that which is the opposite of weak. What you must do tonight is to try and catch the message of the Wind, of the one Spirit, rather than to center attention on the reed. . ."

Brother XII went on to outline the Work in general, and to talk specifically about the importance of group work in the new era. He told his listeners that the Aquarian Foundation was an actual physical counterpart of the Great White Lodge—a replica of its organization on the higher planes and that its work would be accomplished by group action, rather than by the action of individuals:

"At this time, there are in the White Lodge twelve great groups which are specifically concerned with the evolution of humanity. We may say that, in a general sense, these correspond in their nature to the twelve astrological houses. The Aquarian Foundation is especially the work of the 'Nine' and 'Twelve' groups. These two groups are always active in periods like the present, the closing of one age and set of accounts and the commencement of another. The work of the 'Twelve' group is synthetic; its present business is to 'link and to bind,' and the personal use of that numeral in my own case *is due to my connection with that special Group and its work.*"

Brother XII stressed to his listeners the importance of the Work, urging them to come together at once to form groups of the Aquarian Foundation—"the time left is terribly short, and the work to be accomplished is vast beyond belief." He told them that the Masters would fill each group with their knowledge and power, so that each group member would have access to far greater spiritual force than was available individually. Groups would act as transformers: they would receive energy from the Masters, then project it outwards as a potent, practical force in the world of human affairs.

Brother XII told his listeners that as members of the Aquarian Foundation they would constitute a select mental and spiritual aristocracy: "You are Knights of the Grail, or of the Round Table. You are pledged to your own Higher Self to lead His life, the Higher life—thus shall we carry into the world the tremendous force of Example."

After his talk, the members crowded around, asking questions and seeking to become part of the Work. Brother XII's talk was so effective that nearly all of the members of the Ottawa Lodge joined the Aquarian Foundation.

A few days later, Wilson arrived in Toronto, the stronghold of the Theosophical Society in Canada, with more than 250 members. There was tremendous interest in this new "Messenger of the Masters," but Albert E. S. Smythe, the General Secretary of the Society and editor of *The Canadian Theosophist*, was sceptical of Wilson's claims. He'd sent *The Message* to several old-timers in the Society and published their comments about it:

"My opinion of this is that the writer of the circular is a deluded, hallucinated person. . ." wrote one.

"I would have more confidence in it if it were not advertised in *The Occult Review,*" observed another. "I cannot imagine a Master advertising in a magazine. . ."

But in spite of these critiques, Smythe conceded that *The Message* had "more of the spirit of the early days than anything that has appeared from Adyar [Theosophical Society headquarters in India] in recent years."

Brother XII gave several talks to the Toronto Lodge of the Theosophical Society. He asked the members to give him their support in founding a "Center of Safety" in British Columbia. His call to action galvanized the members, many of whom felt that the Lodge had become little more than an intellectual debating society.

Herbert Jefferson was impressed. A commercial artist and active member of the Toronto Lodge, he remembers Wilson as a lean figure with a powerful face and sensual mouth.

"He propounded this scheme of a 'zone of safety,' as he called it," Jefferson recalls. "He was also going to start a school to train people who wanted to help humanity during this crash that was coming. He was very persuasive. He had his detractors, of course, but it sounded alright to me."

In Toronto, Brother XII stayed with George Hobart, an advertising executive and the Secretary of the Lodge. As a souvenir, he gave Hobart a photograph of himself. Hobart loaned it to Jefferson and some other curious members. When Wilson found out, he flew into a rage and demanded the photograph back. "My picture is not public property!" he declared. "It is to be issued by no one but myself!" Hobart was taken aback by Wilson's reaction. The incident, however, did not deter him or Jefferson from making plans to move to British Columbia.

Brother XII spoke to Theosophical Lodges in Hamilton, London, and Windsor, Ontario. The response was also positive. In fact, his trip to eastern Canada was an astonishing success—in one fell swoop, he'd captured much of the

Canadian membership of the Theosophical Society for the Aquarian Foundation. This development did not please the General Secretary of the Society, Albert Smythe.

In Windsor, Wilson spent the day with Joseph S. Benner, owner of The Sun Publishing Company in Akron, Ohio, and the author of the metaphysical classic, *The Impersonal Life*. A gentle, unpretentious man, Benner was a mystic with a Christian orientation and a small but devoted following of his own. He offered to publish Brother XII's writings in the United States, and discussed with him how to best organize the Work in America. Benner left the meeting convinced that Wilson's link with the Masters was genuine.

"It is most amazing to me to see what has been accomplished within the short space of six months through the efforts of this quiet little man," Benner wrote to an associate. "I found, of course, that he has been given to know the whole Plan, but that back of what he himself knows is a great reservoir of knowledge and power which is poured through him as the need and time manifest. I have no doubt that he will carry through and accomplish that which he has been sent out to do, if we who also have the vision prove true and faithful to it."

Brother XII now boarded the train for the three thousand mile trip across Canada to the Pacific Coast. He planned to stop at various places en route to meet personally with readers of *The Message* who had written to him in England. Every prospective member was important, no whistlestop too small to visit. One can imagine him standing beside the tracks in the Canadian Shield, exchanging a few words with a solitary disciple who had made a special trip to meet the train. Or being driven by burly Saskatchewan farmers to their homes for a hot supper and an overnight stay. Or speaking impromptu in a train station in the Rockies to a hastily assembled group of earnest souls. At last, the train rolled into the Canadian Pacific Railway Station in Vancouver. Wilson had accomplished much, but he was exhausted from the journey.

The following afternoon, Wilson stood on the deck of the

Princess Louise as it plowed through the waters of the Strait of Georgia to Vancouver Island. As the ferry slipped past Protection Island into the harbour of Nanaimo, Wilson could see the massive chimney of Nanaimo's largest coal mine, the Number One Esplanade, spewing smoke into the air. Formerly the coaling station for the British fleet in the Pacific, Nanaimo had once exported coal up and down the Pacific Coast, from San Diego, California, to Anchorage, Alaska, and to destinations as far away as Hawaii, Russia, and China. Seven miles of tunnels honeycombed the ocean floor beyond the harbour, and miners toiling far out beneath the Strait of Georgia could hear the ships' engines throbbing directly above them as they worked. The *Princess Louise* docked and Wilson descended the gangplank into Nanaimo.

He was noticed at once by a local contractor named Daniel Egdell, who struck up a conversation with him. When he learned that Wilson needed a place to stay, he arranged for him to rent a house in Northfield, a mining district outside Nanaimo. And so it was that a small, run-down frame house in the middle of a field became the first headquarters of the Aquarian Foundation.

A few days later, Wilson sent a telegram to Edward Lucas, a Vancouver lawyer who'd written to him in England, offering him a place to stay when he arrived. A genial family man and light-hearted spirit, Lucas was an independent thinker, interested in new ideas. He wired back, telling Wilson he'd meet him the following Sunday in Nanaimo.

On March 13, Lucas stood at the rail of the *Princess Louise*, searching the faces on the dock. "WILL MEET BOAT. WILL STAND WITHOUT HAT," Wilson's telegram had read. As Lucas strode down the gangplank, he saw a "slight, tired, delicate man" waiting to greet him, with "iron-grey hair brushed stand-up pompadour, short clipped beard, very kind, very grave eyes—and such a charming smile."

The rapport between the two men was immediate—they talked for eight straight hours. An ardent sailor and member of the Vancouver Yacht Club, Lucas enjoyed taking a nautical line with "The Skipper," as he was soon calling Wilson. He likened working with him to being in the navy: "I'm an officer, kinda. I'm like a Temporary Supernumerary Acting Oiler's Mate. But I'm in the Navy. And War has been declared." All joking aside, Lucas was profoundly impressed by Wilson: "I have met a Messenger. . . I have met a direct, personal Ambassador of the Great White Lodge. And that's that!"

The following weekend, Wilson visited Lucas at his home in Vancouver. Lucas's legal expertise was an asset. He advised Wilson to incorporate the Aquarian Foundation as a society under the Societies Act of British Columbia. The two men sat down at the dining-room table, rolled up their sleeves, and went to work drafting the constitution and by-laws of the Aquarian Foundation. The Society had four objects:

1) To give teaching and instructions to its members upon philosophical and occult subjects, and upon all matters concerning their physical, mental, and spiritual welfare; and to print and publish such books, magazines, or documents as may be necessary for that purpose.

2) To form and operate one or more central communities to be conducted upon mutually beneficial and fraternal principles, and to provide for the education of its members and their children in accordance with the general principles herein laid down.

3) To provide for the pursuance and carrying out of such actions and policies as may be deemed advisable for the welfare of the society and its members.

4) To cooperate directly or indirectly with all other societies, orders, or organizations which are activated by the same principles of Truth, Justice, Brotherhood, and mutual service; to the end that all may share in that greater strength and solidarity which is the outcome of unity of effort and purpose.

The Society was organized around a board of seven directors known as the Governors of the Society—the illumined Brothers referred to in *The Message*. There would never be less than seven nor more than twelve Governors, and any decisions affecting the Society would be arrived at by a vote among the Governors, and would not be dependent upon a vote of the members at large. Ideally, the voices of the Governors would be unanimous, but in the case of a divided opinion, the final decision would always rest with the president of the Society. The constitution made Edward Arthur Wilson president for life; he thus exerted absolute legal control over the affairs of the Society.

Wilson stayed overnight with the Lucas family and proved to be the perfect house guest. He charmed Lucas's wife, Marion, who was an avid astrologer and found their conversations fascinating.

"His voice was a light baritone," Edward Lucas recalled, "and he spoke with a curious, explosive hesitancy—stabbing at you with the first finger of his slender right hand. After every few words, his voice would rasp. He suffered from angina pectoris and took nitroglycerine pills."

The crowded supper table was good-natured bedlam—the Lucases had five children—as food passed back and forth across the supper table and the adults' enthusiastic discussion of the Work competed with the clatter of dishes and the cries of the children. Lucas chuckled at the idea that Southern British Columbia—his own backyard, as it were—had been chosen by the Masters as the cradle of the sixth sub-race and birthplace of the Avatar. "We're really getting in on the ground floor!" he joked.

He also felt as if the friendship of a lifetime had blossomed in a single weekend. "Strange how we feel like protecting this man from harm," he wrote. "With me, it is a strange uprush of love and loyalty such as I have not experienced in years—forty-three the other day—and I don't give in to so many raptures as I used to. But now, it's as though I were seventeen again and had just met my best high-school friend. . ."

Wilson also made time for the Lucas children, letting the younger ones climb up on his knee and play with his watch, and helping fourteen-year-old Frances Lucas with her Llewellyn George astrology course.

"I remember he showed me how to set up a horoscope," she recalls. "He was being nice to me; just a charming English gentleman. But formal—he always kept his tie on! He didn't talk about anything else but the Work—he was pretty well obsessed with it."

After Wilson left, the Lucas family unanimously agreed: "You couldn't possibly find a more friendly and sincere gentleman."

△   △   △

At twelve noon in the second week of April 1927, Will Levington Comfort stood on a dock in San Francisco, waiting for the passenger steamer from Seattle. He'd arrived an hour earlier from Los Angeles—an intense wiry man tanned by the sun and hardened by hours on the tennis court. A former war correspondent, Comfort's stunning first novel, *Routledge Rides Alone,* had been an extraordinary success and hailed by the peace movement in the United States. The author of over a dozen adventure novels and a frequent contributor to *The Saturday Evening Post,* Comfort was a mystic in the tradition of Walt Whitman and Edward Carpenter, a man with a passionate belief in the spiritual destiny of America. *The Message* had worked its uncanny magic on him: he'd been spellbound by it, and had unhesitatingly surrendered himself and his group of workers to Brother XII's cause.

Months earlier, Wilson had written to Comfort from England, saying he hoped that the two men could meet in San Francisco at the turn of the new moon in April. Now the meeting was happening to the day.

The steamer from Seattle docked with a sharp blast of its whistle and Wilson stepped off. For Comfort, this moment marked the end of a long search:

"If you had long been looking for someone, searching the faces of crowds and congregations, peering under the cap of the lone passerby . . . if you had looked in vain for him at the city gates, where the camels and elephants come and go . . . giving up at last, and turning to find him at your side— no giant, no stranger, no king—a voice familiar, a laugh identified again that has never for ages quite died out of the heart—a man whose glove fits your hand—"

Comfort was a romantic, but he was also a shrewd judge of character. He intended to scrutinize "The Messenger" carefully to see if his actions were consistent with his claims. The first test came that evening in a San Francisco hotel. In his magazine *The Glass Hive,* Comfort described the scene:

The man is no orator or lecturer. In fact, he has not spoken in public more than four or five times in his life, and these were recent affairs while crossing Canada; practically virgin he was, therefore, to meeting a crowd when he faced the turn-out in a San Francisco hotel hall. As he rose, sounds of a gala marriage festival began to break in from a banquet hall next door. No dry time they were having in there, and the band had caught the spirit. A change of halls was not feasible, and The Brother XII began to speak in an incredible jangle of laughter and jazz. His isn't a clarion voice, his speech not even oracular. We saw his face set like a swimmer's in the midst of the surges of distracting sound, and heard his words—some of them—the story of the beginnings of the Work, carrying steadily on.

The audience was in torment, partly because it was unable to hear or fix itself to listen, but mainly in pity for him. Yet amazement softly grew, for the voice carried steadily on. No irritation, no resentment: the steady advance of a man who had long since forgotten how to quit. To most, it would have been a shattering of inimical force, but this man was quite unruffled; his mind, turned inward to listen, did not give ear to outward disturbance. . . until we suddenly realized that it was calm outside, that a battle had been fought and won.

The following day, another incident occurred which seemed a further test of Wilson's character:

Among The Brother XII's mail when he reached San Francisco was a letter from a magazine editor, intimating possibilities of an article from him concerning the nature of the Aquarian Foundation. He considered this of immediate importance, groped his way out of the dim room of a hotel, and was sitting bare-headed on the benches of a park— Union Square, in fact—where I found him. He passed over to me the editor's letter and an outline of the article already set up. Now it happened that I knew the editor, something of the temper of the magazine, and what would happen in the editorial offices if an article like this were turned in. At the same time, when a man is hot in a work, pouring his powers into the form, it is about as pleasant a task to tell him he is off the track as to tell a mother her new-born shows signs of reversion to type. I handed the paper back, wondering how I could side-step.

"It does not appeal to you as quite the proper way to approach them?" he gently questioned.

"It does not," said I.

He listened carefully. "I am grateful to hear," he said. "I will try it from a new angle."

An hour or two later, he put into my hands a second budding manuscript. This time, he had a line on the subject, but his way into it would still make it impossible in that certain office in downtown New York. Again, he waited for me to speak; again, eagerly listened to years' experiences boiled hard: "Thank you," he said; "I see it more clearly, and shall try along a slightly different line."

A third time, the writing was brought . . . Through timed exposures, we are now able to witness the opening of a flower that requires days, magically reduced to a matter of seconds on the screen. It was like that, in a way, with the article he was writing. He was able to use the experience of another—in fact, the experience of another had flowed into him and become working knowledge in a forenoon. The point of the incident to me was that a difficult situation had been passed without the faintest wearing red of friction; no preconception on his part, no attachment to his own ideas, and he classed as an Englishman. This, and the banquet hall incident, made positively electric that day a later utterance from his lips—and his hand shot out as he said it: *"Brother, there can be no personality!"*

In Santa Cruz, Comfort and Wilson spent the day with Coulson Turnbull. A big white-haired man with a booming voice, the former Chicago policeman was regarded as one of the foremost astrologers in North America. The author of *The Solar Logos, The Divine Language of Celestial Correspondences,* and a number of important translations of eighteenth-century astrological texts, Turnbull had his own publishing company, The Gnostic Press. He was acting as the Western Divisional Secretary of the Aquarian Foundation and vigorously promoting Brother XII's work among his numerous clients.

Brother XII had brought with him on the trip the Act of Incorporation that he and Lucas had drawn up in Vancouver. Turnbull signed it, as Comfort had done before him. Wilson had told Lucas earlier that they had to have the actual signatures of the Governors on the document "for occult reasons." Turnbull's appointment as Governor brought the number to five, including Wilson himself, Joseph Benner, Edward Lucas, and Will Levington Comfort.

From Santa Cruz, an excited group breezed down the Pacific Coast, stopping every so often to meet other Foundation members in places like Monterey, San Luis Obispo, Oceano, and Arroyo Grande.

"We drove down from Arroyo Grande to Los Angeles,"

Comfort reported in *The Glass Hive*, "and he was not in the least dismayed by some fast going, relishing it keenly when we touched sixty-five. I counted it a most valuable point that he did no front or back-seat driving of any kind—a ready and racy human being who would rather eat a cracker or two in the open than the best of dinners in a restaurant. So long as there's tea . . ."

In Los Angeles, Brother XII stayed with Comfort at his home at 5336 Abbott Place, meeting Comfort's wife Penelope and his recently married daughter, Jane Comfort—also a writer.

"Everybody loved him," Jane recalls. "He was stimulating and wise, and always spoke carefully and with sensitivity. He wasn't overbearing—if he'd acted like an authority, he would have been much less appealing. But you felt his presence—he was carrying a lot of voltage!"

During his stay, Brother XII gave a number of talks at Comfort's home. He spoke to small groups and to people individually if they wished to have a private audience with him.

"When I went in to see him," Jane Comfort remembers, "he asked me, 'Do you have any questions?' I said, 'No, I have no doubts.' He talked on for a while, then he leaned forward and kissed me on the cheek. The kiss was lovely—it was very pure. It was a tribute, really. 'Steve will not mind that!' he said, referring to my husband. Then he took me by the shoulders and looked straight into my eyes. *'You are a living flame of Truth!'* he said, practically shaking with the intensity of his emotion. Then he let me go. 'Now, go!' he said. *'Go!'* And he practically shoved me out the door!"

Comfort and Wilson spent a great deal of time together. "They were marvelously and deeply drawn to each other," Jane recalls. "They were simply—'Brothers.'" Through hours of discussion, Comfort learned more about the experiences which had shaped Wilson's character:

"He has been a great deal apart, many years at sea. He has learned the coasts of the continents as many of us have learned the cities and plains and mountains. He has dealt with contours—even entering the tiny, stillest inlets. He is equipped with a strange, almost uncanny knowledge of boundaries, yet at the same time his sentiency is literally alive at the heart of things. . . He has known the childish ache for understanding and the bitterness of puritanical repressions, known the dissatisfaction of nomadic wanderings—the outcast on life's highway ceaselessly 'moved on' by Karma. . ."

A frequent visitor to the house during Wilson's stay was Baron Maurice Von Platen, a wealthy German-American who had retired to Pasadena with a sizeable fortune. Von Platen, who had made his money in the lumber business, was a philanthropist. He had turned his factory over to his workers when he'd retired, and his hobby was building pipe organs, which he donated to churches. Von Platen was interested in applying occult laws to the world of business in order to improve social conditions. He and Wilson conferred at length during their walks around the property, and Von Platen became the sixth Governor of the Aquarian Foundation.

Some of Comfort's other friends were less taken with Brother XII. Manly P. Hall, the highly respected occult scholar and editor of the journal *The All-Seeing Eye,* wrote to Comfort: "No one should be in a hurry to go forth serving humanity, lest in his impetuosity he destroy others and himself with them. The groundwork should be laid first . . ."

Alice Bailey, head of the Arcane School and a disciple of the Master Djwhal Khul, who dictated *Initiation, Human and Solar* to her, also wasn't prepared to endorse Brother XII unconditionally. She wrote to Comfort that while she was sympathetic to the aims of the Aquarian Foundation, her organization would only recognize it as a divinely inspired group "when it has proved its value and established its position other than by proclamation."

But in spite of the critics, Brother XII's California trip had been a resounding success. Many new groups had been formed and the interest in the Work was intense—in the five week period before and after Wilson's visit, Comfort had sold

300 copies of *The Three Truths* from his book room alone.

When the time came to leave Los Angeles, Brother XII was offered a ride back to San Francisco by a young bohemian couple. As the three drove north, Brother XII and the girl discussed astrology—she was a serious astrologer, and later married the eminent American astrologer Paul Case. They compared their horoscopes and discussed the astrological factors governing reincarnation. When the trio arrived in San Francisco, they stayed at the home of the girl's wealthy mother. After supper, Wilson and the girl talked late into the night and during their conversation, he made a startling proposition to her—he suggested that they have a child together. It would be a great soul, one of the adepts who was waiting to incarnate to take charge of the Work in the future. He had even calculated the exact moment when conception should occur. The girl was flattered—and shocked. She refused his offer.

A few days later, Brother XII boarded the steamer to return to British Columbia. The girl wrote at once to Jane Comfort, telling her about the incident. Although perhaps not completely innocent herself—she may have purposefully set out to try to seduce Brother XII—she took delight in exposing Wilson as a fraud and pretender.

"She felt she was saving us from a charlatan," Jane Comfort recalls. "She was certain she'd discovered a weakness in him—a sexual proclivity that would disillusion us all."

Will Levington Comfort apparently dismissed the incident; he continued to regard Brother XII as "a man beyond tampering."

△   △   △

On April 30, 1927, the group from England arrived in Vancouver, where they were met by Wilson and Lucas at the Canadian Pacific Railway Station at the foot of Granville Street. The new arrivals were a motley crew. Barley looked like the typical absent-minded professor, standing with a bemused expression on his face amidst his trunkloads of books. Annie Barley and Elma Wilson were anything but glamorous in their strange hats and dowdy English overcoats. Frederick Pope was frail and shy, and lacked personality. Sidney Sprey-Smith was obviously an eccentric. A bumbling, comical figure with a pronounced English accent, he kept telling Lucas he was a Buddhist. Lucas regarded him as "one of the world's worst god-damn fools!"

Lucas later described the new arrivals in the most unflattering of terms. Annie Barley was "a crank of the first water," and Elma Wilson "an emaciated old biddy with thin hair and a look about her resembling a reformed witch."

From Vancouver, the party proceeded directly to Nanaimo, where the women set up housekeeping in Northfield. The cramped accommodation led to some friction. According to Lucas, "the two women scrapped continually over who was the boss housekeeper."

Shortly after the group settled in, Wilson decided that the Aquarian Foundation needed an automobile. He and Sprey-Smith returned to Vancouver and set off with Lucas for a used car lot. After looking over a number of cars, they picked out a Reo touring sedan. Wilson decided to have some fun at Sprey-Smith's expense. He told the salesman that Sprey-Smith was an automotive expert and would examine the car.

"Hrumph, oh yes, a car!" stammered Sprey-Smith. "Well now, let me see, that is a nice car now, isn't it? Yes, indeed it is! Hrumph, now I'm supposed to examine the rear-end of this car. Can any of you gentlemen please tell me which end is the rear-end?"

After purchasing the Reo, the group began to search for a suitable site for the new colony. One excursion was made to an abandoned lumber camp south of Nanaimo, which Wilson claimed to have seen in a vision. It was a logged-over area and "bloody desolate," as Lucas put it, and he was able to talk Wilson out of it. He was also able to persuade him to drop his original condition that the site of the colony be exactly twelve hundred feet above sea level.

Another trip was made to a piece of land near Mount Benson, five miles west of Nanaimo. It too was judged unsuitable, much to the relief of the Barleys, who had "heaved a sigh at the thought of having to live in such a desolate and far-away spot."

In the middle of May, Wilson learned of some land for sale in the farming district of Cedar, nine miles south of Nanaimo. The group climbed into the Reo again and followed the Vancouver Island highway to the Cedar junction. Turning onto Holden-Corso Road, they drove through a pastoral landscape of green fields and old farmhouses reminiscent of England. They soon arrived at Cedar-by-the-Sea. Stepping out of the car, they gazed around at the breathtaking natural beauty of the site and unanimously declared, "This is the spot!"

The property was partially cleared, but thick stands of maple, alder, and cedar framed a stunning view of the offshore islands. The land sloped to a pleasant shingle beach, where only a hundred yards offshore, tiny Round Island was set like a jewel in the dazzling blue water. Looking through Dodd Narrows—formed by adjacent Gabriola Island—they could see the waters of Northumberland Channel, which provided a protected passageway to Nanaimo.

"Some lumbering was going forward at the time," Barley recalled, "and E. A.W. had his leg rather badly bruised by a log being dragged against it when the team was turning." Despite the mishap, everyone felt tremendously elated at discovering the ideal location for the settlement.

The next day, Lucas wired Comfort in Los Angeles: "The Head Center has been located as was provided in the Master's Plan. It is a place of incomparable beauty on the sea, surrounded by mighty ranges of green and white mountains, and lying snug among the Gulf Islands. It is a magnificent park—a fit and lovely setting for the work that is to be done there."

On May 17, Wilson signed a contract with the Western Fuel Corporation to purchase 126 acres at Cedar-by-the-Sea for $20 an acre. The money was to be paid in three installments: $842 was paid that day and two installments of $841 each were to be paid, on the same date, in the following two years. The Western Fuel Corporation reserved mineral rights.

The money for the first installment was provided by two persons: one, a civic official from Birmingham, England, and the other, Phillip Jutson Fisher, the balding thirty-five-year-old son of a wealthy Birmingham manufacturer. Separated and with a young son in England, Fisher was a manic type: he would play the piano for hours on end, often leaving the impression of his sweat-soaked plaid pants on the piano stool. He threw himself into the Work with fierce enthusiasm. Brother XII welcomed Fisher's energy and made him the seventh Governor of the Foundation.

Everything was now in place for the work of the Foundation to begin: the land had been acquired, the Governors appointed, and on May 16, 1927—the day before the property was purchased—the Aquarian Foundation was legally incorporated as a society by the province of British Columbia.

Brother XII wanted to start building on the property immediately, but he lacked the necessary funds. After discussing the situation with Lucas and the others, he decided to issue a General Letter to appeal for contributions:

Your Position—and Ours

To all Members:

We have to put this work upon a solid basis, and the first requirement is a suitable place to work, and some tangible means to carry on that work. We have to establish the Northern Center—that is Foundation work and it must be properly and effectively carried out.

At Nanaimo, there are six of us who are giving all our time and all our means to this Work; we are living in a small rented house and sleeping two in a room. The living room has been turned into an office, a desk in one corner and a multigraph machine in another, and most of the work is done on the dining room table. No salaries of any kind are paid— our weekly provision bill is divided into six equal parts and paid for out of our own slender resources: these are coming to an end.

About a month ago, it was proposed to put the position fairly and squarely before our members, but this suggestion was disapproved; a request for real help and cooperation was considered to be "Piscean," i.e. a method belonging to an Age and an order now passing away. We do not contest the point, but as most people are using Piscean brains and thought-processes, we must use Piscean methods if we are to reach them at all. That is common sense. Our work is to show them the new method and the new means, but we must begin at the beginning; mental telepathy is still an unknown quantity to most of you.

Our intention was to ask each member to contribute a small fixed sum each month—a voluntary offering, and without obligation. Again, this was objected to in certain quarters; we were told, "The Masters do not ask for money." In reply to this, our Brother E. A. Lucas of Vancouver said: "No, but the carpenters and plasterers and plumbers do." He prepared a frank statement of the case to put before you all, but this also was disapproved and again we did not press the point. What we have done so far has been made possible only by the generosity of TWO of our members—two out of many hundreds. It is now necessary that we put the position before you immediately and exactly—we believe that all will rise to the occasion if they understand the need.

(1) We have purchased 126 acres of land; one third is paid for, the balance is still unpaid and must be made secure.

(2) We have let the contract for fencing, $450, and the wire and other materials will cost about the same again.

(3) The Center Building will consist of a general office, small office, lecture-room, lobby, book-room, and six small rooms for workers. This will cost $4,500 at the lowest. Today,

I have to order a thousand dollars' worth of lumber and to pay cash for it—we have not got a thousand dollars. In addition to this, we need a large tank for central water supply, a furnace for central heating; we have to build a garage and other out-buildings. These are the barest actual requirements and allow nothing for office furnishings, etc.

To establish our Center will cost not less than eight thousand dollars: if eight hundred members will give ten dollars each it can be done, but some will be unable to do so; therefore, if you have freely received, then freely give. The Aquarian Foundation is not ours individually, yet we, as individuals, have had to contract liabilities for you all. Someone must be responsible, for workmen and firms will not deal with aspirations or helpful thoughts for currency—they need cash. Having thus explained the need, we believe that each of you will do his part, even as we strive to do ours. It calls for some personal sacrifice, but that is the duty and privilege of every disciple. This is a statement of facts; the appeal to help will come from the highest in yourselves—do not turn from that inner self.

Donations for the Center Fund should be by check or draft to either of the following names:—Maurice Von Platen, 1091 Oak Knoll Avenue, Pasadena, California; J. S. Benner, The Sun Publishing Company, Akron, Ohio; or to The Aquarian Foundation, P.O. Drawer 23, Nanaimo, B. C., Canada. LET THE WORK GO FORWARD.

The Brother, XII

The appeal for funds brought a generous response from the membership, although it upset some members who felt that funds shouldn't be solicited in such a manner. Wilson replied by saying that the appeal had been sanctioned by the Masters, that it was necessary, and that—perhaps most importantly—it had generated results.

His sensitivity to the criticism is evident in a thank-you note he wrote to a member who contributed ten dollars:

Dear Brother,

Our grateful thanks for your donation for our Center Building Fund. If others do their bit in a like spirit, we shall be able to provide for the physical and material needs of the Work. One of the favourite devices of the enemy is to spread the fallacy that the Work of the Lodge can be organized and accomplished on earth without material support. They cannot defeat our work on the higher planes, so they plot to cripple it outwardly and financially. This they do by sophistry, branding any outer need as the hallmark of insincerity.

Yours in Service,
The Brother, XII

Construction proceeded rapidly over the next several months. The site was cleared and the foundations laid for the Center Building. Lumber was hauled to the property on scows from the mill at Chemainus, and carpenters framed up houses for Wilson, Fisher, and the Barleys. A Delco power plant was installed; wells were dug and a water tower built. The entire property was fenced, and ten-foot-high gates were raised at the entrance.

The Lucas family moved from Vancouver to Cedar-by-the-Sea for the summer holidays, putting up two large tents in a lovely grove of maples. Lucas placed a wooden sign over one of the tent flaps, "CAMP EARLY DAWN," choosing the name because it was the early dawn of the Aquarian Foundation. Phillip Fisher noticed the sign and in the same spirit named his house "SUNRISE."

It was an idyllic time for the Lucas children. They played on the beach and swam every day. Wilson's elderly neighbour George Fiddick kept sheep, which often ran wild on the property before the fence was built—to the great delight of the Lucas children. "We used to chase one cranky old ram named 'Shorty,'" Frances recalls. "But whenever the sheep came on the property, Mr. Wilson would get very angry indeed!"

The land at Cedar was originally the home of the Cowichan Indians. The line of clam shells in the cliff marked the site of the midden, while the petroglyphs carved in the rocks outside the Center Building were evidence of an even earlier Indian culture. According to legend, five Indian nations had met on the site to end their tribal wars (the word "Nanaimo" is derived from "Sne-ny-mo," meaning "the whole" or "a big strong tribe"). The land at Cedar had become known as a place of peace, a sanctuary where no evil spirit could dwell. In the evenings, the Lucas family would sit on the wooden platform in front of their tent and gaze out across the clearing. Their dog, Wiggles, would cock his head, prick up his ears, and peer intently into the dark. "We'd all laugh," Frances recalls, "and say, 'Wiggles is seeing the Indians!'"

Wilson was well liked by the workmen. "The old man was a perfect gentleman," recalls Dick Nicholson. " 'Could we build a fence?' 'Sure, we'll build you a fence!' We built that fence in a month—840 rods around the property, sixty-five cents a rod. He never flickered once about wages."

"I can see his face plain as day," recalls another. "I used to call him the little bantam rooster—short, but just the same, he was a smart bugger! He knew about that big rock city in Australia, those tunnels in South America. He'd been everywhere. He was a skipper—slave-ships. He told me they had barbed wire on the decks all around the boat."

"They had a young Chinaman named Git working for them," another workman recalls. "I went to get some wedges from Wilson. He asked this Git, 'Where are those hammers and wedges?' He'd left them somewhere. Oh, he raised hell! He called him a slant-eyed, yellow-bellied Chinaman—or words to that effect. *You get them right now!'* he said. I guess a Chinaman was pretty low to him, but it seemed strange—the leader of an organization like that, and here he was cussing his head off!"

Lucas was amused rather than puzzled by Wilson's idiosyncrasies. "He used to drive the Reo at an alarming speed,"

Frances recalls. "Daddy used to laugh; 'Oh, you should have seen the Skipper,' he'd say, 'sitting up there behind the wheel, with his beard sticking up in the air!'"

Wilson had two twenty-eight-foot sailboats built in Victoria—one for himself and the other for Phillip Fisher. They were built from his own design, since, as Lucas put it, he considered himself "the dean of naval architects."

"Another one of my father's nicknames for him was 'Frankie,'" Frances explains, "because he was Francis Drake in his last incarnation. And I think Phil was Walter Raleigh."

"He knew his onions when it come to sailing," one workman recalls. "Did he ever! We'd go off to Valdes just for the heck of it. It didn't seem to matter to him that my pay was running on."

"He liked to be on the water," says another. "If you were steering his boat, he'd tell you which way to go. He'd say, 'Don't hit rocks and don't hit bottom.'"

Wilson's relationship with Elma was a subject of speculation. Although not legally married, they'd been together for about fifteen years. A librarian by profession, she had followed Wilson around the world, a steadfast and loyal mate. Despite Lucas's unflattering description, she had lovely eyes and was gracious and well-spoken. She was a bluestocking, prim and proper, "the soul of respectability."

"We had the notion he was kind of henpecked," Frances Lucas recounts. "He hinted that she wasn't an easy person to get along with. I remember him saying to my father that she was a wife in name only, that sex constituted no part of their life together."

"She was very prudish," recalls a woman whose mother and grandmother both knew Elma. "When they were building the colony at Cedar, she told my mother, 'We don't have locks on all the doors yet. We have a sign we put outside the bathroom, but I'm terrified of anyone coming in and seeing me in my knickers!'"

But in spite of their differences, Wilson and Elma treated

each other with respect and consideration. "Mrs. Wilson always referred to him as 'The Brother,'" adds the woman. "My grandmother would say, 'Don't say that; you mean, Mr. Wilson.'"

$$\triangle \quad \triangle \quad \triangle$$

During the summer of 1927, the Foundation's membership rapidly increased. *The Aquarian Foundation: A Movement for the Unification of All Men of Good Will* was published by Joseph Benner's Sun Publishing Company. A forty-eight page booklet, it contained *The Message,* as well as Brother XII's general letters from England, and included an application blank for those who wished to become "active servers in the greatest of all WORK—the saving of humanity." Individuals who joined the Society were put in touch with other members in their area. By the end of the summer, about 125 groups, composed of ten members each, had been formed in the United States and Canada.

Foundation Letters and Teachings was also made ready for publication. It was a collection of Brother XII's letters, articles, and teachings, and featured an introduction by Will Levington Comfort. Comfort described the first eighteen letters in the volume as "the burning words of one freshly emerged from a vision of the Plan. . . They carry the very light of Contact— from a personality aligned, inspired. We now read in them the Story of the Age, of all ages—the drama of an individual called to specific action for the whole of humanity." Five thousand copies of *Foundation Letters and Teachings* were published. It became the bible of the Aquarian Foundation, referred to constantly by members on matters of doctrine.

From all across North America, letters began pouring into the Foundation headquarters. Edward and Marion Lucas helped with the flood of mail. Wilson would read each letter and write instructions in the margin for how it should be answered. Lucas would then dictate a reply to Marion. Wilson's margin notes were often amusing, sometimes sarcastic. When a Vancouver group secretary informed him she planned another visit to the colony, he scribbled "God help us!" And when she told him she was using group meetings to pray for a sick member, he instructed Lucas: "Tell her this Work has nothing to do with personalities—she is utterly wrong to introduce such an element into a group meeting—it is not a glory hallelujah outfit. She will have to change her views and *actions* entirely. *Tell her so.*"

"Brother XII has asked me to reply to your letter," Lucas tactfully answered. "He wants me to remind you that we should not concern ourselves, as groups, with the personal problems or difficulties of anyone. One of the earliest and most emphatic pronouncements with respect to the Work was that in it, there can be no personalities."

Lucas also explained to members who had been accustomed to receiving personal replies from Brother XII that the pressure of his work now made this no longer possible: "This does not mean that The Brother XII ceases to take a personal interest in those he has formerly corresponded with; it means that his time and energy belong to this Work as a whole, and at present, he is very intensively engaged."

△   △   △

In a remote part of the estate at Cedar-by-the-Sea, a figure in a brown monk's robe glided silently through the patches of afternoon sun and shadow that dappled the forest floor. Passing beneath the dogwood blossoms that studded the green canopy above, it followed a winding path that led down into a wooded ravine. At the end of the path a small cabin stood nestled in a grove of maples. Taking a key from the folds of its robe, the figure unlocked the door, stepped inside and lay down upon a narrow cot. Night soon fell. As the trees glimmered in the moonlight, the figure lay motionless in a state of deep meditation, its consciousness transcending mortal embodiment until it merged with the Absolute.

So might one imagine one of Brother XII's periodic retreats into the House of Mystery. The little cabin in the woods had been built especially for Brother XII's use; it was the colony's *sanctum sanctorum,* and the disciples were forbidden to approach it, lest their vibrations disturb Brother XII's meditation. The House of Mystery was where he experienced *samadhi,* the highest state of consciousness that an individual can achieve.

Inside the House of Mystery, Brother XII also received his inspired writings, as well as instructions from the Masters of Wisdom for carrying out the Work. An important prayer that he'd received in this manner was "The Invocation of Light," which he claimed to have "recovered" at 5:00 A.M., April 27, 1926: "This is the Great Invocation repeated daily in the Temples for thousands of years."

THE INVOCATION OF LIGHT

O Thou Who bringest the Dawn,
Who renewest the day without ceasing,
Whose splendour is the Brightness of the Morning;
Fountain of Life and Source of Light Eternal,
Increase in us Thy Knowledge and Thy Strength.
Thou Who shinest in the East,
Who showest the West Thy glory,
And art supreme in the high heaven;
Thou fillest Thy Houses with Light,
And Thy Mansions with hidden Power.
Thou sustainest the Seven Lords,
The Shining Ones Who keep Thy Path,
And we, who serve Thee through Their Ray,
O Light ineffable.
Increase in us Thy Wisdom and Thy Power,
Dwell Thou in us, as we are One in Thee.

In a General Letter issued to members in July 1927, Brother XII announced that he planned a one week retreat into the House of Mystery:

"The time has come when he whom you know as The Brother XII must take another step, withdrawing for seven days from outer contacts. From sunset on the 14th until sunrise on the 22nd of July, give much time to Silence; in that way, you too may benefit from the Work which will then be done."

On the morning of his retreat, Brother XII joined the Lucas family on the wooden deck in front of their tent. He was wearing a brown monastic robe. He told them he would fast for the entire seven days. After having a last cup of tea with them, he bid farewell and vanished into the forest.

The days passed and everyone assumed the retreat was going well. One afternoon, Edward Lucas and Fred Pope were walking in the woods some distance from the House of Mystery when they heard the sound of sun-dried twigs snapping underfoot. Thinking that an intruder had scaled the fence surrounding the property, they quickly hid. A moment later, Brother XII appeared, hurrying along in a most earthly manner. Lucas and Pope looked at each other in astonishment. Wilson didn't see them and continued on his way, plowing through the underbrush.

"Well, one thing's certain," Lucas snorted. "The old man's in no trance!"

"We're not supposed to see that," whispered Pope.

A few days later, pale and drawn, Brother XII appeared at the Lucas tent. He asked Marion Lucas to make some custard for him, which he greedily devoured.

Brother XII announced to the members that the retreat had been a success. He had passed the "Fifth Initiation." He celebrated the attainment of his new occult status in the poem "Greeting." Two of the stanzas describe his ordeal of initiation:

And now this body!

Seven times seven years have I trained it, taught it,
Urged it to effort, tried it to the limit of its strength.
Knowledge I gave it—a little at a time,
And as the brain could bear it.
With my aid, it climbed steps—easily,
For I had known and climbed them long ago.
Four Gates I opened for these, my new bodies,
Lifting the latch easily, and passing through.
Now, almost within the hour, the Fifth Gate passed.
That body which was mine in part
Is now mine utterly.
Through the Dark Valley it passed,
Straight on, unwavering, fearless.
Fire, Water, Earthquake, Whirlwind –
All these it has passed unshaken,
The Great Ordeal –
The Ordeal of utmost surrender,
Ordained since the beginning of Time –
Is passed. . .

Three days after Brother XII's retreat, the Governors assembled at Cedar for the first annual General Meeting of the Aquarian Foundation. It was held on July 25, Wilson's birthday. Will Levington Comfort, Coulson Turnbull, Maurice Von Platen, and Joseph Benner each arrived from the United States to attend, joining Wilson, Lucas, and Fisher. It was the first time the seven Governors had all been together at the same time. The object of the meeting, as Comfort saw it, was for each Governor to break through "to that plane where our separate rays converged."

The evening before the meeting, six of the Governors talked quietly together outside the Center Building, and passed around the galley proofs of *Foundation Letters and Teachings*. "Our remarks were very casual," Turnbull observed. "We spoke of the nimble, clear and pungent style of our Brother's writings, the creative vitality in the almost magical words; his ability—we never doubted it—to execute the monumental task he had undertaken, and the swift and striking achievements already accomplished." In the deepening twilight, the six fell silent as they contemplated the beauty of the islands. The sound of the waves breaking on the shore drew them into meditation. Brother XII appeared unexpectedly. "He greeted us," Turnbull wrote, "and we were greatly touched with that 'Greeting.' Half-reflected or unreflected memories of the Past became ours. The Brother had attained the vision. Could he impart it to his lay Brothers? A little girl played innocently in and around the Seven, unconscious of the solemnities. 'God love her.' A new rhythm of unfoldment was born."

The day of the General Meeting, Wilson arose early. Today was his forty-ninth birthday, and he had every reason to feel satisfied by what he'd accomplished in the past twelve months. The colony had been only a dream then; now the large Center Building was almost completed, and he was the leader of one of the fastest growing spiritual groups in North America. It was a remarkable achievement.

Later that morning, at eleven o'clock on a perfect summer's day, the Governors and members of the colony gathered together on the grass under a great oak tree, which spread its branches over them like a protective canopy. Brother XII welcomed everyone to the meeting. After a few introductory remarks, he gave a short address, explaining the significance of the occasion. The destiny of mankind was guided by an association of highly evolved Spiritual Beings, he stated, known collectively as the Great White Lodge. These Beings worked in groups, many in number and almost infinite in their activities, but of these groups, twelve were especially concerned with the evolution of humanity and of the planet:

"Each of these twelve groups of Spiritual Beings have— or will shortly have—a focal point upon the physical earth; that is to say, will function through an incarnated physical body, so that there will be twelve men, in the literal human sense, who will in themselves embody the knowledge and power of those

Groups of Spiritual Beings they represent.

"Representatives of seven of these twelve groups have already taken—and are now using—human physical bodies. For many years past, they have schooled and trained these bodies, bringing them slowly, gradually, and by devious paths to an understanding of Who and What they are. Brothers and Sisters, it is my privilege to call together from widely separated points those six representatives of as many Groups now in physical embodiment—"

He then named the six representatives: Joseph Benner, Will Levington Comfort, Coulson Turnbull, Maurice Von Platen, Edward Lucas, and Phillip Fisher. These six Governors of the Aquarian Foundation had been drawn together by a common interest and were working in a common cause, he said, but their collaboration would go beyond this. They would soon become conscious Instruments of the Masters. As a result of the meeting, their consciousness would be raised and extended. Together, the Seven would work as One: "One Spirit, One Mind, One Purpose—Seven Groups working consciously through seven focal points, with One Mind and to One End."

The purpose of the Work would be fulfilled through the meeting that day, Brother XII declared. It was indeed a historic occasion—one for which Earth had waited for thousands of years: "Later, when men come to understand its true significance, the twenty-fifth day of July in the year 1927 shall be commemorated for long ages to come."

When the meeting ended, Von Platen asked Brother XII to sit with the other Governors for an informal group portrait. The seven men posed together in the shade of the magnificent oak. Wilson sat in his shirtsleeves in the center, flanked by Benner and Comfort, sunlight dappling his shoulders, his tie knotted loosely at his throat. It was one of the few times that he consented to be photographed.

After the picture was taken, Frances Lucas moved among the various Governors, asking them to contribute their signatures to her autograph book. Coulson Turnbull wrote a note of encouragement to his favourite student, jotting down the aspects for the day: Sun in Leo trine Saturn in Sagittarius; Sun and Saturn trine the conjunction of Jupiter and Uranus in Aries—a Grand Trine.

Frances approached Brother XII and asked him to sign her book. Taking it from her, he turned to a fresh page and crisply wrote: "A little line for Fran to commemorate a great day for us all, and for the world at large, from The Brother, XII."

The little group slowly dispersed. They were, they all believed, about to embark upon a magnificent spiritual adventure, one they would remember for the rest of their lives.

CHAPTER
III
Empire of Evil

On the first day of August, Edward Lucas climbed into one of the colony's rowboats and pushed off from shore. It was seven days after the General Meeting, and he still felt deeply affected by it. He rowed out into Stuart Channel towards the Strait of Georgia, the sun hot on his body as he dipped the oars into the glassy green water.

"I rowed until the horizon was a circle, of which I was the center," he later wrote. "The sun in the water slid every which way into crazy phantasmagoria, until I could not bear to look at it and shut my eyes. The sun went down and I was in the center of the night. My body, burdened with the past, slewed and slumped and failed me."

Lucas spent the night alone on the water. The next morning, as he watched the sun rise, he felt a renewed sense of purpose:

"I knew again the Light of Eternal Purpose.

"*I know.*

"I know that the wavering reflection of the sun in the water is not real. . . I know that all the works and activities of personalities are but the wavering of the sun in water, and have no existence. I may again be defeated and desolate and alone, but I will remember that in my hour of uttermost desolation, my integrity was established at the Center."

Lucas rowed back to shore, inspired by the experience. He later wrote to Will Levington Comfort: "Do you remember what Pompey said before his last battle—ringed with spears, his last hope gone? 'There are two Romes, Metellus: one built of bricks by hodsmen; but the Rome we serve glimmers in the uplifted heart. Let us not shame that city.'"

Brother XII had told the Governors they would experience an expansion of consciousness as a result of the General Meeting. Coulson Turnbull, like Lucas, had a visionary experience, which confirmed to him that he was Brother IX. Joseph Benner also felt his spiritual powers increase. He was certain that "the vision shining brightly before us" would be rapidly brought into physical manifestation.

Will Levington Comfort, who had some earlier misgivings about Brother XII, wrote that the experience of the General Meeting was "priceless. . . not without splendour. In the South again, the air seemed extra clear. . . The Brother's vibration [had] charged us electrically."

The work at the headquarters steadily progressed as summer turned to fall. In November 1927, the first issue of *The Chalice*, "The Herald of the New Age," was published. The content of the Foundation's monthly magazine surprised many members as they realized for the first time that the Aquarian Foundation was a militant political organization with an unusual philosophy. Brother XII's political beliefs could be summed up in a single word—*conspiracy*.

In his article "What Is the Aquarian Foundation?" Brother XII wrote about a grand design which had existed throughout history to enslave the masses: "Is the financial world the product of the servants of God, or the children of Mammon? What is there that is not controlled, directly or indirectly, near or afar, by the hidden hand of finance?" The real rulers of the world, he claimed, were the servants of the Antichrist, and they controlled everything—from the price of bread to the policies of nations. "No President is ever elected, or King crowned, no treaty ever signed, or army moved, unless it be at the bidding, or at least with the knowledge and consent, of this unseen power which controls prince and president and peasant alike."

The modern world, he explained, was almost entirely the result of the successful plannings of a sinister and merciless power—an invisible "Empire of Evil." It deliberately fomented hatred and strife among the peoples of Earth, setting labour against capital, and nation against nation. By skilful manipulation of the press, it promoted national hatreds, which often culminated in war. In order to wage these wars, countries were forced to borrow—not paper money, but gold—at high rates of interest from those who controlled the supply. No matter which side won or lost, the interest piled up and the gold-getters secured a fresh grip upon their prey. This same hidden power also insisted—again, through a controlled press—on the necessity for huge armaments, which kept the people impotent under the burden of an enormous taxation. The crazy emphasis given in the newspapers to "sport," divorce cases, lost heiresses, channel swimmers, and the details of sordid crimes, was part of a deliberate plan to keep the masses blinded with non-essentials, distracted and amused, so that they would not think for themselves and investigate the varied and significant moves of the "Big Steal."

Brother XII claimed that this "Empire of Evil" had existed for thousands of years. It was the product of a patience that counted centuries as men counted years. In one form or another, it had existed since the time of Atlantis. Kingdoms and empires rose and fell, but the "Empire of Evil" endured unchanged, its teachings, aims, and methods handed down to chosen successors from age to age. It had engineered the fall of the Roman Empire, the death of Jesus of Nazareth and the corruption of His Teachings. It had produced the French and the Russian Revolutions; and Bolshevism—that insidious and hateful poison which was undermining all rule and authority—was its last and most fatal production.

What was the ultimate goal to be attained by this invisible "Empire of Evil"? asked Brother XII:

> It is this: when the peoples of the Earth have been drawn into the net which is spread for them, when the nations are bankrupt and disorganized, when the machinery of government has failed on every hand, and the masses of the people have been decimated by murderous wars, bled white and crazed with accumulated miseries; when they are unable to resist an open and organized attempt upon their liberties—THEN will this Invisible Empire step into the light, its own system of government ready-made, all wealth and resources in its own control, and will say to the distracted nations: "All your schemes have failed and your resources are at an end; therefore, accept our government which is wise and benevolent and, above all, powerful." Resistance will be impossible, and self-interest will dictate surrender; the Invisible Empire will have become visible, openly acknowledged and irresistible, and A WORLD DICTATORSHIP WILL BE SET UP.

Brother XII assured his readers that this "Empire of Evil" would not remain unchallenged. It had been decreed from age to age that the forces of light would intervene at the moment when the powers of darkness were near to final mastery. This divine intervention was once more to be manifested in the present day. The Aquarian Foundation was the coming into physical embodiment of those spiritual Beings who would save mankind in its hour of greatest need. As Brother XII explained in *The Chalice*:

At every critical period in world history, certain individuals are born into the world with a distinct mission, and furthermore, they come fully equipped with the knowledge or the power needed for the accomplishment of that mission.

Such persons are not ordinary persons in the accepted meaning of that term: they are rather Powers or Potencies which have taken physical embodiment the better to perform the task allotted to them. They are unmoved by personal power, untouched by the desire for wealth or personal possessions, which might deflect them from the path marked out. They shun publicity, and desire only that personal seclusion which is an indispensable factor in their Work.

Such is The Brother XII. . .

Brother XII concluded that whether men knew it or not, they were rapidly approaching the most terrible conflict in the history of mankind upon the planet. They were moving swiftly towards the culminating struggle between two great opposing powers—the powers of darkness and the forces of light.

The final battle was about to be fought—Armageddon.

△　　△　　△

Brother XII's beliefs were extreme, but not uncommon for the 1920s. It was the era of trusts and mergers. United States Steel, General Motors, and General Electric were only a few of the companies formed by gigantic mergers. Oil companies, railroads, banks, food and drug companies had followed suit. Merger seemed to have become a mania. Many contemporary observers felt that such concentrations of wealth and power had sinister implications, since a few key individuals could exert tremendous control over every aspect of economic life. Many of the great mergers were handled by Jewish banking houses, such as Goldman, Sachs and Company, Lehman Brothers, and Kuhn, Loeb and Company. The directors of these banking houses were suspected of plotting to control world capital, and of manipulating international politics in order to achieve their goal of world domination. This supposed plot was known as "The International Jewish Conspiracy."

The major document purporting to expose this conspiracy was the infamous *Protocols of the Elders of Zion.* Allegedly the notes of a secret meeting of Jewish Elders held in Basel, Switzerland, in 1897, *The Protocols* outlined a program to overthrow Christianity through subversion and sabotage, and to control the world. Translated into English in 1920, they caused a sensation. American industrialist Henry Ford printed a series of articles based on them in his newspaper *The Dearborn Independent,* and published them in a book, *The International Jew,* of which over a million copies were distributed. *The Protocols* were later discovered to be a forgery, written by members of the Russian secret police, but Ford and others continued to insist they were genuine.

Brother XII believed in the authenticity of *The Protocols,* using them as evidence to bolster his own theory of conspiracy:

"This plot is a *Jewish plot*; it is a small group of International Jews who control practically every banking house in the world. Big business is no longer done by banks, but by chains of banks, and these various chains are all, in their turn, under the control of this one small group of men, whose aim is the absolute domination of the Earth, and the enslaving of every nation, every people, every race except their own."

In addition to the Jews, Brother XII believed that there was another force at work which sought to enslave the human spirit—the Roman Catholic Church. It wasn't a religion at all, he argued, but "a system of cruel and relentless political intrigue, which uses the spiritual aspirations of millions of human beings to its own vile ends." He chronicled the Church's history of intrigue, persecution, and slaughter—including the Gunpowder Plot to blow up the British Houses of Parliament, the Inquisition with its infamous "Star Chamber," and the slaughter of thousands of French Protestants in the St. Bartholomew's Day Massacre of 1572. He claimed that the bloody cruelties of Rome—conversion or extermination—hadn't changed over the centuries, and that now the Church had turned its attention to the United States, where it was relentlessly pushing forward its plans to "Make America Catholic."

In the summer of 1926, a million and a half Roman Catholics had attended the Eucharistic Congress in Chicago. On his way to the Congress, Cardinal Bonanza, the Papal Legate, stopped in New York, where he was received at City Hall with all the pomp and ceremony accorded a prince of the Vatican. A devout Roman Catholic, Governor Alfred E. Smith knelt down before the magnificently robed Cardinal and kissed his ring—a public act of obeisance that touched off a storm of controversy across the United States. Smith was the leading contender for the Democratic presidential nomination; his ring-kissing raised the spectre of Papal interference in the affairs of the nation.

Would a Roman Catholic President not owe a dual allegiance—to both the United States Constitution and to the Roman Catholic Church? The Constitution provided for separation of Church and State, and guaranteed religious freedom. Roman Catholic doctrine, on the other hand, claimed Church sovereignty over the State, and demanded absolute obedience from its subjects in all matters temporal as well as spiritual. Would Alfred E. Smith be able to resist pressure from the Vatican in matters vital to the interests of the Roman Catholic Church? A prominent Methodist Bishop expressed the prevailing Protestant sentiment: "No Governor can kiss the papal ring, and get within gunshot of the White House!"

Writing in *The Chalice*, Brother XII warned that if Smith were elected, Mexico would be annexed, Britain financially crushed, and the fate of Protestantism sealed. The presidential election of 1928 would decide not only the destiny of North America, but that of the entire civilized world.

The Republican Party offered no better alternative. In Wilson's opinion, Herbert Hoover, the bland and uninspiring Secretary of Commerce, was the instrument of the Jewish Money Hierarchy, and not the choice of the majority of Republicans. He'd been foisted upon them in the same way that Smith had been manipulated into place by back-room party politics. The people didn't have any real choice: "Elect Hoover, and you will be plundered in a thousand ways. Elect Smith, and freedom will become only a memory in the land."

Brother XII had devised a plan to defeat both Hoover and Smith. He would go to Washington, D.C., and form his own political party. He believed that there were people dedicated to the ideals of democracy and freedom who would join him in setting up a Third Party. With their support, he would achieve political power, and, guided by the Masters, would establish "The Kingdom of Righteousness" on Earth.

△   △   △

At the Aquarian Foundation headquarters at Cedar-by-the-Sea, snow covered the giant firs. Two figures in heavy overcoats made their way towards the waiting car. Brother XII and Phillip Fisher were leaving on their long journey to Washington, D. C.

The car wound through the winter landscape towards the Vancouver Island highway. In his luggage, Brother XII carried "The Big Document," his plan for the formation of a Third Party in the United States. Copies of it had already been sent to all United States congressmen and to key political organizers in the Capitol. The Third Party would run its own slate of candidates in the upcoming 1928 election. It would be a coalition, drawing together disaffected elements from both the Democratic and Republican parties, as well as other political minority groups. Brother XII believed that the immediate formation of the Third Party was the only hope for the nation—he planned the biggest political upset in American history.

△　△　△

In Washington, D. C., President Calvin Coolidge was facing a crisis. On January 7, 1928, he'd dispatched two battalions of marines to Nicaragua to help the ruling military dictatorship put down a popular uprising. Six American marines had been killed in the fighting and twenty-six wounded. The lights in the White House burned late into the night as debate raged in the Senate over the President's action. Coolidge was accused of waging war in Nicaragua without the consent of Congress in order to protect American financial interests.

Brother XII and Phillip Fisher arrived in Washington and met Joseph Benner, who'd come from Akron, Ohio, to join them. The three men discussed strategy in a hotel room, then began contacting those senators and members of the House of Representatives they thought would be sympathetic to a Third Party. The present crisis only underscored the corruption of the present administration and the vital need for political reform. Brother XII planned to exploit the antipathy many Protestants felt towards Roman Catholics. Already, a protest movement was building across the United States against the nomination of Alfred E. Smith for president. Political cartoons crudely depicted the New York Governor as the puppet of corrupt big city bosses and a willing pawn of the Vatican.

Brother XII enlisted the support of a number of Protestant groups in Washington. He talked to Gilbert O. Nations, editor of *The Protestant*, who was enthusiastic about the plan for a Third Party. He also recruited James S. Vance to his cause. A flamboyant former drugstore magnate, Vance edited the Ku Klux Klan newspaper, *The Fellowship Forum*. The Klan had claimed five million members at its peak in 1924, and although its power had declined, it was still a potent force in American politics. *The Forum* was publishing front page diatribes against Smith's nomination, and Brother XII arranged to reprint several of its articles in *The Chalice*.

The Klan's unofficial spokesman in Congress, and a key individual in Brother XII's plans, was Senator James Thomas Heflin of Alabama. A colourful figure in his black Prince Albert frock coat, cream vest, and flowing black tie, "Tom Tom" Heflin was famous for his fiery oratory, and notorious in the Senate for his fulminations against the Roman Catholic Church. He'd repeatedly denounced the Church hierarchy for its interference in American politics—in particular for its repeated attempts to pressure the Administration to invade Mexico. Heflin had been slandered by the Hearst newspapers, and threats had been made against his life. Attacked as a bigot and accused of fanning the flames of religious intolerance, he remained undaunted. He claimed to have received thousands of letters of support from across the United States, and declared that two-thirds of his fellow senators supported his views in private, but were afraid to speak out in public on such a controversial issue.

When Brother XII arrived in Washington, Heflin's denunciation of the Administration's policy in Nicaragua was on the front page of *The New York Times*. He accused the Coolidge Administration of being controlled by "the golden wand of Wall Street," and charged that American boys were being butchered in Nicaragua so that greedy New York bankers could reap profits from the oppression of the Nicaraguan people. Heflin claimed that an "unholy alliance" existed between the "money-changers" of Wall Street and the hierarchy of the Roman Catholic Church.

Brother XII admired Heflin for his fearless political stand. The two men met in the Senator's cluttered office in the Senate Office Building. They made strange political bedfellows—the heavyset Dixie demagogue and the ascetic English mystic. No details of this extraordinary meeting are known, but in all likelihood, Wilson asked Heflin to be the Third Party candidate for president, no doubt invoking the vision of a stunning victory in the 1928 election, and of a Protestant America united under Heflin's leadership. At the very least, Wilson must have assured the Alabama senator that unseen powers would assist them, crowning their efforts with success.

On January 18, Heflin stood up in the Senate and launched into a tirade against the Roman Catholic Church and the candidacy of Alfred E. Smith. "Talk to me about Al Smith!" he thundered in a voice that could be heard in the rotunda of the Capitol. *"He will never be nominated!"* In the packed galleries high above the Senate floor, Brother XII undoubtedly nodded his approval as Heflin assailed the secret political program of the Roman Catholic hierarchy. Two hours later, his face dripping perspiration and his big frame quivering with emotion, the Alabama senator finished his oration and sat down, exhausted.

The Senate chamber was silent. Then all heads turned as Senator Joseph T. Robinson of Arkansas asked permission to speak. Turning to his colleague, he condemned his speech as utterly unworthy of a senator. It was the first time any senator had dared to rebuke Heflin. "I have heard the senator from Alabama denounce the Catholic Church, and the Pope of Rome, and the Cardinal, and the Bishop, and the priest, and the nun, until I am sick and tired of it!" exclaimed Robinson. Heflin fumed in his seat, while Robinson went on to praise Roman Catholics for their contribution to America.

Finally, Heflin jumped to his feet. He was livid. "I'd like to see you make that speech in Arkansas!" he shouted at Robinson.

"I'll make it in Arkansas—and in Alabama, too!" Robinson retorted.

"Yes, and if you do, they'll tar and feather you!"

Heflin's remark brought immediate cries of protest from the other senators, who were appalled by the utterance. The Senate was gradually restored to order, but the bitter exchange between the two senators was splashed across the front pages of every newspaper in America. The smoldering religious issue had erupted into public debate.

Two days later, at separate times, Heflin and Robinson reiterated their views on religion before the lights and cameras in a "Movie-Tone" studio in Washington, D. C. In theatres across the United States, the American public watched as Robinson argued for religious tolerance, while Heflin vehemently declared he was opposed to having the United States Army fight religious battles in foreign countries. The debate generated further publicity and served to make religion a major issue in the approaching election.

As the "Protestant Crusade" rapidly gained momentum across the United States, there was considerable speculation about its leading spokesman. Was Senator Heflin acting on his own, or were his outrageous public performances and inflammatory speeches masterminded by a sinister influence working behind the scenes? The Catholic magazine *Commonweal* wondered if Heflin's present attitude in the Senate had been cleverly assigned to him by forces which preferred to remain incognito. Such forces, if they existed, have never been identified. The extent of Brother XII's involvement with Senator Heflin is still uncertain. Six months after his meeting with the Alabama senator, on the occasion of the second annual General Meeting of the Aquarian Foundation, he stated:

"In Washington in January last, I told Senator Heflin to get into the limelight as the champion of Protestantism, and to stay there. He has since done that very effectively, and is still doing it. At the same time, I set certain experienced political organizers at the work of forming the Third Party, or rather at laying the wires for its formation later. That work has also been done. In other ways, I have worked ceaselessly to make this 1928 campaign appear what it really is—a religious issue, a struggle between Popery and Protestantism."

△   △   △

Brother XII was also attempting to start a political organization in England. Before he left for Washington, he had submitted an article to *The Referee*, a politically independent newspaper with a circulation of over a million readers.

"I have written a BIG article for the leading Sunday newspaper in Britain (at the request of the editor)," he informed Lucas. "If it is published, and I think it will be, it will cause the most profound effect in that country. In other words, the people of England will themselves take charge, and we shall get something done."

When Brother XII returned to the headquarters, a letter was waiting for him from Albert Laker, editor of *The Referee.* Laker said he'd expected Wilson's article to treat of occult signs, but had found instead "a frank attack on Roman Catholics and Jews, and we endeavour in *The Referee* to avoid any attacks on religious bodies." He told Wilson it was out of the question for him to publish the article.

There was also a letter from Sir Kenneth MacKenzie of Tunbridge Wells, who'd arranged for Wilson to submit the article in the first place. A renowned engineer who'd played a key role in introducing electricity into Great Britain, MacKenzie was one of Brother XII's most ardent supporters in England. He expressed his regret at Laker's decision and suggested Wilson send the article to *The Morning Post*, whose editor had expressed even stronger sentiments in his preface to *The Cause of the World's Unrest.* "I might get him to accept it, for *it ought to be published,* and *in England,* but you do not seem now to want my help in any way! You treated me differently this time last year! No matter, I am still & always with you in our MASTER'S SERVICE, whatever happens."

Sir Kenneth's letter, with its puzzlement at Brother XII's changed attitude, should have been a warning to Wilson. Already his arbitrary conduct had alienated Will Levington Comfort. He'd objected to Brother XII's money-raising methods, and to his policy of having groups follow exact instructions from headquarters. The two men clashed outright when Comfort edited one of Brother XII's articles for *The Glass Hive.* Wilson insisted it be printed without any changes. Comfort refused—and resigned from the Foundation.

A saddened Comfort later described the July General Meeting at Cedar-by-the-Sea to his daughter Jane in a single sentence: "*We gathered together under a dead tree.*" His wife, Penelope, was more cryptic: "In Nanaimo, even the sharks are toothless!"

Edward Lucas was caught in the middle of the dispute. Comfort urged him to break with Wilson—"He's not what he claims to be!"—but Lucas wouldn't hear of it. He was fascinated by the political aspects of the Work, and besides, he was having too much fun.

In one of the monthly Instructions issued to Aquarian Foundation members, Brother XII denigrated Comfort. He accused him of using the Work as a means of "enhancing such small glory as he may have gained by lecturing or the writing of books," and said that Comfort's constant stressing of the personal showed that he'd never really understood the purpose of group work at all: "Personal viewpoint, personal reactions, personal 'clean-up'; thus speaks Mr. Passion-for-the-personal."

Comfort's departure caused the members to wonder: Why would a man who'd been such an enthusiastic supporter of Brother XII now repudiate him? And Brother XII's bitter attack on Comfort also gave them pause. This split among the Governors did not augur well for the future of the Foundation.

Despite these setbacks, Brother XII pressed on with his work. In February 1928, he received a letter from an eighty-five-year-old retired lawyer in Carthage, Missouri, named Oliver G. Hess. He'd read some of Brother XII's writings, and wanted to contribute twenty thousand dollars to the Foundation. But when he later vacillated, blaming his infirmities for his failure to send the securities, Brother XII dispatched Edward Lucas to Carthage to personally explain the Work to Hess.

Lucas and Hess had two things in common: they were both lawyers and they both had a fascination with the American Civil War. Lucas had a library of books on the subject, and Hess was a veteran—he'd fought with the Union forces in Illinois and been wounded at the Battle of Beverly Ford.

Lucas spent several days with Hess, explaining the nature of Brother XII's work to him. He told Hess that the entire financial system in the United States was built up as slenderly as a house of cards, and that the whole structure was about to come crashing down. It was too late to prevent the utter financial demoralization of the United States, he said, but the work of the Aquarian Foundation would prevent the forces of evil from achieving their ultimate objective of world domination. Impressed by the gravity of the situation, Hess promised to execute a trust agreement, transferring twenty thousand dollars in securities to the Foundation.

In due course, the bonds comprising "The Oliver G. Hess Trust" arrived at the Canadian Bank of Commerce in Nanaimo. Brother XII was the sole trustee, authorized to use the funds as he saw fit to advance the work of the Aquarian Foundation. In accordance with Hess's express wish, one set of bonds was put aside to provide Wilson with a small, personal income for life, so that his time would always be available for the Work.

Wilson wrote at once to Hess, assuring him that the management of the Trust would be "a stewardship that will be very sacredly regarded." He expressed a desire to know more about the lives of Hess and his elderly wife, and invited them to the Center for an extended visit:

"I cannot bear to think of loneliness touching you, and you will remember that I once said that I thought we would soon see each other face to face. Well! It is on the knees of the Gods, and you must do as you feel able, but at least I want you to know that this request of mine is from the heart. After Easter, the weather will be beautiful, and it is never really cold. This is one of the most *lovely* spots on Earth, and there are other things connected with it that you will understand fully only if you can come and see us."

Wilson also sent Hess a photograph of himself taken in Italy two years earlier. He told him it was a personal memento for him alone, and asked him not to show it to others:

"Personalities are the bane of this and every other work, and so far as I am concerned, I wish to keep in the background as far as is humanly possible. That snapshot you got of a number of us here taken last summer was, in my estimation, a mistake. I will see that they do not get me in any more snapshots that may be taken here because it defeats that intention of personal effacement which is a sort of protective armour in my own case."

Hess was deeply touched by Wilson's letter, and replied that nothing in the world would give him greater satisfaction than "seeing you and sitting at your feet and learning from your lips the mysteries of Godliness." But he didn't think he or his wife could survive the journey to the Coast in their frail condition. He sent Brother XII his love, and wished "God's blessing upon your noble and self-sacrificing work."

Brother XII continued to solicit support for his Third Party. In the spring of 1928, he took another major step in advancing his political work by forming the Protestant Protective League. The P.P.L. was designed to coordinate the activities of the various Protestant groups that were mobilizing for the upcoming American election. Advertisements in *The Chalice* stated: "Romanism is organized. Protestantism is unorganized. The P.P.L. exists for the purpose of organizing and combining all Protestant elements in the face of a common menace and a common foe." Brother XII intended to use the P.P.L. to build up the Third Party—and the Third Party to build up the P.P.L. He hoped that, together, the two organizations would generate the popular support he needed to ensure the nomination of a Third Party candidate for President.

Brother XII worked quickly to get the P.P.L. off the ground. He arranged for an individual named C. J. Wright of Houston, Texas, to head the League in the United States, and for the "news and views" of the P.P.L. to be printed in *The Pro-Protestant*, a weekly newspaper published in Chicago. Closer to home, he appointed a Vancouver department store executive named John Harrison to run the League in Canada. A bluff

Englishman and hail-fellow-well-met type, Harrison rented an office in the Shelly Building in Vancouver and began drumming up support for the League both locally and nationally.

In late March, eighteen-year-old Eric Davenport, a recent graduate of the Pitman Business College, arrived at the P.P.L. office to apply for a job as a secretary. The first question Harrison asked him was "Are you a Protestant?" Assured that he was, the interview commenced. Harrison dictated a letter which Davenport took down in shorthand, then typed up on the office's new Corona typewriter. Pleased with his accuracy and speed, Harrison hired him on the spot and told him to start work on the first of the month at a place called Cedar-by-the-Sea, outside Nanaimo. His salary would be fifty dollars a month, with room and board. As Davenport was leaving, Harrison handed him a small printed card which stated that he was a member in good standing of the Protestant Protective League.

Two days later, Davenport clutched anxiously at the dashboard of Phillip Fisher's pickup truck as it barrelled along the twisting road towards Cedar. It was night—the ferry had arrived late—and the glare of the headlights startled deer feeding at the side of the road. Fisher talked incessantly as he drove, explaining the work of the Aquarian Foundation to the new employee.

"He practically raved!" Davenport recalls. "He was talking all about Brother XII—and American politics—and all the great things that were going to happen. Then he turned to me with an odd look and said, 'You don't understand any of this now—but one day you will.'"

The headquarters was in darkness when they arrived. Candles flickered in the windows of the houses, and in the moonlight the trees cast gigantic shadows on the ground as Davenport stumbled out of the car and followed Fisher across the clearing to Wilson's house. In the eerie, candlelit interior, he was introduced to Brother XII.

"I was never so scared in all my life," he recalls. "I didn't know what I was getting into—I thought he might be a murderer or something!"

Wilson quickly put the nervous youth at his ease, explaining that there'd been a power failure at the Center—the Delco generator had broken down. Had he had anything to eat? he asked. The next thing Davenport knew, he was over at the Hobarts' house, tucking into a big plate of bacon and eggs, while George and Louise fussed over him like a long-lost son. He was soon fast asleep in a snug little bedroom upstairs in the Center Building.

In the morning, Davenport reported for work in Wilson's office. His job was to take dictation and type up Brother XII's letters. "He was writing to American senators, a police chief in Chicago—people like that," he recalls. "All 'big shots,' high 'muck-a-mucks'!"

Davenport enjoyed working for Wilson, who was usually in good spirits and had an engaging sense of humour. "He had the sweetest laugh," he recalls. "He'd throw his head back and chuckle—it was really catching!

"One time, I had a terrible headache. When I told him I couldn't finish the letters, he said, 'That's all right, Eric; you go upstairs to bed; I'll type them.' And he did—I could hear him going like a bat out of hell!"

In warm weather, the two worked outdoors in front of the Center Building. Wilson would sit cross-legged on the grass, guru-style, and dictate to his young secretary, while Davenport would lie on his stomach with his shorthand notebook propped up in front of him:

"I remember one letter took up thirteen pages—both sides— of my shorthand notebook. He'd go on and on—he'd elaborate tremendously. It was marvellous to hear him. That letter was my prize! I kept it for years!"

Many of the letters Brother XII dictated concerned the P.P.L. He was trying to persuade other Protestant organizations to join the League, so that the separate groups battling the political program of the Roman Catholic Church could be

combined into one united, effective whole. He didn't intend
for the P.P.L. to be only "one more berry on the bush," as he
put it. He reminded his various correspondents of the maxim,
"In unity is strength."

Brother XII was also laying in large quantities of supplies at
the headquarters—flour, sugar, salt, matches, needles, and a
variety of building materials.

"I spent all day helping him store sugar in the attic of his
house," recalls Davenport. "We took turns throwing ten-
pound sacks of sugar up to each other. He even had big bolts
of blue cloth stored in the Center Building—you could've
made dozens of suits from them. He was stockpiling it all for
Armageddon!"

The spring of 1928 also saw a group of new arrivals take up
permanent residence at the headquarters. In April, Maurice
and Alice Von Platen drove up from Pasadena, hauling a
trailer loaded with furniture. Brother XII greeted the distin-
guished-looking retired businessman and his elegant wife as
they pulled up in front of the Center Building, and showed
them to the new home that Von Platen had arranged to have
built for them. It was a spacious two bedroom house with a
stone fireplace, large sundeck, and twin garages. The Von
Platens settled into their new home, delighted to be at the
Center, since they'd dreamed for many years of living in a spiritual community.

The Von Platens were soon joined by their friends, the
Squiers. Ethel Squier and Alice von Platen had been lifelong
companions—they'd attended the same girls' school in Albany,
New York—and had been neighbours in Pasadena, where
Ethel and her daughter, Lucita, ran a successful weaving business. Von Platen had also built a fine house for the Squiers,
complete with a weaving studio, since they planned for their
work to provide a source of income for the colony.

Another friend of the Von Platens' arrived, an astrologer
named Robert DeLuce. A lanky, slow-speaking former mining

engineer from the Midwest, DeLuce had taught astrology at First Temple and College of Astrology in Los Angeles. He'd tried to start a colony similar to the Aquarian Foundation several years earlier in Pasadena without success. He was interested in using the occult sciences to extend the human lifespan, and his article on this topic, "Physical Regeneration," had appeared in *The Chalice* under the name "Lux." DeLuce and his family moved into the house which Von Platen had built for them. Brother XII was pleased to have a man of DeLuce's reputation at the Center and made him a Governor of the Society, filling the vacancy created by Comfort's resignation.

Arriving at about the same time as DeLuce was Coulson Turnbull, who drove up from Santa Cruz with his wife, Cecilia. It was a honeymoon and the start of a new life for the couple, since Turnbull's first wife had recently died after a long illness. Already considered one of the leading astrologers in the country, Turnbull became a regular contributor to *The Chalice*. Brother XII informed the members: "There are few men in America with insight so keen and knowledge so comprehensive as that possessed by Dr. Turnbull."

Another important addition to the community was a former secret service agent with the United States Government who had also been a detective with the William S. Burns Agency and an accountant for the U. S. Treasury Department. Robert England arrived at the colony from Oceano, California, packing a pair of Colt 32s, and amazed everyone with a demonstration of his lightning-fast draw from a shoulder holster. Despite his adventurous background, England was an introspective man whose life had been marked by the tragic death of his wife and daughter several years earlier. In Frances Lucas's autograph book, he wrote: "May life's purpose prove itself to you without the harshness and the sting I felt for many years. The motive will bring the counterpart of itself into every aspect of life. May your motive be above the worldly concerns so common." England soon made himself indispensable to Brother XII, who appointed him Secretary-Treasurer and later a Governor of the Foundation.

And lastly, one of the most enthusiastic members of the Foundation arrived after a "Keystone Cops" chase up the coast from Los Angeles. James Janney Lippincott, a distant relative of the publishing family, was a draftsman whose passion for astrology—to the complete neglect of his domestic responsibilities—had his wife Louise at her wits' end. Lippincott described himself to Brother XII as "a regular 'blood-hound' for Truth," and wrote that he wished to make "an ORDERED and LOVING" separation from his wife, so he could devote himself completely to the Work. When he finally fled to British Columbia, Louise followed in hot pursuit, trying to have him committed, so that she could obtain a financial settlement from him.

"He joked about it," Eric Davenport recalls. "Whenever she caught up to him, she'd go to the police, claim he was crazy, and have him thrown in jail. In Seattle, he was given this pair of denim coveralls to wear. He was six feet six, and they were so short, the sleeves only came up to his elbows. They wouldn't let him shave. 'Just imagine what I looked like when I went before the judge!' he said. 'You see, I *looked* crazy!'"

Lippincott took refuge at the Center, where he did astrological charts for Brother XII and helped with *The Chalice*. His wife returned to Los Angeles after her claim for support was thrown out of the British Columbia courts on a technicality.

Once they were settled at the headquarters, the new arrivals worked hard to make the colony a thriving success. Maurice Von Platen spoke for them all when he wrote to Oliver Hess: "I'm sorry your advanced years do not make a trip here possible, since only in person can you know the thrill of personal contact with the life here."

Brother XII now purchased four hundred acres on nearby Valdes Island. He planned to build a new settlement here in the tradition of the *ashram*, the Hindu equivalent of the monastery. It would be a separate community for selected disciples,

distinct from the colony headquarters at Cedar. The land was
park-like, with grassy open spaces and great groves of cedar,
maple, and madrona. The Indian lands to the south would
give him seclusion and the freedom from outside interference
that he desired. He planned to build a wharf, a freight shed,
a blacksmith's shop, and a small schoolhouse; otherwise, he
would keep the property as natural as possible. He told Hess
he'd start a herd of Angora goats for their wool and plant
flax for linen. The soil was rich and there was an inexhaust-
ible supply of fish along the coast. There was also excellent
water on the property: "I know of one natural spring where
the water is ice-cold even on the hottest days." Brother XII
planned to get the settlement started in the next few months:
"This Center is intended to be an actual place of refuge, where
may come some of our people as are prepared to actually live
the true Aquarian life; it goes without saying that they will be
very carefully selected."

The careful selection of candidates for the Work was a
growing concern of Brother XII's. He believed that every
effort by the White Lodge for the helping of humanity was
opposed by the forces of evil, and that "enemy agents" would
inevitably try to infiltrate the Aquarian Foundation groups
and nullify their work. For this reason, he insisted that every
member take an oath of allegiance called "The Obligation,"
swearing not to create dissension within the group or to hide,
under the guise of a seeming loyalty, secret doubt or disloyalty
to the Work. Anyone who refused to take "The Obligation"
was expelled from the Foundation.

The members of the Aquarian Foundation who met weekly
across the United States and Canada practised a form of group
meditation. For twenty minutes each meeting, they sat in a
circle with their eyes closed, their minds raised to contact the
higher planes. They believed that through a kind of "spiritual
alchemy" their Higher Selves would blend together, the vibration of the group would be raised, and each member would
be able to obtain direct enlightenment. It was thought that

an individual working with a group could attain higher consciousness much more easily and rapidly than an individual
working alone.

This work of the groups was threatened, however, by the
so-called "Brothers of the Shadow," Black Masters who were
trying to invade the groups from the astral plane. In one
of his monthly Instructions, Brother XII identified a well-
known Rosicrucian teacher in California as one of these Black
Adepts. He described the tall, Mephistophelian figure to the
members, warning them not to be deceived by the impressive
helmet, robes, and purplish and yellow light that illumi-
nated this praying "Master": "Stripped of its false beauty of
colouring, the likeness of THE BEAST is found beneath. THE
REAL BROTHERS OF LIGHT, OF THE GREAT WHITE
BROTHERHOOD, WEAR NO HELMET TO PRODUCE
THE STAR."

Should this figure be seen psychically by any member of
the group during meditation, it was to be challenged at once
in the name of the Great White Lodge. If it refused to make
the sign of the Cross and declare its allegiance to the White
Brotherhood, it was to be disintegrated:

> Inhale a deep breath, at the same time mentally asking
> for and drawing down the force of the White Lodge
> into yourself. Then extend the right arm and point the
> finger at the suspected figure. Now exhale, and *with all
> the mental concentration possible,* say: 'I repel you, I resist
> you; by the power of the White Brotherhood, I disinte-
> grate and drive asunder your body of evil—GO!' Make
> the sign of the Cross. When sending out the disintegrating
> power, *visualize it* as issuing from the center between
> your eyebrows and following the course of the extended
> arm and finger. SHOOT IT INTO THE SUSPECTED
> FIGURE WITH ALL THE FORCE YOU CAN MUSTER!

Brother XII urged the members to practise drawing down

the force of the White Lodge daily, not only so they could disintegrate malevolent astral entities, but also so they could send the energy out on missions of help and healing: "Remember that these are real and potent POWERS, and that limitation is only in the instrument, for the power itself is unlimited."

A real-life attack on the Work was made at this time by someone Brother XII was quick to accuse of being an agent of the "dark forces"—none other than Albert E.S. Smythe, the General Secretary of the Theosophical Society in Canada. Smythe had been suspicious of Wilson's motives from the beginning, and now his skepticism had turned into open hostility. In an editorial in *The Canadian Theosophist*, "Blind Leaders of the Blind," he denounced Brother XII as a charlatan and ridiculed his claims to be a member of the Great White Lodge. He called Aquarian Foundation members "boobs," "dupes," and "cuckoos," and claimed that Brother XII was trying to break up the Theosophical Society in Canada so that he could draw disaffected members into his own organization. He also condemned Brother XII's political views and his "diabolical" policy of promoting religious intolerance by setting Protestants against Catholics. He accused Brother XII of being an imposter, one of the many occult frauds who preyed on the weak and ignorant, "wolves in sheep's clothing, who devour widows' houses and batten on the possessions of the simple-minded."

Brother XII was enraged by Smythe's attack. He published a refutation of it in *The Chalice*, answering Smythe's charges point by point. He accused Smythe himself of being responsible for breaking up the Theosophical Society, and quoted letters from former executives who claimed that Smythe's dictatorial conduct had driven them to resign. The most revealing feature of Brother XII's reply was the invective he heaped upon the editor of *The Canadian Theosophist*:

> This hate-inspired misanthrope. . . this Jesuitical prevaricator. . . this cowardly traducer. . . He is a pusillanimous

mouther of empty words. . . a typical Mr. Facing-both-ways
. . . so far as any official recognition is concerned, this man
will die, choked by the lies he utters. . . the man is already
dead to truth, to honour, and to Brotherhood. . . *Those who
have vision* know that the lower astral worlds already yawn
for him. . . *What can be the mental attitude of such a monster
of hatred and slander?* . . the loathsome maggots which infest
his brain. . . this venom-infected creature. . . this creature of
poisoned fangs. . . Albert E.S. Smythe has made the Theosophical Society in Canada a house of lies. . .

Brother XII's vicious attack upon Smythe's character appalled everyone who read it. Henry N. Stokes, an astute
observer of contemporary Theosophical issues and the editor
of *The Oriental & Esoteric Library Critic,* published in Washington, D.C., commented on Brother XII's article in his
editorial, "The Brother XII Bursts Into Billingsgate."

"Is this the sort of language which is to be handed out to
the disciples?" Stokes asked. "Is returning evil for evil one of
the principles of that Lodge which is supposed to include the
Buddha and the Christ? If so, may the gods spare us from such
a Lodge and from such a Messenger. It is too much to look for
perfection in a leader, but one has the right to expect something more than an exhibit of bar-room language in lieu of an
argument."

Stokes concluded that either Brother XII's claim to com-
munion with the White Lodge was a delusion—he would not
go so far as to say a conscious fraud—or that the members of
that Lodge had been "singularly unfortunate" in their choice
of Messenger.

△   △   △

The 1928 American presidential election was now less than
six months away. On June 12 in Kansas City, and on June 26
in Houston, the Republicans and the Democrats, respectively,

were holding their conventions to nominate their candidates for president and vice president of the United States. Two weeks before the Houston convention, Brother XII wrote to Hess:

"I have a pretty big finger in the Houston pie, and I may tell you that the results of the Democratic Convention will be both unexpected and startling. Quite likely, Al Smith will get the nomination, and that will suit our plans perfectly."

His prediction proved correct. Smith was easily nominated on the first ballot when the last-ditch "Stop Smith" drive failed to materialize. And in Kansas City, Herbert Hoover, promising four more years of Republican prosperity, was nominated by acclamation on the first ballot.

As the campaign moved into high gear, Brother XII stepped up his efforts to make the Protestant Protective League and the Third Party a major political force. In Washington, D.C., his organizers worked feverishly to enlist support for the Third Party. At the same time, thousands of copies of Brother XII's articles from *The Chalice* were reprinted and distributed across the United States. They were also published as a book, *The End of the Days*. Its title was taken from the last verse of the Book of Daniel: "But go thou thy way till the end be; for thou shalt rest, and stand in thy lot at the end of the days." In the foreword, Coulson Turnbull called the articles "history-making" and depicted Brother XII as the agent of destiny, leading humanity forward into a new era of truth and enlightenment.

Brother XII now sent a letter to U.S. senators and members of the House of Representatives, appealing for their support. The letter was published in *The Chalice* as "An Open Letter to Certain Senators, Representatives, and Leaders in the United States of America," and was described in advertisements as "the most important and vital document issued in the United States since the Declaration of Independence."

Brother XII warned in the letter that the United States was facing one of the greatest crises in its history—the threat of another civil war. He predicted that if a Roman Catholic were elected president, the people of the United States would rise up in arms to resist religious domination. If, on the other hand, the Roman Catholic hierarchy did *not* win to power electorally, civil war was still inevitable, since Catholics—led by the Knights of Columbus—would mercilessly slaughter millions of Protestants in order to gain supreme control. "All the preparations for this holocaust are made," he declared, *"and the date is set."* The existing government would be powerless to prevent the slaughter and would be swept away "in a tempest of blood and destruction."

This disaster could only be averted if the congressional leaders gave their immediate support to the formation of a Third Party.

The instrument that could secure the formation of the Third Party and guarantee the safety of the nation already existed, Brother XII announced. It was politically untainted, uncompromised by any stigma, and ready to thoroughly purge the rotting evils from national life:

> The Instrument prepared for your use is both keen and clean; it is new-born, a child of Power and of the Cleansing Fire, an offspring of that new Spirit whose winds already sweep across the world. . . The name of this Instrument which shall yet prevail in the Cause of Righteousness is:
> THE PROTESTANT PROTECTIVE LEAGUE.
> *Will you use it or refuse it?* But be sure of one thing; whatever may be your choice—*the people will use it.*

Brother XII urged the senators to take instant and decisive action, since very little time remained to accomplish the work:

> Between this date and the month of October 1928, the League must have its lodges in every State, city, town and hamlet in the Union. We must number these lodges by thousands, and the total membership by millions. That task may

sound formidable to you, yet it can and shall be done; its success is already assured by the publication of these words. You have only to combine in cooperative action and *to circulate this communication by the million*; that is your part— *the nation will do the rest.*

Let each Senator or Representative be allotted one State, so that all are covered. Let one newspaper publish this appeal in every State. Let the Senator or Representative appoint efficient lieutenants in the State allotted to him, and let them create an efficient field-organization. Do this now, and the work will be accomplished in sixty days.

Brother XII was certain that the response to his letter would be overwhelming—great enough to meet all the preliminary financial needs of both the League and the Third Party. He predicted that the League would make the Third Party effective and then sweep it forward into power with an irresistible majority—a majority unequalled in the political history of the nation.

It was a dramatic appeal; how effective it would be remained to be seen. The events of the next few months would determine whether or not Brother XII's political vision would become a reality.

△   △   △

On July 5, the members of the Aquarian Foundation at Cedar gathered together in the auditorium of the Center Building. One year ago on the occasion of the Foundation's first annual General Meeting, Brother XII had talked of the Great White Lodge and the powerful spiritual forces that lay behind the Work. Today, his address was concerned with more immediate and practical concerns—the political situation in the United States.

Brother XII told the assembled members and Governors that the present situation in the United States was actu-

ally much worse than he had stated publicly. The nation
was threatened not only by civil war, but by an even more
horrible threat—an uprising of twenty-odd million Negroes
in the South, armed and led by the Communists. Behind this
"devil's work" were the Jews: "The Jewish world-dictatorship
is about to be set up, and the head—the Jewish Messiah—is a
member of the Rothschild family long resident in Paris."

Moving from racism to religious paranoia, Brother XII then
discussed the work of the Protestant Protective League and
the Third Party. He claimed that many prominent leaders
were now committed to the Third Party. The nomination of
Smith had clinched the issue, since they'd made their support
conditional upon his selection by the Democrats. Hoover's
nomination by the Republicans meant further support.
Publicity was now their most powerful weapon—their hope of
success lay in rousing the nation:

"I purpose within the next sixty days to have the League
known and discussed in every home in the United States, to
have lodges in every town and state in the Union. . . If this
League goes as I think it will go; if the people respond as I
think they *will* respond, then in a few months we will be in control of the most powerful single political factor in the country.
The success or non-success of any political party will depend
largely upon the support of this League, and the League will
be non-partisan. Behind the National Council of the League
stands the Supreme Council, and the bidding of the Supreme
Council will be the will of the Regent of the Lodge."

Brother XII then spoke of his plans to attend the Third
Party Convention in Chicago:

In a few days, I expect to go down into the arena; I
expect to go to a certain city in the Middle-West and there
to arrange for the Conference of the THIRD PARTY to
be held. I expect to have some part in the selection of the
Committee—of the men in whose hands the fate of the
Convention will lie, and *I expect to select, and will select, the*

man who is to be the next president of the United States, and also the next vice president. That is where I need the whip, and that is the occasion upon which I will use it. Either these men shall do the will of the Lodge or I will loose plagues and desolations upon them beyond all telling. It is better that they should suffer than that infinitely worse horrors engulf the nation as a whole.

Brother XII concluded by giving a brief review of what had been accomplished in the past six months:

In November 1927, we had nothing. Politically and every other way, we were weaponless and defenceless—we did not even have any means of publicity—and that is why I started *The Chalice*. We had to forge our own weapons; we had to work with unwilling, or indifferent, or even hostile instruments, and at every stage, we have lacked money and any adequate financial support.

In November 1927, I had to sit into a big game—the biggest game in the world today. I had a poor hand, almost no hand at all, so I went to Washington to draw cards. I drew three aces, though I will confess to you that I was dishonest enough to manufacture them myself. These were—(1) a crimp on the politicians; (2) the Third Party; and (3) the League. I went to Washington to draw them; now I will shortly go to a certain city in the Middle-West to play them.

If these are not enough, then I have two others—I have got five aces in this game and that is a pretty dangerous hand to hold, as many people have found to their cost. I hope I may not have to show the fifth because if that has to be played, there will be very little left of either the game or the players—the FIFTH ACE is a Joker; it is called, "The Ninety percent."

Gentlemen, I have ended on a note which is light because we always fight best if we go into the fight with a laugh. But our task is no light one, and as I have told you so often before, we can accomplish it only if we are utterly selfless, utterly impersonal, utterly true. I have told you much, but I cannot tell you all. The eyes which look into the future and see the whole of it must be incapable of tears; the vision must be clear, undimmed by sentiment of any kind, even as the decisions must be final and inflexible. Therefore, I look to you for your trust, your support, and for a loyalty which may not be shaken. Give me these, and we shall win.

The speech was over. Brother XII stood alone, the spiritual warrior girding his loins for the battle. He was certain the Masters would lead him to victory.

Madame Helena Petrovna
Blavatsky, author of *The Secret
Doctrine* and founder of
the Theosophical Society.
Brother XII believed his
mission was to carry forward
her work into the year 2000.
(Bettmann Archives)

Membership application from
The Aquarian Foundation
booklet, published by
Sun Publishing Company,
Akron, Ohio,
April 18, 1927.

APPLICATION FOR MEMBERSHIP
in
THE AQUARIAN FOUNDATION

Date. . . . .

Desiring to be enrolled as an Active Member
of the Fraternity and as a Server in the Cause of
Humanity, and wishing to do my share in providing for the expense of the Work of THE
AQUARIAN FOUNDATION, I will gladly
send each month until further notice for such pur-

pose . . . .

Name . . . .

Address . . . .

Mail Application to
THE AQUARIAN FOUNDATION
P. O. Box 23
Nanaimo, B. C., Canada

On this wooded shoreline at Cedar-by-the-Sea, Brother XII set up his spiritual community, declaring that his work was "the first Trumpet-blast of the New Age." Round Island is directly offshore. (*The Daily Colonist*)

Workmen unload lumber from a scow for the Aquarian Foundation headquarters, Cedar-by-the-Sea, Spring, 1927. (Author's collection)

THE
THREE TRUTHS

A SIMPLE STATEMENT OF THE
FUNDAMENTAL PHILOSOPHY
OF LIFE

IX XII

AS DECLARED AND SHOWN TO
" BROTHER XII "
(the personal Chêla of a Master)

THE CHALICE PRESS
18 ERSKINE RD., LONDON, E.17

Title page of *The Three Truths*, which Brother XII claimed was dictated to him by his Master in Genoa, Italy, in the spring of 1926. Its lyrical style and profound spiritual insights helped to attract members to the Aquarian Foundation.

Shortly after arriving in British Columbia, Brother XII purchased a Reo automobile, shown here parked in a clearing at Cedar. He enjoyed driving it at a high rate of speed. (Author's collection)

Relaxing at the campsite. Frances Lucas facing camera; Edward Lucas to the left wearing hat. The bearded figure in profile at the right is Brother XII. (Courtesy Frances Lucas)

Aquarian Foundation children at Cedar-by-the-Sea prepare for a spring pageant. (Courtesy Frances Lucas)

The House of Mystery. In this secluded cabin in the woods, Brother XII would retreat to meditate, receiving his inspired writings and communicating with the "Masters of Wisdom" who were allegedly guiding the Work. (Author's collection)

Printed in blue and gold on stiff cardboard suitable for framing, "The Invocation of Light" could be purchased by members for fifteen cents a copy.

THE INVOCATION OF LIGHT

THOU Who bringest the Dawn,
Who renewest the day without ceasing,
Whose splendor is the Brightness of the Morning;
Fountain of Life and Source of Light Eternal,
Increase in us Thy Knowledge and Thy Strength.
Thou Who shinest in the East,
Who showest the West Thy glory,
And art supreme in the high heaven;
Thou fillest Thy Houses with Light,
And Thy Mansions with hidden Power.
Thou sustainest the Seven Lords,
The Shining Ones Who keep Thy Path,
And we, who serve Thee through Their Ray,
O Light ineffable.
Increase in us Thy Wisdom and Thy Power,
Dwell Thou in us, as we are One in Thee.

This is the Great Invocation repeated daily in the Temples for thousands of years. Recovered at 5 a.m., April 27th, 1926.

Akhenaten, 18th Dynasty pharaoh who ruled Egypt from 1351–1334 B.C. and established the worship of the sun god Aten. Brother XII strongly identified with him and claimed to be restoring to the contemporary world the esoteric knowledge underlying the ancient Egyptian Mysteries.

Akhenaten and his family make offering to the sun disk Aten; the god's life-giving rays end in hands which extend the *ankh*, symbol of life, to the nostrils of the King and Queen. Brother XII's "Invocation of Light" was evidently inspired by Akhenaten's famous "Hymn to the Sun."

Edward Arthur Wilson's father, Thomas Wilson, was a prosperous manufacturer and deacon in the Catholic Apostolic Church in Birmingham, England. He named his son after the Church's founder, Edward Irving, raising him in an atmosphere of strict religious devotion. (Courtesy Margery Rowe)

Prior to becoming "The Messenger of the Masters," Wilson abandoned his wife and children, shown here in a photograph taken in Auckland, New Zealand. Margery was eight when her father left; Rupert was six. They only learned of their father's notorious career in their latter years. (Courtesy Margery Rowe)

Brother XII and the Governors of the Aquarian Foundation photographed at the first Annual General Meeting, July 25, 1927. Left to right: Edward Lucas (back to camera), Joseph Benner, Maurice Von Platen, Edward Arthur Wilson, Phillip Fisher, Will Levington Comfort, Coulson Turnbull. (Author's collection)

Another photograph of the seven Governors taken on the same occasion. Wilson is third from the left. (Author's collection)

A family grouping of Foundation members taken the same day. Left to right: Elma Wilson, Joseph Benner, Marion Lucas (rear), Edward Arthur Wilson, Phillip Fisher (rear), Penelope Comfort (rear), Will Levington Comfort, Coulson Turnbull, Sidney Sprey-Smith (standing), Frances Lucas, Alice Von Platen. (Courtesy Schwarze Photographers)

Wilson in close-up. Those who met him remarked that his eyes were his most compelling feature. Edward Lucas described him as "a little brown leaf of a man with a small spiky beard and hypnotic dark eyes that did strange things to you."

Robert England, Foundation Secretary-Treasurer and Brother XII's right-hand man. England was the conscience of the Foundation, but disappeared shortly before he was to give testimony against Brother XII, leaving the Governors without a case. (Courtesy Frances Lucas)

Twenty-year-old Eric Davenport worked as Brother XII's secretary for six months. He left abruptly after Wilson threatened him with a Colt .32, accusing him of colluding with the dissenting Governors. (Courtesy Eric Davenport)

Eric Davenport on the front steps of the Center Building with Norman Williams, a theological student from England, one of the numerous seekers who visited the headquarters to experience Brother XII's work firsthand. (Author's collection)

The Canadian Bank of Commerce at the corner of Church and Front Street in Nanaimo was where the Aquarian Foundation did its banking. (Courtesy Nanaimo District Museum)

Herbert Jefferson was typical of the idealistic individuals who responded to Brother XII's teachings. Jefferson and his wife Dora came to British Columbia from Toronto as part of a large contingent of Theosophists who defected from the Canadian section of the Society to join the Aquarian Foundation. (Author's collection)

Robert DeLuce, prominent Los Angeles astrologer, who Brother XII believed to be the reincarnation of an Aztec sacrificial priest. He played a key role in toppling the "Messenger of the Masters." (Author's collection)

Wealthy Asheville, North Carolina, socialite Mary W.T. Connally is pictured here in this photograph from *The Star Weekly* of May 20, 1933, wearing the same dress that she wore when she met Brother XII for the first time in the lobby of the King Edward Hotel in Toronto. The dress has half-moons on it, which particularly intrigued Brother XII.

This towering moss-draped maple on the Foundation property at Cedar, known as the Tree of Wisdom, was where the faithful gathered at the feet of Brother XII to listen to his words of wisdom. The figure in the photograph is Roger Painter. (Author's collection)

A group of land-working disciples pause for a photograph at Cedar in happier days. Alfred Barley at right, Roger Painter extreme left. Second from left is Dion Sepulveda, who was allegedly groomed to become Brother XII's successor. (Author's collection)

Alice and Carlin Rudy (center), Chicago Forest Preserve, 1927. Their stay at The Brothers' Center turned their lives upside down and broke up their marriage. (Author's collection)

A photograph of the Center Building taken shortly after its construction. It contained an assembly hall, offices, a bookroom and four guest bedrooms upstairs. The man wearing the hat on the porch is believed to be Brother XII. (Courtesy Jean McMorran)

The beach at Cedar-by-the-Sea. It was here that the children of the colony played, swam, boated and dug for clams during its halcyon days. (Photo by James A. Santucci)

The eroded cliffs of DeCourcy Island, carved by the wind and waves and topped by twisted arbutus trees, provided an eerie backdrop for Brother XII's mystical pursuits. (Photo by James A. Santucci)

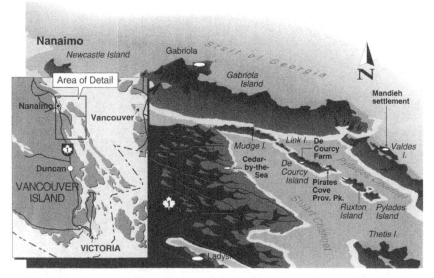

Map of the settlements showing Cedar-by-the-Sea, Valdes Island and DeCourcy Island. Members were assigned to the various properties in accordance with their spiritual status in the Work. (Courtesy Rob Struthers)

CHAPTER
IV
Osiris and Isis

T he Great Northern passenger train, the Oriental Limited, stood on the tracks of Seattle's King Street station on the morning of July 6, 1928, and blew a final blast of its whistle. Porters hurried baggage down the platform and the last stragglers clambered aboard. At 8:15 A.M., the powerful Baldwin locomotive sent a plume of steam curling into the air. As the sunlight glinted off the gold Roman lettering on the sides of its Pullman coaches, the Oriental Limited rolled slowly out of the station. Picking up speed, it bumped through the switches and curved slowly east, beginning the sixty-eight hour, 2,238-mile journey to Chicago.

Inside the swaying coaches, a slender figure in a grey suit moved down the center aisle. Elsewhere on the train, a striking, dark-haired woman named Myrtle Wells Baumgartner sat alone. The wife of a physician in Clifton Springs, New York, Myrtle was returning from a trip to the West Coast. Her husband, Dr. Edwin A. Baumgartner, had injured himself several years earlier playing football. A vigorous, athletic man, his bitterness at becoming an invalid had destroyed their marriage. Myrtle had nursed him faithfully, but the relationship had become an intolerable burden. She desperately yearned for a new sense of meaning in her life.

The Oriental Limited skirted the shores of Puget Sound as Edward Arthur Wilson and Myrtle Baumgartner fell into conversation. She was soon telling him about herself and the details of her unhappy marriage. As the train wound through the snowy passes of the Rocky Mountains, Myrtle talked to her new companion about her aspirations and her spiritual search. Wilson, in turn, told her of his years of solitude and struggle, and of his own spiritual awakening. He spoke of his contact with the Masters and his work as Brother XII. Time passed and the rapport between them grew. The Oriental Limited left the Cascades behind and descended into the high plains of Montana. In the great vault of the sky above, the stars glittered. The stillness of the night seemed to make their choice for them. As the train moved out across the vast prairie, they retired to Wilson's Pullman sleeper. The plaintive sound of the whistle drifted back to the hushed compartment as the two explored the mystical bond that had brought them together again in the flesh.

It was no doubt one of the strangest seductions in history. During the two days and three nights of the journey, the couple renewed a love affair which Wilson claimed had originated thousands of years earlier in ancient Egypt. A romance which had been played out in the court of the Pharaoh and celebrated in the shrines of magnificent temples blossomed again in twentieth-century North America. For, in the course of the trip, Edward Arthur Wilson and Myrtle Baumgartner discovered they were soul mates, and learned that they shared a destiny of monumental importance. It is not recorded where on this journey their mystical ecstasy occurred, but somewhere beneath the blazing constellations the two soul mates took the "Sixth Initiation." During this powerful occult ceremony, it was revealed to them that they were the reincarnations of Egyptian divinities: Wilson was the god Osiris, and Myrtle Baumgartner was the goddess Isis. It was also revealed that a son would be born to them who would be the reincarnation of the Egyptian god Horus. This child would become a World Teacher in 1975 and lead humanity into a new spiritual age that would usher in the Millennium.

Did Myrtle Baumgartner really believe that she and Wilson were the reincarnations of Osiris and Isis? Was she an initiate, as he later claimed? Or was she merely a victim of Brother XII's charisma and of her own desire for an exalted destiny? The answer will probably never be known. In any event, Myrtle did not question the truth of these awesome revelations or balk at their implications. She enthusiastically embraced her role as mother of the next World Teacher, and gave herself utterly to Brother XII.

The blues and golds of the morning light streamed into the compartment as the Oriental Limited sped towards the twin cities of Minneapolis and St. Paul. The fields and farms flashed past. Through the dairy country of Wisconsin the train fled, following the Mississippi River south towards Chicago. Into the outskirts of the city it swept, past warehouses, factories, and stockyards, finally plunging into the dark cavern of Union Station. The journey had ended, but the romance of the ages had been consummated—Myrtle Wells Baumgartner had conceived the next saviour of the world.

△   △   △

Brother XII arrived in Chicago in the middle of a heat wave. The grass had turned brown in the parks along Lakeshore Drive and the great canyons of the downtown core were like ovens. Hundreds had collapsed from heatstroke and there had been ten deaths in a single week. Into this sweltering crucible poured the delegates from three American political minority groups, each of which was holding its own conven-

tion in Chicago to nominate candidates for president and vice
president of the United States.

On July 10, the 152 delegates of the Prohibition Party
opened their convention at the LaSalle Hotel. The ornate
ballroom was ringed by a battery of fans to keep the sweating
delegates cool as they called for a more rigorous enforce-
ment of Prohibition. Herbert Hoover was regarded as being
too weak on the issue, while Alfred Smith was anathema—he
wanted to repeal Prohibition altogether.

Nearby in the more modest Stevens Hotel, the delegates of
the Farmer-Labor Party opened their convention. A smaller
group, they mopped their brows and sipped ice water from
big tumblers as they discussed labour issues and the need for
farm relief. They regarded both Hoover and Smith as unsympathetic to their concerns.

The third group meeting in Chicago was something of a
political mystery. The Jefferson-Lincoln League, composed
largely of dry Democrats from Washington, D.C., had delegates in each of the other two conventions. It wanted to unite
the Prohibition Party and the Farmer-Labor Party into a Third
Party coalition. Brother XII intended to use the Jefferson-
Lincoln League as the vehicle for his own political agenda.

Brother XII moved between the two hotels, lobbying delegates. He repeatedly stressed that there was only one issue
in the coming election—not Prohibition, not farm or labour
concerns, but religion. If Hoover were elected president, economic chaos would sweep the nation. If Smith were elected,
the United States would be plunged into civil war. The fate of
America was at stake, he warned. And there was only one man
who could lead a Third Party coalition to victory—Senator
James Thomas Heflin.

The Jefferson-Lincoln League scored an early success when
the Prohibition and Farmer-Labor parties agreed to strike a
special committee to discuss a possible Third Party merger.
Delegates from the three groups retired to work out the details of the coalition.

In the LaSalle Hotel, the religious issue erupted in the Prohibition Party convention when a delegate from Oklahoma vigorously attacked the Roman Catholic Church.

"We have to beat the Roman Catholic hierarchy that has been responsible for the assassination of our presidents and the slaying of five million Protestants!" he cried. "Al Smith must be defeated, even if there's bloodshed—even at the cost of our lives!"

The hall was in an uproar. Many delegates echoed their agreement, while others tried to shout the speaker down, calling him a bigot.

"*Senator Heflin is my candidate!*" he shouted as the other delegates clamoured to speak.

Was this Brother XII's moment of opportunity? In the sea of frantic faces and waving arms, as scores of delegates tried to make their voices heard above the pandemonium, did he struggle forward to speak? If he could have spoken, could he have swayed the convention with his powers of rhetoric, uniting the delegates around the issue of religion and winning their support for Heflin and the cause of a Third Party?

History does not record him doing so. If he indeed tried to speak, it was too late. The moment was lost. The chairman called the convention to order and the commotion gradually subsided. The opportunity did not repeat itself as the religious issue was not raised again.

That evening the members of the Third Party committee talked late into the night, but they were unable to reconcile their differences. The next morning the effort at unification was abandoned. And with it disappeared Brother XII's hopes for a Third Party coalition.

The following day, the delegates seemed to lose heart. Attendance at the two conventions dwindled. In the LaSalle Hotel, less than fifty delegates of the Prohibition Party remained to cast their ballots as the fans whirred inside the nearly empty hall. In the Stevens Hotel, even fewer Farmer-Labor delegates lingered to nominate their party's candidate for president. After the voting, a forlorn group passed the hat, collecting less than one hundred dollars to pay expenses. It was a humiliating finale.

Reporting the fiasco, *Time* magazine observed that the delegates had accomplished "just about as little as several hundred adult citizens could possibly have accomplished had they set out purposefully to be futile for several days."

The outcome of the conventions in Chicago was surely disappointing to Brother XII. But for him, the debacle was made worse by the fact that his Protestant Protective League was attracting much less support than he'd hoped. He must also have been discouraged by the response to his "Open Letter." A number of influential senators had already declared that it was too late to put the political machinery in place to field a third-party ticket. It was now obvious that Brother XII's program would never be realized. His grandiose dreams of political power had proved to be a delusion.

Brother XII's political work was in disarray, but he continued to press forward with his other plans. Before returning to the headquarters in British Columbia, he arranged to meet the wealthiest member of the Aquarian Foundation, a prominent socialite from Asheville, North Carolina, named Mary Wortham Thomas Connally.

"Lady Mary," as she was known to her friends, was the scion of one of the most illustrious families in the American South. She lived in a fifty-room colonial mansion called Fernihurst, located in the exclusive Biltmore Forest district of Asheville. The house overlooked the French Broad River and had a magnificent view of the Blue Ridge Mountains and Mt. Pisgah. Mary's ancestors had arrived in America in 1608, twelve years before the *Mayflower*, and had sat in the House of Burgesses, the first governing body in America. Mary's father, Colonel John Kerr Connally, was a Civil War hero and a prominent lawyer in Richmond, Virginia. After narrowly escaping death when the floor in the Capitol collapsed, he renounced law and entered the ministry, becoming an eloquent preacher of the Gospel. Colonel Connally was rigid in his beliefs and disapproved of drinking and social gaiety. His socialite wife, Alice Coleman Thomas, daughter of an English tobacco merchant, loved to entertain. She often held parties at Fernihurst that lasted for several days and were attended by as many as five-hundred guests, including her friends the Vanderbilts. On these occasions the Colonel would retreat to the small house behind the mansion or ride out to his property in the Black Mountains to meditate. Mary was influenced by the twin but contradictory values of her parents: her mother's love of society and self-indulgence, and her father's self-denial and religious discipline.

The eldest of three daughters, Mary was raised at Fernihurst in a world of wealth and privilege. Each of the girls had her own servants, even a personal maid to help her dress and undress. Mary travelled widely as a girl, often visiting her uncle, the American ambassador to the court of Spain at Madrid. An excellent horsewoman, she won many trophies at horse shows. Married twice—both times to wealthy and prominent men—and twice divorced, Mary's greatest loss in life came with the death of her only son, Tench Francis Coxe. Only twenty-nine years of age, with a young wife and twin daughters, he died of pneumonia in 1923.

Mary continued to travel and to read extensively. She was sixty years old when she discovered Brother XII's writings. "I was interested in world conditions," she later recalled. "I had studied religions and philosophies and systems of economy and financial conditions everywhere, and nothing seemed to be very satisfactory, and quite by accident, in November 1927, when I was in the West, I was given a book called *Foundation Letters and Teachings*, and I was absolutely amazed at what it contained."

The teachings in the book coincided with Mary's own ideas about how society could be changed. She immediately joined the Aquarian Foundation and studied the monthly

Instructions and other literature she received. These intensified her desire to become involved in the Work. In June 1928,
she sent a cheque for two thousand dollars to the headquarters. She received a personal reply from Brother XII, thanking
her for her donation. Mary wrote back, requesting a meeting
with him.

In August 1928, Mary was staying in Washington, D. C.,
where she kept an apartment, when she received a telegram
from Coulson Turnbull advising her that Brother XII was in
the East on business. Could she meet him in Toronto on the
fourteenth of August? Mary quickly replied that she could, and
the meeting was arranged that would change her life forever.

In the elegant lobby of the King Edward Hotel in Toronto,
Mary Connally waited expectantly for Brother XII. An aristo-
cratic woman with flaxen hair, she wore a special dress for the
occasion—dark blue, with a pattern of half-moons. Wilson arrived, impeccable in a tweed suit and soft felt hat, and greeted
Mary. He was intrigued by her dress and remarked that she
must have worn it because the moon was entering the first
quarter the next day. Mary thought him charming.

The two discussed Brother XII's work, perhaps over a leisurely meal in the hotel dining room. Mary told him of her
amazement upon reading *Foundation Letters and Teachings* for
the first time. "Why, at the risk of being thought presumptuous,"
she declared, "I might have written that book myself!" Wilson
outlined to Mary his plans for a new settlement on Valdes
Island. He described the school he wanted to build there, and
said that food, clothing, and shelter would be provided free
of charge to the children of Foundation members. He spoke
of how traditional education interfered with the natural unfolding of innate character, smothering a child's spiritual
perceptions. Mary told him about her own grandchildren and
how difficult it was to raise children in the jazz atmosphere of

modern times. She was impressed by Brother XII's emphasis on the importance of children to the Work.

"I was convinced that this was the Work which I was going to do in the world," she later recalled. "He had it in a nutshell, so to speak. It was as if different architects had offered you a plan for a great world-building or temple. I accepted his drawings, which were outlined in *Foundation Letters and Teachings* and the letters which followed. They were the specifications and the blueprints. I then realized that he was to be the contractor as well as the architect, and that he, and he alone, could carry out those plans."

Mary explained that she wanted to make a further contribution of twenty-three thousand dollars to the cause, bringing her total donation to twenty-five thousand dollars. Brother XII expressed his profound gratitude and briefly discussed with her the terms of her donation. The meeting lasted a little over three hours. At the end of it, as they were saying goodbye, he thanked Mary again and told her that she had a "special place" in the Work.

Mary returned to Washington, D. C., convinced she'd found her life's purpose. She made out a cheque for twenty-three thousand dollars and mailed it to Brother XII at the Aquarian Foundation headquarters at Cedar.

△　△　△

Brother XII returned to Cedar at the end of August, accompanied by Myrtle Baumgartner. The two arrived late at night, while the members of the Foundation were asleep. In his bedroom upstairs in the Center Building, Eric Davenport was awakened by the sound of voices.

"I recognized Wilson's voice, but not the woman's," he recalls. "I never saw her. The next morning, she was gone. He hustled her over to Valdes Island to give birth to the next Christ."

Brother XII installed Myrtle in a two-room log cabin at

the top of a ridge on the east side of Valdes. The cabin had a kitchen and bedroom and was sparsely furnished with a cast-iron stove, table and chairs and a large double bed. Myrtle remained there in seclusion, while Brother XII returned to Cedar to resume control of the daily operations of the Foundation.

Brother XII kept Myrtle's presence at the settlement a secret, telling only Robert England and the Turnbulls. He asked Coulson and his wife to move to Valdes, so that Cecilia could be a companion to Myrtle and look after her during her pregnancy. Like some royal magician in an ancient kingdom, Turnbull cast the horoscope of the unborn child. His calculations confirmed that the child was indeed an adept, the World Teacher and Avatar that Brother XII had predicted would come to found and stabilize the sixth sub-race.

Upon his return, Brother XII met with a small group of disciples waiting with questions about the outcome of the Third Party convention in Chicago. "He was very matter-of-fact about it," recalls Eric Davenport. "He said that things hadn't gone as expected, but that the plans of the Lodge would still be brought into effect—only at a later date. He talked of returning to the East, and said that the predictions he'd made would ultimately be fulfilled."

On Valdes Island, Myrtle contemplated her future and that of the child she was carrying. She took long walks on the beach, past tide pools teeming with life and twisted red arbutus trees that clung to the shore. She explored the woodland paths that led to lovely groves of maple, spruce, and alder in the center of the island. She read books that Wilson brought her from his library, and sometimes passed the time of day with the workmen he had employed to build the cabins for the new settlement on Valdes.

"We used to see her when we were carrying lumber up and down the beach," one recalls. "It was damn lonely for her over there. She had no one to talk to."

Word soon spread about Myrtle's presence on Valdes. There

were murmurs of indignation among the disciples when they discovered that Brother XII had taken a mistress. Elma Wilson was shocked. Maurice Von Platen and Robert DeLuce demanded an explanation. Brother XII impatiently told them that Myrtle was his soul mate and that they had important work to accomplish together. Their relationship was a necessary part of the plan of the Masters, he claimed, and couldn't be judged according to the usual conventions of society.

But Brother XII now made a strategic mistake. He brought Myrtle to Cedar, so that they could meditate together inside the House of Mystery. The two retreated into the cabin to continue their esoteric work. Under the dark trees and the starry sky, they embraced—Osiris and Isis in union with the Absolute. The disciples were scandalized: Brother XII's use of the House of Mystery for sex desecrated the sacred retreat. Their indignation flared into open revolt.

A little group of idealists grimly confronted Brother XII and Myrtle when they emerged from the House of Mystery. The whispering of the forest was the only sound in the tense moment before they condemned the conduct of their leader. But Brother XII, as always, justified his actions. His relationship with Myrtle was not the mere infatuation of two personalities, he explained, but existed on a higher plane. He and Myrtle were initiates engaged in work that was presently beyond the understanding of the disciples.

Brother XII responded to criticism of his affair by publishing an article in *The Chalice* about marriage. It was a vigorous attack on what he claimed was the dictatorial jurisdiction assumed over marriage by Church and State. In the article, he identified three types of marriage. The first type was based primarily upon sexual attraction, and included the vast majority of marriages. It was, by its very nature, impermanent, yet the Church committed the partners in such a marriage to a lifetime sexual contract, terminable only by death. An arbitrary system tried to make permanent and exclusive an attraction that was by nature ephemeral and transitory: "That this should be perpetrated and erected into a national institution is nothing less than a tragedy." If the sex-attraction were rightly understood and appreciated, he argued, then unwise and consequently unhappy marriages would be eliminated. Marriage would no longer be the sole passport to a mutual sex-relationship, and young people would not suffer the appalling effects of repression imposed by centuries of theological dogma. Although he favoured a larger degree of emancipation in sexual matters, Brother XII stressed that he was not advocating sexual licence or lawlessness.

The second type of marriage he described was the marriage of companionship. It was not the result of a passing sexual emotion, but was founded upon a mental and spiritual affinity. It was likely to become permanent as the bonds of true companionship strengthened over time, "especially if it be not jeopardized by the imposition of a galling 'legal' yoke."

The third and highest type of marriage was the marriage of two initiates. This type of marriage, he explained, could only be consummated by couples who understood the hidden influences and invisible laws which affected the union of the soul with the physical body:

> In such a case, physical union is undertaken deliberately and for the express purpose of providing a particular kind and quality of physical vehicle for *a known type* of incoming soul. The question of sexual gratification does not enter into such a union at all—it is, in effect, a dedication, the payment of a debt to that soul for whose benefit the act is undertaken.
>
> When the purpose of such a union has been accomplished, there is no obligation for its indefinite perpetuation; that is a matter which must be decided by the individuals concerned—no third party has any shadow of right to interfere in this decision or to dictate it. Such a marriage as this is concerned exclusively with spiritual verities—its physical aspects are merely incidental.

If Brother XII intended the article to silence his critics, he miscalculated. It had the opposite effect, creating still more controversy. His detractors seized upon it, accusing him of promulgating a doctrine of free love. There were others, however, who did not think it strange that the birth of certain highly evolved souls should take place outside the conventional social contract of marriage.

In an article in *The Chalice,* "Incoming Souls," Coulson Turnbull elaborated upon Brother XII's teachings. He explained that these revolutionary souls would be conceived in accordance with an exact astrological knowledge and would be born only to parents with higher mental and spiritual faculties. He said that such souls would choose their parentage and time of birth. Such unions would demand a new understanding of ethics and would not always be sanctioned by convention. "This will bring a clash in the near future," Turnbull predicted, "between civil and ecclesiastical laws of man, if unchanged, and the rights of Those who enter on the path of the very gods."

$\triangle \quad \triangle \quad \triangle$

The Aquarian Foundation was in crisis. Brother XII's relationship with Myrtle Baumgartner and his teachings on marriage had left the members divided. While some of them continued to support Brother XII unquestioningly, others like Von Platen and DeLuce were increasingly critical of him.

The establishment of the Mandieh Settlement on Valdes Island also caused friction. Brother XII didn't discuss his plans for Valdes with either Von Platen or DeLuce. He didn't even mention them to Edward Lucas. He seemed determined to proceed with the new settlement on his own, without consulting the other Governors.

"We'd hear a truck rumbling down the road to the waterfront in the middle of the night," Frances Lucas recalls. "He was taking building materials and supplies over to Valdes Island."

Brother XII would navigate with precision across the dark water, skilfully guiding his vessel through the treacherous narrows to Valdes Island. He'd unload the supplies in the tiny bay on the east side, then make the return trip to Cedar the same night.

"I'd be asleep in the Center Building," remembers Eric Davenport, "when I'd hear a rap on the window. It would be Brother XII and Robert England. I'd go downstairs and let them in. It would be pitch-black. They came and went in the dead of night."

In order to provide himself with transportation to the new colony, Wilson ordered a powerful tugboat built at Foster's Shipyard in Victoria at a cost of five thousand dollars. Von Platen and DeLuce were alarmed when they learned that such a large expenditure had been made from Foundation funds without their knowledge.

Brother XII called the new settlement on Valdes Island The Mandieh Settlement after the birthplace of the god Osiris in the Nile delta in Egypt. In an article in *The Chalice,* he explained that the new colony was the next step in the development of the Work. It would be the place where disciples would receive the practical occult training that would prepare them for their future work. Applicants had to be willing to entirely abandon the life of the outer world: *"This means the renunciation of worldly possessions. . .* The aspirant upon this Path must strip himself before he may pass through the eye of the needle—the gate which admits one to association with the inner Brotherhood of the world. If there is a position you value or hope to attain, if there is a sum of money you wish to obtain or to retain, if there is the marriage you have set your heart upon, then the Path is not for you—yet."

Brother XII explained that the nativity of the individual would be of key importance: "He or she must have brought over the needed qualifications from a former life, as there is not time to develop them in this. Also, 'the stars do not lie'; there is no possibility of deception or of self-deception if the chart of the soul is made the chief determining factor."

On a more mundane level, he assailed what he condemned as two of the most devastating evils in modern society—curiosity and criticism. In order that the right conditions could be maintained at the colony, "the very first rule of the Mandieh Settlement will be MIND YOUR OWN BUSINESS." He itemized the essential qualifications for admittance. The applicant had to be:

> Broad minded
> Unconventional
> Unselfish
> Courageous against 'opinions'
> Uncritical of others
> Not curious
> Free from garrulity
> Naturally silent
> Loyal to associates
> Not to be turned aside.

Although few would qualify to live at the Mandieh Settlement, Brother XII explained that souls of the incoming sixth sub-race would soon be incarnating in increasing numbers as children of the colony's members. The Mandieh Settlement would be the physical entry point for these adepts, an environment where they would have the proper physical, mental, and spiritual conditions for their development. He concluded: "Some time ago, I said—'We have to change the thought-currents of the world.' If we change the thoughts of men, we change all the forms and institutions they have built up—we substitute good for evil in every department of human life. The foundations of this Work will be laid here at The Mandieh Settlement."

On September 15, 1928, the Governors of the Aquarian Foundation held an urgent meeting in Edward Lucas's law office in the Standard Bank Building in Vancouver. DeLuce told Lucas that the workmen on Valdes thought Wilson was crazy—he was giving contradictory orders and would fly into a rage over the smallest thing. Turnbull said that despite his articles in *The Chalice*, he had serious doubts about Wilson's sanity, which was why he and Cecilia had returned to Cedar. Von Platen was angry about the money he'd given Wilson for the P.P.L.—it had all been spent, and the organization was a shambles. He said they had to prevent Wilson from squandering the remainder of the Society's funds and suggested they take out an injunction against him. DeLuce wondered if they could have Wilson certified insane and committed to an asylum. Lucas advised against such an extreme action. He suggested the Governors hold a meeting with Wilson to give him a chance to explain himself. If they weren't satisfied with his answers, they could then decide how best to extricate themselves from the situation.

Three days later, six of the Governors filed through the French doors inside the Center Building, past Wilson's office, and down the hallway to the auditorium. In their suits and ties, they looked like executives attending a board meeting, rather than the earthly representatives of an occult hierarchy responsible for the destiny of the planet. They seated themselves around the table: Wilson and Robert England on one side; Von Platen, DeLuce, and Turnbull on the other. Ostensibly neutral, Edward Lucas would mediate the dispute.

Lucas opened the meeting by explaining that the dissenting Governors felt that Wilson had radically departed from the original tenets of the Society. Von Platen and DeLuce demanded an explanation for Wilson's recent conduct. Wilson bristled at this challenge to his authority. He declared that his actions were directed by the Lodge and were the next stage in the development of the Work. The meeting quickly got out of control as the Governors voiced their disapproval of the way in which Wilson was running the Foundation. When his affair with Myrtle Baumgartner was raised, Wilson became irate. He accused the other Governors of being traitors to the Work. Von Platen demanded that he surrender control of the Foundation or agree to dissolve it. Wilson refused, abruptly declaring the meeting adjourned.

The Governors emerged from the Center Building, their faces telling the story to the disciples waiting outside. Lucas stayed behind to talk to Wilson. He suggested that they take a walk around the property. Wilson agreed. As the two men strolled side-by-side past the neat houses of the community, Lucas recalled their early days together, when they'd drawn up the Society's constitution on his dining room table. He reminisced about the discussions they'd had and the excitement he'd felt at watching the colony grow. And finally, he quietly explained why he and the others could no longer, in conscience, continue to act as Governors of the Society. Wilson listened carefully. He replied that he understood Lucas's concern; nonetheless, he couldn't let control of the Work pass out of his hands. Lucas was amazed that Wilson expected the others to function as dummy Governors of the Society. Lucas told him that such an arrangement would never work.

The two returned to the Center Building. Wilson was quiet for a moment. Then he announced that he'd changed his mind—he was willing to dissolve the Foundation after all. Lucas was greatly relieved. It was the only answer: Brother XII could go his way and the other Governors could go theirs. The two men shook hands—they were still "Brothers."

That afternoon Brother XII sent a notice, much less amiable in tone, to Von Platen, DeLuce, and Turnbull, informing them that their membership in the Foundation had been cancelled: "By reason of your recent attempt to overturn the constitution of the Aquarian Foundation and to seize control of our Order, you are one and all the self-declared enemies of this Work. Your nominal membership in this Order is cancelled as from noon on the 18th of September, 1928." He also informed them that if any other members of the Foundation communicated with them or set foot upon their property, that individual's membership in the Society would be automatically cancelled.

Wilson was up early the next morning. He typed a letter to Lucas, explaining that the recent events had been a test. Von Platen, DeLuce, and Turnbull had failed it: "Treachery and instability have been revealed and those who would have betrayed this Cause, or deserted it in a moment of stress, have been broken." He assured Lucas, "As for yourself, good Brother, unless I mistake it, you will have come through the testing; you will have qualified to pass from the nominal to the real."

Lucas replied that although he was gratified the Skipper felt this way about him, he still couldn't continue with him in the Work. Dissolving the Foundation meant the end of their voyage together:

> In short, this cruise is over. The ship we have made it in will be laid up and the crew paid off. And if I, as a mate, contemplated the possible painful duty of putting the Skipper in irons, I am happily spared from such a task. . . You will carry on in the service in a new ship. I do not see my way clear to sign on for the new cruise, but I certainly have no kick coming now about the voyage that is closing. If I have thought the Old Man was loony and finally up and said so—well, I suppose that is a way mates have. I am well content that what you would have regarded as mutiny will not now have to take place.

Wilson wasn't ready to let Lucas go. He wanted him as a friend and ally, and believed their work together was not yet finished:

> Good Brother, a word to you as to the Realities. . .Without realizing it *yet*, you are taking part in the fulfilment of a certain passage from Revelations. Read what is said about the two Witnesses—how they were slain, and their bodies lay

in the streets *for three days*. I ask you, *have we not borne witness?* Is there any other witness comparable to it in these last days? Our witness to the world of soul and spirit is this Work—the Aquarian Foundation. Our witness to the world of outer affairs was the P.P.L. Read *The End of the Days*, and see if any other witness is equal to it. Both of these have now been "slain."

Brother, follow your intuitions and they will not lead you wrongly. You have seen my actions, and you can gauge whether I am honest or not. You have seen also those others. Make your choice. Remember that on the third day, the Witness shall arise again. It is for you to have a part in that resurrection, and part in its preparation, for much will be done in silence during the "three days." You may have a part in it, and in that which follows, *because you are honest.*

Lucas was no doubt puzzled by Brother XII's cryptic utterance. He would soon discover there was more to the prophecy than rhetoric.

△   △   △

A week later, Wilson and Robert England met Lucas at the Hotel Georgia in Vancouver to discuss the legal ramifications of dissolving the Aquarian Foundation. Wilson asked Lucas what would become of the assets when the Society was dissolved. Lucas explained that by law they would have to be distributed equally among the seven Governors. Wilson protested that this was unfair and would defeat the intentions of the various donors who had contributed to the Society.

"I'm perfectly convinced there's a scheme on between DeLuce and Von Platen to split the outfit and get control of the finances," he said. "I'm taking pains to see there'll be nothing left to plunder."

"Well, you needn't be concerned about finances being plundered," Lucas answered. "Von Platen is a man of means."

If the assets were divided, Wilson argued, people who'd worked hard for the organization wouldn't receive proper compensation. Robert England, for example, was being paid only fifty dollars a month. "Bob is entitled to at least three-hundred dollars a month from the time he first came to us," Wilson said, "and I want to make sure that he gets it!"

Lucas asked about Mary Connally's donation, but Wilson cut him off—"Nothing doing! That twenty-five thousand dollars is mine!"

Lucas brought up the Hess Trust: What did Wilson intend to do with it?

"I'll arrange that as best I may with Mr. Hess," Wilson replied. "I'm satisfied that he'll want to divert those funds into my own hands."

Realizing that Wilson was in no mood for debate, Lucas went ahead and explained the legal procedure that would have to be followed to dissolve the Society. The Governors would have to formally pass a resolution, then make application to the Supreme Court of British Columbia, requesting that the Society be dissolved. Lucas advised him that the notices calling the meeting had to be sent out two weeks in advance. He suggested that Wilson mail them out immediately, before any further misunderstandings could arise.

The meeting ended. Lucas returned to his office, and Wilson and England went up to their rooms in the hotel. Wilson was obviously upset at the prospect of having his work brought down in ruins by what he considered the treachery of his fellow Governors. He felt a particular enmity towards Coulson Turnbull. Snatching up some hotel stationery, he scribbled a memo to his former associate, threatening to expose intimate details of his personal life:

"The attempt of yourself and co-conspirators to intimidate me has failed. How completely it has failed, I will now prove to you. I (not you) am going to force a full disclosure of everything, and myself publish all the facts. I mean EVERYTHING—not what you call everything."

Wilson threatened to take Turnbull and the others to court and to reveal Turnbull's liaison with a woman living in Victoria: "I will show (prove) that you had been living with her as your mistress, and I will show the connection of this frame-up with the present plot.

"I will also relate what you told me of your 'vision' of Cecilia on the stairs, in all its indecency, and if you are hardy, will force Cecilia to testify under *oath* as to whether or not she knows of that vision."

Running out of stationery, Wilson tore off a couple of blank CN telegraph forms and finished off:

"Lest you should think I am trying to intimidate you, I repeat that whatever you do, or do not do, I will force a full *public disclosure* of everything—of many other matters also which will hit some of the others fatally. Your safest course is to disappear from Vancouver and from this province while you can—your shortest way would be over the end of the wharf. Whether you go or stay, I will force *everything* into the open."

There was one Governor at the headquarters who took no part in the dispute. Phillip Fisher had resigned from the Aquarian Foundation on September 8, but for some time before that had been acting strangely. Hyperactive by anyone's standards, Fisher had become completely manic, talking incessantly and not sleeping for days.

"I remember him dashing up onto the porch of the Center Building," Eric Davenport says. "His eyes were bugged out like saucers. He told us he'd had a message—he'd been chosen by the Masters to be the next leader! He was so excited, he was drooling. Then he dashed off. *Boom! Boom! Boom!* Just like that!"

Sixteen-year-old Frances Lucas became the object of Fisher's romantic affections. "Poor Phil really went off the deep end," she recalls. "He had a crush on me. He wrote me letters full of astrological symbolism, hinting that we were to have a child together—one of the great souls of the sixth sub-race.

My father soon put a stop to that!"

Fisher's delusions eventually became obvious even to himself and he entered an asylum. The little poem he inscribed in Frances's autograph book before he left the colony gives a glimpse into his exalted state of mind:

> Oh hail O Earth that gave me birth,
> I stand upon my feet,
> I bring again the Laws of Love,
> Venus returns complete.

> "See that ye love one another."

Fisher's injunction was ironic, given the present state of affairs at the headquarters. The atmosphere was one of suspicion and hostility. The road which ran past the Center Building and down to the water marked the dividing line between the enemy camps. The houses of Von Platen, DeLuce, and the Squiers stood on one side of the road; those of Wilson, the Barleys, and the Hobarts stood on the other. The two groups confined themselves to their individual properties in a state of uneasy truce.

Brother XII, meanwhile, drew up the notices calling the General Meeting at which the Governors would vote to dissolve the Foundation. He explained to Lucas that dissolving the Society was an important step in a new stage of the Work and was "part of the Plan itself." It would have been undertaken "quite independently of any of those treacheries and deceits of which Von Platen and his associates stand convicted," and like every other important matter connected with the Work, would be done at the proper time: "The date of the actual meeting will accord with the correct planetary influences for that work. It will be done during the month of October and neither Von Platen, nor anyone else, will put it forward or delay it because it must be done at the appointed time and no other."

He advised Lucas that he intended to shut down *The Chalice* and refund the subscriptions. In addition, he wished to refund the donations of a number of individuals who'd contributed their savings to the Foundation, expecting to live indefinitely at the Center under the shelter of the Work. It was his responsibility, he said, to safeguard their interests and see that they did not suffer any financial hardship as a result of the Society being dissolved.

The next issue of *The Chalice* was at Filmers Printers in Nanaimo, about to be printed. It contained an extraordinary article by Brother XII. Eric Davenport had proofread it:

"Oh, it was a fabulous thing! It was about this magic ring that had been given to him by the Masters. Somehow, when he was on the ship coming to America, he lost this ring in the middle of the ocean. But then, by means of the white *chelas*, as he called them, he came into possession of it again when he was in *samadhi*. He gave this ring to Myrtle Baumgartner. It was the most fabulous ring you could imagine! He showed it to Bob England and some other people there. I never saw it, but it was supposed to be something fantastic—one of these rings that has magic powers associated with it.

"But when this trouble came up with Von Platen, this Osiris-Isis business, I guess he thought they'd use this article against him as proof of his being demented or something. So he drove straight to Nanaimo and had it destroyed. He told us the printers had broken up the plates, put them in the melting pot. He had the only copy—the galley proof. But oh! I wanted a copy of that article! It was a fabulous thing!"

Brother XII now issued a General Letter to the members, informing them of the crisis at the headquarters. "A small group, driven by pride and personal ambition, have tried to seize by fraud or force the leadership of the Aquarian Foundation and the chief places in it," he wrote. He identified the conspirators as "Moritz" Von Platen, Robert DeLuce, and Coulson Turnbull, and explained that they'd all known each other in Pasadena, had formed a distinct group at the Center, and had never assimilated.

"These people, thinking they saw a 'good thing' in the A.F., joined the outer Society, and were profuse in their protestations of loyalty and service. EVENTS HAVE NOW PROVEN BEYOND DOUBT OR DENIAL that their plan was to work themselves into positions of confidence or responsibility. DeLuce was to use his work in the Aquarian Foundation to spread his ideas on 'physical regeneration' and, incidentally, to 'boost his own stock.' We have no interest in regeneration—our interest is in spiritual truths, and we will not have this work brought down to any other level."

He accused DeLuce of wanting to have his wife installed as his own confidential secretary, and Von Platen of making a bid to gain financial control by suggesting that he be made Secretary-Treasurer. "All of these moves were, of course, made in 'a spirit of service' and with a view to 'lightening the heavy burden' I was personally carrying. Every one of these plans failed—Robert was given no chance to spread his theories; Myrtle DeLuce got no 'confidential' position; and I refused to give Von Platen any voice in the financial affairs of the A.F. When they realized that guile had failed, they decided to throw off the mask and to obtain by force what they had failed to get by fraud. They determined to depose me, if possible by a general vote and on the grounds of maladministration, or by any other charges they might bring against me."

Brother XII claimed that he'd been aware of the plot since May, but he had allowed it to develop so that the exposure of the conspirators might be final and complete. "I have de-cided to cut all knots at one blow. I SHALL SHORTLY TAKE STEPS TO DISSOLVE THE AQUARIAN FOUNDATION AS A LEGALLY INCORPORATED SOCIETY. There will be nothing to shoot at, nothing to plunder, nothing to trap by legal trickery, and no 'Society' to tempt men to scheme for personal place and leadership." The outer organization had served its purpose, he declared—that of a drag-net into which had been drawn the fit and the unfit. It was now the time of winnowing and separation. The present crisis was a test. It would decide which members were of the sixth sub-race spirit, and which were "self-deceived, conventional, bound by tradition, entirely of the fifth. . . Those who have in them the nature and spirit of the Work, and who remain faithful, shall go forward to better things—they shall 'pass over to the other side.'"

At the same time, Brother XII wrote to Oliver Hess with news of the crisis: "Dear Brother, I have no time to provide you with complete details, but you will recall I wrote you earlier about Von Platen, who wished to take over the financial management of the Work. He is now heading what is practically a revolution—has tried to get me deposed and contemplates an injunction so as to tie up all the funds." He explained that he had to dissolve the Aquarian Foundation to rid himself of the rebellious Governors, but that unfortunately, upon dissolution, the Foundation's assets would have to be divided among the statutory Governors of the Society. The Hess Trust would be disbursed. To prevent this calamity, Hess would have to sign the new Trust Agreement he enclosed, which would convey the securities to Wilson personally. He urged Hess to execute the document without delay, thereby safeguarding the securities for the future Work: "Brother, the moment is critical and calls for instant action. If you would help me to save the Cause, act at once."

Brother XII also wrote to Mary Connally in Asheville, North Carolina. He explained that he needed to protect her twenty-five thousand dollar contribution from being divided among those who sought to destroy the Work. He included an affidavit which stated that her donation was intended for his exclusive use, in order to forward the Work in whatever way he judged best, and that without his consent, no other person or organization should participate in it:

"I told you when we met that what you could do for this Work would soon be made clear. This is at once your testing and your great opportunity. Have faith in the righteousness of our cause, and of my own motive, and—*you will have saved the whole of our Work on the physical plane.*"

He urged Mary to return the executed document to him immediately in case any attempt was made to tie up the funds. "That done, good sister, pack your bags and come here as quickly as you may. I want you to see everything for yourself, to see these others, their work and their methods, just to judge as between them and ourselves. Only thus shall you judge clearly between the truth and a lie, between the true man and the traitor."

He also explained to Mary that he'd known about the plot against the Work from its very inception:

Sister, all was foreseen, foretold, and prepared for—it is part of the Plan. The purpose of the outer work is done; the real work, the work of the inner order, is about to begin, and in that work, you shall have your part. Unconsciously, our enemies are playing into our hands. When the truth is revealed, they will see that they have not even touched our Work, while they themselves will have lost all.

As for ourselves, we fight the good fight, neither discouraged nor dismayed. Those who are for us are greater now, far greater, than those that be against us.

"If you can hear the words which you have spoken
Twisted by knaves to make a trap for fools,
If you can see the things you gave your life for, broken,
And stoop and build them up with worn-out tools. . ."

CHAPTER
V

Charges and Counter-Charges

The small town of Nanaimo bustled with activity on the last Saturday morning of September 1928. Inside Spencer's Department Store, families stocked up with their weekly groceries, while across the street at Fletcher's, mothers purchased sheet music for young prodigies and exchanged gossip with the ladies from the church choir. At Billy Gray's tobacco store, Nanaimo's gentry mixed with coal miners in blackened coveralls to choose from an aromatic selection of cigarettes, cut plug, pipes, and expensive imported tobacco. Nearby at the Palace of Sweets, children begged their parents for licorice sticks and aniseed balls, and at the Windsor Hotel, thirsty patrons quaffed their first draught of the day. Motorists in caps and goggles headed out of town for the ball game, while at the corner of Commercial and Church streets, local businessmen settled up their weekly accounts in the impressive, classically columned edifice of the Canadian Bank of Commerce.

On this morning of September 29, Robert England, Secretary-Treasurer of the Aquarian Foundation, walked purposefully across the threshold of Nanaimo's main temple of finance and into the cool marble interior. The tellers working briskly behind the counters knew England well, since he was in practically every day on Foundation business. When he stepped up to the wicket and greeted Albert Hazell, the teller noticed that the usually cheerful and self-confident England seemed nervous.

Today, England had an unusual request. He passed across to Hazell two cheques endorsed to himself. One was for $2,000; the other for $800. Hazell remarked that it was a large withdrawal. England replied that he needed the money to put a deal through. Hazell suggested certified cheques or a bank draft, but England insisted that he needed cash. Overhearing the exchange, the manager came over and asked England why he needed such a large sum in cash.

"I need it to make a deposit on something," England replied, looking quite uncomfortable.

Hazell replied that he had no large bills—only twenties. England deliberated for a moment, then took back the cheques and left.

Robert England had been the one Governor who had supported Brother XII during the crisis at the headquarters. He'd been Wilson's staunch friend and ally, and his contribution as Secretary-Treasurer had been invaluable. A brilliant accountant with a shrewd business sense, he had purchased equipment and supplies for the Foundation at bargain prices and had often provided Wilson with key financial advice. But England had recently decided that he could no longer work with Brother XII.

On the fifth of October, England returned to the Bank of Commerce, and again presented the two cheques to Albert Hazell.

"I will have the cash now," he said.

Hazell explained that he still didn't have any large bills—all he had was twenties.

"They will do," England replied.

Hazell counted out $2,800 in twenty-dollar bills. England pocketed the money and left.

The next morning, England made a special trip to Seattle, where he rented a safety deposit box in a downtown bank. He put the $2,800 into the box, and returned to Cedar the same day.

On the ninth of October, England walked into Wilson's office in the Center Building and announced that he was resigning from the Aquarian Foundation. At the same time, he explained to Wilson that he'd taken $2,800 from the bank as payment for services rendered. England's resignation took Wilson completely by surprise. He asked him what right he had to the money. England replied that he was entitled to it, and reminded Wilson of his statement to Lucas and Fisher—when he'd made England a Governor of the Society—that his work had saved the Foundation from ruin. He also recalled the recent meeting at the Hotel Georgia at which Wilson had told Lucas that England was easily worth $300 a month, and that when the Society was dissolved, he was going to make sure that he received it. England explained that as a bookkeeper he was normally paid $250 a month, $600 a month when employed by the United States government. He'd been receiving a salary of only $50 a month from the Foundation, he pointed out, and had served for fourteen months with an altruistic motive, only to discover that he'd been unwittingly assisting Wilson in building up a large sum of money for himself. Therefore, since he was entitled to $250 a month for his services, he was taking the balance of the amount that was owed him—$200 a month for fourteen months. England attached two receipts to his resignation: one for $2,000, as payment for his services to the Aquarian Foundation; another for $800, as payment for his services to the Mandieh Settlement.

Although caught off guard by England's defection, Wilson quickly recovered. That evening, he discussed England's resignation with Edward Lucas, explaining that England had taken the $2,800 from the Mandieh Settlement Fund—the account to which Mary Connally's $25,000 donation had been deposited.

"I have this document," he said, showing Lucas the affidavit which Mary had sent to him. "Will it hold water?"

Lucas read it over. The affidavit stated unequivocally that the $25,000 Mary had contributed was for Wilson's own personal use and did not belong to the Aquarian Foundation.

"Certainly," he replied. "It seems to solve your difficulties."

The following evening, England said farewell to Wilson in his office in the Center Building. He planned to leave the headquarters the next morning. Whatever resentment or bitterness Wilson might have harboured towards his former Secretary-Treasurer was not expressed.

"My bedroom door was open," recalls Eric Davenport, "and I heard voices coming from the office. I crept out onto the landing and listened to the conversation for awhile. They were discussing this money Bob had taken, but Wilson seemed pleased enough about it. 'Yes, Bob; that's fine,' he said. I even heard him chuckle a few times. He thanked Bob for his services and wished him luck."

At six o'clock the next morning, Davenport was warming up the car in front of the Center Building. England carried two suitcases to the waiting vehicle and stowed them in the back seat. He climbed in beside Davenport and the car slowly drove out through the Foundation gates. It made the turn onto Holden-Corso Road, its wheels scattering the morning mist. Picking up speed, the car headed towards Nanaimo.

England's disillusionment with Brother XII had been gradual, forced upon him by an accumulation of small but telling incidents. He was grateful his departure had been amicable. His immediate destination was Seattle, where he planned to retrieve the $2,800 from the safety-deposit box before returning to California.

At the CPR dock in Nanaimo, the *Princess Elaine* was taking on passengers for the seven o'clock sailing to Vancouver.

Davenport helped England carry his luggage to the ferry and told him he'd miss him. The two shook hands and said goodbye. In a sombre mood, the young secretary drove back to Cedar.

Brother XII was also up early that morning. His good humour of the night before had vanished. The underlying hostility he felt towards England had erupted into vindictive rage. He sat at his typewriter and hammered out a letter to this final Aquarian Foundation Governor who had betrayed him:

"Some time ago, I gave you a position of trust, and my full confidence in the handling of funds and accounts. You have deliberately betrayed that trust."

Wilson charged in the letter that England's action of taking the $2,800 was illegal, and that his refusal to refund it convicted him of embezzlement. He demanded that he return the money immediately:

> The purpose of this letter is to give you a chance to make full restitution of the money you have illegally taken. I ask, and expect you to answer the following questions—
>
> 1. Have you deposited the money in any bank; if so, in what bank and in whose name?
>
> 2. Have you retained the notes yourself or have you given them, or any part of them, into the hands of a third party to hold?
>
> 3. Will you repay the full amount of two thousand, eight hundred dollars into the account from which you drew it, before noon today, October 11th, 1928?

After finishing the letter, Wilson frantically searched the premises for England, not realizing he'd intended to leave so early. When Eric Davenport pulled up in front of the Center Building, Wilson hurried over to him. The young secretary was barely out of the car before the furious leader confronted him.

"He was fuming, absolutely fuming!" recalls Davenport. "He asked me where Bob was. I said I'd driven him into town.

Then he asked me how many grips he'd taken. I wondered just what—if anything—he could do to Bob, so I said, 'One grip.' But, of course, there were two."

Wilson realized England was leaving the country. Grabbing the keys from Davenport, he jumped into the car and drove off.

Twenty minutes later, Wilson was in the Nanaimo police station, laying a charge of theft against Robert England. Immediately afterwards in the police court next door, he swore out a warrant for his arrest before Magistrate C.H. Beevor-Potts.

Sergeant Jack Russell placed a phone call to Vancouver. When the *Princess Elaine* docked at the CPR wharf, two police officers were waiting to take England into custody. To his chagrin, they informed him he was under arrest.

That evening, England was taken back to Nanaimo under police escort and was locked up to await his preliminary hearing. In his cramped cell, he had plenty of time to adjust to the fact that his association with Brother XII wasn't over yet.

After returning to the headquarters, Wilson went looking for his secretary. He found him outside the Center Building.

"He threatened me," recalls Davenport. "He said he'd seen a great many people railroaded—innocent young people sent to jail for years. And all the time he was talking, his hand was on the handle of this Colt .32 sticking out of the inside pocket of his suit jacket."

Wilson stalked off, leaving Davenport to imagine the worst. The terrified youth spent a sleepless night, dreading what Brother XII might do to him.

The following morning, Wilson came up to Davenport's room. His demeanour was quite different—not menacing at all. He just wanted to borrow a cigarette. Summoning up his courage, Davenport confronted him:

"I said to him, 'You threatened me yesterday, Brother XII, and I didn't like it!'

"Oh, he was as charming as he could be! 'No, Eric,' he said,

'I didn't threaten you; I wouldn't do such a thing!' And he cackled this cackly kind of laugh."

The next morning, Davenport received a letter from Wilson, informing him that his services were no longer required. Davenport was hugely relieved: he was too unnerved to work anyway. He packed his bags, said goodbye to the Barleys and the Hobarts, and hopped into Jim Lippincott's truck for the ride back to Vancouver.

"I was scared to death!" he recalls. "Just a little greenhorn kid fresh out of school! I was a nervous wreck by the time I got home!"

The strain of events was taking its toll on Wilson, too. He took to his bed in a state of nervous exhaustion. Sitting up in his dressing gown, he wrote a general letter to the group secretaries of the Aquarian Foundation. "As all my help has quit, being involved in the present attack upon our Work, it is *impossible* to attend to any correspondence," he advised them. "Please wait for general letters, as I can deal with the present crisis only in that way."

Wilson also drafted a letter to Oliver Hess, attempting to convince the elderly lawyer to sign over the Hess Trust to him, "so that I might bring it into the safety of the present phase of this Work, and not to get anything for myself personally." Hess had refused to sign the new trust agreement, saying that he considered it fraudulent and deceitful. Wilson repeated that he was single-handedly fighting a tremendous attack on the Work, and promised Hess a "full and satisfactory answer" to the "wicked charges" that had been made against him when he had more time to write: "I am almost distracted with the incessant work each day."

He also begged Hess not to be swayed or deceived by the letters he was certain the other Governors had written him: "Remember, Brother, that our simplest obligation is to hear all the story before reaching a decision. You have heard the lies which are being circulated, and you should be able to judge of the motives and the character of those who would circulate them. As for me, read what I have written in the past, and the record of my work."

At the Mandieh Settlement on Valdes Island, work came to an abrupt halt. The workmen packed up their tools, dismantled their tents and left. The rain poured down on the deserted colony, soaking through the tarpaulins covering the unfinished cabins and dripping down onto piles of stacked lumber and rusting nails. For the time being, the Mandieh Settlement remained unfinished—a mournful cluster of buildings on a rocky hillside, abandoned to the wind and rain.

Myrtle Baumgartner also left Valdes, her dream of bearing the next World Teacher shattered by a miscarriage. Cecilia Turnbull had nursed her through it, but the loss had devastated Myrtle and pushed her to the brink of insanity.

When the other Governors discovered that Horus had "slipped his moorings," as Lucas put it, they took it as further evidence that Brother XII was off the track. "If this thing has been decreed by the gods," Lucas bluntly asked, "how does it happen that Horus is a miscarriage?"

Brother XII and Myrtle had tried again, instructing Coulson Turnbull to cast a new horoscope for the child. But when Myrtle suffered a second miscarriage, her disillusionment and grief resulted in a complete mental breakdown.

"I only saw her once," Frances Lucas remembers. "She was kind of wild-looking and lost—not at all attractive. I remember this strange, sad-looking creature with dark hair parted in the middle.

"Afterwards, I said to Maurice Von Platen, 'Mrs. Baumgartner didn't look like much of an "Isis" to me.' He just said in a joking kind of way, 'Well, you never saw her with her war paint on!'"

How much emotional support Myrtle received from Brother XII is difficult to say, for the relationship between them rapidly disintegrated. She remained in seclusion in the House of Mystery, struggling to recover from her breakdown, her future uncertain.

△   △   △

On October 19, 1928, Robert England's preliminary hearing was held in the police court in Nanaimo before Chief Magistrate C. H. Beevor-Potts. A stern arbiter of justice, the grey-haired magistrate was almost an institution himself, running the court with the rigid discipline of a British military officer. England stood as the clerk read the charge. Acting on his behalf was Thomas P. Morton, also known as "The Egg" because of his shiny bald head. Local gossip had him spending nights on his office couch to escape a nagging wife; taking solace in the bottle, he'd emerge rumpled and dishevelled the following morning to face the new day. He was perhaps not the wisest choice of legal counsel.

Representing Wilson was Nanaimo's leading lawyer, Frank S. Cunliffe, who had articled in Lucas's law office in Vancouver. The thirty-six-year-old Cunliffe was tall and slender and had a keen intellect. His razor-sharp and logical mind invariably demolished his adversaries' arguments with ease. He was a formidable courtroom opponent.

Albert Hazell was called as the first witness. He testified that he was a teller at the Canadian Bank of Commerce, and that England had authority to draw cheques on the Mandieh Settlement Fund account. He described the two occasions when England had appeared at the bank and identified the cheques Cunliffe showed him as the same ones England had cashed.

"And in payment of these two cheques he received altogether how much?"

"Two thousand, eight hundred dollars."

Cunliffe called Wilson to the stand. He testified that England had been employed by him as a clerk and bookkeeper. He said he'd given him the authority to sign cheques as a convenience to himself in handling the accounts. Cunliffe asked how the Mandieh Settlement Fund had originated.

"The Mandieh Settlement Fund was a sum of money donated to myself for the purpose of carrying out my work. There were no strings attached to it. I talked over the question of the settlement itself with the donor, but otherwise there were no conditions attached to it."

"What amount of his time would be taken up in connection with this Mandieh Settlement Fund?"

"I should say that the whole of the work done could have been completed in a very few days if it had been done consecutively. It could have been done by anybody with any knowledge of bookkeeping at all. In addition, he went to Vancouver to buy stores, and he was over there several days."

"The bulk of his work consisted of what?"

"The bulk of his work was clerical work for the Aquarian Foundation."

"What was the accused paid for his services to the Aquarian Foundation?"

"Fifty dollars a month."

"Did he live out there at the settlement at Cedar district?"

"Yes Sir."

"Who paid for his board and provided his lodging?"

"They had arrangements of their own about board."

"Did he pay for it out of his fifty dollars?"

"He got fifty dollars a month, clear."

"In other words, he got his board free?"

"Yes Sir. I would like to qualify that by saying that that is my understanding of the situation."

"Was the Mandieh Settlement under any financial obligation to the accused?"

"No Sir."

"Was the Aquarian Foundation under any financial obligation to the accused?"

"No Sir. Nothing beyond whatever salary may have been due to him at the rate of fifty dollars a month."

"As a matter of fact, had that salary been kept up to date by regular monthly payments, do you know?"

"Yes Sir."

Cunliffe held up the two cheques that had been submitted as evidence, so that Beevor-Potts could see them. He then showed them to Wilson.

"Dealing with these cheques: Exhibit One is for two thousand dollars and is marked 'Full payment for all interest in A.F.' Did he have any legal or financial interest in the Aquarian Foundation?"

"None that I know of."

"Exhibit Two is for eight hundred dollars and is marked 'Payment in full for all interest in Mandieh Settlement.' What do you say to that?"

"He had absolutely no interest in the Mandieh Settlement."

Cunliffe then questioned Wilson about the conversation he'd had with England when England announced his resignation. Wilson claimed he'd never given his consent to England to take the money:

"I told him he had no legal right to it. He said he had, and that he was going to retain it, and that he would decide what he would do with it."

Wilson made no mention of any previous understanding he might have had with England about salary, or of his conversations with Lucas in the Hotel Georgia and earlier when England had been made a Governor of the Society.

T.P. Morton cross-examined Wilson, but didn't question him at any length. He asked about England's missing diary, but Wilson said he had no knowledge of it. Morton sat down, obviously not intending to continue. Beevor-Potts asked England if he had anything to say in answer to the charge.

"I have nothing to say, Sir," replied England.

Beevor-Potts ordered England to stand trial at the next criminal assize court in Nanaimo, to be held on November 20. He adjourned the court.

The accused was led from the courtroom back to his cell. If convicted at the assizes—and it appeared as if Wilson had a strong case against him—England faced a prison sentence and future criminal record. It was not a pleasant prospect and he realized that in the circumstances, Wilson was unlikely to show any mercy in demanding that justice be served.

△   △   △

Shortly before 11:00 A.M. on October 24, 1928, Maurice Von Platen, Robert DeLuce, and Edward Lucas entered the Center Building. They were hopeful that the General Meeting would be little more than a formality, and that the motion to dissolve the Aquarian Foundation would be quickly passed. Of the original Governors of the Society, only Wilson, Lucas, Von Platen, and DeLuce would be attending. Joseph Benner had sent his power of attorney to Von Platen; Comfort, Turnbull, Fisher, and England had resigned. The dissenting Governors were looking forward to putting the entire episode of the Aquarian Foundation behind them.

When the three entered the auditorium, they were amazed to see Wilson flanked by Alfred and Annie Barley and George and Louise Hobart. Wilson explained that he'd appointed them Governors of the Foundation. This meant that he was assured a majority: he would have five votes to the dissenting Governors' four. Wilson called the meeting to order and announced that in accordance with the by-laws that gave the president the power to increase the number of Governors to twelve, he'd appointed the Barleys and Hobarts Governors of the Society. He then read from a prepared statement:

"I am keenly sensible of the responsibility which rests upon this Order to see that the monies donated to us from time to time to carry on our work are properly applied for the purposes for which they were donated. It has been suggested that in view of the dissension which has been raised by some of the Governors, this outer Order as a legal entity should be dissolved, but such a course would automatically involve a compulsory realization of the assets and a distribution of those assets among those holding legal membership in the Society.

I am impelled to the conclusion that dissolution is not, at the present time, the proper remedy for whatever troubles may exist, and would certainly be a very unfair proceeding having regard to the wishes of those who have donated to this Order as a whole the funds and assets of which it has control."

DeLuce, Von Platen, and Lucas looked at each other in alarm—their worst fears had been realized. But Brother XII had another, less obvious reason for stacking the meeting in his favour. He believed that the Governors didn't really wish to dissolve the Society, but intended instead to pass a motion deposing him as president, so they could seize control of the organization themselves. His appointment of the Barleys and Hobarts as Governors defeated this stratagem.

Brother XII proceeded to dictate three terms which would have to be complied with before he would agree to dissolve the Society:

"First, there must be refunded to the Mandieh Settlement Fund the sum of $2,800, which Robert England, the erstwhile Secretary-Treasurer of this Order, wrongfully abstracted. It is my firm conviction that his action was instigated by some of the Governors, or at least is now supported by them.

"Secondly, all attempts to depose me and obtain control of the Outer Order and to obstruct our work must cease, and harmony must prevail.

"Thirdly, proper arrangements must be made to safeguard the monies donated or loaned to this Order, and if no other solution can be arrived at, then such monies should be returned to the donors or lenders."

The three dissenting Governors looked at Wilson, their faces set. Von Platen told him they couldn't accept his conditions.

Wilson tabled the motion to dissolve the Society. With the Barleys and the Hobarts voting with him, he outvoted the others five votes to four, defeating the motion. He then declared the meeting adjourned.

The dissenting Governors left the auditorium. Outside the Center Building, they climbed into Von Platen's car and drove off, leaving Wilson and the others to congratulate themselves on their victory.

Von Platen's car arrived at the Nanaimo police station and the three men climbed out. Inside the station, a hurried conference took place as they put into effect a contingency plan they had devised for just this situation. Lucas and Robert DeLuce put up a bond for England's bail; England then laid a charge of theft against Wilson, accusing him of stealing $13,000 from the Aquarian Foundation. England also swore out a warrant for Wilson's arrest.

Wilson had left the headquarters immediately after the meeting. He was driven to Nanaimo, where he boarded the *Princess Elaine* for Vancouver. Three hours later as he stepped off the ferry, two officers closed in on him. They informed the startled Wilson he was under arrest, then unceremoniously hustled him off to the police station. The details of Wilson's arrest no doubt pleased England. Ironically, it had taken place in circumstances identical to his own—a fitting case of poetic justice.

That evening, Wilson was so weak he could barely stand as he faced Magistrate Beevor-Potts in the dimly lit Nanaimo police court. Frank Cunliffe had acted quickly for his client, using $10,000 of the Hess Trust as a security deposit and arranging for Alfred Barley and George Hobart to furnish the balance of Wilson's $20,000 bond. Late that night, Wilson was released, shaken by his ordeal.

George Hobart drove the exhausted guru back to Cedar. Slumped in the back seat of the car, Wilson was shocked by the treachery of his enemies. His arrest was proof to him that they would stop at nothing to destroy him and his work. In his own house at last, he collapsed into bed and slept.

The next day, Von Platen and DeLuce met Lucas in his office in the Standard Bank Building in Vancouver to discuss the situation. Wilson had outmaneuvered them at the meeting and still retained control of the Foundation funds. They decided that their next course of action would be to apply to the Supreme Court of British Columbia for an injunction to restrain him from dealing with any of the funds of the Society.

That afternoon in the court house on Georgia Street, Edward Lucas presented the case for the injunction to Chief Justice F. B. Gregory. He explained that for some time Wilson had been carrying on the affairs of the Aquarian Foundation against the wishes of the other Governors. He'd refused to dissolve the Society at a general meeting called for that purpose, and had seized control of the Society's funds, amounting to $45,000, using them to build a separate settlement on Valdes Island and for other purposes unknown to the Governors.

Lucas read from the affidavit: "The defendant, Edward Arthur Wilson, has obtained control of the monies of the Aquarian Foundation and is systematically and continuously misapplying the same, and unless a Receiver be appointed and an injunction granted, all the monies of the Aquarian Foundation will be misapplied and totally lost."

After a brief hearing, Justice Gregory granted the injunction. It went into effect immediately, freezing the assets of the Society, including Wilson's personal account. The injunction prevented him from holding any meetings of the Governors or from otherwise transacting any business of the Society.

Lucas rushed to telephone Nanaimo Printers. He threatened the manager with dire legal penalties if he printed a general letter that Brother XII had written to the membership, answering the charges against him. Lucas so intimidated the manager that he even refused to give Wilson galley proofs of the letter. Wilson was thus prevented from defending himself or explaining his actions to the Foundation members.

Robert England, who had been released on bail furnished by Lucas and DeLuce, now laid a second charge of theft against Wilson. He charged that on October 5, 1928, Wilson had removed $5,000 from the Aquarian Foundation bank account and deposited it to his own personal account. This increased the amount Wilson was accused of stealing to $18,000.

At Cedar, Brother XII was still recuperating from his arrest. He was confined to bed, too ill to sit up to a typewriter. Propped up by pillows, he wrote in longhand to Oliver Hess, telling him about the recent events. He said that both Robert England and Edward Lucas had betrayed him: "Lucas, who also had my confidence, as you know, has deserted me and is retained by the German and his money. He has advised them all along."

He explained that the injunction prevented him from using any funds—even those in his own bank account—and had been deliberately timed to coincide with his arrest:

> This was to cut me off from the possibility of bail, so that I would be forced into the common gaol. This they knew would kill me physically as I am an invalid, and can only keep my body going with the greatest care. They issued a second charge (more money), and their lawyer asked the magistrate *to increase the bail. This he refused to do:* even the magistrate can see it is a plain case of malicious persecution. Then they took exception to one of the bondsmen in the bail already issued in the hope that they could force me into the gaol in that way. By the mercy of God and the help of loyal friends, that move was defeated and I came home last night to go to my bed—very ill.

Brother XII advised Hess that the securities in the Hess Trust which he'd donated to him personally—and not to the Aquarian Foundation—had provided him with his bail money: "These are the only means I have of protection, or of continuing this fight to protect our Work. They have saved me from imprisonment and, I believe, physical death. You can thank God that such is the case."

The next day, Wilson got up from his bed to attend two separate court cases in Nanaimo. In the morning, he appeared at his preliminary hearing to answer the charge of stealing $18,000 from the Aquarian Foundation. Standing in the dock, he looked tired and drawn, and he seemed relieved when the hearing was adjourned for three days. It was a sorely needed reprieve for a man in his condition.

In the afternoon, Wilson testified against James Lippincott and a workman named Perry More. He'd brought trespassing charges against the two men when they'd refused to leave the premises at Cedar after he'd ordered them off the property. They had retaliated by bringing lawsuits of their own against Wilson. Lippincott was suing Wilson for $450, representing three months of work at the Mandieh Settlement. More had filed a claim for $1,000 in unpaid wages.

In the trespassing case, the debate became acrimonious as accusations and counter-accusations flew bitterly across the crowded courtroom before Magistrate C. H. Beevor-Potts. T. P. Morton infuriated Wilson by calling him an "upstart" and by saying he had no right at the Center and ought to "get off." These and other insulting statements made by Morton in front of the court had Wilson practically beside himself with rage. Over Cunliffe's vigorous protest, the case was adjourned.

From his bed that evening at Cedar, Wilson penned a furious rebuttal to Morton's comments. He claimed that his statements were either "malicious and intentional lies calculated to prejudice me with the court, or the man knows not what he is talking about." He vehemently denied Morton's charge that the only money he had, had been taken from the Aquarian Foundation:

"In order to start the Aquarian Foundation, I had to sell my only possessions in order to publish the preliminary *Message* and my first small book, *The Three Truths*. I gave all that I had, about $1,700 all told. . . I have a small income, possibly averaging $50 a month, derived from royalties on the books I have written. This has paid all my personal living expenses to date, and I have never drawn one penny of recompense or salary from the Aquarian Foundation at any time."

Wilson emphasized that he alone had created the Aquarian Foundation: "The entire Work has been planned and built up by myself. I have written every book, every pamphlet, and every Instruction printed or issued in connection with our organization. It is the literal truth that *I am* the Aquarian Foundation and it has no existence apart from myself."

The dissenting Governors, on the other hand, had no possible claim to anything in the Work: "Any 'rights' they may claim as nominal Governors of this Society, they derive from myself alone—I appointed them and made them such. In return, they are using the legal machinery of a British court of justice in an effort to persecute and hound to his death a British subject, a man whom they well know is innocent of the charges they have brought forward."

Wilson sank back in his bed, exhausted. He felt a sudden pressure in his chest and had difficulty breathing. The pressure increased and he felt a shooting pain in his left arm. His panic mounted as he realized he was having a heart attack.

Dr. Ross Lane rushed out from Nanaimo to examine Wilson. He confirmed that he'd indeed suffered a heart attack—but a minor one, not serious enough to disable him. He ordered Wilson to remain in bed for three days of complete rest. Helpless and frustrated, Wilson lay on his pillows, powerless to act against the enemies who were bent on destroying him.

The same day in Vancouver, Von Platen, DeLuce, and Lucas launched another legal action against Wilson. Since he had refused to dissolve the Aquarian Foundation voluntarily, they attempted to force its dissolution by petitioning the Lieutenant-Governor of British Columbia to revoke the Society's charter.

Standing on the front steps of the provincial court house, Lucas told a group of reporters, "The storm about the Aquarian Foundation has been brewing for some time. It broke upon the establishment by Mr. Wilson of the Mandieh Settlement, and his announcement of his views on marriage."

Lucas briefly explained why he and his fellow Governors were filing the petition. He said he felt it was important that the public at large, as well as the members of the Foundation, be informed of Brother XII's activities.

The petition summarized the charges against Wilson in the matter of the $25,000 donation by Mary Connally:

> The said Wilson wrongfully diverted a great portion of the said fund to an account in the Canadian Bank of Commerce at Nanaimo, called the Mandieh Settlement account, and proceeded to purchase in his own name, or jointly with others unknown to the petitioners, a piece of land on Valdes Island which was called the Mandieh Settlement, and to store there large quantities of food, and make other large capital expenditures from the funds belonging to the Aquarian Foundation.
>
> The Mandieh Settlement has no connection with the Aquarian Foundation save that the said Wilson is the proprietor and owner of it.
>
> The said Wilson left Cedar on a trip to the East in July, 1928, and returned to the Mandieh Settlement accompanied by a woman who is the wife of a professional man in the State of New York. The said Wilson established her at the said Mandieh Settlement as his mistress; and this notwithstanding the fact that in the house occupied by him on the property of the Aquarian Foundation was living at the same time a woman who had been introduced by Wilson to your petitioners as his wife.

The petition stated that Wilson had since been arrested on two charges of theft of the Society's funds: "More of the nefarious practices of the said Wilson will be given by your petitioners by way of verbal evidence as is required to establish the position that it is not in the interests of decency and order that the said Society should continue to exist."

The petition also stated that Joseph Benner of Akron, Ohio, had written to express his accord with the action of the Governors; the petitioners therefore comprised all of the original Governors of the Society with the exception of Wilson. The petition concluded by asking the Lieutenant-Governor to cancel the incorporation of the Aquarian Foundation and declare the Society dissolved.

Edward Lucas was always one to appreciate the humour in a situation. Brother XII had often predicted that Armageddon would occur in 1928. Lucas realized that the prophecy had come true, although not in quite the way Brother XII had foretold:

ARMAGEDDON

"Maurice von Platen
Without any excuse,
Proceeded to fatten
With Robert DeLuce
 The magic Aquarian Golden-Egg Goose,
 And to put it to premature death!"
The Skipper grew wrath,
And the Skipper grew stern –
"The grim aftermath
They will presently learn!"
 He added with sibilant breath.

"Neither Robert DeLuce
Nor Maurice Von Platen,
So long as I'm loose,
Will plunder or batten
 (The fire he put the traditional fat in)
 On the riches I've painfully stored.

I have plans of my own
To prevent them from leaking,

Distinctly alone
(In a manner of speaking)
 I will handle my husbanded hoard."

Thus did he say,
Thus did he write 'em,
So to put him away
Where the dogs would not bite him,
 They decided without more ado to indict him,
 And appealed to the nearest police.
Thus Robert DeLuce
And Maurice Von Platen
Without parley or truce
Proceeded to flatten
 The white-bedecked Angel of Peace.

They said that a Master
Ought not to fear
Financial disaster
Or accumulate gear,
 Or dally with truth or act on the queer
 And this was the message they brought:
Without Sanskrit or Latin,
But plain as the deuce,
Maurice Von Platen
And Robert DeLuce
 Said the Skipper's pronouncements were rot.

And the state of affairs
At the moment of writing
Is that very few prayers
And some fairly hot fighting
 And the mutual clangor of legal indicting
 Vibrate the Aquarian cash.

Thus "the unification
Of men of good will"
Suffered inflation
Unduly until
     It burst with a terrible crash.

CHAPTER
VI
Weird Occultism Exemplified

A black 1928 Ford sedan motored along Holden-Corso Road through the farming district of Cedar. Up and down the hills it went, winding its way through leafy groves of maples and sumacs ablaze in the scarlet and gold colours of autumn. The cattle grazed behind split-rail fences and the rolling green fields were dotted with farmhouses and barns. Inside the car, Nanaimo lawyer Victor B. Harrison and *Vancouver Province* reporter Bruce McKelvie discussed Brother XII and the court cases they'd attended the day before. Harrison turned down a leafy road towards the sea, glinting a vivid blue between the trees. Following the road to its end, the car came to a stop in front of the massive wooden gates of the Aquarian Foundation.

The two men stepped out of the car. Harrison, a powerful and heavyset man with a large nose and strong features, was a prominent figure in Nanaimo; he'd been elected mayor several times and was a partner in Harrison and McIntyre, one of the town's leading law firms. He was also related to the former president of the United States, William Henry Harrison. His companion, Bruce McKelvie, was a robust individual with a ruddy complexion. He wore thick spectacles and resembled Dickens's famous character Mr. Pickwick. A veteran reporter with *The Vancouver Province*, McKelvie had been covering the legislature in Victoria when he'd been assigned the story about the Foundation. He stepped forward and rattled the nine-foot gates while Harrison stood back, thumbs hooked in his vest. On the other side of the stout wire fence, they could see the houses nestled among the trees—an idyllic scene this quiet Saturday morning. Seeing no one about, McKelvie called out to attract attention.

Moments later, a dignified elderly gentleman emerged from one of the houses and approached the gates. George Hobart greeted the two strangers in a friendly manner. Harrison and McKelvie introduced themselves and asked if he could give them some information about the Aquarian Foundation. Brother XII was in bed that morning, still recuperating from his heart attack. Had he known about the visitors, one may be certain he would never have admitted them or allowed anyone to speak with them. But Hobart was open and trusting. Unlocking the gates, he let the two men inside and offered to give them a tour of the premises.

Hobart showed Harrison and McKelvie around the property, letting them view the fine houses with their handsome workmanship, the communal dining-room and cookhouse, the power plant, the garages and vegetable gardens, and the "Pepper Pot"—a quaint little cabin that different members used as a writing studio. Inside the Center Building, he introduced them to a young Scotsman named Herbert Cameron, whom Brother XII had recently hired as a bookkeeper to replace England. The two men inspected the offices and workrooms, including the auditorium with its polished hardwood floor and raised platform from which Brother XII addressed his followers.

Leaving the Center Building, they walked down to the waterfront, where they met Perry More and James Lippincott. The two Americans were sharing a small cabin, refusing to leave the property until their trespassing case was settled. A cement contractor from Los Angeles and a nonstop talker, More enthusiastically expounded on the Aquarian Foundation philosophy. Lippincott showed McKelvie his chart, "Astrology is the Clock of Destiny," which was advertised in *The Chalice*, and explained the astrological significance of the teachings. In answer to McKelvie's questions, Hobart outlined the reasons for the split between Brother XII and the other Governors. He discussed the dispute over the new settlement on Valdes, and spoke candidly about the scandal that had erupted around Brother XII's relationship with the so-called "Magdalene from Chicago." McKelvie and Harrison listened with intense interest.

Hobart even led the visitors past the tangled blackberry bushes and down the path to the ravine where the House of Mystery stood masked in a clump of trees. He explained that in this cabin, Brother XII would leave his body and while in the state of *samadhi*, communicate with the Masters of Wisdom and receive instructions for the Work. Hobart added that other members had also achieved *samadhi*, and that it wasn't necessary to have a retreat for the purpose.

The group returned to the Center Building. McKelvie asked the disciples there how they regarded Brother XII now. Several remarked that they'd observed a change in him. "He is not like the man I knew in California at all," said one. "A friend of mine saw him there when he was in *samadhi* for six days, and his face was wonderfully beautiful. He is different now."

Although one section of the Foundation was trying to put Brother XII behind bars, most members viewed him more in sorrow than in anger. It wasn't really his fault, one of the disciples explained: "He took the 'Sixth Initiation,' and he should not have done it. He failed the test, and his Black Adept is the cause of it."

What did a Black Adept have to do with it? asked McKelvie. The disciples informed him that on the higher planes to which a spirit could project itself, there were Black Adepts or influences—what the orthodox mind would call devils. One of these adepts had taken possession of Brother XII, and it wasn't "The Brother" that the fuss was about, but his black familiar.

"I have seen the Black Adept," whispered one of the disciples. "And so did another member of the Foundation. We both saw him—the other man saw him twice—and we compared notes. It was the same one all right. He wore a black cowl that came down to his shoulders and his face was like leather that had been smoked for a month."

The visit ended, and Hobart escorted Harrison and McKelvie back to the gate. Before he said goodbye, he gave them several of Brother XII's books and some copies of *The Chalice*. The two men thanked him and drove off. McKelvie was delighted by their good fortune—they'd succeeded in getting an inside look at the Foundation and he had everything he needed for his story about Brother XII.

△   △   △

Bruce McKelvie began his newspaper career as a schoolboy selling rags to *The Province* to clean the printing presses—when supplies ran short, the ladies of the neighbourhood wondered why their laundry kept mysteriously disappearing from their clotheslines! As a youth, McKelvie worked as a "printer's devil" on Texada Island, feeding paper into a flatbed press, but when the family returned to Vancouver, he got a job working for *The Province* on the police beat. It was the days when reporters were issued guns and rode in squad cars, and McKelvie made his reputation as a crime reporter of legendary skill. During his career, he'd covered every major story in the province, from murders to mine disasters, and he was on a first-name basis with premiers, police chiefs, and underworld figures. He was also an expert on Native Indian culture, having been made a blood brother of the Sliammon tribe after saving the Chief's daughter from drowning. His novel *Huldowget* vividly portrayed Indian customs and magic; he'd also written a boys' adventure novel, *Black Canyon,* based on an Indian massacre of gold miners in the Fraser Canyon in 1858, as well as a book on the early history of British Columbia. McKelvie brought his considerable talents as a reporter to the Brother XII story, so much so that he himself would become an important figure in the drama.

That night, McKelvie typed up his article about the Aquarian Foundation for *The Province's* Sunday edition. When he'd finished, he wrote to his friend Harry Pooley, the Attorney-General of British Columbia, telling him about the colony at Cedar and joking that there were some aspects to the story "that even my ingenuity could not manage to put into a family journal." It hadn't taken McKelvie long to make up his mind about the Foundation. He informed Pooley:

It is nothing more or less than a free-love colony, and the resort of weak-minded, money-mad Americans who have been resorting there by the hundreds. If not checked, I am sure that British Columbia is going to be put to the expense of maintaining a number of them at Essondale [the provincial mental hospital]. In fact, one young fellow named Fisher went raving mad in Nanaimo a few days ago and was sent to an asylum. This fellow invested anywhere from $15,000 to $20,000 in the erection of a magnificent house in the colony with its own electric light system, etc. A German-American millionaire named Von Platen is another who has a home there that cost many thousands.

There are about twenty persons at the colony now, but during the summer months, they numbered hundreds. The manager of the Malaspina Hotel told me that he was crowded with them, mostly wealthy men and women from

California, who went out there daily to imbibe the wisdom of Brother XII, and swallow his doctrines, hook, line, and sinker.

The teachings seem to be a jumble of all the occult doctrines from ancient Egypt to the present day, with special instructions from "The Master Minds" given to Wilson while he is "samadhi" or in a trance.

McKelvie quoted an excerpt from Brother XII's article on marriage, saying it was "too hot for the sedate columns of *The Province,* so I'm giving it to you to show the real trend of affairs there." He told Pooley that marriage laws and conventions were derided, and that Brother XII was carrying on an affair with a married woman, even though he had a wife living at the headquarters at Cedar.

"This new love-nest on Valdes Island, as well as money, seems to be at the bottom of the court charges and counter charges that are to be heard Tuesday. . . To me, it looks as if it might develop into another Aimee Semple McPherson case on a larger scale, AND WE DON'T WANT THAT IN B.C."

McKelvie urged Pooley to launch an official investigation into Brother XII's activities: "I hope you take some action to preserve decency in our regard for morality. As a father of a growing family, as well as a citizen of British Columbia, I don't want to see that kind of a cult grow up here."

On Sunday, October 28, McKelvie's story appeared on the front page of *The Province* under the headline: WEIRD OCCULTISM EXEMPLIFIED IN AMAZING COLONY AT CEDAR-BY-SEA.

Revelations Follow Dissension in Cult of Aquarian Foundation, Which Has Been Flourishing in Pretty Vancouver Island Village—Chief "Master of Wisdom" Prefers Trespassing Charge Against Former Disciples of Peculiar Order—"House of Mystery" Amid Mansions of

Wealthy Adherents, All Enclosed by Barbed Wire Fence.

Revelations that will startle the public are promised when the charges and counter-charges that have split the Aquarian Foundation at Cedar wide open are aired in court here next week. Weird occult doctrines suggestive of the teachings of Buddha and half a score of other theosophical and astrological teachers from Zoroaster to Madame Blavatsky, with new and incomprehensible additions claimed to be recent personal instructions from some "Master" will be unfolded. Mingling of the sexes under plea of spiritual duty and in defiance of recognized marriage laws will be told, for it was upon this doctrine of freedom, agreed to in theory, but objected to in practice, that the Aquarian movement has apparently crashed.

McKelvie gave an account of his visit to the Foundation headquarters, and said it was a mystery "how a retired sea-captain managed in this age and generation to gather about him from the four corners of the continent and Europe a following of apparently intelligent men and women who accepted him as a superior being in personal contact with 'The Masters' on spiritual planes far removed from this mundane sphere." He described Wilson as "a spare, slightly stoop-shouldered, pale-faced and ascetic-looking man, who sports a thick square-cut greying beard," and stated that the cult had approximately two thousand members throughout the United States and Canada. Wilson's antagonist, Robert England, was a "clean-shaven, sunburned young man in his thirties. . . He is a prepossessing chap with more than the average share of good looks."

McKelvie quoted at length from Brother XII's articles in *The Chalice*, including his attack upon marriage: "'The idea that participation in such a ceremony (a recognized marriage ceremony) confers exclusive and possessive rights over the person and affections of another can never be substantiated. It cannot be so because it is not in accord with the facts; if it is backed by a man-made law, the law will not prevail because it is at variance with the laws of Nature.'" McKelvie reported that members of the Foundation had predicted sensations when the court cases opened. He concluded his article by calling for an immediate government investigation into the activities of the colony: "There is a strong feeling in Nanaimo that enough has already been revealed to warrant prompt and speedy action by the Attorney-General to find out what kind of a cult has been established in British Columbia."

McKelvie's story was picked up by the Hearst newspaper chain and appeared all across the United States. It made the front pages of *The San Francisco Examiner* and *The Los Angeles Examiner,* headlined: FREE LOVE CULT LAID TO CALIFORNIANS and CALIFORNIAN CALLED HEAD OF LOVE CULT. The Hearst story identified Brother XII as a former resident of California and Spain, and claimed that many Californians were included among his disciples:

> Cloistered in a sylvan Eden among remote forests of Vancouver Island, far from plebian eyes, is a magnificent retreat where wealthy Americans, particularly from California, are wont to retire to study "occult mysticisms."
>
> But Canadian authorities, called upon to settle a rather worldly dispute among denizens of this synthetic paradise, have scratched beneath its esthetic exterior. And their official delving is said to have revealed, under the surface of its neo-mystic labels, a startlingly elaborate "free love" colony.

The Nanaimo newspapers eagerly seized upon the story. *The Daily Herald* informed its readers that the members of the new religious sect sequestering itself in the leafy, almost impenetrable seclusion of Cedar believed that the world was going to the "demnition bow-wows," and that after the cataclysm, the Aquarians would take charge of the earth. The writer ridiculed Brother XII's pretensions: "President Wilson is one of the Twelve Masters of Wisdom. Who the other eleven are does not matter, for the whole idea is absolutely ridiculous." He said it was impossible to define occultism ("They [sic] are no words to explain those things what [sic] cannot be grasped, or which do not register in the mind. . ."), but said it was good enough to "cheat and cozen some of Barnum's daily arrivals out of their wits, their minds, and their earthly possessions." He demanded that the Aquarian Foundation be investigated, deported from Vancouver Island, and "stamped out."

Bruce McKelvie remained in Nanaimo, waiting for Wilson's preliminary hearing. While he was there, he interviewed the local people to get their reaction to the startling developments of the past week. The following day, his story appeared on the front page of *The Province:*

CULT'S REVOLT EYE-OPENER TO OLD NANAIMO. People of Island City Thought at First That Aquarian Foundation Had Something to Do with Fish, But Now They Know Otherwise, and the Happenings at Cedar-by-the-Sea Furnish Biggest Sensation in Years.

Citizens of Nanaimo are watching with keen interest the struggle that has centered about the Aquarian Foundation by the seashore and in the maple groves of Cedar district, which is reflected in charges and counter-charges in the courts of British Columbia. In the seventy-five years since the coal mines of Nanaimo were opened, there have been many sensations and excitements in the Coal Capital of the Pacific Coast—but this war among the devotees of a new cult is something novel and entertaining, and its progress is being observed with attention. The whole thing is so unexpected and surprising that the good people of Nanaimo do not quite know what to make of it.

McKelvie reported that the colonists had previously been regarded by their neighbours as a harmless lot of faddists who were good spenders at the local stores. They had referred to them as "the Aquariums" and had left them alone, not prying into their affairs. Now, however, they felt a new and justifiable curiosity: "'I thought,' observed one old resident of the district as he lighted his pipe, 'that they had something to do with fish. You see, on the other side of the town, at Departure Bay, the government has a place—a biological station it is called—and I've heard some call it an aquarium. Well, naturally, I thought that this bunch at Cedar was another outfit like that, only run by rich Americans who made a hobby of studying fish life.'

"But," continued McKelvie, "the good people of Nanaimo are learning a great deal, and the new importance of the place is a subject of general discussion.

"When one man who had read some of the Aquarian literature told his friend that the selection of Cedar as the home of the cult had been dictated by a higher authority on an advanced plane, the answer was given: 'Well, can you blame the Spirit? Ain't this district the finest in the world?'"

While interviewing people in Nanaimo, McKelvie met a man who claimed to have known Wilson thirty years earlier. He told McKelvie that he'd encountered Wilson on the street only a few days ago and had greeted him by name. Wilson had looked at him blankly. The following exchange had taken place:

"Don't you know me?" the man asked.

"No," replied Wilson. "I never saw you before."

"Oh yes, you did. You recall when we worked together for the Dominion Express in Victoria."

"I never worked for the Dominion Express," Wilson answered.

At this, the man became somewhat annoyed, since he was certain Wilson had recognized him.

"You did work for the Dominion Express," he continued, "not only at Victoria, but also at Calgary. We roomed in the same house in Calgary. At Victoria, you asked for an increase in wages and when you were refused, you quit and went to sea. You remember me all right!"

Wilson was nonplussed for a moment; then, seeing it

was useless to further deny his identity, replied: "Yes, I remember; but for God's sake, don't say anything about it."

McKelvie had every reason to believe the man's story, since he was still smarting from Wilson's rebuff. He also told McKelvie that Wilson was fond of the sea and had owned a small sailboat in which he had explored the coastal waters off Vancouver Island. He was therefore well acquainted with the locality. McKelvie was puzzled: Why would Wilson wish to conceal the fact that he'd lived in British Columbia before?

McKelvie then recalled a statement Wilson had made in a letter written from Southampton, England, on January 15, 1927, and reprinted in the booklet, *The Aquarian Foundation: A Movement for the Unification of all Men of Good Will.* Announcing the location of the colony in North America, he had informed his disciples:

"The Center chosen by the Manu (Vaivasata) to be the cradle of the coming sixth sub-race is neither Mexico nor California, *but Southern British Columbia.* . . This locality has been actually and definitely selected—it is his choice alone, and while it is already known to me, *I have not seen it in the physical body as yet.* " [McKelvie's italics]

McKelvie couldn't reconcile the statement in the letter with the story the former express clerk had told him. He concluded that Wilson had lied in the letter and that many sincere people were being deceived by him. McKelvie decided to investigate Wilson's past. In the meantime, he was certain of one thing— Brother XII's claim to have never been in southern British Columbia in the physical body was "poppycock."

△ △ △

On Tuesday, October 30, 1928, Wilson's preliminary hearing was held. By ten o'clock, every seat was taken as curious spectators jammed the courtroom seeking a glimpse of the mysterious cult leader. McKelvie was covering the hearing for *The Province,* and Victor B. Harrison was watching the proceedings on behalf of the Attorney-General's office.

Magistrate C.H. Beevor-Potts brought the court to order with a sharp rap of his gavel. T.P. Morton acted for the prosecution and Frank Cunliffe represented the accused. Beevor-Potts read the charge that Wilson "on or about August 28th in the said county of Nanaimo unlawfully did steal $13,000, the property of the Aquarian Foundation."

Cunliffe wanted the second charge of theft of $5,000 to be heard at the same time. Morton insisted they be tried separately. "But they are bound up together," protested Cunliffe. Beevor-Potts convinced Morton that the evidence given in the $13,000 charge should apply to the second charge as well.

Robert England took the stand and was sworn in. In answer to Morton's questions, the former secretary-treasurer described the circumstances surrounding Mary Connally's $23,000 donation. He explained that Wilson had given him the bank draft on Valdes Island.

"The draft was taken to the bank under instructions from Mr. Wilson?" asked Morton.

"Yes. He wrote on the back of the envelope what to do with it."

England stated that he'd deposited the cheque in the Canadian Bank of Commerce in Nanaimo, dividing it three ways: $10,000 into the account of the Aquarian Foundation; $8,000 into the account of the Mandieh Settlement Fund; and $5,000 into Wilson's own personal account. The entire $23,000 should have been deposited to the account of the Aquarian Foundation, he said, since it had been given to further the work of the Society.

Morton's strategy was to show that Wilson was using the funds for purposes other than the declared objects of the Foundation. Leaning towards England, he asked him about the property on Valdes:

"This land that was purchased on Valdes Island, in whose name was it purchased?"

"The actual deed was made out in the name of Mr. Wilson,

and not in the name of the Aquarian Foundation."

"What did he build there?"

"The first thing he built there was a log cabin."

"Was it a large building?"

"The actual body of the cabin was about eighteen feet inside."

"Is it furnished?"

"Yes Sir."

"How many rooms?"

"Two."

"What are they used as?"

"General living room and a bedroom."

"What furniture is in the bedroom?"

"Two or three chairs, cooking utensils, dishes, and one bed about three-quarter size."

"Did Mr. Wilson live there?"

"Sometimes."

"Did he live there alone?"

"Not all the time."

"Who was living there with him?"

Frank Cunliffe sprang to his feet: "I object that this is not relevant to the case."

The bald, round-faced Morton shook his robes indignantly and drew himself up to his full height to address Beevor-Potts:

"I wish to show that in no way can it be shown that the monies that Wilson was spending on that island were being spent for the benefit of the Aquarian Foundation. I say that Wilson was using that island for his own purposes and not for the purposes of the Aquarian Foundation—and that those purposes were immoral purposes!"

Beevor-Potts shook his head: "I am going to rule that out. It is doubtless very sensational and would make good copy for the newspapers, but I cannot see that it has anything to do with this case at all."

Morton appealed to Beevor-Potts: "I have no idea of providing sensational news, but at the same time I wished to endeavour to show that Wilson was using the monies of the Aquarian Foundation absolutely and solely for his own purposes."

"I rule it out," Beevor-Potts snapped.

Morton was determined to bring out Wilson's affair with Myrtle Baumgartner one way or another. He asked the Magistrate for permission to question the witness about a certain conversation he'd had with Wilson on Valdes Island. It had a bearing on the money stolen, he explained; if the prosecution could show that Wilson had used the money for purposes other than those of the Aquarian Foundation, then the evidence should be admissible. Beevor-Potts allowed Morton to proceed.

"What were the details of the conversation?" Morton asked England.

"Well, he stated that he had, on one occasion, on a trip to Chicago from Seattle—"

"I object to that!" Cunliffe interjected. "What can that have to do with Valdes Island?"

Beevor-Potts overruled the objection. He gestured towards England:

"Proceed, witness."

"He told me that when travelling from Seattle to Chicago, he had met a woman and that they had been together, and that they had both taken the 'Sixth Initiation.' He said that he himself was the reincarnation of the ancient Egyptian god named Osiris. The woman was the reincarnation of the goddess Isis. There had been a conception, and a son would be born to them who would be the reincarnation of Horus. The object of this settlement on Valdes Island was that as the result of the union between the reincarnation of Osiris and Isis, they would bring into the world a son who would be the reincarnation of Horus, who in the year 1975 would be a world leader."

There was dead silence in court. Morton smiled in triumph. England added that Wilson had told him he planned to bring a woman to Valdes to rear the child.

"I object that this has nothing to do with this alleged theft," Cunliffe interjected.

Beevor-Potts sustained the objection. He agreed with Cunliffe that the testimony shouldn't have been allowed as it had nothing to do with the charge.

Cunliffe approached the witness box to cross-examine England.

"Where did you get the idea that this money belonged to the Aquarian Foundation?"

"Because it was sent to the Aquarian Foundation."

"Is that the only reason you thought it belonged to the Aquarian Foundation?"

"I have always understood that money so forwarded belonged to the person or corporation to whom it was addressed."

"So because it was addressed to the Aquarian Foundation, you say it belonged to the Aquarian Foundation?"

"No, there were other reasons."

"Did you report to your fellow Governors the way in which this twenty-three thousand dollars was handled?"

"No Sir, I did not."

"You said nothing to any of them?"

"I had instructions from Mr. Wilson to say nothing about it to anyone."

"Did you have any other instructions from Mr. Wilson?"

"I had all kinds of instructions from him. I was under orders from Mr. Wilson all the time."

"Did you consider that he was doing right or wrong?"

"I thought that he was doing wrong."

"In that case, why did you not refuse to carry out his instructions?"

"You don't know Edward Arthur Wilson like we do. He is a man who will not tolerate any opposition to his slightest whim."

"Who is the owner of the Mandieh Settlement Fund?"

"Mr. Wilson claims to be."

"Who was the owner of the money in the Mandieh Settlement Fund?"

"I considered it belonged to the Aquarian Foundation ever since the day it was created. I always understood in my mind that it belonged to the Aquarian Foundation."

"Why was this ten thousand dollars put into the account of the Aquarian Foundation?"

"I don't just remember why."

"I suggest to you that it was to be considered as a loan?"

"He said that to me afterwards."

"How long afterwards?"

"I think within a day or so after the visit of myself and Mr. Wilson to Vancouver."

"Was there any document drawn up with reference to that ten thousand dollars, showing that it was intended to be a loan?"

"Not that I can remember."

Cunliffe held up a receipt to the court. He showed it to England.

"Is this your writing and signature?"

"Yes Sir."

Cunliffe read the receipt aloud: "'Received from E. A. Wilson (The Brother XII) the sum of ten thousand dollars exactly, as a temporary loan to the Aquarian Foundation, to be repaid without interest upon demand of the said E. A. Wilson, the sum being from funds advanced to him by Mary Connally.'" The receipt was dated August 28, 1928, and was signed by England.

"Do you remember that now?"

"I do. Yes Sir."

Cunliffe moved towards England, speaking louder and more forcefully.

"What did you do with this document after you drew it up?"

"I think it was in the files in the desk in the ordinary way."

"How often do you clean out the wastepaper basket?"

"I never clean it out myself."

"Who did clean it out?"

"Mr. Davenport."

"How often?"

"I don't know."

"And I suppose you cannot account for the fact that that receipt was found in the wastepaper basket all screwed up into a ball?"

"No Sir."

There was silence in the courtroom. Cunliffe paused before taking careful aim with his next question.

"In view of that receipt, you could not seriously lay a charge of theft, could you?"

"Yes, because I was instructed by Mr. Wilson to write that receipt."

"And you did not tell any of the Governors?"

"No Sir. I was acting under his instructions."

"And you took no steps whatever until after you had been arrested on a charge of stealing $2,800?"

"No, I did not."

Cunliffe produced a resolution from the Governors of the Aquarian Foundation to the Canadian Bank of Commerce authorizing the opening of a new account, the Mandieh Settlement Fund. The resolution was signed by Wilson and England.

"If this was not authorized by the Governors, why did you sign it?"

"It was Mr. Wilson's instructions."

"Did Mr. Wilson instruct you to sign false documents?"

"Not in so many words."

T.P. Morton called Edward Lucas to the stand. Lucas explained that there had been no meetings of the Governors during 1928 and that no bank resolutions had been passed: "The Governors of the Aquarian Foundation have certainly at no time authorized the creation of the Mandieh Settlement or the Mandieh Settlement Fund, or any diversion of the funds of the Aquarian Foundation to the Mandieh Settlement, the Mandieh Settlement Fund, or to Mr. Wilson personally."

Cunliffe cross-examined Lucas. He showed him the affidavit which Wilson had received from Mary Connally, giving him jurisdiction over her twenty-five thousand dollar donation. He then read it aloud to the court:

> "In view of the fact that an attempt is now being made by certain persons to gain control of the Aquarian Foundation, to depose its founder and to attach its funds. . . in the matter of my personal donation of twenty-five thousand dollars, I, *as donor*, declare that it is at the sole disposal of The Brother XII (E. A. Wilson) in whole or in part, and that I hold him and no other responsible for its disposition and administration. . . The sum of ten thousand dollars which he advanced to the Aquarian Foundation for the furtherance of that section of his work may, at his discretion, be recalled and otherwise applied. . . It is my purpose and intent that the full amount of my donation be held personally by The Brother XII (E. A. Wilson), and that without his consent, no other person or persons, or any organization whatsoever, shall participate in it."

Mary's statement was unequivocal. Beevor-Potts turned to Lucas, puzzled: "Is this not a question of a difference of opinion between two factions as to which of the two should control the funds? Is this not a simple question between the members?"

Lucas insisted it was not: "As a member of the Order, I would say that a sum of money having been received by the Aquarian Foundation could not have been diverted to any other account without authority—without a theft being committed. The question is whether the money has been stolen or whether it has not. The accounts are simple enough."

"Is it not purely a civil matter?"

"No Sir, I should say not. I think it was purely criminal. I should say that nobody on earth, outside the Aquarian Foundation, could do anything with that money. Not even the donor."

Beevor-Potts looked dubious.

Lucas gamely continued: "The fact was that the Aquarian Foundation received twenty-three thousand dollars from Mrs. Connally, and that twenty-three thousand dollars went into E. A. Wilson's pocket. It is either theft or it is something incomprehensible."

T.P. Morton summed up the case for the prosecution. He stated that he had argued the main point: he had demonstrated that Wilson had used the funds of the Aquarian Foundation for purposes other than those for which they were intended. He asked Beevor-Potts to commit England for trial at the fall assizes.

It was now late in the afternoon, and Frank Cunliffe asked for an adjournment. He told the magistrate that the defence needed until Thursday morning to prepare its case. Over Morton's objections, Beevor-Potts granted the adjournment.

The magistrate asked the accused if he wished to say anything in answer to the charge. Wilson appeared startled by the question. He slowly stood and faced Beevor-Potts. Pale and thin, he made as if to speak—but did not answer. Frank Cunliffe quickly replied for him: "He has nothing to say at present."

△   △   △

Bruce McKelvie's account of Wilson's preliminary hearing appeared on the front page of *The Province* the next day, headlined: "OSIRIS AND ISIS MET ON TRAIN BETWEEN SEATTLE AND CHICAGO. They Were Brother XII and Lady Friend Reincarnated, Says Witness at Aquarian Proceedings— New Messiah Was to Come Out of Valdes Island by 1975, According to Plan—Weird Story Told at Police Court Hearing of Cult Troubles at Cedar-by-the-Sea."

McKelvie added his own touch of colour to the story, saying that the romance between the two reincarnated Egyptian divinities "linked the sunny sands of ancient Egypt and the blue waters of the Nile with the wooded slopes of Valdes Island and the dancing waves of the Strait of Georgia." He described the love affair between the two soul mates as "the twentieth-century version of the love story of the gods," and marvelled that a little two-room log cabin on Valdes Island was to be the home of the reincarnation of Horus, a future world leader and great religious teacher like Christ.

These latest disclosures about the preference of the Egyptian divinities for the pleasant shores of the Gulf Islands astonished the local residents and inspired even more comment and speculation. According to McKelvie, however, old-timers in the district accepted the news philosophically. As one elderly resident sagely observed: "Ah, think, as 'ow yon lad Wilson got 'is wires twisted, like, an' instead o' gettin' 'old o' Mrs. Hises, the gypsy goddess, 'e got ol' Mother Eve 'erself."

Not everyone in Nanaimo approved of all the publicity the case was getting. The editor of *The Nanaimo Free Press* commented: "We are indebted to B.A. McKelvie for the assurance that the affair is a local sensation, and this looks like a dirty crack at our rustic emotions. Importance is only relative, and as no local person seems to be adversely affected by the operations of the practical occultists, I suggest the scene of court activities be moved to Vancouver, which has had no sensations since good civic government was established there."

But Bruce McKelvie wasn't interested only in the sensational aspects of the story. He wanted to find out the truth about Brother XII, so he set to work to learn all he could about his past. In Victoria, McKelvie confirmed that Wilson had, in fact, worked for the Dominion Express company as a baggage clerk and also as the driver of a delivery wagon. A fellow employee remembered him as a dapper man with a sallow complexion who often wore a red rose in his lapel.

Wilson had handled the important Wells Fargo account, but quit when he was refused a two-dollar-a-week raise in pay. Then he'd worked for a time on a coastal steamer running between Victoria and San Francisco. Next, he'd tried ranching in the Okanagan, but when that venture was unsuccessful, he'd returned to Victoria and worked for the express company at the Edgewood Station. In 1912, Wilson had left Victoria on a ship bound for the Orient. From time to time he'd returned: once, it was as the first officer of a passenger ship; another time, it was to try to persuade a former fellow clerk to join him in a South Seas trading venture; still later, it was to enlist support for the establishment of a ship chandlery. On the basis of his investigations, McKelvie concluded that Wilson had an intimate knowledge of British Columbia. Convinced that he was misrepresenting himself to his followers, he decided to do everything he could to unmask him.

In Nanaimo, Brother XII was suddenly the object of intense interest and curiosity. Many of the stories told about him corroborated McKelvie's findings about Wilson's past, since a number of local people claimed to have a vivid recollection of Wilson as a young man.

Alva Shaw's father owned the IXL Stables on Skinner Street. According to her, Wilson had worked at the stables years earlier, and had made an extraordinary impression upon her father and the people of Nanaimo.

"He could hypnotize you as quick as look at you!" she recalls. "I was afraid to look at him; there was something about his eyes that scared me. The horses would kick with everyone else but him—he'd calm them down like magic. My dad would say, 'I think he hypnotizes the goddamned horses!'"

Alva claims that Wilson even put on a stage show as a hypnotist in the local Orpheum. "The theatre was packed," she reminisces. "All the miners wanted to see it. *Oh, he was good!* He went down into the audience and picked out the people he wanted, then brought them up on stage. One man bet him a dollar he couldn't hypnotize him—he lost his bet! The girl played the piano and everyone sang. Then he'd bring them out of it and they wouldn't know they'd sung. They told him he was a damned liar! Some of them got mad and said they didn't sing. The audience all clapped and said, 'Yes, you did! Yes, you did!'

"There were these two fellows who worked in the stables—Claude Peck and his brother. They were darn good workers, but oh! they used to drink—they used to drink cruel! He said to my dad: 'You watch, I'm going to stop them!' My dad said, 'The Pecks have drunk for years; you'll never stop them.' And by God, he stopped them! And I don't know to this day how he stopped them, but he did! Them fellows turned out to be wonderful fellows. My dad said he didn't hypnotize them either; he could tell by their eyes. It was the power he had—my dad said he had a lot of power.

"He preached in the church too, if the minister was sick. He preached as good as any minister—he didn't even need a Bible. He could speak three or four different languages. He could talk Chinese. He talked to the Chinaman that used to run the laundry. Oh, he amazed my dad something terrible! He was thunderstruck to think he was so clever! He was *so interested* in him. Later on, he went out to Cedar to see him, and when he came back he said, 'Yes, it's him!'"

Mervyn Wilkinson's father worked as a locomotive engineer at the Number One mine in Nanaimo. "Wilson was the lamp-keeper in the mine," Wilkinson recalls. "He had a little cabin next to the pit-head. All the lamps that went down into that mine were inspected by him. His job was to make sure they were working properly and had enough fuel. He apparently worked quickly and efficiently and had plenty of time to read. His cabin was always stocked with the best of books."

A music teacher in Nanaimo named Peggy Reynolds boarded Wilson briefly in the spring of 1927, while he was getting established at Cedar. Her daughter, Margaret Salwyn, remembers Wilson as a polite upper-class Englishman, a bit on the "shabby genteel" side.

"He tried to be friendly with me as a child," she says. "He knew I was very fond of cats, so he drew a picture of a cat for me. He had very artistic-looking hands. I remember he used to point at you when he spoke. We thought it was rudeness, but it was just a mannerism of his. He could speak well. My grandmother said, 'He'll get by—he's got the gift of the gab!'

"It must have been around Easter that he stayed with us. I remember he laughed and said, 'We used to sing a song at home in England:

Hot cross buns,
Hot cross buns,
If your daughters don't like them,
Give them to your sons.'

"My grandmother didn't approve of some of his behaviour. After dinner, he'd come downstairs in his dressing-gown to stand near the fire. He felt the cold a lot. She'd say, 'Now, Mr. Wilson, you cannot come out of your room in your dressing-gown. Put on your proper clothes!' It was considered quite vulgar to do that.

"Or if the telephone rang, he'd come downstairs and ask if it was for him. My grandmother would say, 'If the call were for you, we'd tell you!'

"One evening, everyone was talking in the living room. 'You know what I'm doing out at Cedar,' he said, 'I'm starting a new religion.' My grandmother thought it sounded a bit batty, but was probably harmless enough. Then he said, *'I tell you frankly, Mrs. Reynolds, it's all a skin game.'* My grandmother and mother were quite disgusted when he said that. He only said it once, but the moment he made that declaration, they vowed to warn everyone against him."

△   △   △

The big locomotive roared through the night, its huge head-light cutting through the darkness as it left the lights of Reno far behind and raced up the Pacific Coast towards Seattle. In a first class compartment on board, Mary Connally waited impatiently for the train to reach British Columbia. Only a few days earlier in Asheville, she'd received a desperate telegram from Wilson telling her he'd been arrested and imploring her to come to Nanaimo at once. Mary's response was immediate— she was on a train the next day, making a last-minute dash across the continent to appear in court on his behalf.

In his office in the Imperial Building at 97 Commercial Street, Frank Cunliffe prepared Wilson's defence. Notified by Mary that she was on her way, he sent two telegrams to the Union Pacific station in Everett, Washington. One was from himself; the other was from Wilson, who wanted Mary to know how grateful he was that she was coming to his aid.

"Just before his trial, he sent for me," Annie Barley recalled. "He told me he wanted me to go to Vancouver and meet Mrs. Mary Connally, who had been providing funds for his work. He said, 'I want you to go and meet her and be very nice to her.'"

The train arrived in Vancouver that evening. Annie Barley met Mary Connally at the railway station, and the two women stayed overnight in the city. At 3:11 P.M. the following afternoon, Mary sent a telegram to Frank Cunliffe from the Canadian Pacific telegraph office in Vancouver: "TAKING 5:30 BOAT. CAN YOU MEET ME? HAVE BLACK WHITE FUR COAT."

Cunliffe was waiting on the wharf with his car when the *Princess Elaine* docked. After the tension of the past few days, the Nanaimo lawyer no doubt felt an enormous sense of relief when the patrician figure of "Lady Mary" Connally stepped off the boat—his star witness had arrived.

On Thursday, November 1, Wilson's preliminary hearing resumed. There was an expectant hush in the court, for in spite of the defence's secrecy about the presence of an important witness, the occasion was, as McKelvie described it, "something in the nature of a surprise party where the host and hostess meet the guests in evening dress." The court was ready for the surprise, and—true to its hopes—Frank Cunliffe produced it.

"Mrs. Mary Connally," he called.

All eyes turned to watch as a nattily dressed woman with baby blue eyes and flaxen hair stepped into the witness box. Although she was of uncertain age, it was obvious that a few years earlier Mary had been a woman of rare beauty.

Mary was sworn in. When she gave her address as Reno, Nevada, famous for its "divorce colony," a murmur rippled through the courtroom. In answer to his questions, Mary told Cunliffe that she'd arrived in Nanaimo the night before, coming directly from Asheville, North Carolina.

"You are the lady who has been referred to in these proceedings as having made a donation of twenty-three thousand dollars in August of this year?"

"Yes Sir."

"There was an item before that of two thousand dollars?"

"Yes."

"Tell us, briefly, how it came to be made."

"I was a member of the Order and very much interested in its future development, of which the Aquarian Foundation was simply the beginning and 'outer heart.' This was to be followed by further developments, other settlements and places to be used as refuge places from life's storms. I wished to help develop the new work of the Order, the present work and the future work, in which I am greatly interested, as I believe it is one of the most beautiful and idealistic programs in the world."

"Do you know the accused?"

"I have that honour."

"Did you have any conversation with him?"

"Yes."

"Where?"

"In Toronto."

"When?"

"On August 15th last."

"And was that the occasion when this donation was decided upon?"

"It was."

"To whom was this donation to be made?"

"The donation was made to E. A. Wilson personally."

"Did the Aquarian Foundation have any interest in that money?"

"It should not have done. It was made to him direct, personally, entirely for him to do with as he pleased in connection with his work."

"Now it appears that the draft was drawn payable to the Aquarian Foundation?"

"That was entirely Mr. Wilson's desire. I would have preferred to make it payable to E. A. Wilson, but he said no, to let it go in the usual way to the Aquarian Foundation."

"Was anything said as to the manner in which the twenty-five thousand dollars was to be dealt with?"

"I told him he had absolute control, and that he could do what he wished with it. I approved of his principles and do so still. His proposal was to have a new settlement which was to be a place of refuge for people in time of trouble—this money was to help his work along."

"It was to help what part of his work?"

"Any part of his work. I left it absolutely to him as I had every confidence in him and still do."

"Was anything said as to the division of the money in actual amounts?"

"Yes, it was proposed that ten thousand dollars should go as a loan to the Aquarian Foundation; eight thousand dollars was to be put into the new settlement; and five thousand dollars was to be invested by Mr. Wilson at six percent for his own use entirely. This last suggestion was entirely my own. This suggestion I made in Toronto."

"In other words, the personal donation of five thousand

dollars was your own proposition voluntarily made?"

"Oh yes. I still wish it, and I only wish I had made it more. I believe in Mr. Wilson's principles and his integrity, and I have come a great many thousand miles to testify on his behalf."

T.P. Morton cross-examined Mary. He asked her if she knew the objects of the Aquarian Foundation.

"I am not a Governor," she replied.

"For what purpose are these people carrying on?"

"They are carrying on to help mankind."

Morton read aloud the objects of the Society: "'To give teachings and instruction to its members upon philosophical and occult subjects, and upon all matters concerning their physical, mental, and spiritual welfare; and to print and publish such books, magazines, or documents as may be necessary for that purpose.' As far as you know are those the objects of the Aquarian Foundation?"

"That is only the beginning."

"What are the other objects?"

"I am not ready to discuss that with you except to say that it is a good work and for the betterment of mankind."

"I suppose that in carrying out these objects it is purely humanitarian and the members would naturally live decent moral lives?"

"I have nothing to do with that whatever. I made a donation to Mr. Wilson to assist him in his work."

"The objects of the fund, to your mind, do not include immorality?"

"No, certainly not. But I would like to know your definition of immorality—"

"There has been no evidence here of immorality," Frank Cunliffe interjected.

"I have already told you," Mary impatiently explained, "that the money was given to Mr. Wilson to be used at his discretion. I asked him if I should make the cheque payable to him personally. He said, 'No, make it out to the Aquarian Foundation.' I now believe I should have followed my own intuition in the matter and made the cheque payable to him personally. The money was to be spent by E. A. Wilson as he saw fit. He could spend it in any way—personally, if he wished. It was a straight gift to him."

"You gave it to him as a straight gift?" asked Beevor-Potts.

"Yes."

"If you had known that this money was to be used for immoral purposes, would you have donated it?" asked Morton.

"It all depends on what you call 'immoral' purposes. I have not come here to discuss why I gave this donation. I have come here at considerable inconvenience and expense to make a statement that this money was given by me to E. A. Wilson to do with as he saw fit, and I still believe in Mr. Wilson's integrity."

"That is all the defence, Your Worship," Cunliffe stated.

Mary stepped down from the witness box. Frank Cunliffe summed up the case for the defence. He said that everything had been done in accordance with the understanding of the donor, and that the twenty-five thousand dollars had never actually been placed in the Aquarian Foundation account—the ten thousand dollars that had been deposited was a temporary loan only. It was clear that the money hadn't been stolen, he said, and that Wilson should be acquitted.

Morton pointed out that although Mrs. Connally had donated the money for purposes outlined by Wilson, he hadn't told her of all his activities on Valdes Island. There was no question, he said, that Wilson should be committed to stand trial.

In reviewing the evidence, Beevor-Potts stated that there was one vital point: the money had been forwarded to the Aquarian Foundation as a bank draft, unaccompanied by any letter of instruction. A month later after the trouble had developed, Mrs. Connally had written a letter setting out her intentions. Beevor-Potts said that in view of the circumstances, he didn't think it was a case of a straight committal. He therefore bound Wilson over on bail of five thousand dollars to appear at the fall assizes to answer any indictment that might be preferred against him there.

The next day, Bruce McKelvie's account of the hearing appeared on the front page of *The Province*, headlined: "DRAMATIC SURPRISE AT AQUARIAN HEARING."

> The dingy courtroom of Magistrate C.H. Beevor-Potts Thursday would have made an admirable setting for a movie drama or a scene for one of the old-time plays of the coal-oil circuit, where at the crucial moment of the trial of the hero, the heroine, blonde and blue-eyed, bursts into the group of serious-faced officials, lawyers and spectators to proclaim the innocence of the accused.
>
> Such indeed, in brief, was what happened in fact when Edward Arthur Wilson, otherwise Brother XII of the Aquarian Foundation, was called for his defence to the charge that he had converted $13,000 of the funds of the Foundation to his own personal uses.
>
> The only difference in the ending between this real-life drama and the popular plot of playwrights was that the magistrate did not wholly free the accused from the toils of the law, but bound him over in the sum of $5,000 to appear at the assizes in Nanaimo later this month. Nor did he follow the stage custom and descend from the bench to grasp the hand of the hero and express his great gratification at his deliverance from his accusers. With these minor exceptions the situation was one that might have had its counterpart on the boards.

Frank Cunliffe was satisfied with the judgment. His client hadn't been committed for trial, but had simply been placed under bonds to answer a charge if the Attorney-General should prefer one against him. "I do not expect anything further will be done in connection with the charge," he wrote to a colleague, "as it is quite obvious there has been no theft."

Beevor-Potts's decision to refer the case to the assizes caused considerable surprise in legal circles, especially in view of

Mary's statement that her donation was an outright gift. The judgment was accepted to mean that the provincial government intended to fully investigate the activities of Brother XII and the Aquarian Foundation.

The Ku Klux Klan was a powerful political force in the 1920s. Brother XII solicited Klan support for his own political aspirations. This Klan march in Washington, D.C. took place August 8, 1925. It was estimated that nearly sixty thousand Klansmen marched in the parade, while nearly a million persons watched the spectacle.

Senator James Thomas Heflin, who Brother XII hoped would be the presidential candidate for his Third Party, speaks at a Klan rally in this photograph taken June 18, 1928. Original caption: "Invading his opponents' territory, Senator Thomas Heflin of Alabama addressed some 10,000 Ku Klux Klansmen and their associates in a huge natural amphitheater at Hurstville, near Albany, N.Y., and renewed his attack on Catholicism and Smith. The Governor ordered State Police to guard the loquacious Senator." (Corbis)

Senator James "Tom Tom" Heflin was key to Brother XII's political plans. In a speech at the Foundation headquarters, Wilson stated: "In Washington in January last, I told Senator Heflin to get into the limelight as the champion of Protestantism and to stay there. He has since done that very effectively and is still doing it." (*The U.S. Senate Historical Office*)

In the August 1928 issue of *The Chalice*, Brother XII urged U.S. congressmen to support his Third Party and Protestant Protective League in order to prevent a civil war from erupting in the United States. The quotation "Give up thy life if thou would'st live" is from H.P. Blavatsky.

A collection of Brother XII's political articles published in book form. His "Open Letter to Certain Senators, Representatives and Leaders in the United States of America," reprinted in this volume, was described as "the most important and vital document issued in the United States since the Declaration of Independence." In other articles, Brother XII warned about the power of the press to shape public opinion, a prophetic injunction in light of the contemporary manufacturing of consent by corporate media.

The End of the Days

by
THE BROTHER, XII

These history-making documents set forth a warning of the darkening period of the future. They cover problems concerning chiefly the United States of North America and Canada.

ISSUED BY
THE CHALICE PRESS
P. O. BOX 595, NANAIMO, B. C., CANADA

This low relief from the temple of Horus at Edfu, carved between 181 and 145 B.C., shows the god Osiris receiving the double crown of Upper and Lower Egypt from the goddesses Isis and Nephthys. Filmmaker David Cherniack, who produced a Brother XII television documentary in 2002, felt that the carving could represent Brother XII and his two consorts, Myrtle Baumgartner as Isis and Mabel Skottowe as Nephthys, his seducer and destroyer.

Osiris and Isis Met on Train
Between Seattle and Chicago

They Were Brother XII. and Lady Friend Reincarnated, Says Witness at Aquarian Proceedings—New Messiah Was to Come Out of Valdez Island by 1975, According to Plan—Weird Story Told at Police Court Hearing of Cult Troubles at Cedar-by-the-Sea.

By B. A. McKELVIE.

NANAIMO, Oct. 31.—That a little two-room log cabin on Valdez Island was to be the home of the reincarnated spirit of Horus, son of the Egyptian god Osiris and the goddess Isis, who were represented in this day and generation in the persons of Edward Albert Wilson, otherwise Brother XII, of the "Aquarian Foundation," and a woman whom Wilson met last summer on the train between Seattle and Chicago, was the story retailed to Magistrate Beevor Potts and a crowded court-room Tuesday.

The occasion of the unfolding of the twentieth century

version of the love story of the gods was the appearance of Wilson in court to answer to a charge of misappropriating $13,000 from the funds of the Aquarian Foundation, with headquarters at Cedar, eight miles from here, to his own uses.

The romance that linked the sunny sands of ancient Egypt and the blue waters of the Nile with the wooded slopes of Valdez Island and the dancing waves of the Strait of Georgia was revealed only after a long wrangle between lawyers and the quoting of authorities on evidence as set out in weighty tomes.

(Continued on Page 15, Col. 3.)

This bizarre headline appeared in the Vancouver *Daily Province* on October 31, 1928, in an article describing the affair between Brother XII and Myrtle Baumgartner, the wife of a New York physician. The two believed that the child of their union would be the reincarnation of the Egyptian god Horus and beome a World Teacher in the year 1975.

Veteran reporter Bruce McKelvie sought to expose Brother XII as a charlatan. His colourful articles about Wilson's activities appeared in newspapers across North America. (Courtesy Katherine McKelvie)

Man From Carthage, Mo., Helped
Reincarnated B. C. Egyptian God

By B. A. McKELVIE.

WITH the filing of affidavits and counter affidavits in the injunction proceedings, the Aquarian Foundation battle that has claimed public attention for more than a week enters upon another phase. The proceedings thus far have been for the most part confined to the police court at Nanaimo where cross charges of theft and misappropriation of funds have been aired before Magistrate C. H. Beevor Potts.

With these temporarily out of the way, pending the opening of the assizes in the coal city later this month, interest has switched to the application being made by three governors of the foundation, Maurice Von Platen, Robert de Luce and E. A. Lucas for an injunction to restrain Edward A Wilson, Brother XII, founder of the cult, from disposing of the assets.

Wilson has answered the application by charging two of the three governors, Von Platen and De Luce, with conspiring to obtain possession of the property at Cedar-by-the-Sea and the donations that have been made towards carrying on of the work.

Robert England, erstwhile secretary-treasurer and governor of the organization, has filed in the Supreme Court registry in support of the application of his co-governors an affidavit in which he supplements somewhat the story he told in the police court proceedings of the affinity of the reincarnated spirits of the Egyptian divinities Osiris and Isis, and reiterates that Brother XII used assets of the foundation for his own purposes on Valdez Island.

(Continued on Page 2, Column 1.)

A follow-up article in the same newspaper on November 4, 1928, referred to Oliver G. Hess of Carthage, Missouri, a retired lawyer and Civil War veteran who contributed $20,000 to the Aquarian Foundation, one of the sums under dispute in the action of the Governors against Brother XII.

This lip ornament worn by a Haida medicine woman, which Bruce McKelvie gave to the disciples as a protective charm, helped them to overcome their fear of Brother XII's magic. (Photo by author)

cont'd

Lest you should think I am trying to intimidate you I repeat that whatever you do, or do not do, I will force a full public disclosure of everything — of many other matters also which will hit some of the others' fatally. Your safest course is to disappear from Vancouver and from this Province while you can — your shortest

way would be over the end of the wharf. Whether you go or stay; I will force everything into the open.

XII

At the Hotel Georgia in Vancouver, Brother XII dashed off an angry memo to Coulson Turnbull, written in part on blank CN telegraph forms, threatening to disclose intimate details of his personal life.

Black Magic, Gold and Guns
Feature Strange Cult Case

(Special to The Colonist)

NANAIMO, April 27.—How the arts of Egyptian black magic were invoked by Brother XII, self-styled chela of a divinity, in order to rid himself of those whom he disliked, was disclosed to Chief Justice Morrison in Supreme Court here, today, when further revelations were made concerning strange happenings at the Aquarian cult domain near Nanaimo. His Lordship was told of orders being issued by Brother XII in a letter from England to Roger W. Painter, learned in the dark mysteries of the East, to kill Hon. R. H. Pooley, Attorney-General for British Columbia; Hon. Joshua Hinchliffe, Minister of Education; E. A. Lucas, Vancouver barrister, and Maurice and Alice von Platen, wealthy California couple.

The "etheric" assassinations failed, the witness explained, for at that time he did not know how to go about such things; and if he did, he would not have done so.

ETHERIC ASSASSINATION

At a later date, however, he said, following the return of Amiel de Valdes, sometime Edward Arthur Wilson, but more commonly known among the cult members as Brother XII, he had witnessed an attempt "to sever the etheric and physical bodies of George Hobart."

With some detail the witness explained, at the request of the Chief Justice, the mechanics of etheric assassination. The spiritual body of Hobart was summoned, and was supposed to be standing in front of Brother XII, who called on invisible powers to smash and break the body of Hobart, accompanying the invocation with vertical and horizontal motions of his hands, as if quartering the torso of the object of his wrath. Incidentally, Hobart did not die.

In answer to questions by V. B. Harrison, counsel for Alfred H. Barley, cultured Englishman, who was the plaintiff in the suit against Brother XII for the return of $14,232, Mr. Painter explained further.

"What is an etheric body?" he was asked.

"It is a finer spirit than the bodily life."

Mr. Harrison: And how would it affect a person?"

Witness: The idea was to destroy the etheric body, and then the physical body would wither and die.

FAILED IN TRUST

The revelation about black magic came during the course of the hearing of Mr. Barley's claim for a return of the money he had given to de Valdes to carry out specific works, such as constructing a school and Greystones, a palatial building on DeCourcy Islands. These works were not done. Mr. Painter was called, and in his examination by Mr. Harrison, he said that in 1930, while Brother XII was in England, he wrote him, telling him to "sever the etheric and physical bodies" of the Attorney-General and Minister of Education, and the others.

"Why?" interjected His Lordship, in surprise.

"He did not like them."

"How was it to be done?" asked His Lordship.

"By black magic."

Continuing, on answer to questions, the witness said that he did not attempt to commit these assassina-

Continued on Page 2, Column 3

Aquarian Group Attending Nanaimo Trials. Left to Right: A. H. Barley, Mrs. Barley, R. W. Painter, Mrs. Mary Connally, Miss M. White, Mrs. Bruce Crawford, M. Hirst, Bruce Crawford.

The court action against Brother XII was reported in *The Victoria Colonist* on April 28, 1933. During the proceedings, the mechanics of "etheric assassination," as practised by Brother XII against his enemies, were explained by Roger Painter, who participated in the nocturnal rituals: "The idea was to destroy the etheric body, and then the physical body would wither and die."

A relative of former U.S. president William H. Harrison, Nanaimo lawyer and mayor Victor B. Harrison represented the disciples in their court action against Brother XII. (Author's collection)

Aquarian Farms Show Appalling Work of Vandals

Buildings Wrecked on DeCourcy and Valdes Islands While Lawsuits Are Pending—Big Vessel Scuttled—Horses Stolen and Fruit Trees Uprooted

(Special to The Colonist)

NANAIMO, April 28. — Desolation stalks on DeCourcy Islands and the Aquarian lands of Valdes. Brother XII, otherwise Amiel de Valdes, or Edward Arthur Wilson, self-styled chela, or representative of a divinity, has gone. He has vanished from the pleasant acres where he reigned with the power of a potentate, and his conquerors in the courts of the land do not know where he has gone.

The DeCourcy Islands, where a City of Refuge was to be built, and where a palace to be called Greystones was to be erected and Valdes Island, where the Mandieh Settlement for the elect of the Aquarian cult was to be established, today presented scenes of wanton destruction. These lands were awarded by Chief Justice Morrison to Mrs. Mary W. T. Connally. The lands are there, but the buildings and farm appurtenances stand out damaged and destroyed beyond estimation.

GREAT DAMAGE

At the DeCourcy farm, windows of buildings have been smashed, doors torn from their hinges, water tanks and cisterns have been hacked and punctured, fencing ripped up and, in some cases, carried away. Fruit trees have been uprooted, and fifty walnut trees have been removed.

From the barn there has disappeared a mowing machine, seed cleaner, root slicer and cultivator, while other equipment has been rendered useless.

Two horses and a flock of chickens have vanished.

In the farmhouse linoleum was found to have been torn up, crockery stolen or broken, while in a smaller house even the sink had been taken away, other supplies were ruined with evident malicious intent.

At The Point, near where Brother XII had caused fortifications to be erected, as would a feudal baron of old to protect his lands, further

Continued on Page 2, Column 5

Delegate of Gods Has Vanished

BROTHER XII
The erstwhile leader of the Aquarian cult, near Nanaimo, who did not appear to defend himself against claims of the former disciples. His whereabouts are unknown.

This article by Bruce McKelvie from *The Victoria Colonist* of April 29, 1933, detailed the destruction that had been wreaked on the colony by a vindictive Brother XII and his henchmen before he fled the premises. "Desolation stalks on DeCourcy Islands and the Aquarian lands of Valdes," it read. "Brother XII, otherwise Amiel de Valdes, or Edward Arthur Wilson, self-styled chela, or representative of a divinity, has gone. He has vanished from the pleasant acres where he reigned with the power of a potentate, and his conquerors in the courts of the land do not know where he has gone."

The disillusioned disciples pose outside the Nanaimo Courthouse, April 28, 1933, after winning a civil lawsuit against their former leader. Left to right: Bruce Crawford, Morgan Hirst, Georgia Crawford, Margaret Whyte, Mary Connally, Roger Painter, Annie Barley, Alfred Barley. (Author's collection)

Alfred Barley, sub-editor of *Modern Astrology* and close associate of Alan Leo, the so-called "father of modern astrology," first met Brother XII in Southampton and was perhaps the most loyal of all the disciples. He eventually sued Brother XII for the return of the funds he had given him, obtaining a judgment for $14,232. (Author's collection)

Roger Painter, the "Poultry King of Florida," brought $90,000 in cash to the colony, equivalent to well over a million dollars in today's currency. He testified that Brother XII ordered him to kill B.C. Attorney-General R.H. Pooley and others with black magic. (Author's collection)

Mary Connally, photographed outside the Nanaimo Courthouse. She described Brother XII as "very much like the exhibited picture of Mephistopheles" and stated that he had cruelly defrauded her, telling the court: "The damage to my physical body is something that cannot be paid for." (Author's collection)

The Nanaimo Courthouse where "the strangest cases ever to come before a Canadian court of law" were heard before Chief Justice Aulay M. Morrison and an astonished gallery. (Courtesy Nanaimo District Museum)

The *Lady Royal* scuttled in the lagoon at DeCourcy Island. One of the masts was blown off with a charge of dynamite; another explosion damaged the hull. (Author's collection)

Another view of Brother XII's beached flagship from the Summer 1941 issue of *The Shoulder Strap*, the official journal of the B.C. Provincial Police. Original caption: "The hulk of the once glorious *Lady Royal* lay a smashed and battered thing." (Photo by Cecil Clark)

The fort which guarded Brother XII's house on DeCourcy Island was entered through a trap-door in the ceiling. The man in the photograph is shown about to descend into the gun emplacement. There were five forts constructed on the island. (Author's collection)

A sniper's nest on Valdes Island is inspected by a member of the B.C. Provincial Police. The colony's arsenal consisted of a British .303 and a case of twelve 6.5 mm Italian Mannlicher carbines. (Photo by Cecil Clark)

Inspector Cecil Clark at the site of Brother XII's headquarters on DeCourcy Island. Intruders were discouraged from landing and sometimes warned off with rifle fire. The area is now a provincial marine park. (Author's collection)

In September, 1935, Bill and Mary Lowell and Sarah Puckett departed from Cedar-by-the-Sea for Oceano, California, their belongings packed into a trailer. (Author's collection)

The colony's school as it looks today. At one time, the building was also used as a dormitory for the female members of the community. Brother XII is believed to have concealed his gold in an underground vault in the basement. (Photo by Cecil Clark)

Treasure hole where Brother XII hid perhaps half a million dollars in gold and banknotes. Chemainus historian Harry Olsen lifts the concrete lid to the empty vault. (Photo by Cecil Clark)

Georgia Crawford demonstrates how she was forced to paint a shed at the edge of a cliff on DeCourcy Island, risking serious injury should she fall to the rocks below. (Author's collection)

The contemporary remains of a stone fort on DeCourcy Island. Most of the disciples were unaccustomed to wielding weapons and only reluctantly carried out their guard duties. (Photo by James A. Santucci)

Illustration by Victoria artist Miles Lowry for the opera *Brother XII*, composed by Wes R.D. Wraggett and previewed in Victoria, British Columbia, December, 2002. Using both contemporary idioms and period styles, the work explored the dramatic and mystical dimensions of the Brother XII saga. (Courtesy Miles Lowry)

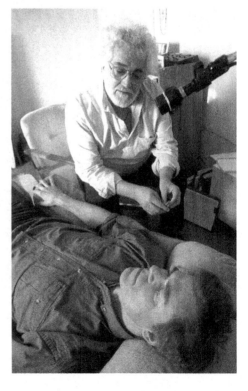

The author undergoing hypnotic regression under the guidance of transpersonal psychologist Richard Clarke in an attempt to discover what past-life links he might have had with Brother XII. The session yielded a provocative account of murder in ancient Egypt and provided tantalizing clues which helped to explain his present fascination with Brother XII. (*The Vancouver Sun*)

CHAPTER
VII
The Storm of Personality

Across the United States and Canada, the members of the Aquarian Foundation were confused by what was happening at the headquarters. They'd received Brother XII's General Letter telling them about the crisis, as well as a letter from the dissenting Governors. Many had read about the petition to dissolve the Society in the newspaper, since the story had been reported in *The New York Times* and other large American dailies. But most members didn't know who to believe or what to think. Many simply resigned from the Foundation, but a surprising number wrote to Brother XII at the headquarters, expressing their support and affirming their loyalty to the Work.

Brother XII read the letters in his office in the Center Building. The mail had poured in from across the continent, from addresses like the prestigious Cosmos Club in Washington, D. C., the Security Building in Tulsa, Oklahoma, the Cotton Exchange in Memphis, Tennessee, and the

headquarters of the Knights of American Protestantism—
a splinter group of the Ku Klux Klan—in Muncie, Indiana.
Foundation members in Florida, Texas, Kentucky, Kansas,
Missouri, Illinois, Michigan, California, Colorado, Virginia,
and numerous other states rallied to the cause. A note of encouragement even arrived from Dr. Carl Ramus, a physician
working on Ellis Island in New York. Brother XII was gratified
by this strong show of support.

In Los Angeles, a car sped along the Santa Monica freeway
past rows of white stucco buildings and pastel bungalows.
Inside was a determined trio of Brother XII loyalists, led by
Ida Mary Trask, the Divisional Secretary of Los Angeles. The
tall English teacher and lover of Milton and Dante had immediately responded to Brother XII's predicament. Together
with fellow members Ned Barmore and W. J. Barnett, she
drafted a resolution in support of him. In the form of a proxy,
it protested the Governors' court action against Brother XII,
expressed confidence in his leadership, and gave him the
legal right to represent each person who signed it. Along the
palm-lined boulevards of greater Los Angeles the three drove,
taking the resolution before groups in Pasadena, Hollywood,
Santa Monica, Redondo Beach, and Long Beach. The pile
of resolutions in Ida's lap grew steadily smaller as she distributed them to the group secretaries and urged the members
to carry on during the crisis, so that the Los Angeles division
could continue in harmony.

Ida wrote to Brother XII, telling him that the Los Angeles
members had been following the court cases in the Vancouver
newspapers. She enclosed a copy of the resolution and told
him: "I believe that nearly everyone in this Division will sign
it without question. I am going to tell them all that it is a
voluntary matter on their part, and *that you have not asked for
it.* The Division here is sticking to 'The Message.' They know
THE MASTER *is the head of the Work.* They know the 'storm'
was one of *personality,* that if one understands 'The Message,'
personal issues should not be considered at all."

Brother XII appreciated Ida's spirited defence of him. With its more than fifty groups, California was a stronghold of the Foundation and he wanted to retain as many members there as possible. He made copies of the resolution and sent it out to other groups across the continent to collect additional signatures, which he could present as evidence when the petition to dissolve the Aquarian Foundation was heard by the government.

In the Everett Building in Akron, Ohio, a frosted-glass door engraved with the words "Aero Rubber Company" opened into the reception area for Joseph Benner's two modest businesses. A door beyond led into a large room with several desks and a typewriter. Here, Benner's assistants put up orders for his specialty rubber business, while in an adjoining office, Benner himself operated the Sun Publishing Company, publishers and distributors of books on the inner life. The quiet but intense author of *The Impersonal Life* was both a Governor and the Eastern Divisional Secretary of the Aquarian Foundation. In his book-lined office, Benner conducted the business of the Society, keeping membership records, holding group meetings, and receiving patrons. Over the past few weeks, he'd dispatched urgent letters and telegrams to Brother XII, asking for an explanation of the recent events at the headquarters. He'd received no real answers, only promises to explain. Unsatisfied by Brother XII's replies and weighing the evidence the other Governors had sent, Benner decided that Brother XII had failed and was unfit to carry on the Work.

Benner wrote a general letter to the members in his division, explaining that although it seemed inconceivable, Brother XII would no longer be with them in the Work. He asked the members to be as understanding and lenient as possible: "If our Brother has sinned and failed in his Trust, it is because he is still human and essayed the heights before he had purified his nature of elements that could not stand the brilliant Light of the Impersonal Power of such heights." Benner told the members he would soon issue a series of monthly Instructions.

He exhorted them: "Hold steady and know that what is of God will stand forever, and that error will fall of its own weight."

Benner also wrote to Earle and Josephine Coffin, divisional secretaries in Dayton, Ohio, asking for their help in carrying on the Work. "Additional confirming evidence has come to me to prove that the Brother has run amuck," he told them. "The Power that came to him was too much for him to stand and it has broken him, as it will break all those who are not firmly established in the *Christ* consciousness, recognizing no source or authority but our loving Father in His Kingdom within each one of us."

Benner pointed out that Brother XII's General Letter had been a subtle appeal to the members to sustain him *personally* in the wrong path he'd chosen, and said that they must be true to principle, not personality. "From now on," he urged them, "the work of self-training must become a real and daily act, inspired with the fiery zeal that alone will win to the Kingdom of Heaven."

But the Coffins were unsympathetic to Benner's new program. While they did not doubt his sincerity, they saw his hasty effort to start his own organization as an obvious grab for power. How could he possibly claim to know all the facts in the case, they asked him, when he hadn't been at the headquarters himself? His "facts" were only the opinions of the other Governors. And by *what* authority had he assumed the leadership? Why couldn't he at least have waited for a general call from the membership? The Coffins immediately wrote to Brother XII, telling him of Benner's attempt to usurp the leadership of the Foundation.

Brother XII now faced another legal battle in his attempt to regain control of the Aquarian Foundation. On October 25, 1928, Von Platen, DeLuce, and Lucas had obtained an injunction preventing him from using any funds in the Foundation bank accounts and from transacting any business of the Society, including issuing general letters to the membership. It was critical to Wilson's plans that he succeed in having the injunction overturned.

On the afternoon of his preliminary hearing on November 1, both Wilson and Mary Connally had filed affidavits in the injunction proceedings. Mary reiterated the testimony she'd given in court and swore that she was well aware at the time she'd made her donation of the manner in which it would be used by Wilson. She stated that the Aquarian Foundation had no right to any part of her $25,000 donation, other than such interest as the defendant chose to give it. In his affidavit, Wilson discussed the Hess Trust, saying he'd converted some Grand Trunk Railway bonds into money, obtaining for them $2,446.14, but that he'd deposited a certified cheque for that amount in the Canadian Bank of Commerce in Nanaimo, and that the Trust fund was intact. He charged that the plaintiffs had entered into a conspiracy to entirely destroy the Aquarian Foundation and the work upon which he was engaged.

Von Platen, Lucas, and DeLuce filed counter-affidavits, stating that they only wanted the Society's funds to be returned to their respective donors. Lucas said he'd been instructed by Oliver Hess to secure the return of the Hess Trust, and that it would be contrary to the interests of justice if Wilson were once more clothed with the power to dispose of the securities in the fund. Robert England and James Lippincott also filed affidavits in the case. England repeated his Osiris-Isis charge, while Lippincott offered the following glimpse of Wilson and Myrtle together:

"In the house occupied by the said Wilson at the said Mandieh Settlement, there was but one bed, which I verily believe was occupied by the said Wilson and the woman who lived there with him. On one occasion, having taken my leave of the said Wilson and the said woman, I stepped out of the house and as I passed the window of the said house, I observed said Wilson and the said woman in close embrace."

Bruce McKelvie continued to cover the story for *The Province*. In a front page article, headlined: "MAN FROM

CARTHAGE, MO. HELPED REINCARNATED B.C. EGYPTIAN GOD," he reported Wilson's financial dealings with Hess and described the contents of the various affidavits filed in the proceedings. McKelvie explained that some members' faith in their leader had been shaken by Brother XII's claim in his encyclical letter from England that he'd never been in southern British Columbia in the physical body: "Later discovery that he had been employed by the Dominion Express Company in Victoria, and had lived about twenty years ago in Vancouver and Calgary, shattered to some extent the ethereal romance suggested in his Southampton declaration."

In Carthage, Missouri, Oliver Hess laboriously typed a letter to Brother XII, asking for the return of his securities. He explained that he wanted the fund to be spent for the benefit of mankind, "not for the glorification or credit of personality." Hess told Wilson that the other Governors had written of him only in the kindest of terms, "but as I think you have, in a measure, failed so far, we had better commence anew, and with better understanding than we had at first."

Hess's lawyer, Howard Gray, also wrote to Wilson, requesting the return of the bonds, though he advised him that once he straightened out his problems, "it is more than likely that Mr. Hess will again donate the bonds for the purposes mentioned."

On Tuesday, November 6, the injunction proceedings were held in Vancouver before Chief Justice W.A. MacDonald. Frank Cunliffe was facing Edward Lucas, who was appearing in the dual role of plaintiff and counsel. Cunliffe opened the proceedings, arguing that the facts in the case clearly showed that the plaintiffs were not entitled to an injunction. The terms of the injunction were also wider than justified, he said, since it denied Wilson access to his own bank account—he couldn't even use his money to buy a meal. Lucas agreed to amend the injunction to release sufficient money for Wilson's immediate needs, but Cunliffe rejected this concession. Instead, he argued that the injunction had been improperly granted in the first place. It was on this argument, bristling with legal technicalities, that the two lawyers fought it out in a formidable display of rhetoric. Cunliffe also argued that the injunction seriously affected the rights of individuals not before the court, since the Aquarian Foundation was a world-wide organization, with branches in the United States, Great Britain, South Africa, Australia, and New Zealand. Lucas responded that the Governors represented the membership and he could supply the evidence to prove it. The battle raged until late in the afternoon, when the magistrate adjourned the proceedings.

On Friday, November 9, after Cunliffe and Lucas had summed up their arguments, Chief Justice MacDonald announced his decision. "In my opinion, the injunction should be dissolved," he declared. "Simply put, the framework of the action is wrong. It is alleged in the affidavit that the Aquarian Foundation is a Society incorporated under the Societies Act of British Columbia. If its rights were invaded, it should be a party to the action. Without it being a party, any order deciding its rights would be unwarranted."

It was a crucial victory. A jubilant Wilson congratulated Frank Cunliffe on a brilliant courtroom performance. He was in control of the Foundation again and could now write to the members explaining his actions.

△   △   △

Brother XII immediately issued a General Letter addressed "TO MY BROTHERS AND SISTERS IN THIS WORK." He thanked everyone who'd written to him and told the members they were to consider this a personal letter to each and every one of them:

"We have all passed through, and are now passing through, a time of terrible trial and testing, but we should remember that those who endure to the end *must* be tried as by fire, for is it not written—'these are they who have come out of great tribulation'? This fierce attack has been allowed to develop against us for two reasons: (1) that each may be proven in the matter of loyalty to our Cause, of faith in our own integrity of purpose, and of unselfish devotion to the Right. (2) that the treacherous, the disloyal, and the self-interested may depart from us in this hour."

He advised the members that the official Society known as the Aquarian Foundation belonged to the first stage of the Work, and that the time was nearly ripe for the disintegration of its outward form:

The outer Society was the means we used for the collection of material; the present crisis is the means used for the detection and rejection of those weak and faulty elements which are always attracted to any "new" movement. *With that which remains, we are about to commence the building of the Temple.* If to you is given a part in this glorious work, know that it is because you have earned the right and have passed the preliminary testing. Take to yourselves that verse which says—"Him that overcometh will I make a pillar in the temple of my God, *and he shall go no more out.*" (Rev. III., 12). The clamour, the uncertainties, and the bitter strife of personal lives will surge around you, but you shall remain unmoved and undismayed, your feet set upon a sure Foundation.

From that date forward, Brother XII told the members, the Work would take a different form:

There will be no material or outward organization: the bonds which knit us together will be invisible to any but ourselves; they will consist of Faith, Loyalty, and the Will-to-serve. The mind will know, the heart will respond, the individual will serve. Learn to regard this Society known as the Aquarian Foundation for what it is; it is now but the chrysalis, the soon-to-be-empty shell. You who issue from it shall shortly emerge into a world of sunlight, of spiritual consciousness hitherto unknown to you.

Nature and super-nature have set their guards about this transformation, so that none but the sincere may pass. The shell is broken and that which it contained must sink or rise according to laws as inexorable as that of gravity in the material world. There will be no chance for deception, and no mistaken judgments. Wait in patience for our further word.

Your Brother in Service,

XII

Just as this letter was going to press, Brother XII received the letter from Earle and Josephine Coffin in Dayton, Ohio. They enclosed a copy of the letter Joseph Benner had issued to members and explained that he was attempting to take over the leadership of the Foundation.

Brother XII was furious. Benner's action was the last link needed to prove the nature and extent of the conspiracy against him. He stopped the press and added a ringing postscript:

Brothers and Sisters, hear the truth. At the very moment Benner wrote his letter, he had in his possession a copy of my General Letter for November in which I took up specifically every personal charge against myself. We could not issue it here owing to an injunction of the court secured by these traitors expressly to prevent us taking any action to make the real facts known. The letter was, therefore, sent to Benner, asking him to print it in Akron and distribute to all our members.

BENNER HAS DELIBERATELY SUPPRESSED THAT LETTER, and has not given you the slightest hint that it was ever written. I ask you if such an action would be taken by an honest man? Do you think that a man who stoops to such infamy is a fit leader for our own Work? His letter breathes the very spirit of hypocrisy and contains deliberate lies. Read the fourth paragraph on the first page: it is Benner and these infamous conspirators who "will no longer be with us

in the Work he (myself) established in our hearts and lives."
Here he unconsciously admits a little of the truth—he and
these others established nothing; they have only torn down
and destroyed. . .

The truth that this whole tragedy is a deep and cunning
plot is now overwhelming and indisputable. My November
Letter suppressed by Benner will follow immediately; when
you have that you will be in possession of the true facts; *then*
shall you make your choice, whether you will stand with
The Brother XII and this Work, or with those traitors who
are trying to destroy it for their own personal gain and ambition for leadership. Our associate Benner has earned a
new name—not Joseph Benner but JUDAS Benner from
henceforth.

Brother XII now issued the November General Letter, in
which he answered the charges that had been brought against
him. There were three basic charges: first, that he'd lost all
knowledge of the plan of the Lodge—if he'd ever had it;
second, that he was wrongfully using the funds of the Aquarian
Foundation to further his personal plans; and finally, that he
was openly immoral in his personal life. These charges were
summed up in the more general charge that he was "black"
and had been abandoned by the Elder Brothers because of
personal failure.

Brother XII emphatically denied the charges. "There has
been no personal failure," he declared, "and there shall be
none, unless it be the breakdown of the physical body under
the tremendous strain now put upon it."

He claimed that upon close examination, none of the
charges were supported by any evidence. In answer to the first
and second charges, he explained that the founding of the
Mandieh Settlement was part of the original plan—it was the
actual "Center of Safety" referred to over and over again in
earlier writings, the manifestation of the program announced
in *The Message*. The donation given by Mary Connally was spe-

cifically for that purpose, he said, and wasn't intended for the Aquarian Foundation. He had the signed declaration of the donor upon that point.

In answer to the charge that he was openly immoral in his personal life, Brother XII replied by giving an account of the circumstances of his relationship with Myrtle Baumgartner— although not identifying her by name. He made it clear that he considered her a fellow "Brother" and initiate:

> The first stage of this Work was individual—I alone gave "The Message," built up the outer organization, and gave the subsequent teachings and instructions you have received. These writings are my witness—a living witness that will endure long after those who try to destroy it are forgotten. My work will live.
>
> The second stage of this Work is not individual, but dual in its nature; its labours and responsibilities are shared by another of our Inner Order. Together, we have to teach the laws governing the true relationship of man to man, of parents and children, and of that alliance between man and woman which we are used to call marriage. That this work may be done with a perfect understanding of every angle of the problems involved, it was essential that one of us should take a feminine embodiment. This my Brother has done.
>
> For many years past, *we have worked together on inner planes*; but the time has now come when we must work as one, outwardly and in the life of the physical world. We have to teach by example and action, not only by words. We have to *live the life*, and that means to show men and women what the true marriage relationship is, as distinguished from the conventional and the false. That brings us into conflict with the standards, conventions, and prejudices of the existing order. It cannot be otherwise, for these represent conditions which are characteristic of fifth-race methods and misinterpretations. If we were conventional, careful of personal reputation, no work could be done, and

we would be spiritually dead, or at least in bondage to the old order, impotent to lead the way or to declare the truth that makes men free.

I am charged with maintaining a marriage relationship with one to whom I am not legally married. It is quite true, and some, though not all, of the reasons for this course, I am now putting before you. But the charge that my course is immoral is not true. It is unconventional, and the world at large confuses morals with conventions. The existing marriage laws of civilized countries are demonstrably immoral and at variance with the divine scheme. A young girl may be married to an old man of seventy (for wealth or worldly position), and the relationship be considered entirely moral and proper. But should she love one of her own age outside the conventional marriage tie, she is damned socially and morally by the conventionalists of all classes. To inferentially sanction the existing scheme by subscribing to it ourselves would be a hypocritical surrender of principle to expediency.

In forming your judgment in this matter, remember that the course I have to follow *was chosen deliberately*. We who must together tread this road met for the first time in our physical bodies recently, and discussed it fully. We considered the sacrifices it demanded, the bitter trial to ourselves and others, and the terrible personal sufferings involved in the loss of friends, and the condemnation of almost all others. We looked these things in the face, we counted the cost fully, and *we are willing to pay the price*. Never for one instant was it a matter of an ordinary personal attraction. This is what our enemies would have you believe, and what most of you *will* believe. For both of us the personal equation is the one thing that has been set aside. We are willing to sacrifice all for the sake of the work we have undertaken.

You cannot judge of this matter as though it were an ordinary personal delinquency. It is nothing of the kind. It is a necessary and exceedingly bitter experience—a hard, rough portion of the path I have undertaken to tread. It is not self-gratification. It is self-immolation on the part of those who would, if need be, give their bodies to be burned that we may bear witness to the truth.

Brother XII then answered the most controversial charge brought against him, that he'd claimed to be a reincarnation of the Egyptian god Osiris:

An untruth which is now being circulated amongst our members is that I have stated that I am "an incarnation of Osiris" and that my helpmate in this work is Isis. I never at any time made that statement. The story was started by Robert England and is part of the plot to discredit our Work. Such things could only be said or inferred by persons utterly ignorant of spiritual verities. Osiris-Isis are living *Principles* in Nature, not personal god and goddess. In the Mysteries, they symbolized this very Principle of Duality of which the modern world is entirely ignorant. The worship of Osiris-Isis was really a study of, and an understanding of the dual aspect of the spiritual Monad, inseparable from manifestation *in form*. To that extent, every person is an "incarnation" of one or other of these dual Principles. But there are few today who have any knowledge of the "dual law," and it is our work to restore in part that knowledge to mankind. The "divine child" Horus symbolized the concrete brain-knowledge of those truths, which are "born" into the world of men as the result of a knowledge of the Dual Law which governs the *union* of the Osiris-Isis Principles in nature.

This close association, which the ignorant and the uncharitable label as "immoral" is in reality a very sacred thing—far more so than the ordinary, conventional marriage tie, and having claims which are immeasurably greater. Also, it is a matter of the greatest significance to mankind generally at this time. You may gain a hint of that significance if you know where to look for it. . .

Brother XII referred members to *When the Sun Moves Northward,* a mystical treatise that linked the stages of human initiation with the solar year. He quoted the following passage:

> "It is only in the occult ceremonies and vigils that the recognition of spiritual comrades can take place. If, when the consciousness comes to you of those who are your true companions, you find one who is a friend on earth, then may you know that you have gone far indeed upon the path. To be powerful enough to attain an association with a companion on the physical as well as on the psychic plane means that the divine part of the man has been able to unfold a petal of its lotus flower and to permit its sweetness to become a fragrance that can reach the outer sense. For this so wonderful thing must come from on high; it means that two initiates are fated or permitted to meet upon earth—a marvel in an aeon."

> When this tremendous thing referred to as a "meeting of two initiates" takes place in physical bodies, it is the sign and symbol of a mighty work. It is not only a "marvel in an aeon" but it marks in this case the beginning and the end of an aeon. How many of you will ignorantly misjudge this significant event as a mere vulgar personal delinquency? Upon your judgment and decision of this event your own spiritual standing will be decided, as will also your progress or your retrogression through many future lives.

Brother XII advised the members that further information regarding the second stage of the Work would be available shortly. He closed by thanking "the many friends and members who have sent me such splendid letters of loyalty and encouragement during this dark time of trial. I thank you all from my heart."

△   △   △

Conspicuously absent from Brother XII's General Letter was any mention of his recent involvement in American politics. Only a week earlier, on November 6, 1928, a record number of Americans had flocked to the polls and elected Herbert Hoover president of the United States in a national landslide. Alfred Smith won only eight states, losing even his home state of New York. Convinced he'd been defeated because of his religion, he announced he'd never again run for public office. Brother XII no doubt felt vindicated by the election results, believing that together with other Protestant activists, he'd contributed to the defeat of the Roman Catholic candidate. But even so, the election underscored the fact that none of his predictions had come true: the P.P.L. and the Third Party had been dismal failures; he hadn't selected the next president of the United States; and Roman Catholics hadn't slaughtered Protestants in the bloody civil war he'd predicted. In the aftermath of the election, he quietly abandoned any further political plans.

Two days after the election, as the *Princess Charlotte* plowed through the waters of the Strait of Georgia, John Harrison performed his last official act as Secretary of the Protestant Protective League. In his ornate handwriting, the florid Englishman and former department store executive wrote out his resignation from the P.P.L. on B.C. Steamship stationery. Harrison had relentlessly pushed the interests of the League for the past year and was exhausted by the effort. "I finally broke!" he wrote Wilson, "and brought on my old trouble of *shell-shock,* with complications." He explained that he'd shut down the P.P.L. office in Vancouver, since it seemed pointless to continue. But although disenchanted by the League's failure and the political infighting at the headquarters, he assured Brother XII: "I am with you," and added, "*Brother,* I think of you as I knew you at first, and no one can take that from me!"

Brother XII was unmoved by Harrison's expression of loyalty. "I have your letter of recent date," he replied. "It is evasive to a degree and the concluding sentences are an insult to my intelligence. I estimate your 'love' for me at exactly its true value." He went on to accuse Harrison of misappropriating seven hundred dollars of P.P.L. funds and of conspiring with Robert England against him. He also threatened him with legal action unless he swore out an affidavit giving full particulars of the plot: "I am determined to sift every phase of this conspiracy and to convict every person concerned therein. I am not inclined to take definite action against yourself PROVIDED you assist me to bring these others to justice."

Astonished that Brother XII should turn against him, Harrison wrote back, giving the accounting he'd demanded and explaining: "The two hundred dollars was to meet current expenses then overdue, and the five hundred dollars was sanctioned by you to carry on over the crisis, as the P.P.L. was at that time to go ahead at all costs." He also reminded Wilson he'd given up a lucrative position with the department store to work for the League, and the consequent neglect of his personal affairs had cost him about two thousand dollars. "It was just over a year ago that we started, and today I haven't the price of a streetcar fare!"

Harrison wasn't taking sides in the dispute. "I was approached in Victoria to give evidence for the Lucas-Von Platen outfit," he told Wilson. "I refused. They had better keep away from me. I have finished with the whole thing, and I hope no one ever mentions it to me again!"

In the Belvedere Hotel in Sooke Harbour, on the outskirts of Victoria, Mary Connally waited for the opening of the fall assizes in Nanaimo. The hotel was an old hunting lodge, with a totem pole out front and stables in the back. It was a favourite hideaway for wealthy tourists who hunted deer, bear, and cougar in the surrounding woods. The Belvedere was a sanctuary for Mary, a place where she could retreat from the glare of publicity surrounding Wilson's preliminary hearing. She dreaded the prospect of appearing in court again at the

Nanaimo assizes. On November 13, a week before the assizes, she wrote to Attorney-General R.H. Pooley, requesting a meeting with him. She enclosed a copy of a clipping from *The Nanaimo Daily Herald* about Wilson's hearing.

"I came a great many miles at a very inconvenient time to testify to the innocence of Mr. Wilson," she explained, "and my own specific instructions at the time I made my gift. I was amazed to find my word doubted and a further hearing demanded. I have been quite stunned by the newspaper reports which have been broadcast in the Eastern papers. My family are sending frantic letters and telegrams offering—even threatening—to send out family lawyers. I have been staying as quietly as possible in this little hotel waiting for the 20th, when it occurred to me that perhaps you might be able and willing to help me avoid another courtroom ordeal. Am coming into Victoria for the day tomorrow early, and hope you can spare me half an hour. . ."

Although there's no record of what transpired during the meeting, it's unlikely that Pooley could offer Mary any assistance beyond the assurance that Wilson would receive an impartial hearing. He may have also explained that given her earlier testimony on Wilson's behalf, and the ambiguous nature of the charge against him, it was by no means certain that she would be called as a witness. In any case, Mary could at least take heart in Wilson's oft-repeated utterance that these events were a test, and that once the crisis was past, she herself would play an important part in the next stage of the Work.

△   △   △

In Nanaimo, on the morning of November 20, 1928, the fall assizes opened. The courtroom was packed, since the criminal and civil cases that were tried during the week-long hearings were always a major source of interest to the residents of the colliery town. At eleven o'clock, Chief Justice Aulay M. Morrison, an imposing figure in his black robes and wig, called the court to order. After swearing in the members of the grand jury, he reviewed the cases on the docket. In addition to the charges against England and Wilson, the week's cases included rape, assault, perjury, opium smuggling, and the sexual abuse of a ten-year-old girl. When Morrison had finished, Victor B. Harrison, Crown Counsel, stepped forward and stated that the Attorney-General's office had instructed him to have the charge against Wilson traversed to the next assizes because the principal witness for the Crown, Robert England, had not appeared. Harrison explained that England was out on bail and the police had been searching for him.

"Has he absconded?" asked Morrison.

"I do not know, Your Honour," replied Harrison. "I only know that he cannot be located."

Lucas and DeLuce were obviously perturbed by England's absence. As England's bondsmen, they stood to forfeit their bail if he didn't show up. Lucas could lose his house in Vancouver, and DeLuce twenty-five hundred dollars. England's failure to appear seemed like an admission of guilt, and without his testimony they were certain the charge against Wilson would be dismissed. Chief Justice Morrison told Harrison that he'd postpone England's case until the next afternoon and hear the charge against Wilson later that week.

The following day, England still hadn't been located. Morrison announced that he'd be tried *in absentia*. Lucas stood up and told the magistrate he had some material evidence that should go before the grand jury. The magistrate directed Harrison to endorse Lucas's name upon the bill. The grand jury filed out to hear Lucas's evidence *in camera*.

Wilson immediately suspected a trick. According to his own account, he slipped out of the courtroom and made his way down the hall to the grand jury room. Pausing outside the closed chamber, he listened at the door. The voices were muffled and he couldn't hear them clearly, but he could tell that Lucas was "jollying along" the members of the jury: "I myself heard roars of laughter as he was addressing them. . ." It seemed obvious to Wilson that the charming and witty Lucas had the grand jury eating out of the palm of his hand.

The jury members returned to the courtroom and the foreman announced the verdict—"No Bill" against Robert England. Wilson could only turn helplessly to Frank Cunliffe, appalled by what he considered a travesty of justice.

Cunliffe was also dismayed by the judgment, since he considered England guilty of theft. After the assizes were over, he wrote to the Attorney-General, drawing his attention to the matter. "It seems to me astounding to think that where a man jumps his bail, all his bondsmen have to do is to get themselves before the grand jury on the pretext of giving evidence, and then in the course of that secret proceeding induce the jury to bring in a 'No Bill.'" He pointed out that Lucas could not in any sense of the matter be regarded as a Crown witness, and that his only interest in the matter was to save his own pocket. "I certainly would not have liked to have seen Mr. Lucas obliged to put up the amount of the bail, and in a way, I suppose he can hardly be blamed for taking the steps that he did to rid himself of that obligation. . . I do, however, feel strongly that in this respect, there has been a gross miscarriage of justice."

The next day, the grand jury considered the charge against Wilson. Chief Justice Morrison made it clear to the jury what he thought the verdict should be. He explained that the trouble was basically a squabble among the members of the Foundation over who should control the assets: "In my opinion, there are other courts in the land to settle such disputes. It is up to you to decide whether or not the time of the Assize Court should be taken up with such matters."

After the briefest of deliberations, the grand jury returned and announced its verdict: "No Bill" against Wilson.

Wilson was relieved and so was Mary Connally. The weeks of legal struggle had ended in another decision in Brother XII's favour. His victory, however, was not the story of the assizes. The real story was the mysterious disappearance of Robert

England:

"AQUARIAN TREASURER IS MISSING. ROBERT ENGLAND, EX-OFFICER, FAILS TO APPEAR AT ASSIZES. LAST SEEN IN SEATTLE. FRIENDS BELIEVE HE WAS CARRYING $2,800 ON HIS PERSON."

In a front page story in *The Province*, Bruce McKelvie asked: "What has become of Robert A. G. England, erstwhile Secretary-Treasurer of The Aquarian Foundation at Cedar-by-the-Sea?"

When he failed to turn up at the opening of the Nanaimo Assizes on Monday to face a charge brought against him by E. A. Wilson, leader and Brother XII of the Aquarian cult, the suggestion was made that he had feared to face the court, but this his friends declare to be untrue. They contend that he had no reason to doubt the outcome of the case, and this has been borne out by the fact that the Grand Jury returned "No Bill" in the indictment.

Those who are intimate with England fear that he has met with foul play in Seattle. England was formerly a secret service agent for the United States Government, acting under William J. Burns, and as such became a more or less familiar figure to denizens of the underworld. He was last heard of in the Sound City on November 3, when he checked out of the Calhoun Hotel, announcing that he was returning to Vancouver. It was known, reports from Seattle state, that he was carrying $2,800 on his person, and friends there had remonstrated with him for so doing. This fact, together with surrounding circumstances, has aroused the fears of his friends in British Columbia.

Edward Lucas was one of the most puzzled by England's disappearance. He couldn't believe that a man of England's character would skip out and leave him and DeLuce to forfeit their bail. England had been staying with Lucas in Vancouver, and the lawyer had advised him to go to Seattle to bring back the twenty-eight hundred dollars he'd placed in the safety deposit box.

"At first, my father thought Bob had run out on him," Frances Lucas recounts. "He felt sick about it—he couldn't believe he'd do that. Then, in the long run, I think he decided something must have happened to him. Bob's clothes, typewriter, and notebook—which I'm sure he must have treasured—were all left at our home."

Frances recalls that there may have been another reason why England took the twenty-eight hundred dollars from Wilson's bank account: "I think it had something to do with the strategy in the court case, apart from the fact that the money was owing to Bob. My father and the others felt the money should be sequestered, so it was removed from the account to put it beyond Brother XII's reach. It seems to me that Bob took that money to Seattle for a specific reason, which wasn't only personal to him. But this is vague in my mind; I don't know the details."

The last person apparently to see England was Nellie Little, a young woman whose family owned the general store at Cedar.

"She was visiting her sister in Seattle," Frances says, "when she saw him at the bus station. He showed her the money he was carrying, which was in cash. 'You know, I think I'm being followed,' he said. He got on the bus to come north, and from that day forward, not one of us ever heard from Bob again."

Rumours about England's disappearance quickly spread. Some people said he'd gone missing off the B.C. Steamship ferry between Vancouver and Nanaimo—that his luggage had arrived, but he had not; he'd either been pushed overboard or dumped off a pier. Others claimed he'd disappeared on the Vancouver Island highway somewhere between Nanaimo and Victoria. But England's body was never found and none of the rumours could be substantiated.

There was even speculation that Brother XII might have had a hand in England's disappearance, since he stood to gain the most if his former Secretary-Treasurer failed to appear at the assizes.

"I seen a couple of guys come over to Valdes in a speedboat right around that time," Arthur Nicholson recalls. "They were talking to Wilson—left again the same day. They looked pretty peculiar to me. I call them 'no good suckers.' You know what I mean? I think he was bumped off."

Another workman met with Brother XII the day before the assizes opened. He could tell that Wilson had more on his mind than the work they discussed on Valdes Island.

"I walked over to the old man's house at Cedar on Sunday morning," Dick Nicholson recalls. "Heavy snow on the ground. He was in his pyjamas, and he seemed pretty upset about something. England's name came up, but he wouldn't talk about him. He seemed afraid of something. He said he'd been to Victoria that week. I thought later, well, if he went to Victoria, what was to stop him from going to Seattle, cause that's where England disappeared."

In light of all this speculation, it should be noted that evidence exists to suggest that England did, in fact, choose not to face the court. It does not prove, however, that a more sinister explanation might also be possible.

An undated note from John Harrison to Wilson, discovered in Frank Cunliffe's files, reads: "England has jumped his bail and gone. Lucas and DeLuce will have to find the amount. This information is confidential to you."

And in his letter to the Attorney-General, written after the "No Bill" judgment was brought in against England, Cunliffe writes: "Some days before the assizes opened, it became more or less common knowledge that England had gone to the States and would not return for his trial, and I passed along to Mr. V. B. Harrison, Crown Counsel, such information as I had in this respect."

England's fate remains a mystery. Among the papers he left at the Lucas house were the astrological charts of a woman named Marie Belle Abbott and her two children,

Frank Abbott—born in Fresno, California in 1909—and Forrest Abbott—born in Los Angeles in 1911. England and the forty-one-year-old Marie Belle Abbott had both joined the Aquarian Foundation in Oceano, California, and it's possible they were romantically involved. Perhaps England returned to California to be with her; and maybe Frank Abbott or Forrest Abbott, if they're still alive, know whether or not their mother saw him again—and what eventually became of him.

△   △   △

Robert England had been Brother XII's closest advisor and confidant for over a year. Working with him daily, he'd had a unique opportunity to observe Wilson close up. When he resigned, England wrote a letter to Wilson, telling him, with unflinching honesty, exactly what he thought of him and why he believed Wilson had failed in the Work:

To

Edward Arthur Wilson
President of The Aquarian Foundation
and Owner of The Mandieh Settlement:

This declaration is addressed to you in the form of a letter in order that I may make plain to you at this time the results of my fourteen months of incessant labour for a principle, fourteen months of constant observation of your works, fourteen months of a steady listening to every word you have spoken to me regarding the work of the Brothers of Light and their plans for humanity, and also the part or parts the Brother XII had, and still has, in the carrying out of those plans.

Because I am possessed of an excellent memory, a desire to always find out the why of everything, and a belief that the higher the work and worker, the more careful we must be in proving them and their works, due to these, I have been gradually and very surely forced to come to the following conclusions that: –

(1) The Brother XII is no longer working in or through the body and faculties of Edward A. Wilson.

(2) That the Master's Consciousness was gradually withdrawn during the period from the latter part of January to about the first day of July of this year, 1928.

(3) That the present plans of E. A. W. are not from the Master, nor are they any part of the Plan of the White Lodge, but are rather the plans of two ordinary human beings possessed of very keen and active brains, namely Edward Arthur Wilson and Myrtle Baumgartner.

There are many incidents which I could recite, dating from early in 1928, which to me are proof of the above three points because they show, even though they are often small things, the inconsistency in many of the actions you have said were for other purposes, and the following are some of the most vital points to be considered, namely: –

1. A consistent and repeated failure to know or recognize the very obvious characters of individuals met with at the Center from time to time in past months who have expressed a desire to take up some phase of the work, such as:—(a) Maurice Von Platen was always held in very high esteem by you until he expressed a desire or wish to control, or at least handle the finances; (b) You told others as well as myself that Ross Humble was a chela of the White Lodge when he first came here, but you later on condemned him as a thing of evil, and said that you had always known he was black; (c) When Thomas Smith first came here, he appeared very foul to me at first sight, and has remained so, but you took him into the office and after being shown about ten thousand dollars' worth of letters of credit, you brought him back out and asked me to look again and meet

a real brother, with the results that he is making merry with the women in Victoria; (d) It looks to me that you knew Robert DeLuce had reason to believe that he would be appointed your successor in the outer work, for you had yourself led him to believe that it would be so. I saw by your own thoughts when I told you that he planned to take control by force that you had no idea of such a move. His plan was helped along by Maurice Von Platen realizing that you had used his money to take a trip with a woman, instead of for political work. The idea that Robert DeLuce was the reincarnation of an Aztec sacrificial priest had never occurred to you until I told you of my own convictions in the matter which were, and still are, true so far as I am concerned, but a few days later, I heard the story from J. J. Lippincott that you had told him you had traced Robert's past incarnations and had found that he was the reincarnation of an Aztec sacrificial priest. . . and (e) Your repeated failure to realize that I was very carefully cataloguing all these for my own protection later on, my reasons being that where the higher things are concerned, I must be certain, and I had to prove to myself whether you were who and what you claimed to be.

2. The many attacks you have made upon individuals in your published writings and in private letters has shown me there was none of the love in you or the compassion an Adept of the White Lodge should and would show, or that a Master of the Wisdom would show for his chelas. The work done in Washington, and later in organizing the P.P.L. was, so far as I can see, good work and true work, but when the personal ideas and plans of yourself took hold, it was all wrecked. You will perhaps remember that I told you there was nothing to come from any of the P.P.L. work.

3. Your present methods of getting money and property into your own control, without telling those who give it all of the facts connected with your present plans, is one I cannot approve of, for it is quite plain to me from the methods

you employ that you are now concerned only with the getting of money and a place. You added up the total receipts
of cash roughly in your mind one day when we were out in
your boat not many weeks ago, and remarked in a tone of
satisfaction that it was not too bad considering the time you
had been at it. You have not told Mrs. Mary Connally all the
details of your plans for the Mandieh Settlement, nor of
your present life there, nor of your past life. These latter are
your own personal affairs to some extent, but others who
are associated with you are most certainly affected by them
because you are the head of the A.F.

4. When you told me of your trip to Chicago from Seattle
with Myrtle Baumgartner, and that a conception had taken
place, and that the offspring would be the World Teacher,
and that you were the physical embodiment of the ancient
Egyptian God Osiris, and that she was the physical embodiment of the Goddess Isis, and that the child would be the
physical embodiment of Horus, while the trip was said to
have been made in the interests of the P.P.L. and the political welfare of the people of the American continent, I used
a faculty you have never known I possess, and I followed the
actual thoughts in your mind while you were talking to me.
They were very different from the words you spoke; and all
the while you were speaking, you were surrounded with a
dull gray mist or fog, which was filled with hundreds of tiny
imps dashing frantically about, and they were controlled
by a helmeted and evil-faced monk, who stood some feet
behind you with a hellish leer upon his face. You said at the
time that I might not believe what you were telling me, and
I replied that I had worked out a lot of things in connection
with the matter and might believe quite a bit. . .

5. Your present treatment of Elma is your own personal
affair, but it serves as a detail in the measurement that I
must make. "By their fruits ye shall know them." She has
given you fifteen years of her life in faithful service. Even an
ordinary man of the world with a limited sense of honour

would have at least gone to her once it was decided to undertake the present arrangement on Valdes Island, and have told her all the truth in the matter. She knows nothing as yet concerning the trip from Seattle to Chicago. . .

The letter abruptly ends—why England didn't finish it isn't known. Since it was discovered in Frank Cunliffe's files, Wilson must have read it—but under what circumstances? Did England present it to him the night before he left the headquarters? Did its contents trigger Wilson's incredible rage, causing him to swear out the warrant for England's arrest? One can only speculate. In any event, although England disappeared, his letter survived—a revealing insight into the character of Brother XII.

CHAPTER
VIII
Black Magic in Court

At the Belvedere Hotel outside Victoria, snowflakes drifted down from a grey sky, blanketing the former hunting lodge with white and gently filling up the surrounding woods. Men with brooms knocked the snow off the windshields of cars parked out front, while others carried armfuls of firewood into the lobby. In the dining room, waiters set out cups and saucers and brought sandwiches and cakes to the long white buffet as the hotel guests assembled in the warm interior to observe the ritual of afternoon tea.

Mary Connally had returned to the Belvedere after the assizes. She was grateful that the charge against Wilson had been dropped and that she hadn't been required to appear in court on his behalf. But she wasn't able to savour the victory, because he'd immediately called upon her to assist with another crisis in the Foundation.

"He was liberated," she later recalled, "and I went down to Victoria and spent the winter. And I took charge of the woman that was very much in evidence during the trial, named Myrtle 'B.' She was the one they talked about so much and tried to make into so many headlines. She came to me in great distress and said that her name was 'Jenkins.'"

Myrtle Baumgartner's mental state hadn't improved since she left Valdes Island—it may even have deteriorated. According to Mary, her condition was "deplorable," and she gave the older woman a great deal of anxiety and cost her quite a bit of money, since Mary paid for Myrtle's hotel bill at the Belvedere.

Mary wasn't able to rely on Wilson's help either: "He came down a couple of times to see her while she was there—three times," she later said.

Mary was surprised to discover that Wilson also expected her to pay his legal bills. Earlier, she'd given Frank Cunliffe money to purchase *The Victoria Colonist* newspaper, since Wilson wanted to acquire a newspaper in order to further his work. But the owners decided not to sell. When Cunliffe returned the money to Mary, he informed her that he'd deducted his legal fees from the amount she had given him.

"This was a surprise to me from two standpoints," she recalled. "First of all, that I was not consulted about it. And secondly, that he hadn't paid his bills after all I had done."

But Mary put these thoughts aside and did her best to look after Myrtle, accepting the additional financial expense philosophically, since she had the means to do so. Yet she found the experience at the Belvedere disquieting: "That was the first ripple I had of anything that was not quite in order to me."

As the hotel staff prepared for the Christmas season and Mary watched over the broken and pathetic figure of Myrtle Baumgartner, how could she not help but wonder if this troubled interlude were not an ominous portent of the future?

Brother XII couldn't ignore the issue of his relationship with Myrtle Baumgartner, since it continued to be a subject of controversy among the members of the Foundation. In spite of the explanation he'd given in his November General Letter, he'd still been attacked by Joseph Benner, who had vigorously denounced him for his sexual misconduct, refusing to believe that he and Myrtle were initiates:

> Read what is said in reply to the fourth charge and note the fact that no denial is made that the woman came and *lived with* him secretly, while he already had another wife at the Center. Is anything said that this woman was induced to desert a loving husband, an invalid whom she had been nursing and caring for for months previously? Think you, if these were the two "Initiates" claimed, that the Great Law would not have arranged it so that they would have come together in a perfectly natural way—by making each one *free* to do their "mighty work" together, instead of by deceiving a wife and deserting a helpless husband? Think you God or Initiates of the Great White Lodge work that way? Or that God would authorize the taking of both the Law of God and the law of man into their own hands and bending them to fit desire—no matter on how high a plane?
>
> My Brothers, the serpent of sex is the most subtle and deceptive force in man's nature. Wherever sex still lives and is given any prominence in the mind, it insidiously works to maintain its power, and unless the heart has been purified by unselfish love, sooner or later it will bring havoc into the life, and if encouraged and fed, will destroy the mind and body, and almost wreck the soul.

Benner told the members that to be a disciple, self and sex had to be absolutely forgotten, since in "The Kingdom" they did not exist: "When you have found The Kingdom and are abiding There, then and then only are you fit to learn the holy meaning of That which in human terms is called Soul-Mates or Companion Souls." He claimed that Jesus Christ had taught no such doctrine for the New Dispensation, and that, as disciples, they could not enter the New Age that way:

"Do not mistake, The New Age—The Age of Aquarius—is the Age of Love, the Age of the heart and not of the head, and 'He who is to come,' the Blessed Christ, must first have the foundation of love laid for Him in the hearts and lives of every one of his followers before He can come. The Age of Mystery, of Occultism, of Intellectual Knowledge, is passing. They must make way for the clear Light of Truth in Love."

Brother XII wanted to settle the issue of his relationship with Myrtle Baumgartner once and for all. Under the heading "A Personal Matter," he addressed a General Letter to the membership, replying to Benner's new charges. He said he wanted the members to know the real facts, so they could all be sure, in their own minds, that they weren't being led into something opposed to the ideals of true morality:

> That one whom he charges with desertion of a task made, in the first place, a mesalliance. The circumstances of her life were desperately unhappy—it is not for me to state the reasons, except to say that the fault was not on her side. For years she had nursed "an invalid husband," but if you knew the CAUSE of the invalidism, and the conditions under which the nursing was done, the whole case would assume another aspect. The Good Law HAD worked to make each free. An entire separation had been agreed upon between those two before I had ever seen the lady in the flesh or knew that she existed. To say that she was "persuaded to come here" is utterly false. She decided to come to this Center and to devote her life to this Work (either here or elsewhere) before I knew anything of the matter. I did not know she was coming until three or four days before her arrival, and I had never seen her physically in my life. When she did come, THERE WAS A MUTUAL RECOGNITION. Since 1922, we had worked closely on inner planes, and NEITHER KNEW THAT THE OTHER WAS IN PHYSICAL INCARNATION UNTIL THE

MOMENT OF THAT MEETING.

Another point, and one that is important from the conventional standpoint, is this—the lady was a wife only in name, since early in 1925, she had never been anything more than a nurse and attendant to the man whose name she bore. In that year, she experienced very great things in the spiritual world, and as a result of them, she was under an obligation to abstain absolutely from all ordinary contacts until the time came when her life-work could be undertaken. This work, which Benner so sneeringly refers to, was a matter of many years of intense inner training and preparation—even as is my own.

Brother XII dismissed Benner's remarks about sex as typical of his moralizing attitude. He explained that his own teachings were for disciples, not for the masses of humanity. The incident with Myrtle was a special and unusual circumstance necessary for the accomplishment of a particular work; it did not point to a rule of conduct for all.

Benner had accused him of bending both the law of God and the law of man to fit desire. He replied:

What is law? Law is the aggregate of the CONDITIONS of sentient existence in A GIVEN FIELD of consciousness. There is one law for the animal, another for man; one law for the savage, another for the intellectual; there is the Law of the disciple, and the Law of the Initiate, and the Law of the Adept or perfected man. Law is not a rule of conduct but a condition of existence, and it varies with the range of consciousness.

There is a wide difference between the man or woman who has reached the (comparatively) lofty development required in the true disciple, and the rank-and-file of humanity. There must therefore be a CORRESPONDING DIFFERENCE in the laws which rightfully govern these two differing stages of growth. The average man must be governed by and submit to a law imposed from without. Why? Because that law, in theory at least, represents "the greatest good for the greatest number"; it is the corrective for self- ishness. The disciple must be governed by and submit to the Law imposed by the Spirit or Higher Self upon the outward physical man. Thou shalt keep the Law within thine own heart and within thy mind—the Law of thine own being.

Brother XII also took the opportunity to clarify his views on marriage. The essence of his teaching was simple, he said, and he had no wish to make a mystery of it:

The case stands thus: TWO PERSONS SHOULD ENTER A DEFINITE MARITAL RELATIONSHIP ONLY WHEN THE NATIVITIES (BIRTH HOROSCOPES) OF BOTH WARRANT THE UNDERTAKING OF SUCH A MUTUAL RESPONSIBILITY. The nativity is the chart of the Soul, as well as of its outer garment—the physical body. In marriage, we deliberately invoke (stir up) the powers and potencies of the psychic and spiritual worlds—to do so ignorantly, or at the instigation of a mere passing sexual attraction, is always disastrous. The disciple must first KNOW THE LAW, and then bring himself into voluntary and complete accord with it. He differs from the masses of mankind in that he is self-governed.

In closing, he stated: "Reason must control passion; the good of the Race must ever come before mere personal incli- nation. What we have come to declare is THE LAW OF THE ILLUMINATI—of those disciples, Initiates, and Adepts who consciously live the life of the inner world of Reality and are governed by its laws. They are no longer subject to the lesser laws of men—they are the Children of Knowledge."

Brother XII's letter was ironic, given Myrtle Baumgartner's present condition. But he couldn't publicly acknowledge her breakdown, since it was a persuasive argument in itself against his assertion that the Work was proceeding according to plan. His General Letter also contradicted the sworn testimony of Robert England that he'd met Myrtle on the train between Seattle and Chicago. Was he telling the truth or was his version of events a deliberate falsehood? Whatever the case, he obviously did not wish to raise more questions than he could answer.

Myrtle's breakdown, according to Annie Barley, was the result of Brother XII's mistreatment of her. Given his explosive temper and vindictive nature, one can imagine the scenes that might have taken place between them when he realized Myrtle would not fulfill her exalted destiny.

Myrtle didn't remain in Victoria for long. Before the year was out, she was sent back to Toronto in the care of Louise Hobart. After nursing an invalid husband, Myrtle was now an invalid herself.

Dr. Edwin A. Baumgartner, a proud and wilful man, wasn't about to forgive his wife or take her back. He initiated divorce proceedings, sending a lawyer named Harold Potter all the way to British Columbia to obtain evidence. The divorce was granted on grounds of adultery on September 1, 1931, in the County Court in Canandaigua, New York. This is the last known record of Myrtle Wells Baumgartner, whose love affair with Brother XII and dream of becoming the mother of the next World Teacher had led her to a pitiful and tragic end.

Brother XII's disciples believed that as a member of the Great White Lodge, he possessed the powers of an adept. He could leave his physical body at will and travel in his spirit body to any part of the world. He could enter locked rooms, listen to secret deliberations, read sealed documents—nothing could be hidden from him. It was also believed that he could wield powerful occult forces in his battle against the "Brothers of the Shadow," the black adepts who were trying to lead mankind astray.

Brother XII had defined good and evil for his disciples as follows: "'Good' is simply knowledge rightly applied; i.e., directed towards the attainment of the ultimate goal set before humanity. 'Evil' is the same knowledge wrongly applied, and leading through selfishness and greed away from that goal."

But many of the disciples now suspected that Brother XII had been possessed by one of the very adepts he'd warned them about. Robert England's clairvoyant vision of the "helmeted and evil-faced monk" standing a few feet behind Brother XII and inside his aura suggested this, as did the sinister black-cowled figure "with a face like smoked leather" that had been seen lurking near the House of Mystery by two of the disciples.

"He was always talking about the black adepts and the white *chelas*," Eric Davenport recalls. "One time, he was citing an incident at a big convention he'd attended, and telling us how the black adepts, as he called them, could disrupt a meeting by sending out their vibrations against the speaker to make it so he couldn't talk. They could paralyze him or give him a heart attack or even kill him. The white *chelas* would be battling these black adepts, trying to counteract their thought transmissions, these waves they sent out. It sounded like he was demented when he talked like this, but he referred to these adepts all the time."

If Brother XII possessed the powers he described to Davenport would he use them against his enemies?

The answer came during Wilson's preliminary hearing before Judge C. H. Beevor-Potts. Though this particular incident didn't find its way into the official transcripts of the case, Thomas P. Morton, the lawyer acting against Brother XII, was in the midst of addressing the court when he was inexplicably stricken. "He had some papers in his hand and all of a sudden, he started to shake and he collapsed on the floor and lay there as if he'd been knocked out," Victor B.

Harrison recalled, "and a moment or two later, three or four people sitting on the low bench which he had occupied collapsed, some right on the bench, and two, I think, went over the edge of the bench and onto the floor."

Harrison was astonished by what he'd just witnessed. "This is a very extraordinary performance," he recalled thinking. At that moment, Brother XII emerged from the audience and stalked across the police court floor. He approached Harrison and held out his hand to shake hands. "This is an awful state of affairs," he said. "They're trying to prosecute me, but there's nothing in it, and you're going to be appointed by the Crown to prosecute this case at the assizes."

Brother XII's prediction proved correct. "How he knew, I haven't the faintest idea," Harrison later reflected. "He was a most remarkable man."

The lawyer rebuffed Brother XII's conciliatory gesture. "Don't talk to me," he replied. "Go away. I don't want to be bothered by you."

In the midst of the confusion, Brother XII returned to his seat, while Beevor-Potts attempted to restore order. Harrison recalls that the shocked magistrate also succumbed to Brother XII's spell and that he "growled like a dog," but managed to say in a rather shaky voice, "This court is adjourned."

Three weeks later, on December 6, 1928, during the James Lippincott case, Brother XII again lashed out in court with his occult powers. The former Foundation member was suing Wilson for $450 in wages that he claimed was owed to him for his three months of work at the Mandieh Settlement, though Brother XII maintained that Lippincott's work was voluntarily performed.

Lippincott's most important witness was Coulson Turnbull, who'd made a special trip from Vancouver to appear. He probably didn't relish the prospect of testifying, since he'd been badly shaken up by the note that Brother XII had left for him at the Hotel Georgia threatening to disclose the most intimate details of his private life and suggesting he disappear from British Columbia by the shortest route—off the end of the wharf.

Like Benner, Turnbull planned to continue the work of the Aquarian Foundation, but in a new form. He believed that traditional theology would be replaced in the future by a religion based on myth, symbol and allegory. "I am now undertaking the most difficult task in this incarnation," he wrote to one of his students in California. "I shall continue the outer work in a series of monthly Instructions, 'Letters of Understanding.' I have been engaged in research work into the ancient Egyptian Mysteries—this will come out in the Instructions I shall issue."

But Turnbull hadn't impressed Lippincott's estranged wife, Louise, who'd returned to Los Angeles after her claim against her husband had been dismissed. In a letter to Attorney-General R.H. Pooley about her husband's involvement in the Aquarian Foundation, she stated that Turnbull had counselled Lippincott to reject marriage: "He wrote my husband's horoscope, telling him he should be free at any cost and many more things to urge him to leave me. He is a very bad man and goes to any length to further his own ends. He told me himself that he knew Mr. L. was not just right, but refused to help me."

Louise had nothing good to say about any of the Foundation members: "This whole crowd, Mr. Pooley, are a bad lot. The higher-ups are simply preying on weak mental cases for personal gain. Wilson, England, Lucas—they're all the same. In fact, they did all they could against me. Therefore, I was amused when I see Mr. Lucas claims all this trouble in the cult is over the ideas of marriage, etc. Not one of them before felt a married man had any obligation towards a wife."

Judge C. H. Barker called the court to order. Wilson was represented by Frank Cunliffe, Lippincott by Thomas P. Morton. On the stand, Lippincott testified that he'd built a log cabin for Wilson on Valdes, and had generally been at his beck and call, taking supplies to and from the Mandieh

Settlement. He said Wilson had told him he'd pay him well, and had even promised him twenty-five acres of land on the island as a gift because he considered him one of his most trustworthy followers. But whenever Lippincott had brought up the subject of wages, Wilson got angry: "He gave so many contradictory orders that I couldn't get along with him. After a row, we both expressed a mutual desire to quit."

When Cunliffe questioned Lippincott about his wife, Lippincott explained that he'd had trouble with her, that she'd tried to prosecute him, and that the case had been thrown out in the local courts.

"As a matter of fact, you were in hiding from your wife?"

"I was not."

"Didn't you tell Wilson that you wanted to be on the island so that your wife couldn't find you, and didn't you receive a letter from Lucas telling you that you'd better come out and take your medicine?"

Lippincott said he couldn't remember.

In answer to another question, Lippincott acknowledged that the Foundation wasn't supposed to be a remunerative organization. He admitted that he hadn't asked for wages initially, and had turned over the proceeds from the sale of his chart, "Astrology is the Clock of Destiny," to the Society.

Coulson Turnbull was sworn in. Since he'd been living on Valdes during the time Lippincott was working there, his testimony was vital to Lippincott's case.

Morton asked Turnbull about the arrangement that had existed between Wilson and Lippincott with respect to wages.

What happened next has been described by a number of eye-witnesses. The big astrologer was about to give testimony for Lippincott when he started to tremble and suddenly fainted in the witness box, crashing to the floor with a groan and a thud.

The courtroom was in a pandemonium as his wife Cecilia rushed to the witness box to help her stricken husband. She knelt over him as he lay on the floor, wrestling with an imaginary assailant. According to a reporter, she urged him to get a grip on himself and repeatedly assured him that the "evil man" could not harm him.

Dr. Earl Hall was hastily summoned and applied smelling salts to Turnbull's nostrils. The astrologer revived and was slowly helped to his feet, before being taken out of the courtroom.

The commotion gradually subsided and proceedings resumed, but Turnbull did not recover sufficiently to return as a witness.

Edward Lucas was next to take the stand. He described Lippincott's work on Valdes, and said he'd heard Wilson state on a number of occasions that he intended to pay the various individuals who had worked for him.

"You wouldn't say that Wilson's conversation about paying certain ones bound him legally?" Barker asked. Lucas replied that he didn't think it did.

Wilson then took the stand and denied that any contract, either expressed or implied, existed between him and Lippincott. He claimed that Lippincott had volunteered his services, and reiterated that he was under no financial obligation to the plaintiff.

Frank Cunliffe reviewed the case. He pointed out that Lippincott hadn't asked for wages until after the crisis at the headquarters and that the court had to prove that it was the intention of both parties that the plaintiff be paid.

T. P. Morton stood up to summarize Lippincott's case. He had only just started to address the magistrate when he suddenly halted his delivery in mid-speech.

Judge Barker looked at him quizzically, waiting for him to continue, but the lawyer simply stood there, immobilized, blinking in confusion as he tried to collect his thoughts.

The only sound in court was the embarrassed rustling of papers as the court staff waited for him to resume his legal argument.

"This is ridiculous," Morton finally stammered, "but I've forgotten what I was saying!"

"You were telling the court–" Cunliffe prompted him.

Morton shook his head helplessly and shuffled back to his seat, baffled by the loss of his faculties.

Judge Barker announced his verdict. Since there was no significant difference between the evidence of Wilson and that of Lippincott, and since the burden of proof was on Lippincott, he would render judgment in favour of Wilson.

Barker declared the court adjourned. Immediately, conversation erupted as everyone began to discuss Turnbull's collapse and Morton's inexplicable mental lapse.

Wilson and his chauffeur, a burly Swiss named Walter Miller, pushed through the crowd and exited the courtroom. As they started down the courthouse steps, Miller stumbled and fell heavily down the steps, dislocating his shoulder.

Miller was immediately taken to the Nanaimo hospital, while Brother XII was driven away by George Hobart.

The newspaper reporters quizzed the disciples for an explanation of the startling events that had just occurred. Although reluctant to talk, they admitted that they believed the incidents, including the chauffeur's fall, were caused by Brother XII's occult powers, but that was as much as they were prepared to tell the curious reporters.

"TWO COLLAPSE IN COURTROOM," proclaimed the headline in The Province the following day. "DEFENDANT WINS. TALK OF OCCULT POWER WHEN ACTION BROUGHT AGAINST AQUARIAN PRESIDENT."

Brother XII's startling demonstration of his powers wasn't lost on his followers, especially the ones who had broken away and feared his reprisals. Both Frederick Pope and Sidney Sprey-Smith, who'd come out from England with the original party in the spring of 1927, took these latest events as their sign to leave.

Pope, the shy and effeminate interior decorator—he'd been nicknamed "Lucy"—had always wanted to escape. According to Edward Lucas, Wilson had threatened to kill him if he ever tried. Nonetheless, one night under cover of darkness, Pope slipped away from the headquarters and made his way back to England.

"Poor Fred!" Frances Lucas recalls. "I remember my father laughing about it. He chuckled, 'Fred ran like a frightened rabbit!'"

Sidney Sprey-Smith also feared Brother XII's retribution. The bumbling and eccentric ex-British Army captain took refuge at Peggy Reynolds's boarding house in Nanaimo. He stayed on there, unable to make the final break and return to England.

"He was from a good family," her daughter, Margaret Salwyn, says. "He was educated at Sandhurst and had been an officer in the army in India. But Brother XII had such a hold over him, he was terrified to leave. My mother had to buy the ticket for him. Even then, he said to her: 'What if The Brother wills the boat down!' He really believed he had that much power."

The day after the Lippincott case, Lucas and Cunliffe met in Cunliffe's office in the Imperial Building in Nanaimo to discuss a negotiated settlement to the dispute. Lucas explained that Von Platen and DeLuce would submit their resignations as Governors of the Foundation if Wilson conveyed to them the registered titles to their property at Cedar. Wilson was prepared to do this, Cunliffe said, but only if the Governors withdrew their petition to the government to have the Society dissolved. He also insisted they agree to publish a legal notice in the Vancouver, Victoria, and Nanaimo newspapers, announcing their resignations as Governors and disclaiming all interest in the Foundation. In addition, they would be required to sign a quit-claim in respect of any present or future interest in the Society's assets.

The next day, after talking over Wilson's terms with Von Platen and DeLuce, Lucas wrote to Cunliffe, advising him that a negotiated settlement was impossible under the conditions they'd discussed: "Mr. Von Platen takes the position that he has been grossly libelled all over America in the letters circulated by Mr. Wilson, and that the very least he should do is endeavour to compel Wilson to carry out his pledge that the Aquarian Foundation be dissolved."

Lucas, who'd been hoping that the Society could be dissolved voluntarily, was far from enthusiastic about having to spend more time and money on litigation in order to resolve the dispute: "I guess we will have to put on our worn armour and hop into the fray."

△   △   △

At 11:30 on the morning of December 12, 1928, the members of the provincial cabinet, led by Premier Simon Fraser Tolmie, assembled in the executive chambers of the Parliament Buildings in Victoria to hear the application to dissolve the Aquarian Foundation. The cabinet members had already reviewed the evidence submitted with the petition; now they would hear the arguments from the opposing sides. The tremendous publicity given the Aquarian Foundation meant that the government was being closely watched to see whether or not it would continue to sanction the activities of British Columbia's most notorious religious cult.

Edward Lucas spoke first. He argued that Wilson had violated the principles of the Society and wasn't fulfilling the purposes for which it had originally been founded. He claimed that Brother XII's teachings represented a threat to public morality and read excerpts from Wilson's article on marriage to prove his point. He also read extracts from the numerous attacks Wilson had made in his published writings upon various individuals, including Von Platen, Comfort, Benner, Turnbull, and Albert Smythe. Lucas accused Wilson of trying to start a religious war in the United States and of preaching anarchy in pursuit of his political goals. He pointed out that the Society's literature prominently stated that it was incorporated by the province of British Columbia. Lucas urged the cabinet to intervene in order to stop Wilson from spreading his insidious propaganda across America, and asked for the appointment of a receiver to take charge of the assets.

Frank Cunliffe spoke against the application. He argued that the legal grounds given in the petition were not sufficient to justify cancelling the Society's charter, and that a forced dissolution of the Society would violate the rights of its members. His client was not necessarily opposed to winding up the Society, he explained, but wished to do so in a manner which would protect the interests of all parties involved. Cunliffe stressed that where applicable, Wilson intended to return to the original donors the contributions they'd made to the Society.

Cunliffe sat down and the subject of all the controversy rose to speak. Edward Arthur Wilson himself would present the case for the Aquarian Foundation.

"Gentlemen: in the matter of the petition for the dissolution of this Society now before this honourable Council, there are aspects of the greatest importance which must have much weight in your decision, but which we have hitherto had no opportunity of presenting. They are points which are concerned with spiritual and moral values rather than legalities. They are not only of great importance in this issue, they are to us by far the most important aspects of this whole matter. Because of their nature, no legal counsel can present them. I alone and in person can do that, and I ask the opportunity of so doing before a decision is given by this honourable Council."

Wilson told the cabinet members that although he stood alone before them, he was the representative of thousands of people, that he pleaded their cause rather than his own in a case that so dearly affected their happiness and well-being.

"The petition which has been made to this honourable Council *is an instrument of untruth and wilful deception,*" he declared. "The alleged grounds for its presentation are not the real grounds, as I will presently prove. In itself, it is proof of the real *characters and motives* of the petitioners."

He went on to describe the petitioners as "a band of trouble-makers from Los Angeles." He called Von Platen and DeLuce "alien immigrants of more than questionable character," and Lucas "their hired tool—a man who has sold honour, sold loyalty, sold friendship, for a fee." He accused them of attempting to depose him in order to gain control of the Society: "This petition is, so far as they are concerned, a last resort; its object is to bankrupt and destroy what they have failed to steal for themselves."

In proof of his charges, Wilson gave his own detailed account of the events that had led up to the attack upon the Work. He claimed that the petitioners had neither equity in, nor any moral right to the assets of the Society. To support his argument, he gave a brief outline of the history of the Foundation, explaining how he'd established the first groups in England and formed sections in Switzerland and several other European countries. He'd subsequently organized sections in the United States, Canada, South Africa, Australia, and New Zealand, and linked up scores of isolated members in places as widely separated as West Africa, Egypt, India, Burma, and the islands of the Pacific.

"I have written every book and every Instruction ever published by this Society," he declared, "and every article of importance in *The Chalice* magazine. In actual and veritable fact, I AM THE AQUARIAN FOUNDATION, and apart from myself it has no plan, no driving force, and no existence."

What had the petitioners done to entitle them to any right or interest in the Society? he asked. "With one exception only, they have made no material contribution beyond the small monthly payments made by all members, though I am bound, in fairness, to acknowledge the legal assistance rendered to us by Lucas before he deserted this Cause for that of our enemies."

Any "rights" the petitioners might claim, he continued,

they owed to himself alone, since it was he who had appointed them and given them the opportunity to prove themselves in the Work:

"I have been accused by these petitioners of failing to adhere to the principles of our Order and of having made attacks upon certain individuals. In reply to those accusations, I would remind them of the words I wrote long since—'*We fight not for ourselves, but for that which is committed to us.*' I have repudiated more than one attack and lying accusation made against this Work. I have exposed the individuals who brought these accusations against us, even as I will expose these petitioners themselves for what they truly are. Beyond such personal references as are necessary to the defence of this organization, I will make no personal defence. I have in all things a clear conscience—I have no need to make defence."

Wilson told the council that the Aquarian Foundation was an organization dedicated to the uplifting and betterment of humanity. He reminded the cabinet members that he'd given them petitions and written evidence from hundreds of members of the Society who repudiated the action of the petitioners, and that the stigma which would fall upon the Society if the petition were allowed would affect many thousands of earnest and sincere souls.

"Gentlemen, in the interests of equity and true justice, I claim that these thousands have a right to consideration, that their voice should be heard. If the scales of Justice are to weigh with impartiality and righteousness, then the weight of their Cause must be thrown into the scale. They appeal to you that you shall not allow the greed and fear of these conspirators to inflict upon them a grave injustice and a deep distress."

Finally, Wilson reiterated that the claims of the petitioners were a mere legality. He concluded:

"It is still my intention to dissolve the outer Society myself, but under such conditions and in such a manner as shall not subject it to the rapacious plunderings of these petitioners. I am more anxious to be rid of them than they are of me, and if every other measure fails, I will myself petition this honourable council to effect its dissolution at such time and upon such conditions as shall ensure justice for the membership of this Society as a whole, and in every part of the world."

Premier Tolmie thanked Wilson for his presentation, and assured him the cabinet would consider the facts in the case very carefully and reach a decision as quickly as possible. The fate of the Aquarian Foundation now rested in the hands of the British Columbia government.

△   △   △

In the spring of 1928, Thomas Smith, a thirty-six-year-old businessman from Hollywood, California, arrived at the Aquarian Foundation headquarters driving a brand new green and black Oldsmobile roadster. Smith's wife had recently divorced him after only three months of marriage, claiming that he had threatened her with bodily injury, was insanely jealous, bragged to her about his improper relations with other women and had caused her to have a nervous breakdown. Smith showed Brother XII letters of credit worth ten thousand dollars and was invited to join the group at the headquarters. The other members were not so easily impressed—with his deadpan face and coarse manner, Smith was generally considered to be a repulsive character.

"I thought he was a horrible man," Margaret Salwyn recalls. "He'd been in World War I, and I heard him telling my grandmother: 'Men, women, or children; it made no difference—I could take a drink of water afterwards and forget it!'"

Smith's hobby was oil painting. He fancied himself an artist and soon became a familiar figure at Cedar-by-the-Sea, perched in front of his easel, painting the landscape. But he only stayed at the headquarters for a few months; at the beginning of the summer he moved to Victoria, to the great relief of everyone at the Center.

In Victoria, Smith met a twenty-two-year-old movie usherette named Gladys Barlow at a high school dance. He asked her out, and the two were soon seeing each other nearly every day, driving around Victoria in Smith's automobile, going to parties and the beach, and parking in secluded spots at night, where they engaged in heavy petting. The relationship was definitely physical, but was never consummated. Gladys refused Smith's demands for intimacy and rejected his proposal of marriage. At the end of the summer, she broke off the romance and Smith returned to Los Angeles.

Three months later, Smith returned to Victoria, determined to see Gladys again. He'd already sent her an engagement ring, which she refused to accept, leaving it at the Customs House in Victoria. Smith telephoned and begged to see her, threatening to kill himself if she refused. Gladys went out with him two nights in a row. On the third night, on the pretext of taking her to see a friend, Smith drove her to an unfurnished house in Oak Bay, which he'd rented that morning. When he pulled into the overgrown lot beside the dark and vacant house, Gladys immediately suspected something was wrong. She got out of the car and started to run towards the street, but Smith caught up to her, dragged her back to the house, and pushed her through the front door, snarling, "I'm going to get you tonight!"

In the bedroom, he threw her down onto a bare mattress and started pulling off her clothes. "I'll kill you!" he said, "and I'll kill myself—and maybe that is the best way!" Gladys tried to scream, but Smith clamped his hand over her mouth. "You do love me, don't you!" he said. Gladys shook her head. Smith insisted she tell him she loved him. "What is the point of saying it?" she protested. Smith's hands closed around her throat: *"Never mind, I want to hear you say it!"* Panic-stricken, Gladys told Smith she loved him. He then forced himself upon the terrified girl.

When it was all over, Gladys picked up the scattered pieces of her clothing and dressed. She followed Smith into the living room, where he lit a fire and played some gramophone records. In a bizarre engagement ceremony, he then slipped a cheap diamond ring on Gladys's finger. Fearful of provoking him, she pretended to be flattered by his attentions. After planning the details of their wedding, Smith told her he wanted to drive back to her parents' house and announce their forthcoming marriage.

Smith drove Gladys home. As the pair walked up the sidewalk together, Gladys pointed to a rose bush and asked Smith to pick her a rose. When he stopped to pluck it, she rushed up the front steps and into the house. Locking the door behind her, she screamed to her parents, *"Don't let that man in! He'll kill me!"* Smith ran back to his car and quickly drove off.

The following morning, Constable Frederick Boyt of the B.C. Provincial Police noticed a man answering Smith's description standing on the CPR wharf in Nanaimo waiting for the 6:00 A.M. ferry to Vancouver. After questioning him and examining the contents of his car, Boyt arrested him on a charge of rape. Smith was returned to Victoria under police escort to stand trial.

Smith's arrest made headlines in the Victoria and Nanaimo newspapers. The reports identified him as a former member of the Aquarian Foundation who still owned property at Cedar. This publicity linking one of Brother XII's followers to such a sordid incident couldn't have come at a worse time for Wilson, just as the cabinet was in the middle of making its decision about the Foundation's future.

Cyril F. Davie, a Vancouver Island lawyer and member of the legislature, had been lobbying the cabinet on Wilson's behalf. He advised Frank Cunliffe that he'd been unable to influence the cabinet members in light of "a recent development concerning a young girl, now in the charge of the police, whose unfortunate condition the police allege to be traced to the Aquarian Foundation." Davie said he couldn't speak to the truth of the charge, but "the alleged immorality of the whole affair is so strongly entrenched in the minds of the cabinet that it became useless for me to labour any further argument against the dissolution."

△   △   △

As the year 1928 drew to a close, many commentators confidently predicted that Brother XII's career was finished. Henry Stokes, editor of *The Oriental & Esoteric Library Critic*, published in Washington, D.C., reviewed the peculiar events in his article, "The Brother XII Bubble Bursts." Commenting on the Osiris-Isis controversy, he observed sardonically, "Whether there was an effectual guarantee that the proposed son Horus would not be a daughter does not appear." Stokes believed that the entire episode was a useful example of the dangers facing the unwary spiritual seeker:

> Some of the members may have learned a salutary lesson; others being born suckers will continue to be such, and will bite at the next bait offered. There are many who cannot resist the allurements of persons, be they men or women, possessed of self-assurance and of a commanding or persuasive mien, who think, or pretend to think, that they are in communication with beings on a higher plane, especially when they clothe themselves in garments of light and back up their assertions with ancient truths, but always implying, "I am a new Messenger." It is worth thinking over by others than those of the Aquarian Foundation.

Stokes was nevertheless intrigued by Brother XII:

> It is not my business to diagnose the character of the Brother XII. Was he simply a shrewd imposter who finally overplayed his part? Was he really convinced, as many another is, of the reality of his mission and of his psychic revelations, and did he finally fall a victim to them, finding an excuse in the idea that he was the god Osiris incarnated? Was he, as has been maintained, the victim of the "Dark Forces"? Was he simply a fool beguiled by a woman? These are interesting questions which may be left to his followers to settle. . .

Meanwhile, it appears certain that the Brother XII has signed his own death warrant, and as he alone was the supposed link between the Masters and the White Lodge, the affair will go to pieces and leave not a wrack behind. . .

But Stokes, like many others, seriously underestimated Brother XII. The strange career of the retired English sea-captain was not over yet.

△ △ △

The British Columbia government was looking into the legal implications of dissolving the Aquarian Foundation. H.M. Garrett, the Registrar of Companies, advised the Attorney-General that the Society's objects were perfectly legitimate and that dissolving it because of its political or religious tenets would be a mistake. He pointed out to Pooley that if the Society were dissolved, its assets would revert to the Crown, but that such an action would be a novel precedent and perhaps a dangerous one.

"In my opinion," Garrett concluded, "the only grounds on which it would be proper for the Lieutenant-Governor in Council to act is the decency or not of the Society's operations—whether or not it is an immoral organization. Even so, there is nothing to prevent Wilson from reorganizing the Society on an unincorporated basis and doing the same thing again. It seems to me that, if possible, criminal proceedings should be instituted."

Edward Lucas was growing impatient awaiting the government's decision. He had expected an announcement within days of the hearing. The weeks passed and there was still no word. He finally wrote to the Attorney-General, asking what was causing the delay. He urged the government to act quickly in the matter, observing somewhat bitterly that "Mr. Wilson, of course, is carrying on his work both at Cedar and at Valdes Island, and is proclaiming by circulars that his work for the emancipation of humanity has been successfully established."

CHAPTER
IX
City of Refuge

Brother XII's new tugboat, the *Khuenaten*, cast off from the dock below Nanaimo's Malaspina Hotel and headed out into the busy harbour. The little coal town quickly faded into the smoky haze as the fifty horsepower Fairbanks-Morse diesel propelled the sturdy vessel out past Protection Island and the bare rock of Gallows Point. The salt spray fell hissing into its wake as the tug rounded Jack Point and headed south into Northumberland Channel, towards its destination of Valdes Island.

In the first three months of 1929, Brother XII had resumed work at the Mandieh Settlement, transporting supplies there with the *Khuenaten* and rapidly building up the colony. The government still hadn't announced whether or not it would dissolve the Aquarian Foundation, but he was continuing his work regardless. On this particular morning in April, he was taking Mary Connally to Valdes to show her the progress that had been made at the new settlement. With Walter Miller at

229

the helm, Brother XII and Mary could stand in the bracing air of the tug's open afterdeck and drink in the magnificent beauty of British Columbia's Gulf Islands.

The *Khuenaten* moved east, beneath the massive sandstone cliffs of Gabriola Island. Entering False Narrows, it swept past the floating kelp beds that lined the shores of Mudge Island, discharging their pungent aroma into the salty air. Built over the winter in Victoria, the forty-foot tugboat had already proved its worth, hauling supplies to Valdes in the roughest winter conditions. The exact derivation of the name *Khuenaten* isn't known, but Brother XII may have named his tugboat for the Egyptian god of water, *Khnoom*—the moist power. Or perhaps he chose the name in honour of the pharaoh Akhenaten, the religious reformer and mystic with whom he strongly identified.

Emerging from False Narrows, the *Khuenaten* headed across Pylades Channel towards the rocky ramparts of Valdes Island. This coastline had been explored in 1791 by the Spanish captain Don Cayetano Valdes, but thousands of years earlier, some say, King Solomon's navies had sailed here all the way from Africa in search of gold, their crimson sails billowing in the wind. Gliding through the swirling waters of the pass between Cordero Point and Josef Point, the *Khuenaten* headed south along the foreshore, slipping in behind the rocky shelf of Kendrick Island, its sandstone ledges home to nesting cormorants. In a tiny bay known locally as Dogfish Bay, the tug dropped anchor and Brother XII rowed Mary ashore.

A trail led up from the pebble beach into the forest. Salaal and sword ferns crowded the path, and other trails branched off to cabins nestled in the underbrush where individual colonists had chosen to build. After a ten-minute walk, the trail came out into a large open area that faced the Strait of Georgia. There was a thick carpet of moss underfoot and the granite outcroppings were covered with lichens. The sounds of hammering and sawing echoed across the clearing as carpenters framed up an assembly hall and other workers constructed log cabins in various locations around the clearing. Under a tarpaulin that flapped in the breeze, the women of the colony prepared lunch on a large cast-iron stove. Setting down their tools, the workmen seated themselves on either side of a long trestle table, digging hungrily into steaming platters of food. After Brother XII escorted Mary around the settlement, he led her to his house, a five-room log cabin at the top of the ridge.

Inside the comfortable interior, tea was served from a table set with fine linen and Limoges china. Brother XII explained to Mary that the Mandieh Settlement would now be called the Brothers' Center, after those Masters of Wisdom or Elder Brothers who were behind the Work. He'd decided to change the name because of the unfavourable publicity the colony had received, but its purpose remained the same: the settlement would be the actual physical location where the Elder Brothers would incarnate, bringing a new spiritual impulse to mankind and giving instruction to the selected individuals who would take part in the work of restoration succeeding the breakup of the existing order. All this was fully explained in *The Brothers' School,* a paper he issued to prospective disciples, which outlined the requirements for admittance:

"True discipleship means a life dedicated to the service of humanity; it is diametrically opposed to the preferences of the personal self. No compromise between these two is possible. Therefore, the first requirement is THE SURRENDER OF PERSONAL POSSESSIONS, an actual not a theoretical surrender. If the disciple is truly dedicated, it follows that all he has is included in the dedication of himself. This is the first requirement and it constitutes at once a safeguard and a test which the insincere will be unable to face."

The Brothers' Center would be a self-contained spiritual community, independent of the outside world. Individual members would be able to surrender personal possessions because all the needs of the body—food, clothing, and shelter—would be provided for. By putting away the attractions and allurements of the world, the disciple would, at the same time, have loosed from his shoulders the burden of its problems and anxieties. Provisions would come out of a common fund, and all buildings or cabins put up would automatically become the property of the community. Cabins were expected to be simple and unpretentious, avoiding nonessentials. Crops would be cultivated, and everyone would be expected to help in the general work and to comply with the rules and requirements necessary to ensure harmony.

The applicant to the Brothers' Center had to be prepared to completely surrender all other interests and activities: "The disciple must be ready to 'live the life,' a life of service and devotion to one end. None may live this life in part and the life of the outer world in part. The bars have not been let down because we have come into the Western world. Had you essayed to come to us in Tibet or elsewhere, all that would have been taken for granted. Only the gold of pure and unselfish devotion will pass the test."

Brother XII declared that perhaps one person in a million would be able to fulfil the conditions for entry: "The real occultist is born, just as is the musical genius, the artist, or the Teacher." In answer to the question, "Who may qualify?" he replied: "THE CHILDREN." These would be born to faithful members of the group, he explained, and would be raised in an environment conducive to their development, away from the spiritually devastating conditions of the outside world: "The effects of eighteen or twenty years of ordinary training are so terrible from a spiritual standpoint that they permanently disable all but those rare souls, the born Servers of the Race, and even these are hindered to a degree." Brother XII told Mary that the formation of the Brothers' Center was an event of great significance.

Later that day, Brother XII and Mary travelled in the *Khuenaten* southeast from Valdes across Pylades Channel to the DeCourcy group of islands, which lay at the north end of Trincomali Channel. The soft sandstone cliffs of the islands had been eroded into strange shapes by the wind and waves, giving the shoreline an eerie, moonlike quality. The Indians who had inhabited these islands had buried their dead in crevices that ran deep into the rock. Brother XII explained to Mary that there was a deserted farm in the center of DeCourcy Island that had good soil; if it could be made operational, it would provide the colony with all the food it required. He told her that these islands, lying directly between Cedar and Valdes, were strategic. If the Center could acquire them, it would have a self-contained unit of property, and members would be able to come and go as they pleased, free from outside interference.

The *Khuenaten* carefully negotiated the narrow channel between the long spines of rock guarding the entrance to the lagoon at the south end of DeCourcy. This lovely spot was known locally as "The Haven." The waves lapped gently against the warm sandstone and all around the lagoon, the foliage rose up rich and luxuriant. The staccato chatter of kingfishers filled the cove. At the head of the bay, the emerald-green waters shone jewel-like in the sun. Brother XII explained to Mary that he wanted this idyllic sanctuary to be the new headquarters of the colony.

Mary was seduced by the beauty of the islands and by Brother XII's vision of the future of the Work. Returning to Nanaimo, she arranged to purchase DeCourcy and Ruxton Island, the two largest islands in the DeCourcy group, comprising 669 acres, from the estate of Nanaimo pioneer William Minter Flewitt, for the sum of ten thousand dollars. Mary put the title in the name of Brother XII's Secretary-Treasurer, Thomas Cranmer Williams, rather than in her own name.

"I wished my name kept out of it," she later explained. "There'd been so much talk and notoriety, and my family hadn't known anything about what I had done, and I didn't want them to know. The deeds were made out to Thomas Cranmer Williams to keep anything from being known."

A few weeks later, Mary left British Columbia for California.

But the acquisition of the DeCourcy Islands meant that Brother XII could proceed with his plans to expand his work. He now devoted his full attention to establishing his new colony, an island kingdom set amidst the spectacular natural beauty of Canada's Pacific coast.

△   △   △

A number of members of the Aquarian Foundation who had remained loyal to Brother XII through the recent crisis now arrived to take up permanent residence at the Brothers' Center. They included a commercial artist named Herbert Jefferson and his wife, Dora. The Jeffersons had been the secretaries of a Toronto group, but upon receiving Brother XII's invitation, they sacrificed their house for a fraction of its value and boarded the train for Vancouver.

"He always insisted that he be paid in gold," Jefferson recounts. "Before I left Toronto, a woman who was a very keen member said to me, 'Now, Brother, I want you to take this money and give it to Brother XII.' There was about five hundred dollars in gold, so I bought a money belt that I wore around my waist, and put these gold pieces in it so they wouldn't get stolen. I handed it over to him when I got there, but he never invited her out. Ha! She was fanatically attracted to the movement, but she never received an invitation!"

The Jeffersons were met in Nanaimo by George Hobart, who'd known the couple in Toronto. During the drive to Cedar, he told them how disappointed he was with life at the colony.

"He said to me, 'Bert, the whole thing is a wash-out! It isn't what we thought it was!'" Jefferson recalls. "He was sorry he'd come out in the first place, but he said to me, 'Here I am, and here I've got to stay. I'm just going to make the best of it!' That was the first thing that struck me—that people who had gone out early on felt as if they'd been sold down the river."

The Jeffersons were now in much the same situation as

Hobart. They'd left their old life behind, so when they arrived at Valdes they turned over the little money they had brought and joined the community.

Jefferson and his wife were required to sign a paper declaring that they were there as guests, not employees, and that all work they performed was voluntary. This way, Brother XII ensured that no legal claim could be brought against him for wages or any other compensation.

Jefferson, who was forty-six years old at the time, was assigned to a work crew, cutting a trail across the island from the West Bay to the site of the main settlement. Brother XII planned to eventually widen this trail into a road, so that he could truck supplies directly across the island. Jefferson was unaccustomed to hard physical labour—his usual job was drawing illustrations for the Eaton's mail-order catalogue—but, like Hobart, he resolved to make the best of the situation. He worked hard and enjoyed the strong feeling of camaraderie that existed among the men.

Brother XII gave him another job, building a fence across one section of the property to stop the sheep that belonged to his neighbour to the north, an elderly widow named Amelia Wake, from straying onto his land. "He sent a note to her, saying, 'If you don't keep your sheep out, I can be a bad neighbour, too,'" Jefferson says. "I thought it was quite uncalled for!"

He remembers that one day Brother XII accidentally dropped a cigarette end into a wastepaper basket and it burst into flame. He managed to put it out, but the incident triggered Brother XII's fear of fire. He had Jefferson scrape up and cart away all the moss from the rocks surrounding his house so there would be no chance of it catching fire.

Jefferson and his wife were both keen students of metaphysics. Like many of the disciples who'd accepted the invitation to Valdes, they expected there would be more instruction than there was, even though Brother XII had written that the Brothers' Center was not a school of classrooms or of books, but a school for the soul. The occasional talks that he gave were excellent, but they didn't always satisfy his audience.

"Once he was very good," remembered Jefferson," and Dora said, 'Oh, Brother, just go on a little further and explain a bit more, and then I'll have got something really definite!' 'No,' he said, 'I can't—I can't say any more.' And he wouldn't go on, and that was quite disappointing."

For Jefferson, it was the small incidents that served to illuminate Wilson's character, rather than the grandiose claims to knowledge he might make:

"Dora used to cook for us," he recalls. "One day, she was in the pantry when she heard footsteps behind her. When she turned, there was Brother XII taking a dozen eggs out of the cupboard. 'We haven't any eggs,' he said. 'I thought I'd just borrow these.' Dora said, 'Well, these people here have bought these eggs with their own money. They'll miss them, so will you please return them?' 'Oh, I will, Dora!' he said, 'I will!' But that was sneaky of him—to come and take a carton of eggs. He returned them, but he wouldn't have if she hadn't been there.

"Every week or so, we'd send to Mac & Mac's in Vancouver for our supplies. He'd go down to the boat, look at what had been brought in and pick out what he wanted. If he needed a carton of cigarettes, he'd take it. Tom Williams would ask, 'Where are my cigarettes?' Brother XII would say, 'Oh, Tom, I took them. I was out of cigarettes. You put in for another carton next time.' He hadn't ordered them, he hadn't paid for them—but the poor sucker that had ordered and paid for them never got them!"

One day, Jefferson and another worker were sent by Brother XII to DeCourcy Island to clear some land. He dropped them off on the island with a thermos of tea and some sandwiches and said he'd pick them up that evening. But he never showed up at the appointed time. The two men found an old well for drinking water, dug for clams, and slept in the deserted farmhouse, battling hordes of hungry mosquitoes. Three days later, Brother XII remembered he'd left them on the island and returned in the *Khuenaten* to pick them up.

"All these jobs he gave us to do were tests," Jefferson explains. "He'd say, 'Now, you'll be tested. I'll give you something to do which may appear to be hard for you, or unreasonable, but this is my way of testing you. When you come through with flying colours, then you've passed your initiation and you're ready for further work.'"

So Jefferson stayed on at the Brothers' Center and tried to "live the life" of discipleship, even though he'd concluded from his own observations that the Master, in his own daily life, wasn't living up to the high standards he expected of his disciples.

Another new arrival at the colony was Gertrude Phillips, the widow of a U.S. congressman and a former feature writer for *The Washington Post* and *The New Orleans Picayune*. An astrology columnist for *The San Francisco Examiner*, Gertrude had patented a system for charting the horoscope, *Astrology: The Scientific Basis of Prophecy*. After her husband's death, she devoted much of her time to social work, and hoped to meet in the Aquarian Foundation people with ideals similar to her own. Inspired by Brother XII's writings, she'd already made several large contributions to the Work before arriving in Nanaimo on June 6, 1929, to take up residence at the Center:

"He met me at the Malaspina Hotel and he was very cordial," she related. "And he asked me at once at the hotel how much I had brought. Before this, he had written to me to sacrifice all I could, realize all the cash I could and bring it in. I told him I hadn't been able to bring so very much, but that I had stock which I had arranged to sell. Stock was up then, so I expected to realize a large sum on it. I told him I would turn it into the Work, and he was very much pleased.

"The next day, I went with him on the tug, and the woman

whom he'd introduced as his wife accompanied us on the boat. She called herself Elma Wilson—and they were not good friends at all. They spoke very sharply to each other.

"We arrived at Valdes and he lived in a comfortable house, in the front yard of which there was a tent. I had to live in the tent. There was no heat and it was very uncomfortable. He told me I had to live there until I could build a house.

"Then he asked me if I could cook for some of the men whose wives hadn't come. He said they were very much overworked. When I saw these young men that were so wet and tired and overworked, I was glad to cook for them. The cook stove was out at the back, and I could hear him and this woman quarrelling violently most of the time—everyone could hear it. He was cursing and it was simply terrible. It shocked me.

"One day, he came down to my tent with a letter. He sort of confided in me because I had been a welfare worker and he thought perhaps I would understand. He read this letter aloud to me. He said it was from Myrtle 'B,' and that before I came, she had lived in one of the cottages on Valdes. He said she was his soul mate and that she went insane. He told me that she had had two miscarriages, then he sent her away. And he said, 'I am now sending her two hundred and fifty dollars,' as she was begging him for money.

"And then I asked him, 'Can our Work afford it? Are we to give money to everyone we send out?' And he said, 'Mary Connally has given us the money to buy this island of Valdes for our Work. She is very rich. She is worth about three million. In fact, we have plenty of money to use.'

"And I remember when we went into town, he wore a grey suit. He asked me what I thought of his clothes. 'Don't you think I ought to dress better now?' he said. I asked him if that was his best suit. He said, 'Yes, I was a poor man when I came into the Work. I had nothing to bring in except my brains and the work of my hand.'

"Another time, I had to come to Nanaimo to cash some cheques. He brought me over on the tug. We went past

DeCourcy Island, and he showed me a nice little harbour there. He pointed it out, that it was a good harbour. I said, 'What a pity we don't have a harbour on Valdes. We very much need a harbour.' He smiled and said, 'This is our harbour. Mary Connally has given the money to buy these islands for our Work. This is really our harbour.'"

△   △   △

A sinister figure, who would become a major force in the life of the colony throughout its latter days, now entered the picture. Mabel Skottowe was a thirty-nine-year-old redhead with a harsh voice and an abrasive manner. She was adept at manipulating men and using her feminine charms to get what she wanted. Born Edith Mabel Rowbotham in Lancashire, England, in 1890, she'd emigrated to Canada with her parents, settling on a farm outside Lemsford, Saskatchewan. Her father became a prosperous farmer and later a Justice of the Peace. Mabel taught school for ten years in places like Battleford, Broadway, Eagle Hills, Lancelot, Macoun, Marengo, Novar, Zealandia, and other small prairie towns. On New Year's day in 1918, she married John Coulson "Percy" Skottowe, a brash and boastful former North-West Mounted Police constable, who was manager of the Union Bank of Canada at Lancer. When he was fired from the bank for a shady loan scheme he devised, the couple moved to Seattle, where Skottowe worked as a clerk for a steamship company. In 1926, the marriage broke up and Mabel went to Florida to live with Skottowe's father, Reverend John Coulson Skottowe, the Episcopalian minister of Saint Katherine's Church in Pensacola. Considered a nonconformist by his congregation, Skottowe was a strict vegetarian, taught reincarnation, and was regarded as a mystic. The author of *Religious Brevities for Those Who Think*, he undoubtedly influenced Mabel, who had always been an ardent student of the occult. At some point, she adopted the letter "Z" as her mystical name, the significance of which remains a mystery.

In Florida, Mabel met Roger Painter, the owner of a wholesale poultry business that grossed over a million dollars a year. Long-haired, bearded and saturnine, Painter was known as "The Poultry King of Florida." He was a former stage hypnotist with a penchant for magic and the occult. He was also a compulsive womanizer; he'd been married five times and had carried on numerous affairs. He and Mabel were drawn to each other, entering into a stormy love affair. In 1927, the two became the divisional secretaries of the Aquarian Foundation for Florida. They remained loyal to Brother XII throughout the crisis with the Governors, and in the spring of 1929 they received an invitation to come to the headquarters in British Columbia.

By this time, Painter had already been making regular contributions to Brother XII, who often wrote asking for money. Painter would promptly send a cheque for five or ten thousand dollars or more. He kept no track of the amount he gave, but when he left Florida, he turned over his poultry business to his brothers and went north with ninety thousand dollars in cash to give to Brother XII.

From the beginning, the two new arrivals were in a different league from Herbert Jefferson or Gertrude Philips, or indeed from any of the other new arrivals. Brother XII recognized them as fellow "Brothers" destined to play a major role in his future work. Mabel Skottowe was Brother III, and Roger Painter was Brother IX. After the defection of the other Governors, each of whom was to have been the physical channel for the energy of one of the twelve Brothers of the White Lodge, Brother XII needed to find other suitable individuals to fill the vacancies. In any case, their arrival was an event of major importance, sealed for good measure when Painter turned in ninety thousand dollars to the Work.

Brother XII claimed to have known and worked with Painter in a past life. He wrote to Mary Connally: "To me there has recently come a Brother whom in the past I knew and worked with as *John de la Valette*—after whom the old town of Valetta in Malta was named. We have renewed old memories and are now cooperating in the work I have outlined."

Jean de la Valette was the first Grand Master of the Knights of Malta, one of the most powerful religious orders in Europe during the Middle Ages; he had heroically defended Malta against the Turks during the Ottoman siege of 1565.

On the rugged windswept shores of Valdes Island, far from that era in time and place, Roger Painter, true to Brother XII's recollection of their shared past, had a vision of an island in the Mediterranean and a long road winding down from the mountains. Down this road on a hot afternoon, a long train of Knights in plumed helmets, their swords and shields glinting in the sun, moved steadily towards one central point—the ancient city of Valetta on the island of Malta.

In the same letter, Brother XII explained to Mary the significance of this historical period to their own work:

> If you have an opportunity, secure and read a good history of that period, and especially anything dealing with the Knights of Malta or the Knights Templar. It is true that you will only be able to get the *shell* of those great endeavours, but even at that it will be interesting and instructive reading. If you read between the lines, you will be able to understand something of the purity of their aspirations and the selflessness of their devotion to their Order. Histories are biased and politically controlled, and if you remember that the last vestige of that Order was suppressed about the close of the eighteenth century by interested governments, you will understand that history will surely pass over their virtues and enlarge upon their defects. The point is this—*the Knights are gathering again;* they have come into incarnation to take up their place in the line of battle we are forming. Many are scattered through the ranks of Freemasonry, and through them, working with us, that Order will soon receive a new life and a great purifying.

Brother XII also spent a great deal of time with Mabel Skottowe. The growing attraction between the two soon became apparent. Painter brooded about it, his past-life link with Wilson no proof against jealousy, while Elma went about her chores tight-lipped. It was obvious the two were about to become lovers.

"She had a tent in the bush," Herbert Jefferson recalls. "We'd be in bed about ten-thirty at night, and we'd hear him going to her tent. He'd leave late that night or else early the next morning."

A few days later, the colonists heard screams from Mabel's tent and ran to help her. They rushed up in time to see Roger Painter burst out of the tent, shaking with rage, and dart off. Inside the tent, they found Mabel, brutally beaten.

Brother XII banished Painter from the colony. The "Poultry King" returned to Florida, consoling himself with a new mistress, twenty-three-year-old Leona Siever. Painter continued to correspond with Brother XII, however, waiting to be summoned back to the colony.

Elma fled to a sympathetic friend in Vancouver—the same Mrs. Reynolds who had run the boarding house in Nanaimo. "I heard my mother open the door," Margaret Salwyn recalls, "and Elma Wilson fell into her arms in tears. 'How could he do such a thing!' she sobbed. 'After all these years—to think he's really like this!'"

Brother XII was unmoved by Elma's grief. In a letter to Mary Connally, he mentioned that "Elma is very probably going to Switzerland in the near future, as I have a request for help from that section which she is very excellently fitted to answer. Also, she feels that an entire change will be a very good thing for her."

In the same letter, he also referred to Myrtle Baumgartner: "There is no possibility that 'M' will ever be able to come out here again. The rule seems to be inexorable that in this Work, if one once fails, there is no recovery in this incarnation. That is so in the instance to which I refer and *I know it.*"

With Elma conveniently occupied elsewhere, Mabel Skottowe now moved in with Brother XII. She became his personal secretary, taking dictation, typing letters, and advising him on the day-to-day running of the colony. She may even have collaborated with him on a book he announced was in preparation at this time, *The Law of Cycles and of Human Generation.* The advertisements for this work, apparently never published, ascribed its authorship to "Two Brothers of the Twelfth Hierarchy." In any event, Brother XII came to rely on Mabel's judgment, and made her the foreman in charge of the work done at the colony. Mabel instructed the disciples to call her "Madame Z" (using the American pronunciation "Zee," with the accent for "Madame" placed on the first syllable) and even had her table napkins monogrammed with a large "Z."

"She was very feminine and very clever at handling men," Herbert Jefferson remembers. "She was an adventuress, really. She took charge of him and jolly well made sure she got what she was after—money and power. They each helped each other to a lower life—in a respectable way, but nevertheless it was a lower life. She was 'bad medicine' and corrupted the whole concern—but she was pretty deep."

The disciples soon discovered that Madame Z, a tireless worker herself, was a harsh task-mistress. She was impatient, short-tempered, and carried a riding crop or quirt, which she didn't hesitate to use when her temper got the better of her. Many of the disciples resented her interference in the affairs of the colony, but they had no choice but to obey her. Brother XII made it clear to them that he considered Mabel his co-worker, with authority equal to his own. If she told them to do something, it was the same as if he'd given the order himself. "She is my eyes, she is my ears, she is my mouth," he declared. "Her orders are my orders. Whatever she says, you are to take as coming from me."

With Madame Z at the helm, Brother XII had time to devote himself to various domestic projects he was eager to complete.

"Have done such a lot of work since you were here," he wrote to Mary Connally. "You would not know the log house—all stained inside and a garden fenced. I formed beautiful soil by draining that little slough, and I shall plant many things next week. . . Valdes is developing by leaps and bounds—many houses up and many people coming in. Excuse this hurried scrawl, but am perpetrating it just before going to bed. All send you their love."

He also had Alfred Barley do some astrological work for Mary, adding his own interpretation to the chart: "Venus (in this progressed figure) is in the twelfth house, house of occultism *par excellence,* and Uranus is in the tenth, and so dignified and very powerful. I take this to mean that you will come into your own, indeed that you have done so in respect to your relations with the Lodge and all it stands for. Knowing this, it will not be difficult to suffer outer ills gladly if need be, for they are of small moment when weighed in the balance with the Realities."

Mary responded by sending Wilson a number of beautiful gifts, such as a blue glass vase and stand, and a pair of silver candlesticks, which he mentioned in another letter: "I have at last straightened up my room, indeed the whole house on Valdes, so that you would not know it. The teapot and the candlesticks have a shelf all to themselves, and the lotus box is on a small table in the center of the big window with the blue cloth under it. All my books are fixed on a good shelf, so now the place is fit to live in. Love to you from all here, and COME BACK SOON."

Mary owned 160 acres of property in the San Bernardino Valley in California, which Brother XII believed would be an ideal spot for a southern center for the Work. On June 17, 1929, while staying in Reno, she made a further contribution to the cause, deeding the property to him for the sum of ten dollars.

Brother XII was delighted to receive the deed. He immediately wrote to thank her and told her about the progress they were making on DeCourcy: "Have had the hay cut and stacked in the barn—a splendid crop. Dick Nicholson is enthusiastic over the ranch and says he has never seen such a splendid soil or such really wonderful possibilities anywhere else. The old house will have to be *burned* down, as it is very much over-run with live-stock, 'almost walking away' as Nicholson says. One could not even use any of the lumber, so it is best to burn it and salt down the site."

At the same time, he informed her of a major new development he planned for DeCourcy Island, explaining that an important decision had been made at a recent conference of the Brothers of the Twelfth Hierarchy:

> In order to carry forward this Work into its next stage (which will have a bearing on the world situation), certain of our Brothers now in incarnation need to have a central residence from which to work, and in which they may enjoy that retirement from outer world contacts they need. DeCourcy is exactly adapted to that purpose. It has therefore been decided that I build "Greystone," and I have the plans already worked out. It will be a large place—two reception rooms, six or seven bedrooms, three bathrooms, good entrance hall, etc. The servants' wing will be on one side of the house, while my own quarters will be in a separate wing, and so be quiet and private, consisting of a library, bedroom, dressing room, and bathroom. . .
>
> I have chosen the land immediately behind and running up from the middle of the three bays at the south end. The ground slopes easily and has the right aspect, and there is plenty of foliage (oaks, maple, and arbutus) for a shelter against the wind from the south-east, and also for a screen of privacy. The beach is good and there is ample water at no great depth. . .
>
> You will be glad to hear the news, for I know you love a dignified house. Also, the erecting of this one house at once will double the value of the property. If you will also

build a good house on or near the site of the old house in the center of the island, we would have an estate that would be worth—even from the point of view of real estate—not a cent less than sixty thousand dollars.

He told Mary that this mansion would be built out of the granite found on DeCourcy Island. It would have a slate roof and walls of dressed stone, five feet thick. He said it would take him a year to build, but he hoped to get the materials on the site by the end of the summer.

Mary was pleased to hear that DeCourcy would be virtually a private estate for their own residences, and that she would have a place of honour beside him. "In fact," she later recalled, "if I had been inclined to be selfish about it, it would almost look as if I had bought DeCourcy for my place and his place."

The plans for Greystone coincided with another of Brother XII's concerns at this time—his search for a successor. Since Myrtle Baumgartner's miscarriages, he had resumed his search for a child—not his own—who he believed would succeed him, and who had already been born some years earlier. Greystone would also be the residence, he wrote Mary, "of the One who will be in charge of this Work in the near future. Neither I, nor He who will come after me, can long continue in the kind of quarters I now occupy."

In several issues of *The Chalice* in 1928, Brother XII had advertised for this child. Under the headline "IMPORTANT," he explained that a male child had been born July 19, 1917, at 5:20 A.M., somewhere in the United States or Canada, but probably in the Midwest, between thirty-five and forty-five degrees north latitude and at one hundred degrees west longitude. He urged the parents of any child born on that date to contact him, since this child was destined to play an important role in the future work of the Aquarian Foundation.

Coulson Turnbull's birth chart for the child showed him to be a soul of great dignity, poise and self-reliance, one who had incarnated with exceptional mental power and purpose. "We find him to be a fine mathematician, keen scientist, an astrologer, an artist, and a very warm-hearted soul, all necessary for a leader," Turnbull observed. "'He will draw all men unto Him.'" He noted that Pleiades on the cusp of the eleventh house indicated the protection of Higher Intelligences and showed that "the mission of this soul will be a well guarded one." Turnbull advised his students to work out the twenty-ninth and fifty-ninth years' directions, the latter falling in the year 1975.

The search for this child had puzzled Edward Lucas. In the margin of *The Chalice,* next to Turnbull's interpretation of the chart, he made a note: "This boy is said by E.A. Wilson to be a body he is preparing for himself, and will take charge of at the death of his present body, yet he doesn't know where the boy is now—queer, isn't it?"

Brother XII even asked Mary Connally to assist him in locating the child: "Do not forget the search I asked you to undertake. The time is speeding, and *very much* depends upon making that contact without delay."

A few months later, however, he wrote again, telling her he'd decided to postpone the search for the time being, until he had more time to concentrate on it. He would build Greystone first. "First the nest, then the Bird," he joked. "'But you wouldn't call *that* guy a bird, would you?'"

Each month, Brother XII wrote a general letter to the disciples, giving his teaching on a variety of subjects relating to the Work. The letters were subsequently published in London, England, by L.N. Fowler and Company under the title *Unsigned Letters from an Elder Brother.* Their purpose was to help the disciples make the transition to a higher state of consciousness. Brother XII told them that it was not only possible for them to take this step, it was inevitable. They only needed to decide to apply themselves to the task and to let knowledge direct their effort. This is why contact with a Teacher was of supreme value:

> The disciple who is dimly aware of the existence of the worlds of Reality is like a small ship upon an ocean; in all directions he is surrounded by the illimitable; beyond his small horizon lies the unknown. His own efforts may be compared to the winds which drive his vessel forward, variable in force and direction. What is his first requirement? He must be able to steer a straight course. Chart and compass and rudder are essential to success; without them he will be driven in every direction at the mercy of every wind that blows. The chart is prepared by others who have already made the journey and are familiar with those regions and conditions which the voyager seeks. The compass is within yourself—it is the compass of Intuition. The rudder is the rudder of your own Will; you must keep a firm hand upon the helm so that the buffeting of wind and sea shall not deflect you from your course. Of themselves, neither hopes nor aspirations will avail you; knowledge alone can bring you to the port of your desires.

Brother XII stated in the *Letters* that the first requirement of a disciple was that he or she be reborn in a spiritual sense. Once this spiritual birth had taken place, the enclosing walls of personal concerns would have forever fallen away, and the disciple could live consciously in the world of Spirit: "Love, emotion, experience, life itself, all these will be seen in a newer and truer perspective; you will view and understand them from the mountain peaks of reality instead of, as heretofore, from the weary and flattened plains of illusion. Life for you will no longer mean the few brief and perhaps empty years which lie within the span of one short incarnation, for you have now entered consciously into a life that is endless and eternal; you have only to realize the fact."

This same birth was also taking place in the life of the race, he explained: "This our Era is both the ending and the beginning of an Age; all who are born in it are part of it, are factors in the total sum, grains weighed in one or other of its scales. *It is a period of birth for the Race as a whole*—humanity may no longer be carried in the womb of ignorance and darkness; the hour of birth is upon them. It is not a Saviour of men that shall be born, but Man himself."

Brother XII also tried to give a sense to the disciples of how great and vast was the work upon which they were engaged. It stretched back many thousands of years, he said, explaining that in all ages, every great work had been accomplished by a small group of souls under one especial leader. This same group of souls incarnated again and again to carry forward the work to which they were dedicated:

> The commencement of our present effort and association goes back a long way—to the time when a certain Ruler of ancient Egypt withstood the corrupt and materialized priesthood of that day and did restore a knowledge of the Truth to the hearts and minds of men. He was Himself one of the divine Initiates, and in that life it was necessary that He should wield the authority of a great Ruler if the work was to be done. "The Invocation of Light" was one of the products of that earlier striving.
>
> Between that day and this there have been many efforts, each varying with the needs and circumstances of the age which called them forth, but always "for the destruction of evil-doers and for the sake of firmly establishing righteousness," we—you and I—have striven. In the present time, two efforts are, in a special sense, taken up again and carried forward. The first of these I have already referred to; it was the overturning of the state religion of Amon-Ra by the pharaoh of that day, Amenhotep IV, who changed his name to Akhenaten, by which name he is known to historians. The Restoration of the Mysteries, and of that divine

knowledge which underlies them, and which is again to be made known to men, *is the fruit* of that earlier Restoration.

Another and much later work accomplished by this same group, and many who joined with us in that struggle, links us with Europe in the Middle Ages—a period of spiritual darkness almost unequalled in history. I refer to the work of the Knights Templar with their various degrees and associate Orders. That effort, or series of efforts, came in a period when Europe was under the feudal system of government; it was an attempt to purify and uplift it, to restore to it a spirit of devotion to the service of others and that sense of *responsibility in government* which originally characterized it. . .

Today, you will find these brothers of ours scattered through most of the modern orders, and especially are they to be found in the ranks of Freemasonry. Most of them have not yet realized the truth with regard to themselves, but they have an intuitive sense of a change—imminent and desirable. Almost immediately the trumpet-call will be sounded for these, and—they will awake and remember: *Through their efforts the ranks of Freemasonry and other similar orders will know a great Renaissance.*

Brother XII also claimed in *Unsigned Letters* that many outstanding religious figures from the past were part of the Work:

Remember that the physical embodiments of a Regent are practically continuous, and that many notable lives or historical characters are, in reality, but the work of the one life or Consciousness. I will give you an instance—Moses, Samuel, Elijah, Daniel, John the Baptist, and Saint Paul were physical embodiments of THE REGENT OF THE MANU. Note how the qualities of leadership and judgment characterize them all alike, how they arraign the evils of their day, how they exhort, drive, compel, build and rebuild, and in the end—establish. Moses said, "Ye are the Seed of Abraham"; St. Paul said, "Ye are children of one Household" (Hierarchy); and I say unto you—"Ye are members of one Brotherhood." It is the same teaching and the same Work.

A constant theme in Brother XII's letters was the coming collapse of the social order. Three months before the October stock market crash, he wrote:

Often we are asked—"When will this destruction be?" and my reply to you is—*It has already commenced.* Beneath the note of a camouflaged "prosperity" so loudly sounded in the public press, the big operators, the financiers and those who are in key positions see already the terrific cracks and fissures in the economic and financial bases upon which this artificial civilization is up-reared.

Consider past history and you will find that whenever the hour has struck for the downfall of a nation, a group of nations, or an order of civilization, it is brought about *by the crumbling of that upon which it is raised.* The glory of ancient Egypt was brought low by the corruption of her religious life—a slow process but in the end inevitable. The downfall of Rome came with the destruction of her military power, sapped by an effete luxury. This also was a slow process but equally sure. The overthrow of a great system of religions occupied some thousands of years; the destruction of the military power of the Roman Empire was spread over some centuries. In both cases, the superstructure was comparatively solid and enduring; also, in those days, events moved slowly.

Consider now upon what the civilizations of modern nations rest, what is that foundation upon which they are built. They are builded not upon the faith and beliefs of nations, not upon military or naval power, but upon something so flimsy, so intangible, that even a rumour causes the whole to perilously sway. THEY ARE BUILT UPON CREDIT. Consider also that events in this age are *not* slow-moving; they rush upon us with a fierceness of haste and a precipitancy that is bewildering. Know therefore that this completion of downfall which in Egypt took some thousands of years, and which engulfed the Roman Empire after the passage of some centuries, shall sweep away the present order *in a few short months* from the time of the first great crash. . .

Beware the first light puffs which presage the coming storm, the trickle of pebbles and small rocks which precede the landslide. It is but a few weeks since five banks smashed in one district in Florida in one day, and some of our own people suffered greatly thereby. Things are not as secure as they may appear. Do not be deceived by great buildings or the massed traffic of city streets; remember rather their flimsy under-pinning and how their very weight and numbers are chief factors in their destruction. The greater the mass, the greater the panic when it starts. It is the large centers of population that will be a shambles because *judgment will strike at the heart of the evil.*"

Brother XII told the disciples that the present work was one of preparation. They were laying the foundations of the new order which would succeed the present: "We have to form the nucleus of that order which, Phoenix-like, is to arise from the ashes of the tempest of destruction we foresee." He used the expression "City of Refuge" to describe the colony, and predicted that within a very short time, it would become a center of safety in the midst of chaos:

"We are building a City of Refuge, and it has to be built *before* the break; we have to get food, stores, tools and implements, raw materials; we have to build, to make roads and landings, to clear and to cultivate, and we have to do this work and to obtain these supplies now, while we are able to get them."

He asked the members to make a special sacrifice in order

that the work could be accomplished in time. And to each one, he sent a "Card of Recognition" inscribed: "Labour in this Vineyard, and thou shalt eat of its fruit. Build thou the City of Refuge; it shall hide thee in the Day of Adversity."

△   △   △

Mary Connally, meanwhile, was in Washington, D.C. for the hearing of a lawsuit she'd filed against the Southern Railroad Company. She contended that the smoke and cinders from the railroad's shops in Biltmore, where it had built a round-house, had seriously damaged the potential of her estate at Fernihurst for residential development. She was suing Southern Railroad for $250,000, one of the largest claims filed in the federal court in Asheville at the time. The suit had subsequently been transferred to the district court in Washington, D.C. The entire railroad community in the United States was watching the proceedings. If Mary won a large settlement, dozens of similar claims, aggregating in the millions of dollars, were expected to be filed.

Brother XII was very interested in the case and advised Mary at length about it. He predicted: "You will not gain all you hope, but will nevertheless make some gain."

The proceedings opened on August 5, 1929, in the U.S. district court in Washington, D.C. For ten days, the testimony of a procession of witnesses, including Southern Railroad officials, bank executives, Asheville realtors, railroad employees, and local residents, was heard. With so much at stake, the evidence was fiercely contested. After the last witness had stepped down, the jury withdrew to consider the verdict.

The morning of the eleventh day, Mary took her seat in court. Pale but composed, she listened while the foreman of the jury announced the verdict: damages to the plaintiff of one cent. The jubilant Southern Railroad officials congratulated their lawyers. Mary sat stunned by the decision. Her own lawyer moved to have the judgment set aside, but the judge overruled the motion and ordered Mary to pay the costs of the action.

Brother XII reacted to the news with less than philosophical calm. "I got a letter from him," Mary recalled, "telling me that I was doing absolutely the wrong thing, and acting absolutely in the wrong manner, and that I was absolutely responsible for losing my lawsuit, although I had all his instructions as to what to do and how to do it."

Brother XII evidently thought better of his initial response and wrote again to "Lady Mary," expressing his regrets. He added that the decision about whether or not to appeal must be her own, based upon competent legal advice. He also urged her to return as soon as possible to British Columbia:

"You have been through a terrific jam this summer and you need to get right away from it all. . .You need peace and quiet, and a chance to rest, and think, and grow. . .

"Concentrate on settling up outside business and on returning quickly in order to take up that life which is yours in Reality."

Summer faded into fall, and on DeCourcy Island, Brother XII proceeded with his plans to turn the island into the new center of his activities. He had some preliminary clearing done of the site he planned for Greystone, as well as a road of sorts made down to the water. He also continued to rehabilitate the farm in the center of the island, since he planned for it to eventually supply the needs of everyone at the three settlements of Cedar, Valdes and DeCourcy. In addition, he finished construction of his house in the lagoon at the south end of the island. It stood on a grassy bluff overlooking the entrance to the bay. On the opposite shore, he planned to build several houses for the select few who would comprise the inner group that would live near him. This entire area, known as the Point, became the new headquarters of Brother XII's operations.

In the last week of September, Brother XII and Madame

Z moved over to DeCourcy. Delighted to be installed in the new house at last, Wilson wrote to Mary: "The home is indeed a 'haven,' and I am so busy getting all my affairs in running order."

Brother XII's move to DeCourcy marked a definite change in his relationship with his disciples. He advised Mary that he could no longer "mix in" as before, and that he had to "withdraw myself almost entirely from *personal* contact with any of the people here." The retreat was not for selfish reasons, he explained. It was a necessary part of his occult work.

Brother XII claimed that this seclusion was the right of every adept in physical embodiment. In connection with it, he quoted from *Light on the Path*: "'It is part of His inheritance, part of His position. He has an actual title to it, and can no more put it aside than the Duke of Westminster can say he does not choose to be the Duke of Westminster... Unless protected and made safe, Their growth would be interfered with, Their work hindered. The Neophyte may meet an Adept in the flesh, may live in the same house with Him, and yet be unable to recognize Him, and unable to make his own voice heard by Him.'"

But there was another reason for his seclusion. He explained that he was working with a ray of tremendously powerful spiritual force—the Sixth Ray or Red Ray. It would be focused through him as its appointed agent in the outer world; as a result, it would be dangerous for the disciples to visit him or to approach unbidden:

"This seclusion is necessary, not only for the work of the Adept, but FOR THE SAFETY OF THOSE WHO OTHERWISE WOULD COME INTO PERSONAL CONTACT WITH HIM. This Ray will heal and enlighten and uplift that which is attuned to it, BUT IT WILL DESTROY that by which it is opposed... My advice to all who are unacquainted with the nature of the Red Ray and the laws which govern its operations is—stay out of the Powerhouse."

At the Brothers' Center on Valdes Island, the disciples were growing disgruntled. They felt estranged from Brother XII because of his retreat, and many still objected to the harsh rule of Madame Z. The hard work, too, was taking its toll. A number of the disciples began to quietly set aside money from their fifteen dollars' monthly allowance, towards the day when they could leave the colony.

Somehow, Brother XII became aware of the situation and acted promptly to put down the insurrection. On October 11, he made a special trip to Valdes and summoned the disciples into the assembly hall. Herbert Jefferson was among the anxious group who faced him.

"I want each one of you to declare whatever money you've got, up to a dollar," he announced. "I have an idea that some of you are holding back!"

Opening the Bible, he dramatically read the account of Ananias and Sapphira, who had tried to deceive the Apostle Peter by withholding money from the sale of their land:

"'But Peter said, "Ananias, why hath Satan filled thy heart to lie to the Holy Ghost, and to keep back part of the price of the land? Whiles it remained, was it not thine own? And after it was sold, was it not in thine own power? Why hast thou conceived this thing in thine heart? Thou hast not lied unto men but unto God."

"'And Ananias hearing these words fell down, and gave up the ghost: and great fear came on all them that heard these things.'"

Brother XII finished by recounting the fate of the wretched Sapphira, who had also lied to the Apostle: "'Then fell she down straightway at his feet, and yielded up the ghost: and the young men came in, and found her dead, and carrying her forth, buried her by her husband.'"

Brother XII's performance had the desired effect. The disciples came forward and surrendered the money they'd retained. Herbert Jefferson declared thirty-five dollars, although other disciples declared much larger amounts.

But both Jefferson and his wife, Dora, thought Brother XII's attempt to intimidate the disciples was a disgrace. At the end of the meeting, they told him they wanted to leave the colony. Thomas Cranmer Williams and his wife also told Brother XII they didn't wish to remain.

"He was nice to me, mind you," Jefferson recalls. "He said to me, 'I think you're making a mistake, but you're free to go any time.' He let me use the *Khuenaten* to transfer my personal effects to Vancouver, which he didn't have to do. Afterwards, I wrote him a letter to thank him. I was very careful what I said. I didn't heed the temptation to denounce him. I simply said that we'd had a rich experience—that was the way I put it."

Jefferson regards Wilson as a fraud, but a brilliant one, with an extraordinary grasp of spiritual matters:

"He was quite an attractive character until you got to the inner man—then you saw what a rotten person he was. He was a pretender; in that sense, he might be called—in a slight way—a lord of the underworld, but not beyond that.

"All of his disciples were under his hypnotic spell, but only for a time. When you got away from him and saw the thing as it really was, you saw at once how false it was—and how his pretences were all just 'boogie woogie'!"

Brother XII was pleased with the results of the meeting. He wrote to Mary Connally that there had been a "big clean-up" on Valdes Island: "On Valdes, *the whole atmosphere* has been cleared up, and we have at last gotten it clear and free from separateness, and from petty personal planning. At last, we are able to commence to really build (in an inner sense) that environment which is intended. There has been some elimination there. Should it always work that way, for *it is impossible* that the wrong spirit or the wrong attitude can long remain hidden. The vibrations of our work are powerful: they are so that that which is opposed to it is inevitably drawn up to the surface and cast out."

Brother XII informed Mary that she could now have the house on Valdes vacated by Thomas Cranmer Williams and his wife as a temporary residence before she moved to DeCourcy. She'd be comfortable on Valdes, he assured her, and could temporarily store her belongings in a storeroom at Cedar.

At the same time, he told her about Bruce and Georgia Crawford, a young couple who had recently arrived from Lakeland, Florida. The Crawfords owned a small dry cleaning business, and had brought their life savings of five thousand dollars to the colony. Brother XII described them to Mary as "two beautiful souls who are almost purely sixth-race in type and outlook," and said they'd be willing to give her all the help she needed:

"They are quite young, and we call them 'the children.' I know you will love them, and they you. They have been through a great testing since coming here, not in one, but in a hundred different ways, and they have come out with flying colours. Bruce will help you in any way you need in fixing the house and getting settled, and he will look after the wood, etc. for you, and love to do it."

Mary began winding up her affairs and preparing to return to British Columbia. She decided not to appeal the railroad case. In the midst of packing, she wrote to Brother XII, asking what she should—or shouldn't—bring.

He encouraged her to bring whatever she wished, despite the restriction laid down in *The Brothers' School* paper against personal possessions. "By all means," he wrote, "bring your bathroom fixtures and everything else you can, seeing that you are having a car (railway) to Vancouver."

△   △   △

Almost a year had passed since the petition to dissolve the Aquarian Foundation had been heard by the provincial cabinet. The government had decided to let the two parties try to reach a negotiated settlement, but the bitterness and mutual recrimination that existed between Brother XII and the other Governors had sabotaged every attempt. Finally, on

November 15, 1929, the cabinet passed an Order-in-Council dissolving the Society. Attorney-General Harry Pooley explained to reporters when he made the announcement that each landowner at Cedar would be given title to his property and that the amount of land that would revert to the Crown was small.

Brother XII was satisfied with the decision. No assets were attached to the Society, and he was now free to return the Hess Trust. There were nine bonds, each worth a thousand dollars, remaining in the twenty thousand dollar fund. Frank Cunliffe returned them to Oliver Hess, explaining that the proceeds from the other securities had been used "to the very last cent" for the work of the Foundation.

But the government was still concerned about Brother XII's activities and hoped to launch criminal proceedings against him to expel him from Valdes and DeCourcy. On November 24, Corporal W. A. MacBrayne of the B.C. Provincial Police landed on Valdes to have a firsthand look at the community. His cover story was that he was searching for the *Tee-Hee*, a launch that had gone missing with its owner two months earlier. MacBrayne counted the number of houses in the settlement and made a few discreet inquiries of the disciples about their activities. "They were very non-committal and uninformative," he observed in his report.

The next day, MacBrayne visited the farm on DeCourcy Island, where he talked to two workmen who were draining a swamp. They informed him that Wilson lived in the lagoon on the east side of the island. Steering his vessel through the reef, MacBrayne tied up at the float below Brother XII's house. "I had a chat with Mr. Wilson, but did not see the woman he is supposed to be living with," MacBrayne wrote. Again, he gleaned very little information. He returned to Victoria, filing a report of his investigation with the Superintendent of the B.C. Provincial Police.

MacBrayne's visit, coupled with a remark by Pooley to reporters that the government intended to watch Brother XII's activities closely, made Wilson furious. He immediately wrote to Frank Cunliffe, protesting this harassment by the government of a group of innocent settlers, who were minding their own business and interfering with no one:

> For the government to "watch" such a little community is *persecution*. It really means that our enemies, having obtained the "ear of the government," are trying to harm and defame us, and if possible oust and dispossess us, using government officials as catspaws in the furtherance of their own spiteful plans.
>
> Unless the officials concerned recognize these facts and change their attitude, we will take steps to bring the whole matter to the attention of the Privy Council *in Great Britain*. One of the chief instigators and prime movers in this attack is an alien German-American, a Prussian by birth. The writer is British born, a citizen of this Empire, and has a right to justice and a fair consideration of the facts of this case.

Indeed, the government could find no legitimate reason to prosecute Brother XII. H. M. Garrett, Registrar of Companies, studied MacBrayne's report and advised the Attorney-General that, beyond cancelling the charter of the Aquarian Foundation, it wasn't possible for the government to take any further action. Based on the evidence he had, Garrett concluded: "Brother Wilson appears to be leading a quiet if not a proper life."

Brother XII now surprised everyone by abruptly leaving for England. Madame Z accompanied him. In Nanaimo, he met with Frank Cunliffe and made the necessary legal arrangements, drawing up a will and giving Alfred Barley power of attorney. He also put Barley in charge of the colony in his absence.

On December 3, two days before he left British Columbia, he issued a General Letter to the membership, announcing his departure. He explained that he had been called away from the Center "on matters that are vital to the safety and preservation of this whole Work, and I may be away for some months." He instructed the members to make all cheques payable to Alfred Barley, since he himself would be unable to endorse such items in his absence. He promised to continue the monthly letters, although they might arrive irregularly, since he'd be posting them only as convenience allowed during his travels. Assuring the members that all phases of the Work were going forward as planned, he closed his letter by exhorting them:

> We are passing through the final stages of that long fight against those who have sought to destroy this Work. Stand firm and loyal; continue to support our Cause as you have done in the past—now, if ever, our need is great: it is the moment of intensest struggle before the final Victory. Again I say, STAND FIRM—I go to establish that which shall prove a sure refuge for you all.
>
> > Your Brother in service,
> > XII

This drawing by artist Joan M. Smith illustrated an article about Brother XII in Victoria's *Daily Colonist* on September 30, 1962. Original caption: "By charms and incantations, Brother XII tried to kill B.C.'s Attorney-General."

Bruce McKelvie's feature article about Brother XII, written for the North American Newspaper Alliance, appeared in newspapers across the continent, including Toronto's *Evening Telegram*, May 20, 1933.

LEGALS

The first official public notice of the death of Brother XII, identified as Julian Churton Skottowe, Edward Arthur Wilson, and Amiel de Valdes, was this legal notice in *The Vancouver Province*, July 10, 1939.

Now a police training academy, this building in Neuchâtel, Switzerland, was formerly the Clinique du Chanet, where Brother XII was a patient in November, 1934, under the care of Dr. Roger Schmidt. Wilson's death in Neuchâtel remains a matter of speculation. (Photo by author)

The former site of the Mandieh Settlement on Valdes Island, looking towards the Strait of Georgia. In the foreground, the remnants of Brother XII's house on this windswept bluff are all that remain of the settlement. The cabins of the other colony members have long since succumbed to the elements. (Photo by author)

Minard G. Hill, former owner of Yellow Point Lodge in Chemainus, points to the chimney of Brother XII's house overlooking the lagoon at DeCourcy Island in this photograph that appeared in *The Star Weekly* on August 10, 1957.

A five-part series of articles about Brother XII, written by Paul St. Pierre for *The Vancouver Sun* in February, 1952, was illustrated with woodcuts by Richard Bennett. Original caption: "To the crowds who flocked to hear him, the bearded prophet set out the talents required of those who might come to his refuge."

Another woodcut in the series depicted Brother XII using his occult powers in court to disable his adversaries. Original caption: "'This is ridiculous, but I've forgotten what I was saying,' the lawyer said."

Colony members were given various tasks to perform as tests of their fitness for the Work. Original caption: "The colonists on DeCourcy Island cleared the rocks off their fields with buckets."

The last message from Brother XII was found written on a piece of tar paper left under the floorboards of a false floor in one of the colony's buildings: *"For fools and traitors—nothing!"* Original caption: "The caretaker read what was written on the paper."

This caricature of Brother XII by James Ferguson appeared in *The Financial Times* Weekend, May 30/31, 1992, illustrating a review of the original edition of this book. (Courtesy James Ferguson)

Cover illustration from *The Wide World* magazine, December, 1942. The article by W. W. Bride was a florid recounting of the excesses and abuses that occurred at the Pacific Coast colony under the regime of the hypnotic cult leader.

The illustrations accompanying the article took considerable artistic license in interpreting the Brother XII story. In this full page drawing by T.T. Cuneo, the guru sports an imaginative Indian headdress and swirling robes as he berates his terrified followers. Original caption: "Lashing them with withering scorn and dire threats."

Advance notice for *The Law of Cycles and of Human Generation,* the book that Brother XII was working on prior to the colony's breakup. It would have included the esoteric heart of his teachings and though it isn't known if the book was ever published, the manuscript would surely be the rarest and most valuable of his writings.

Psychic James H.P. Wilkie in his consulting room at his home in Vancouver, British Columbia, where he allegedly contacted Brother XII in the spirit world. (*The Vancouver Sun*)

CHAPTER
X
A Test of Obedience

As midnight approached, thousands of excited revellers wearing paper hats and carrying noise-makers crowded into St. Paul's churchyard. In London's West End, the nightclubs were jammed with dancing couples. Claridge's had been transformed into a Persian Garden and at the Berkeley, a midnight tableau featured Father Time and Miss 1930. As the final seconds of the 1920s ticked away, the countdown began all across the great metropolis. As Big Ben began booming the midnight hour, the horns and sirens of the boats on the Thames mingled with the cheers and hurrahs of the exultant crowds singing "Auld Lang Syne." At the Savoy Hotel, members of the D'Oyly Carte Opera Company, dressed as Yeomen of the Guard, led over two thousand guests in song. All across London church bells peeled, ringing in the New Year.

Brother XII and Madame Z also celebrated the beginning of the 1930s in London. Although the "Messenger of the

Masters" did not return triumphant from his crusade to bring the Work of the Great White Lodge to America, Brother XII at least took pride in still having a group of loyal followers here in the land of his birth. He apparently did not try to recruit new members and there is no record of his having visited the Privy Council as he had threatened. He'd written earlier, "The first great battle in this campaign has been fought *and won,* but physically I am worn to the limit and very weary of it all." England provided him with an opportunity to rest after the rigours of the past three years and to simply be himself.

While in London, Brother XII published with L.N. Fowler and Company the monthly letters he'd written the previous year. In the foreword to *Unsigned Letters from an Elder Brother,* he stated: "The writer is not interested in fame or in a personal 'following'—the former is emptiness, the latter mostly unreliable. He will not countenance any organization, nor any attempt to create a cult amongst those who, as the result of reading these Letters, may wish to step out of the rut of men and their affairs. But if any shall come to us in a spirit of teachableness, with a pure desire of Truth for Truth's sake, and the will to unselfish service in the cause of humanity—we will receive them."

The book was judged favourably in *The Occult Review,* although the reviewer noted that the announcement in it that a Center in British Columbia had been formed with strict requirements for admittance seemed curiously inconsistent with the sentiments expressed by Brother XII in the foreword. Still, the reviewer conceded, there was much material for thought and speculation in the pages of this "puzzling yet withal intriguing book."

Brother XII also published with L.N. Fowler *A Primer of Astrology for Children.* The book was written by Annie Barley at Wilson's suggestion and was, he claimed, the first book on astrology written especially for children. In his foreword, he said that the knowledge of astrology would have great importance in the coming age: "Let parents commence this study with the child, and it will often be found that in these things, the child will teach the parent. Has it not been written that 'a little child shall lead them'!"

In London, Brother XII also wrote a General Letter to the disciples in which he reviewed the stages of the Work. Perhaps for the benefit of the doubters or the faint of heart, he told members that powerful forces were protecting their cause. He said that both the Center and his own residence during the months of October and November just past had been *"guarded by hundreds of unseen horsemen;* unseen by the physical eyes only, but visible to such as have the inner sight, and plainly seen by some of our own number. When we left to carry on our Work and this Plan elsewhere, the horsemen disappeared and were seen no more."

At the same time, he used the General Letter to answer criticism that his trip to England was simply to satisfy personal whims. He referred members to their Bibles and the story of the flight of Joseph and Mary into Egypt: "Read these records, and remember that history repeats itself, sometimes almost minutely. Also, had some of our nominal members lived in that day, I fancy they would have whispered amongst themselves— 'What, going to Egypt! How impossible, how *inconsistent* after all these prophesyings by our old friends Hannah and Simeon and others. Evidently things have gone wrong and *they have gone off the track*—we never thought they would go to Egypt; just an excuse for a holiday, no doubt!'"

Despite his disclaimer, Brother XII and Madame Z spent time in one of the loveliest resorts in England, the ancient fishing village and boatbuilding center of Brixham on the Devonshire coast. Brixham was famous as the place where William of Orange had landed in 1688 with fifteen thousand troops, deposing King James II, England's last Roman Catholic monarch, in what is commonly known as the "Glorious Revolution." A hundred years earlier in 1588, Sir Francis Drake, in his flagship *Revenge,* had towed the first warship captured during the defeat of the Spanish Armada into Brixham's harbour. And in 1815, Napoleon Bonaparte had been held prisoner here on board the *Bellerophon*, before being transferred to the *Northumberland*, the ship that would take him to exile on Saint Helena—an exchange eagerly watched through telescopes by an excited populace anxious for a glimpse of the legendary French conqueror.

Brother XII and Madame Z stayed at 37 King Street in a three-storey terrace house overlooking the harbour. They visited the boat yards of Jackman's and Upham's, renowned for their Brixham trawlers. The oak beams used in their construction were buried for years deep in the sand below Torbay Beach, a traditional pickling process that made the wood practically indestructible. Brother XII had come to Brixham to buy a sailboat. He chose a sturdy, seaworthy sixty-two foot Brixham trawler with a gleaming black hull. It had been built in 1919 for three demobilized servicemen who'd named her *Us Dree* (Devonshire dialect for "We Three"). After their fishing venture failed to pay, she had passed into the hands of a wealthy Englishwoman who'd converted her into a yacht, adding handsome furnishings below deck. Wilson rechristened his vessel *Lady Royal* and registered her with the Royal Corinthian Yacht Club at Plymouth.

Brother XII and Madame Z decided to sail the *Lady Royal* back to British Columbia. After testing their vessel off the coast, they filled the water tanks, stocked the hold with provisions, and hired a local sailor named Merle Scott to accompany them. In March, they sailed the *Lady Royal* out of Brixham's harbour and into the English Channel, beginning a voyage that would take them halfway around the world without the assistance of auxiliary power.

△   △   △

During Brother XII's absence, the disciples continued to work towards their goal of making the colony self-sufficient. Roger Painter returned with his new bride Leona and the two became the custodians of DeCourcy Island, living in Brother XII's house at the Point. Harold Krause arrived with his mother-in-law, Anna Wilkerson, from Everett, Washington (Krause's wife had died in childbirth). Sarah Puckett, a spirited seventy-six-year-old retired schoolteacher from San Francisco, joined the group, turning in her government pension to the Work. Bill and Mary Lowell, who had been working as cooks in a mining camp in Nevada, arrived with three thousand dollars in cash. A powerfully-built man, Lowell was a former heavy-weight boxer and sparring partner of Jack Dempsey.

Alfred Barley kept Brother XII informed of the progress the disciples were making at the settlement. The letters he received from him were generally of a practical nature, dealing with various business matters relating to the colony. A telegram sent from Brixham on March 1, 1930 reads: "Have block eighteen registered my name. Lowells belong Valdes."

One night before he left for England, Brother XII appeared at Barley's house, carrying a small, heavy bundle wrapped in a towel. He didn't tell Barley what was in it, but told him to take good care of it as he was afraid of fire. Barley had put the bundle away unopened. He now received a letter advising him that the bundle contained gold coins. Brother XII instructed him to put the coins into a quart mason jar and fill the jar with melted paraffin wax. He was then to have a wooden box made to hold the jar, and to sink the box in the cistern of Wilson's house at Cedar. With his characteristic thoroughness, Barley followed these instructions exactly.

Barley's mother had died the previous December, and he informed Brother XII that he expected to receive an inheritance of ten thousand dollars. He received a letter from Wilson in which, according to Annie Barley, he said, "Don't you think a nice thing to do with that money would be to put it into Greystone that we are about to build, and you yourself would have your apartments there and live with me in that building, and it would be a palatial mansion." When the money arrived in the summer of 1930, Barley banked it, holding it intact for

Brother XII's return.

Mary Connally was probably more surprised than anyone to learn that Brother XII had gone to England. She was in Asheville, North Carolina, preparing to come to British Columbia, when she received a note from him advising her of his trip. Mary finished packing and locked up Fernihurst, leaving the fifty-room mansion standing empty. She took the train to Seattle, where she remained awaiting news of Brother XII's return.

While in Seattle, Mary got a letter from Annie Barley, telling her that for "diplomatic reasons," Brother XII would like her to buy his house at Cedar. Annie explained that this would save him "annoyance and possible embarrassment in the future." Mary was surprised by the request—she had planned to build on DeCourcy, not buy at Cedar. She didn't know that the "diplomatic reasons" were that Brother XII had promised the house to Elma Wilson, but hadn't made a deed of it to her, and that he wanted to get the house into Mary's hands, so that Elma couldn't get it. Mary bought the house for four thousand dollars—although she later claimed it was only worth fifteen-hundred dollars—and in August 1930, she moved to Cedar.

△   △   △

After leaving Brixham, the *Lady Royal* crossed the Bay of Biscay in late March, heading for the Canary Islands. Brother XII reached Las Palmas in April, where he replenished his food and water before launching out into the grey swells of the Atlantic. Setting a course southwest, the *Lady Royal* followed the classic route first travelled by Columbus, who made the crossing in twenty-one days. For weeks, the sturdy little craft was only a speck upon the vast ocean, yet with the trade winds filling her sails, she made steady headway, until the crew could at last make out the islands of the West Indies shining on the horizon.

Brother XII spent two months sailing the turquoise waters

of the Caribbean, with its white beaches and cloudless skies. In Kingston, Jamaica, he took the *Lady Royal* into the dry dock for repairs. But after a quarrel with the owner, he refused to pay his bill and demanded that his vessel be put back into the water. He sailed away, not realizing that the incident would have serious consequences.

On the Isle of Pines, Brother XII recruited another crew member, an Englishman named Edric Douglas Agate. Educated at Lancing College, a private boys' school in Sussex, the handsome and bearded twenty-five-year-old bore a striking resemblance to King George V despite the difference in age, and was often greeted by friends in crowded bars with cries of "Here comes the King!" Agate had worked in a bank in Bangkok and had travelled widely. He was an interesting conversationalist, and Mabel took an immediate fancy to him. "He's just like his name," she remarked to Wilson. "He's like an agate!"

The *Lady Royal* sailed to Panama, where Brother XII hired two San Blas Indians, named Louis John and Charles Foster, in the Canal port of Colon. With their white cotton trousers, straw hats and bare feet, the two muscular and dark-skinned natives added a picturesque look to the crew. After transiting the Panama Canal, the *Lady Royal* left Balboa on July 27, 1930, to begin the long voyage up the Pacific coast to British Columbia.

$$\triangle \quad \triangle \quad \triangle$$

At the Brothers' Center on Valdes Island, meanwhile, a situation had developed that threatened the harmony of the community. It centered around Oliver and Adelaide Heflinger, an older married couple from Los Angeles, and their adopted daughter, a young woman from Haileybury, Ontario, named Regina LaCarte. Before he left, Brother XII had installed the three in a cabin on Valdes and instructed them to remain there during his absence. But for reasons that aren't clear,

Alfred Barley made repeated attempts to separate "Reggie" from the Heflingers. He finally ordered her to move to another cabin on Valdes and live with Sarah Puckett.

Although Barley claimed to be carrying out Brother XII's instructions, Reggie refused to leave the Heflingers. Barley accused the three of forming a clique of their own and of persisting in an attitude of "non-cooperation." In defence of their position, Oliver quoted from *Foundation Letters and Teachings:* "Whenever one is asked to promise unquestioning obedience, either to a person or to a fraternity, something is wrong. No true Occultist, no Brother of the Right-hand path would make such a demand."

The deadlock continued. Barley eventually wrote a curious letter to Reggie which lifts to some extent the veil of mystery surrounding the disciples' beliefs and provides an insight into the peculiar psychology that motivated them. Barley's anti-Catholic bias is evident in his disparaging allusions to the "so-called religion" of Regina's childhood.

PRIVATE AND CONFIDENTIAL

This story is written by one who wrote you formerly in the hope that you would stand the TEST OF OBEDIENCE, and would not be misled and hypnotized by others.

There was a little girl who was born into a family with a kindly mother, but with a very brutal father. This little girl had to work to help support the family, but during the course of her work, she became interested in the higher teachings and aspired for chelaship. Her motives and her aspirations were good, and The Masters decided that it was possible she could take that IMPORTANT STEP, and they called her to their Center.

The first condition that confronted her was rather difficult—very little physical comfort or ease, and this she stood well. After testing on this, she was prepared to take the next step forward to ascertain if the servant (the brain mind) could open that gate which leads to STRENGTH—discrimination—and to test her on opening that door, she was placed with a member of her own sex who had been reared in the same so-called religion as her own. Herein is the wisdom of THE MASTERS—more wise by far than the intellectualists or mentalists. They have their own way of testing, and the mentalists are unable to discriminate for the reason that one is third dimensional, while those who are able to hear the silent voice intelligently are in Fourth Dimensional. So the tempter drew nigh and began to whisper—everything was made smooth for her: ease, comfort, plenty to eat, with very little labour. To her mentality and lower self, things were indeed made very pleasant, as much love (so-called and misnamed) and suave kindness were bestowed upon her, which indeed was pleasing to the consciousness of the body and its senses. She became lulled, failed to exercise the first QUALIFICATION—DISCRIMINATION—became blind as to what was her lower nature or her higher nature.

An order came, conveying to her in exact words, from the representative of the XIIth House on the plane of form (physical plane). But the little girl had become so stupe-fied by suggestions that were more or less hypnotic that she FAILED TO OBEY or even acknowledge receipt of the letter. The quality of the disciple is tested by the degree of his obedience. The Masters then forwarded another com-mand, and this like the first was not heeded, nor the letter acknowledged. But The Masters had heard the call of the heart of that little girl, and decided in their wisdom to give her another opportunity to see if she could be freed from her mental enslavement. They sent another of their chelas, who is OBEDIENT to their thought and who seeks only to serve the HIGHER, and this one being of a great heart and kind nature, was selected to make a final effort to free the little girl from her bondage. When an appeal was made for her to visit for a while, the soul cried out in tears for its re-lease, but again the mental enslavement WON.

A little knowledge is dangerous, and for this reason,

knowledge is withheld from those who are not able to stand it. The little girl was not taught by her so-called religion that the priests have the knowledge as to how to create a tremendous thought-form, and further, that the fanatical of the cult who have passed over become the servants of that thought-form, in order that the adherents may be held to their service. Therefore, in the talking to and fro between the two of this cult, there was formed an entrance for one of those to whisper into the brain mind, instructing and advising them so subtly that it seemed as though they were receiving direction from their higher selves. But remember, the senses had first been lulled and suggested to.

However, The Masters in their great spirit of helpfulness to all those seeking Their WAY determined to make additional endeavour to break this insidious bondage which, if persisted in, ends in total darkness and disintegration of the soul, until its atomic parts are so scattered that it takes aeons and aeons of time for it to rebuild its constituent parts. So another order came, and again was a messenger sent—the one of the heart, who seeks not to serve self, but the brain mind of the little girl had been so instructed by that spirit which opposes humanity and The Great White Brothers that the servant was again disobedient.

This is from one who has travelled a long long path, and who did earnestly seek to free the soul of the little girl from the mental domination, for the cry of the heart in its first call to be carried to the heights had been heard. But it had permitted itself to become stupefied and dulled by the thought-form invoked, and hence it is not well to talk too much unless intelligence and discrimination are used.

If one looks to the personality of The Brother XII in the objective world, they will never know what constitutes The Brother. They MUST look beyond the personality. I who am writing this to you, am still interceding that the door be held open for you. Will you, or will you not, shake free, and be YOURSELF. Failure is indeed a sad affair. FACE yourself and know YOURSELF.

I trust this little story is not too long, and that you will absolutely consider it private and confidential, not to be shown to anyone. The betrayer has always been Judas, and one that betrays another brother can know the spirit of Judas possessed him. A hint should be sufficient.

△   △   △

After leaving Panama, the *Lady Royal* was hit by a storm while coming up the Mexican coast. For days, the little sailboat was pounded relentlessly by huge waves. When the storm finally abated, she had been driven far off course and was in equatorial waters hundreds of miles from land. There was no wind and she lay becalmed for weeks. The storm had damaged the provisions: there was kerosene in the drinking water and worms in the oatmeal, which the crew ate—worms and all. Eventually, the rations ran out and the crew became too weak to even sail the vessel.

On October 5, 1930, seventy-one days out of Balboa, the *Lady Royal* was drifting helplessly six hundred miles southwest of San Francisco. It was 8:00 P.M. and the seas were heavy. Several of the crew were lying on deck close to death. Wilson was considering sacrificing his pet water spaniel for food, when she started to bark furiously—she'd sighted a ship! One of the crew managed to light an improvised flare.

On board the Matson liner S.S. *Wilhelmina,* bound from Honolulu to San Francisco, Third Mate W.P. Peters noticed a flickering light to starboard. The big passenger ship hauled off course and went to investigate. There in the beam of the liner's powerful searchlight lay the *Lady Royal.* According to *The San Francisco News,* which carried a report of the rescue, Captain E.R. Johanson ordered a boat lowered to go to the assistance of the stricken vessel. As his rescuers came on board, Wilson gasped, *"We're thankful you got here!"*

The boat made three trips to the *Lady Royal,* stocking her

hold with fresh fruit and vegetables, two sides of beef, a crate of eggs and other provisions. Wilson sent money to pay for the stores, but Captain Johanson returned it. The lights of the *Wilhelmina* disappeared into the night, leaving the crew of the *Lady Royal* to thank Providence for their miraculous escape.

In British Columbia, the news of the amazing rescue appeared in *The Victoria Colonist*, headlined, "MATSON LINER AIDS YACHT BOUND HERE," alerting the government to Brother XII's return to the province. Attorney-General Pooley sent a clipping to Colonel J. H. McMullin, Superintendent of the B.C. Provincial Police, asking: "Is this not Bro 12?"

McMullin contacted Assistant Inspector George E. Norris of the Customs and Excise Preventive Service and asked him to have the customs officer at William Head Quarantine Station, south of Victoria, ask all incoming vessels if they had seen the *Lady Royal*. McMullin suspected Brother XII might try to smuggle members of his sect into the province.

Sergeant Jack Russell of the Nanaimo detachment of the B.C. Provincial Police made a special trip to Cedar-by-the-Sea, where he interviewed Maurice Von Platen, who informed him that there were about five or six persons on board the *Lady Royal*. But neither Von Platen nor anyone else at Cedar seemed to know when Brother XII was due to arrive in British Columbia.

In his report, Russell commented: "From my own knowledge of E. A. Wilson, who is a very shrewd man, I am of the opinion that he will not try to evade any Customs or Immigration regulations."

On Wednesday, November 5, 1930, a thick blanket of fog covered the Strait of Juan de Fuca. The ghostly silhouette of a two-masted sailing ship emerged from the mist and slipped unseen past the Customs Station at William Head. Vanishing into the eerie whiteness shrouding Haro Strait, the vessel moved steadily northwards towards DeCourcy Island.

Brother XII now encountered his most serious difficulty

navigating. The wind died and the current threatened to drive his vessel onto the rocks. Luckily, the fog lifted and two United States Coast Guard preventive boats spotted the *Lady Royal* in distress and guided her into the safety of Roche Harbour on San Juan Island.

Brother XII and Madame Z left the *Lady Royal* in Roche Harbour and took a launch directly to DeCourcy Island. Returning the next morning in the *Khuenaten,* they towed the *Lady Royal* through the Gulf Islands to DeCourcy.

Mary Lowell was one of the disciples at the Point when Brother XII towed the *Lady Royal* into the lagoon. She went down to the water to help him unload the sailboat, but he swore at her and told her to get away from the boat.

"He had a bunch of parcels on board," she said. "He carried them off and he wouldn't allow anyone to touch them. He hid them in different parts of the island—parcels of different sizes wrapped in black oilcloth. . . I stood on the shore and watched him hiding them in different places, and all the time he was swearing and raving."

While Brother XII was hiding the parcels, Madame Z and Agate stood on the beach, watching for government boats. Z paced up and down in a tremendous state of agitation, afraid that an Immigration vessel would come into the lagoon and seize the *Lady Royal* before it was unloaded.

"He had just finished hiding these things in three or four different places in the bush," Mary recalled, "when a boat did come in and sailed around. We had a bale of green tomatoes on a scow in the bay, and a man got out and looked at these tomatoes, and [Brother XII and Z] were in a terrible state, and then the boat sailed on out of the harbour. And he came up to her and said, 'Well, I will have a cup of tea,' and then they sent me home."

What was in the parcels? Later reports that Brother XII would load a launch and make nocturnal trips to the main shore of Vancouver Island when the blinking headlights of an automobile signalled DeCourcy Island, there to rendezvous with the Oriental occupants of the car, has led to the surmise that the parcels contained drugs. Brother XII's increasingly irrational behaviour is also cited as evidence to support this theory. It is known, however, that at least some of the parcels contained copies of *Unsigned Letters from an Elder Brother* and *A Primer of Astrology for Children,* which he'd had published in England, and which he was no doubt afraid that the government would confiscate.

After the *Lady Royal* was unloaded, Brother XII sent Alfred Barley to Nanaimo to notify Customs Officer H.L. Good that the vessel was in the lagoon at DeCourcy awaiting inspection. When Barley returned with the message that the *Lady Royal* would have to be brought into Nanaimo at once, Brother XII flew into a rage and cursed Good. Nonetheless, the following morning he took the *Lady Royal* into Nanaimo, and passed the Customs inspection without incident.

After making formal entry into Canada, Brother XII took the *Lady Royal* into the Nanaimo dry dock. As his vessel was winched up the stays, he was astonished to see an enormous clotted mass of seaweed clinging to the bottom of his boat. When he hacked it away, he discovered an iron bar sticking out about ten feet on each side of the keel.

The owner of the dry dock in Kingston had devised a unique form of revenge. After his argument with Wilson and before he put the *Lady Royal* back into the water, he'd drilled a hole in the keel and hammered the bar through. Wilson had sailed through the Caribbean and up the Pacific coast, never suspecting that the reason his vessel was so sluggish and unresponsive in the storms that struck her was because she was dragging about five tons of kelp beneath her. By all accounts, he was livid.

Brother XII's return to British Columbia attracted major publicity. Bruce McKelvie wrote a front page story in *The Victoria Colonist,* headlined: "SMALL CRAFT ENDS HAZARDOUS OCEAN TRIP AT NANAIMO." He described Wilson as an experienced navigator and lover of the sea, and observed that his adventurous voyage smacked of "the fanciful undertakings of a Henty thriller or a Clark Russell story."

Maurice Von Platen objected to the publicity given Brother XII's return. He sent a copy of McKelvie's article to the Attorney-General, saying he believed Wilson intended to use such stories as a means of recruiting followers. He asked Pooley to issue a statement making it clear that the Aquarian Foundation had been dissolved in the public interest and that Wilson was prohibited by law from making any further use of the name.

Pooley, who had already received a great number of inquiries about Brother XII's return, called a press conference. He announced that the government wouldn't tolerate any attempt by Brother XII to revive the Aquarian Foundation, and told reporters that as far as the Attorney-General's office was concerned, "the operations of the Aquarian Foundation are at an end."

$$\triangle \quad \triangle \quad \triangle$$

The disciples at the Brothers' Center were glad that Brother XII was back, although for the first week or so they saw very little of him. He secluded himself on DeCourcy Island and didn't speak to anyone.

"He went immediately to DeCourcy with the greatest secrecy," Mary Connally recalled. "The thing I couldn't understand was all the secrecy. The blinds were pulled down and the lights were darkened, and I didn't know anything more that was going on there than if I had been an entire stranger."

On Sunday morning, November 16, Madame Z walked unannounced into Mary's house at Cedar. The two women had a long talk, during which Z told Mary that Brother XII expected her on DeCourcy Island soon. She also invited Mary to attend a general meeting that was being held that morning in the Center Building at Cedar.

At the meeting, Brother XII read an eighteen-page letter

that set out his new plans for the colony. One of the changes he proposed was the formation of an advisory council, to be composed of Alfred Barley, Roger Painter, Bruce Crawford, Bill Lowell, and Sarah Puckett, with himself as chairman. It would allow the disciples to participate in decisions affecting the colony and would give them greater autonomy.

Brother XII spent about twenty minutes after the meeting talking to Mary Connally. It was the last real conversation she was to have with him: "Apart from seeing him about half a dozen times, for perhaps five minutes at a time, I never saw him or talked to him or had any conversation with him. As far as the personnel were concerned, he absolutely ignored me as completely as if I didn't exist."

Roger Painter was another disciple baffled by Brother XII's behaviour. As a member of the new advisory council, he attended a meeting at which a drag-saw was ordered. When the saw arrived, he took it to the Point and was busy sawing wood for the stoves when Brother XII approached him:

"He came up and said, 'Why, this is a fine saw.'

"Then, speaking louder, he said, 'This is a fine saw!'

"And I said, 'Yes, we will cut some wood.'

"He said, 'Isn't this the one that has been rehabilitated and made over?'

"And I said, 'No, Brother; this is a new saw that we bought.'

"And like a flash, he came at me and cursed me for everything under the sun, and called me a dirty low-down sneak, and said that I had undermined him.

"I had forgotten that he had authorized the saw at the advisory council meeting. And I said, 'All right, sir; you can call me what you please, but I am not a sneak!'

"And he talked with me there for three solid hours, and called me every name under the sun, and at last Bruce Crawford happened to remember the case, that he had authorized the drag-saw himself—and that one time, we got the best of him!"

Not long after this incident, Brother XII dispensed with the advisory council, giving as his reason that it had taken action without referring the matter to himself. "In short," as Alfred Barley put it, "it had constituted itself an *administrative* instead of an *advisory* body."

On Valdes Island, the Heflingers and Regina LaCarte remained isolated in their cabin, unaware that Brother XII had returned. Alfred Barley sent them a letter demanding that they quit the premises, but the letter was so ambiguously worded that they didn't know if it was from Brother XII or not, so they ignored it.

At about ten o'clock on the morning of December 19, 1930, Oliver Heflinger heard his dog barking and looked out the window of the cabin. He saw Bruce and Georgia Crawford, Bill and Mary Lowell, Harold Krause, and the two Panamanian Indians, Louis John and Charles Foster, filing down the trail. When he opened the door, Crawford handed him three letters.

"Do you want them or don't you?" he asked.

Heflinger hesitated, uncertain what to say, but Adelaide stepped up behind him and cried, "We don't want any more of your letters! We've had enough of them!"

Crawford slowly put the letters in his pocket, then said, "Come on boys!" He and Bill Lowell grabbed Heflinger and pulled him out into the yard, where Harold Krause and the two Indians tied him up.

"Is this what you call Brotherhood?" Oliver protested.

"Keep still or I'll smash you in the face!" Lowell said.

"Would you hit a man with his hands tied behind his back?"

"If you don't keep still, I'll show you what I'll do!"

Crawford and the others marched into the house and grabbed the two women. Adelaide and Reggie tried to resist, but Crawford and Krause forced their arms down by their sides, while John and Foster tied them with rope around the elbows, then pushed them out the door and into the yard.

"You have been after this girl in a dirty way for a year," Adelaide said as Crawford tied Reggie's wrists behind her back.

"Yes, I have," Crawford replied, "and what are you going to do about it?"

The others went back inside the house and began throwing the Heflingers' bedding and other things into the yard, ignoring their pleas to be careful. When Oliver and the two women agreed to cooperate, Crawford untied them. The three were led single-file down the trail to the landing and were rowed out to the *Khuenaten*, which was anchored in the bay. After their belongings were loaded on board, they were held on the tugboat for three hours before it started for Vancouver Island.

The three were dropped off at Boat Harbour, south of Cedar, where Alfred Barley was waiting with Heflinger's car. "There is your machine," he said to Oliver. "You can get in and follow me for the road out." It was now dark and Heflinger lost sight of Barley's tail-lights on the twisting road. He came out on the main highway and drove to the Cranberry Hotel, where the three spent the night.

In Nanaimo, the Heflingers were interviewed by Sergeant Russell, Staff-Sergeant Owens, and Inspector W. S. Parsons of the B.C. Provincial Police. The three officers concluded that although there was sufficient evidence to warrant prosecution for kidnapping and assault, there could be little hope of securing a conviction. Parsons examined some of the Aquarian Foundation literature in the Heflingers' possession. In his report to Superintendent J. H. McMullin, he observed: "It disclosed borrowings from the precepts of Buddhism, Brahminism, Occultism, Astrology, Theosophy, and the rituals of Egypt. I noticed, too, that what is described as sexual relationship amongst ordinary people is touched upon within the sect as spiritual affinity. Probably, if the full truth is known, the leaders would be found to have more or less free intercourse with the more engaging of their female followers."

The Heflingers had the balance of the money they'd contributed to Brother XII's common maintenance fund returned to them by Frank Cunliffe. They received back $1,320;

Regina LaCarte had forty-two dollars refunded and was given a train ticket to Toronto, which she never used. She and the Heflingers remained in Nanaimo, living together in a tiny apartment on the outskirts of town. Oliver's sister, Lydia Howard, visited them there in the summer of 1932.

"They were living in near-poverty," she recalls. "My brother was very disappointed in this group and was reluctant to say much about it. He was reading a book called *A Dweller on Two Planets* when I was there and he would refer to that a great deal when we were talking.

"Reggie was the delicate, reclusive type. All she could talk about was Mahatma Gandhi—she worshipped the very idea of his name. Her hero worship was so extreme, it seemed to border on mental illness. And she'd say things like, 'This capitalist system is all wrong!'"

When World War II broke out, the Heflingers and Regina LaCarte returned to California. Adelaide died soon after from influenza. Reggie underwent a remarkable transformation: she made herself beautiful, married a lawyer in Oakland, and had a child. Oliver continued working as a house painter in Los Angeles, dying there in 1961 at the age of eighty-one.

"My father always said Oliver was the dreamer of the family," his sister recalls. "But I know he was quite disillusioned with this Aquarian community up in British Columbia. He had nothing good to say about it."

Elma Wilson, meanwhile, had returned from Switzerland after helping to organize a group there, only to discover that Brother XII wanted nothing more to do with her. He made it clear that she wasn't welcome on Valdes or DeCourcy—or even at Cedar, since Mary Connally was now living in the house he'd promised her. Still intimately involved with Madame Z, he had no place for Elma in his life.

Elma didn't completely give up hope. She took lodgings in North Vancouver, where she worked in the reference department of the public library. She remained friends with the

Jeffersons, often going for walks on the weekend with Dora, to whom she confided that she was still deeply in love with Wilson.

"She didn't say very much," Herbert Jefferson recalls, "but I think she must have been terribly let down. I know she wrote a letter to him in which she said, 'If ever you want any help, never mind the past; all will be forgiven. I'm still fond of you, and whatever you've done to me in the way of letting me down, I'll still take you back.'

"I think she must have died shortly afterwards because we never heard from her again. She went back to Scotland, I believe. She was a typical highbrow and bluestocking—the old-fashioned type. A nice person, but not the type that he wanted."

On Sunday morning, December 21, 1930, the Barleys had just finished breakfast when they heard a loud knock on the door. Opening it, they saw Bruce Crawford, Bill Lowell, Harold Krause, and the two Panamanians standing on the porch—a contingent which Wilson afterwards complacently referred to as his "wrecking gang." Crawford presented Barley with a letter from Brother XII which advised him and Annie that circumstances made it necessary that they be transferred immediately to Valdes Island. According to Barley, the letter was "a masterly production, being nicely calculated to remove any tendency on my part to display unwillingness or unreadiness to go."

Barley had no sooner finished reading the letter than "the gang" was hard at work removing him and his wife, lock, stock and barrel, from their house and carrying all of their belongings down to the *Khuenaten.*

In the house next door, Mary Connally was sitting at her typewriter composing a letter when Bruce Crawford and Bill Lowell walked in. Crawford handed the startled woman a note from Brother XII which said that owing to "adverse conditions" at Cedar, she must leave immediately for Valdes Island.

"The note asked me to please give these people all the help I could, as they knew what to do," Mary recounted.

Crawford told Leona Painter, who was living with Mary at the time, that she would accompany her to Valdes Island. With that, the wrecking gang began packing up all of Mary's belongings and carrying them down to the tugboat.

A short while later, bundled up against the cold, Mary and Leona stood on the deck of the *Khuenaten* with the Barleys and watched the houses of the Cedar settlement recede as the tug headed across Stuart Channel towards Valdes Island.

When the *Khuenaten* reached Valdes, the wrecking gang unloaded the tugboat, then stood back. Crawford told the new arrivals that they would have to carry everything by themselves up to the two cabins they would occupy. The *Khuenaten* chugged away, leaving the little group standing in the midst of a huge pile of tables, chairs, dressers and cabinets, clothing, bedding and linen, heavy steamer trunks, kitchen utensils, a sewing machine, boxes of books and other personal belongings. The four began hauling everything across the landing to the trail which led up to the cabins. Mary Connally and Leona Painter's destination was a cabin located a quarter of a mile away at the top of a steep hill. The Barleys had been assigned to another cabin an eighth of a mile beyond that.

The little group struggled valiantly, dragging their things to the beginning of the trail before undertaking the difficult task of lugging everything up to the cabins. The two elderly women and the frail Barley were unaccustomed to physical labour of any kind—Annie and Mary were both sixty-three years of age—but they worked strenuously, awkwardly carrying their heavy burdens up the primitive trail. Stumbling over rocks and tree roots, hands numbed by the cold, limbs aching from the strain, they tried desperately to finish before darkness fell.

At last, they had successfully moved everything into the two cabins. They sank down, exhausted from the ordeal. In spite of their fatigue, however, they must have felt gratified by their effort, for they knew that the transfer to Valdes Island had a special significance.

"It had been generally understood among us," Barley later explained, "that Cedar, Valdes and DeCourcy represented three degrees of discipleship. Cedar was for the merely interested; Valdes was for the neophytes; and DeCourcy was for the accepted disciples. According to one's fitness or adaptability, he or she might be graded to, or maybe de-graded from, one or other of these locations as the general development of the Work might determine. When a sudden removal was insisted upon, it was supposed that the person so moved had in some way 'fallen down on the job,' or else was taking the place of some other who had side-slipped, and the seemingly needless inconvenience was cheerfully accepted."

Acting in this spirit, Barley sat down as soon as the move to Valdes was completed and even before getting a meal wrote a letter to Brother XII. He later recalled: "I cooperated with all my heart and wrote him on the same day, saying it was 'the finest game I had ever played,' lest the kindly heart I then believed in should imagine that I had been put to any discomfort."

In their cabin on Valdes, Mary Connally and Leona Painter were forced to make do as best they could in primitive living conditions. The house had been stripped when its former occupants, the Heflingers and Regina LaCarte, were evicted. It was now little more than an empty shell, with a rough floor and holes in the walls. The cold came up through the floorboards from the frozen ground below, since the house had no foundation of any kind. Mary's bedroom faced north and had huge windows which let out all the heat from the one-hole coal stove she'd brought with her. The only other source of heat was a small cooking stove in the main room. There was no plumbing or running water, just an outhouse and a well for water.

Valdes Island was bleak in winter. A bitterly cold wind blew in from the Strait of Georgia, chilling Mary and Leona to the bone. They spent most of their time wrapped in heavy sweaters and overcoats, huddling around the coal stove, trying to keep warm. At night, the cold penetrated every crack in the house, making sleep impossible. This was not the kind of Christmas to which Mary was accustomed in Asheville. There was no brightly-lit tree, crackling fire or turkey dinner, no family or friends with whom to celebrate the holiday season— only the two of them, alone and miserable in a wretched hovel on Valdes Island.

Mary found her present circumstances ironic, given the fact that Nanaimo residents had thought the "Aquarium Foundation" had something to do with fish: "You can imagine the cold that I suffered," she recalled. "That was an 'Aquarium.' I used to feel that I was in an aquarium of ice-cold water every night."

The Barleys were warmer and more comfortable in their cabin. They had only been on Valdes for about a week when Brother XII invited them over to DeCourcy Island to visit him and Madame Z. In the evenings, the two couples sat around the fire and talked of their mutual interests.

One night, the Barleys were surprised to hear Madame Z complain bitterly about Mary Connally. "You know, Annie," she said, "with reference to this Work, we have some very difficult problems to solve. Mary Connally is our worst problem. She is the fussiest person. She wants her servants. If she wanted a glass of water, she wouldn't get it for herself. She wants this, that, and the other, and she expects us to wait on her. That is all very fine, but we cannot do it."

Brother XII, who was sitting nearby, nodded in agreement. "Yes," he added, "she will never do for this Work. She even wants us to bring her a cup of coffee in the morning before she can get up!"

The invitation to DeCourcy was to prompt more than a social call from the Barleys. Their visit conveniently provided Alfred with the opportunity to turn over his inheritance to Brother XII, as well as the remainder of his savings.

On December 31, 1930, the Barleys made a special trip into

Nanaimo. Alfred withdrew $4,900 from the Canadian Bank of Commerce, the second installment of his inheritance, adding it to the $5,100 that he'd withdrawn earlier. During Brother XII's absence, he'd also put aside $1,855 in gold coins and $760 in two-dollar bills, to make a grand total of $12,615. Barley was acting in accordance with Brother XII's instructions to the disciples that all contributions must be in permanently negotiable securities—the order of preference being gold, dominion currency bills, and bank bills of the smallest denomination.

The Barleys spent the night in Nanaimo, staying at the Globe Hotel. Alfred's solemn mood was in marked contrast to the festivities of the small town welcoming the New Year. "I well remember the noise of the fireworks," he recalled.

On the evening of January 2, 1931, Brother XII rowed Barley out to the *Lady Royal,* which was anchored in the lagoon. Once on board, he asked Bruce and Georgia Crawford to withdraw because he and Alfred had "some business to transact." Barley, who had wrapped the money in brown paper, put several packages on the table. Brother XII didn't open the packages and count the money, but asked Barley to write on each one the amount it contained and his initials. He then locked the packages in the small safe in the cabin of the *Lady Royal.* There were no witnesses to the transaction.

"I noted the strange circumstances of our being alone on the ship," Barley recalled, "and reflected that it was 'open to construction,' as they say, had I been disposed to suspect him. But when you take a man for a spiritual leader, you treat him as one, and therefore I regarded this circumstance as a test of my single-mindedness, which indeed it might have been."

A few days later, Brother XII called Roger Painter on board. He opened the safe, removed a package containing about $4,000 in ten- and twenty-dollar bills, and handed it to Painter with the words, "Here, take this money, Roger, and get it changed into one- and two-dollar bills. I don't see why that fool Barley didn't give me ones and twos, instead of tens and twenties!"

The Barleys returned to Valdes Island. They were amazed to find Mary Connally's things in their cabin and to discover that their own belongings had been transferred to the cabin occupied by Mary and Leona. In short, they'd been made to trade places with them. Barley was mystified. "Here again, no reason ever transpired for this sudden and arbitrary *volte face,*" he recalled. "No reason even now suggests itself to me, beyond finding out just how far we could be played about with, without rebelling."

A few days after Mary Connally and Leona Painter had installed themselves in the cabin, Madame Z appeared and told Mary that she would have to work like the other colonists. Taking Leona aside, she told her that she was not to wait on Mary any more, that Mary had to learn how to do things for herself. "I do not even want you to wash a dish for her," she instructed Leona.

Mary now began to work like she'd never worked before. She cooked, scrubbed floors, washed windows, spaded the garden, painted the floors in two unfinished cabins, chopped and carried wood, and helped the other disciples with their chores. She was also made "the carrier," the person who had to transport the food and other supplies to the different cabins on the island. Bent over from the weight of the heavy loads on her back, Mary staggered along the forest trails, supervised by Leona Painter, who drove her relentlessly, making sure she never stopped to rest.

"I thought possibly it was a test," Mary said later. "I had been raised in great luxury and wasn't supposed to lift a glass of water for myself."

Mary believed that the constant work and physical privation was a form of initiation, which would strengthen her soul and prepare her to take a step forward into higher consciousness.

"It was a species of discipline—discipline to the limit—and I was very proud, I suppose, and I didn't want to think that anybody could do what I couldn't do, and I did push myself to the limit."

On January 30, 1931, after nearly a month of gruelling labour, Mary received a letter from Brother XII:

> Dear Lady Mary:
> After some consideration, it seems to me that the conditions on Valdes are too primitive for you, and although the change from Cedar has, I hope, done you some good, yet I do not think you would be either happy or wise to remain there indefinitely.
> Will you let me know if you would prefer to return to Cedar, because if so, we will arrange to make the transfer for you at the earliest moment. My feeling is that you should return to Cedar and remain there (or at any other outside point you may choose). . .

Mary knew what the letter meant—she had failed the test. She was devastated: "It nearly broke my heart to think that I had failed. Going back to Cedar was a disgrace—it was a disgrace. I was trying to make the grade, and I didn't know what to do. I felt sick. I wished I were dead."

Mary replied to the letter by writing to Brother XII, telling him she was happy on Valdes and wished to remain there: "I was trying to make the grade and I was so sick, I didn't know what to do. I wanted to be dead and I pretended to be happy when I wasn't."

Madame Z arrived at Mary's cabin and told her to be ready to leave at a moment's notice. Mary accepted the situation and packed her things: "There is no Czar in the world that has been more autocratic. I even packed my underdress and toothbrush for a week, so that if they came in the morning, I would be ready."

The days passed and no one came. Two weeks later, Madame Z appeared at the cabin and informed Mary that she would remain on Valdes Island.

Mary resolved to make the most of this second chance to prove herself. She redoubled her efforts, driving herself to the point of exhaustion. Some of the jobs seemed pointless. "I had to walk this trail every day to see if there was any mail," she recalled. "It was a three-mile walk. I walked that trail every day for a period of three weeks—and there was never any mail. But rain or shine, snow or heat, I had to go."

Mary was again mercilessly supervised by Leona Painter, who made sure the older woman carried out all her tasks at high speed and under the most terrific pressure. Leona herself was being driven by fears which Brother XII had planted in her mind. Shortly after he'd returned from England, he'd separated Leona from her new husband and forbade the couple to see each other. He'd told Leona that if she didn't do exactly as she was told, she would lose her soul: "When he told us that we had failed in the Work, why, we were lost for aeons of time— and that would put you through intense agony—and they sent me away, and I didn't know whether I would see my husband again. And that—combined with the other pressure they put on me—made it all I could do to keep hold of my mind."

Mary didn't realize at the time why Leona treated her so cruelly. It was only later that she learned of the young woman's desperation: "She drove me as she certainly wouldn't have done if she hadn't been on the verge of losing her mind. Nobody would have driven a woman of my age—with the weakness of my body—the way she drove me. She was almost insane from being separated from her husband, and from the fear of losing her soul."

Three weeks later, Roger Painter came to Valdes with orders from Brother XII that the two women must return to Cedar. Once again, they had to be ready to leave at a moment's notice. After delivering his message, Painter returned at once to DeCourcy Island—obeying Brother XII's directive not to otherwise communicate with them.

Mary and Leona quickly packed their things and waited for the *Khuenaten*. Several days passed. Then Madame Z appeared at the door and told them to move into a nearby warehouse and to remain there until further notice, since several new arrivals to the colony would be moving into their cabin. Mary and Leona carried their belongings over to a dilapidated wooden building with a dirt floor. Boards were missing from the walls and there was a gaping hole in the roof through which the rain poured. Again, the only source of heat was the one-hole coal stove that they brought with them, and their only source of water was at the top of the hill, two hundred yards away.

Mary and Leona tried to patch the hole in the roof and mend the broken walls. Wet and miserable, they huddled in the dark interior of their squalid home, sleeping on straw mattresses and shivering from the cold. At the end of three days and nights, they were exhausted and demoralized.

The fourth morning, Madame Z suddenly appeared from around the corner of the warehouse. "You have to leave in twenty minutes," she told them. "The Brother is here. I just saw him, just spoke to him. You cannot take any of your things—you can buy others."

The two women desperately began packing up some of their belongings to take back to Cedar. Mary started pulling her dresses out of the trunks she'd put them in, but Madame Z stopped her. She marched Mary and Leona down the trail to the *Khuenaten,* which carried them swiftly away from shore. "I had to leave everything," Mary recalled. "All my dresses and everything I had were strewn out there and left in the pouring rain!"

Mary and Leona were returned to Cedar on March 17, 1931, after spending three months on Valdes. But their ordeal was not yet over. Madame Z commanded them to cultivate a three-acre field in order to "provide food for the destitute." The two women worked seven hours a day, plowing and harrowing the field. They even worked in the rain, wading through the mud like two penitents, in the belief that it was a test to make them fit to serve humanity.

"I still didn't realize," Mary said. "I thought it was a test just to see if I could make good, if there was anything in this world that would hold me back in this work I had come here for—the freeing of humanity from its shackles."

The work took its toll upon the elderly woman. Mary's body ached, her hands became rough and worn, and she lost twenty-eight pounds during the time she worked in the field. The other disciples noticed how frail and ill she looked, but they did not help her, since Madame Z had forbidden them to communicate with either Mary or Leona.

"They instilled in all of us the most horrible religious superstition that could be imagined," a dismayed Leona later recounted. "The others were given instructions that Mary Connally and I emanated such terrible vibrations that they shouldn't come near us or they'd be contaminated, and that we were cheap, common people.

"We did not understand it until afterwards, when we found out that practically everybody was told the same thing about everybody else, and no one felt that they could trust anyone. Usually they told you about some awful spirit that worked through different ones."

For weeks, the pair continued working in the field. Was this brutal labour a final attempt by Brother XII and Madame Z to force Mary to resign from the Work? Rumours that she was even yoked to a plow and made to till the field like an animal make one wonder if the hard labour wasn't part of a deliberate plan to shorten her life.

One day, Mary was told by Madame Z that her work was finished. From then on, she was considered by the other disciples to have been permanently downgraded in the Work. Perhaps to placate her, Brother XII gave her the job of receiving new arrivals to the colony. It was only later that Mary realized she'd been misused. "They knew that the States was in a bad way and that I didn't have any more money—and that they had finished with me absolutely!" she declared.

At about the same time as Mary and Leona were returned to Cedar, the Barleys were also removed from Valdes Island. On March 30, 1931, Madame Z popped her head in at the door of their cabin and informed them they had just twenty minutes to pack and get ready to be taken to DeCourcy Island. They cooperated with "hearty good will," as Alfred put it, since the transfer to DeCourcy meant they'd been "promoted" in the Work: "We felt honoured, for had we not 'attained'?"

On DeCourcy, the Barleys were uncomfortably housed in a small, two-room cabin with the Crawfords—to say nothing of their dog. They tolerated the crowded living conditions in the hope that they'd soon be moved to a cabin of their own.

Instead, ten days later, they were ordered back to Cedar. The ostensible reason was that they could look after the property there, although Brother XII was already paying George Hobart thirty dollars a month as caretaker. The Barleys realized they'd been "demoted," that in some mysterious way, they'd failed to measure up to Brother XII's standards.

This fall from grace was disturbing enough, but to make matters worse, they'd lost many valuable possessions as they'd been shuffled about from place to place. "The consequence of these repeated and French-farce like moves," Alfred recalled, "was that our belongings not only got disarranged, but misplaced, and some of them we never did locate as they passed into general storage in a somewhat promiscuous way."

There now followed a period of relative calm for the Barleys at Cedar. The disciples on Valdes and DeCourcy, however, continued to be subjected to a regimen of hard physical labour. The majority of them submitted to it without complaint, motivated as they were by a spirit of discipline and devotion to a cause. They had, after all, been warned in advance what to expect when they came to the colony. *The Brothers' School* paper clearly stated: "The activities of the Great White Lodge can be summed up in one word—WORK. This work is endless, never-ceasing. . . Those who come to us will be expected to support our Work and our Cause TO THE UTTERMOST."

The disciples believed that the hardships they endured were dictated by Brother XII's zeal for the spiritual welfare of the community. They continued to regard him, for the most part, in the best possible light. He was, as Alfred Barley expressed it, "the representative—the incarnation almost—of our ideal of this new brotherhood movement, which we believed was in the process of being established."

CHAPTER
XI
Amiel and Zura de Valdes

On a crisp morning in February 1931, Fermin Sepulveda and his twenty-one-year-old stepdaughter, Valea, carried furniture out of their house in Monterey to the four-wheeled trailer parked in the driveway. Inside their comfortable home in Franklin Heights, his wife, Isona, and the two younger children, fourteen-year-old Dion and his thirteen-year-old sister, Sereta, packed kitchen utensils into boxes and carried suitcases into the front hallway. After a last look at the house, Isona and the children climbed into the Model T Ford, while Fermin gave a final tug on the ropes of the fully loaded trailer. He then eased the car and trailer out into the traffic on Franklin Avenue and the Sepulvedas began their journey to the Brothers' Center.

Fermin and Isona had been secretaries of an Aquarian Foundation group in Monterey before they were summoned by Brother XII to British Columbia. Formerly an opera singer, Isona had studied *bel canto* under Enrico Caruso and had understudied Amelita Galli-Curci at the New York Met. After a series of tempestuous marriages ended her career, she'd supported herself and her children as a singing teacher in Monterey. Her interest in metaphysics extended to an affair with Dr. Frank L. Riley, a noted Theosophist; she'd accompanied him to Palmito del Verde, an island off Mazatlan, where they collaborated on *The Bible of Bibles*, a sourcebook of the world's religions. A handsome Castilian Spaniard, Fermin Sepulveda was a resourceful and highly skilled handyman, with a strong mystical inclination. He'd met Isona while attending her Theosophy classes in Pacific Grove and become her fourth husband and a good stepfather to her three children.

The Sepulvedas did not proceed directly north to Canada. Instead, they followed the circuitous route which Brother XII had prescribed for them. First, they drove to Salinas, where they picked up an elderly walnut farmer named Edgar Conrow, who slipped an attaché case full of bank notes under the front seat. The little party then crossed the Sierra Nevada Mountains, driving fifteen-hundred miles east to Bismark, North Dakota. Turning north, Conrow and the Sepulvedas entered Canada at North Portal, Saskatchewan, under fictitious names, telling the Immigration officials they planned to homestead in the Peace River district of British Columbia.

"Brother XII was paranoid," Valea Sepulveda explains. "He should have had us sprinkle twists of paper behind us, like the Chinese do, to keep the evil spirits from following us. He probably thought that all the evil spirits in the world were going to trace him to his lair!"

Battling freezing temperatures and a howling blizzard, the Sepulvedas headed west across the prairies. Blocked by a landslide in the Rocky Mountains, they loaded their car and trailer onto a flatcar and proceeded by train to Revelstoke, where they resumed their journey, driving down the Fraser River Canyon on a board road that hung precariously out over the precipice. "There were boards missing from the road," Dion recalls, "so we packed our own two-by-twelve and every time we came to a missing board, we stuck ours in."

When the Sepulvedas arrived in Vancouver, Fermin telephoned Frank Cunliffe's office in Nanaimo and was told to sell the car and trailer and to convert everything the family had brought into cash. Isona kept a few of her cooking utensils, but Fermin sold the remainder of their belongings at a fraction of their value. The Sepulvedas then boarded the ferry for Nanaimo, where Bruce Crawford was waiting for them in the *Khuenaten.*

"I remember when we hit Cedar, the spring flowers were beginning to come up," Valea recalls, "and it was just beautiful there. We stayed at Cedar for a day or two; then we were transferred to Valdes Island, starry-eyed."

One night about a week later, the Sepulvedas and a number of other new arrivals at the colony assembled in the main meeting hall on Valdes Island and turned over all their money to Brother XII. Included were the proceeds from the sale of the Sepulvedas' house in Monterey and the contents of Edgar Conrow's attaché case.

"There was a wad of bills passed out there," Valea exclaims. "I never saw so much money in all my born days! That table was piled high with it, and it was all in cash."

In the days following the meeting, Brother XII assessed the skills of the new arrivals and assigned them to different locations in the colony. "He had a deliberate policy of separating families," Dion recalls. "If there was a tight family group, he'd break it up." Isona Sepulveda and her two daughters, Sereta and Valea, were sent to the farm on the west side of DeCourcy. Fermin went to the Point to build a sawmill at the head of the bay, while Dion was given a special task.

"I had an interview with him, and he said he needed me because no one else could do the jobs he wanted me to do," Dion says. "He wanted me to be the cabin boy on the *Lady Royal.* It was flattery, pure flattery!"

Dion moved into Brother XII's house at the Point and lived with him and Madame Z almost as an adopted son.

"Wilson wanted Dion," Valea recalls. "He was the most good-looking young chap you ever laid eyes on. He was a plum—an absolute plum!"

"My job on the *Lady Royal* was clean-up duty," Dion reminisces, "and he started at the basics with me. He taught me how to scrub the ship, handle the ropes, take out the storm sails and air them in the sun. He taught me the rudiments of shooting a sun-line and a moon-line, and how to navigate by the stars—all the stars I know the names of today are from that time. He'd say, 'Dion, break out the nine canvas!' '*Yessir!*' And away I'd go, racing across the deck to show what I could do!"

For Dion, the experience gave him a sailor's education that ultimately led to a career in the United States Navy. He served on submarines, rising rapidly through the ranks and retiring as a lieutenant commander after twenty-four years of sea duty. Today, he credits the training he received from Brother XII for his success.

"He was an absolute craftsman at sea who inspired confidence in anyone who was with him," he says. "We frequently took the *Lady Royal* out in inclement weather and it didn't bother us a bit. He was not a man to shirk his duties—we careened the *Lady* twice while I was there. Although a lot of it was hard work, it was exciting to a youth of fourteen."

Because Dion lived in the same house as Brother XII and Madame Z, he had plenty of opportunity to observe them in their private lives, when they weren't playing their roles as the colony's spiritual leaders.

"Frequently, Z would visit my room to see that it was 'ship-shape and Bristol fashion,'" he recalls. "She showed me how to make the bed and explained what my other duties were. She was an awfully cold woman, though—I never could understand how anybody could climb into bed with that gal! But he did, so they must have had a pretty strong affection for each other in spite of their frequent quarrels.

"Z was very strong-headed—she was like a Billingsgate fish-wife when she got mad! That was Z! One time, he put a box with a long board on top of it outside a newly constructed cabin that needed a staircase. She stepped on the end of the board and it kranged her kneecap. She flew into a rage at him for putting it there. The argument ended up with Brother XII putting the board back and saying, '*Goddamn it! Leave that board there!*' Just an emotional display! Well, I witnessed all this and wondered about being at the feet of the Master!"

Valea Sepulveda worked at the farm on the west side of DeCourcy, taking care of the animals and doing farm work. "We were a slave troop," she recalls. "I was five-foot-six, and in the time I was there, I shrank three inches from heavy labour!" Valea always did her best to avoid Madame Z. "I was her pet hate. She would lay us out in lavender when anything went wrong, and she was utterly despicable to the horses—she beat them unmercifully!"

Valea was understandably shocked when her mother told her that she must have sex with Edgar Conrow, the elderly walnut farmer who had accompanied them to the colony. Isona explained that everyone had been assigned a partner and that it was part of her initiation.

That night, Valea waited anxiously in her bed. When she heard footsteps on the stairs and saw the silhouettes of the men coming into the dormitory, she jumped out of bed and slipped out the open window. She shinnied down a tree and ran to the barn.

"My partner was an older man," she recalls, "and I admit I wasn't too kind to him when he cornered me in the barn. He came off second-best. I don't know the details of their theory, but it had something to do with the *kundalini*. They believed they could achieve eternal youth through the sex act. I can guarantee you that there were some high times that went on there! My escape route out the window and down that tree was the only thing that saved my skin!"

Isona Sepulveda was a volatile, highly-sexed woman, a seductress who had broken up many homes. Fidelity wasn't an issue between her and Fermin. Most men found Isona irresistible and Brother XII was no exception.

"Brother XII invited my mother to visit him at the Point," recalls Valea. "The two were fascinated with each other. I know she slept with him because she bragged about it—she was never one to hide her affairs of the heart. She didn't go into the physical details too much, but she spoke of it as a great spiritual experience."

Sereta was taken away from her mother and sent to Valdes Island. Alone and unprotected, the innocent young girl was sexually assaulted by one of the disciples.

"What really got me," Valea recalls, "was when my little sister was raped. The whole thing made me ill, because she was only about thirteen at the time. She didn't really understand what had happened and she was a bit bruised up. I don't know whether it happened more than once or not, I only know of the one time."

Brother XII soon tired of his affair with Isona Sepulveda. Exasperated by her demands, he threatened to maroon her on Ruxton Island without food or water.

"Ruxton Island was Devil's Island," Valea explains. "It was the jailhouse. There was a small cabin there and you survived if you could. I know of at least two people from the colony who were sent there, and one of them never came back."

In dread, Isona fled DeCourcy Island. The hysterical woman rowed ten miles across Stuart Channel to Chemainus. Cold and wet, she staggered up the beach to the small lumber town and ran, distraught, along the main street, before slumping down exhausted on the veranda of the Green Dragon Hotel.

When he discovered that she'd gone, Brother XII sent Fermin and the children to Chemainus to bring Isona back. They found her at the Green Dragon, and Fermin pleaded with her to return with them to the colony. Isona refused. Grabbing Dion and Sereta, she swore to protect them and said she'd never permit them to go back to the island.

Fermin and Valea returned to DeCourcy to report to Brother XII, while Isona hurried to the local police station, where she poured out her story to Sergeant Hall. He drove her and the two children to Cedar, where Maurice Von Platen succeeded in calming Isona down enough so that she could give a coherent account of what had happened. Von Platen then took her, Dion, and Sereta back to Chemainus, where he paid for a room for them in the Green Dragon Hotel.

The next day, Sunday, May 25, Von Platen wrote to Attorney-General R.H. Pooley, describing Mrs. Sepulveda's experiences at the colony and asking the government to intervene on the family's behalf:

> From her statement, the conditions at Valdes, and more still, at the DeCourcy Islands, are unspeakable, but the specific charge she makes are that her little daughter was attacked by a person named Bill, and was placed under this brute's orders, and that her boy was taken in by Wilson, and, according to his own statement, slept with Wilson and was made the so-called Sun God, and completely alienated from her. This boy said last evening that he had another disclosure to make which would put the man at the head of the colony under the law, but refused last evening to particularize, but said that the offence was of a nature against morality. He will tell the police.
>
> These people came here ostensibly as agriculturists, are entirely without funds, and as I am satisfied that their story is true, as it confirms the whole dirty mess brought out in the hearing of my case against Wilson, I appeal to you to take such steps as are in your power to assist them in blotting out this cancer in the province.

Brother XII evidently decided that he didn't want Fermin or Valea at the colony after all, so he sent them to Chemainus to join the rest of the family. After a heated argument in the hotel room, Isona finally persuaded Fermin to make a statement to the police.

The Sepulvedas were taken to Victoria by Sergeant Hall and

interviewed by Inspector Thomas W.S. Parsons of the B.C. Provincial Police. After obtaining separate statements from each of the family members, he concluded: "The allegations of Von Platen cannot be proved. There has been no impropriety where the boy is concerned, but there seems to have been an unprovable indecency perpetrated upon the little girl by the man 'Bill,' a resident of Valdes Island." Parsons recommended that the Department of Immigration launch a full inquiry and suggested that perhaps if the American principals of the colony could be deported, the colony would break up.

The Sepulvedas returned to the Green Dragon Hotel. Exhausted by their interrogation, they went to bed early. But Dion couldn't sleep. He lay awake, wrestling with the feeling that he must return to DeCourcy Island. Finally, he slipped out of bed, tiptoed past his sleeping stepfather and crawled through the open window onto the roof of the veranda. Lowering himself off the edge, he dropped down to the ground.

Dion ran down to the dock, where he picked out a likely-looking fishing boat, started up the engine and cast off. He'd nearly cleared the harbour when a police launch cut him off— someone had seen him stealing the boat. Kicking and yelling, he was dragged back to his family.

"I'd been hypnotized," he later explained. "Before I left DeCourcy, Roger Painter hypnotized me and gave me some post-hypnotic instructions to report back to him by any means possible. I fought the idea of going back to the hotel. I think my step dad tied me up that night. Gradually, I was brought back to the realm of normality."

A few days later, Dion knelt in the prow of an Immigration vessel and guided it through the reef into the lagoon at DeCourcy Island. He acted as pilot against his will. "I felt very bad about it at the time," he recalls. Dion stayed on board while the officers went ashore and walked up to Brother XII's house. When there was no answer, they pushed open the front door and stepped inside. Brother XII and Madame Z had apparently fled, leaving everything behind. After wandering through the deserted rooms, the officers inspected the other houses at the Point. They, too, had been hastily abandoned. Leaving the contents of the houses undisturbed, the police withdrew.

After the Immigration boat had gone, the colonists returned from their hiding places in the woods, and the life of the colony resumed. The police didn't come back and no charges were ever laid.

But now an astonishing thing occurred. The Sepulvedas actually *returned* to DeCourcy Island, reconciled their differences with Brother XII, and were reinstated into the community. Dion was taken back into Brother XII's household and remained there for another year. He emphatically denies the allegations contained in Maurice Von Platen's letter:

"There was never any homosexuality on the part of Wilson. He certainly made no overtures towards me; if he did, I would have known it. I was never made the Sun God, and I never slept with Wilson—nor did I ever say I did."

On the whole, Dion's view of his relationship with Brother XII is remarkably positive. "He was more of a father figure to me than anything else," he says. "He taught me a lot, especially about sailing. My only regret is that we didn't put out to sea more often in the *Lady*. I always thought he would have been good at training kids."

Brother XII had ended his affair with Isona Sepulveda, but he continued to entertain other women at the Point. "He had a number of overnight guests," Dion recalls. "I just regarded them as visitors. I don't know for sure that he slept with them, but afterwards, there'd be arguments between him and Z— she seemed jealous."

In the spring of 1931, a young married couple named Alice and Carlin Rudy, both thirty years old, arrived at the colony from Chicago. Although Alice has no particular loyalty to Brother XII, she still defends him against his critics. "It was awfully hard on him because he could *not* get the right people," she says. "They would not cooperate. They thought they knew what this work was about, and they *didn't* know, and he could *not* get through to them!

"A lot of them, even my own husband, were unstable. They were off the beam! They couldn't keep it in the spiritual—they brought it down to the mental, and then it drove them bugs!

"Those Sepulvedas were the worst ones! Mrs. Sepulveda was as crazy as a bed-bug! She was mental—she'd go into hysterical fits! She took any kindness that you tried to show as something dirty. Like one night, the father didn't come home until late. Dion was crying, so I put my arm around his shoulders to comfort him. And she told Mabel that I was trying to seduce him—that's the kind of mind she had!"

Before coming to the colony, Alice had worked for ten years at the Marshall Fields department store in Chicago, supporting her husband while he tried his hand as an inventor, prospector, salesman, pianist, and poet.

"He had a good job with the railroad, but he always quit it," she says. "They took him back five different times! Oh, he was always going to invent something or find gold, or write something, but he never did. Even his own mother told him, 'One of these days, Alice is going to wake up and you're going to lose your meal-ticket!'"

Browsing in a Chicago bookstore one day, Carlin found a copy of *The Three Truths*. He began writing to Brother XII, who was so impressed with his letters, he invited Carlin and his wife to the colony. "My husband corresponded with these people for two years and I knew nothing about it," Alice recalls. When Carlin announced that they were going to British Columbia, Alice didn't object; she was so disillusioned with the marriage, she felt anything would be better than their present situation.

"We didn't put in a dime," she recalls. "They sent us $385 in Fargo, North Dakota, so we'd have enough money to get into Canada. My husband splurged all the way. He stayed in the best hotels and ate in expensive restaurants. Even going over on the ferry from Vancouver to Victoria, he went to the dining room for a regular meal, while I went to the lunch counter for a sandwich. 'That isn't your money,' I said, 'You have no right spending it!'"

The Rudys arrived in Chemainus, where they were met by Madame Z. "She and Carlin clashed from the start," Alice remembers. "She was mad when she found out he'd spent all the money they sent him. And when she told us the men and women slept in separate dormitories, he battled her on that! 'What kind of outfit is this,' he said, 'where a man can't even sleep with his own wife?'"

It was soon apparent that Carlin wasn't going to fit in at the colony. He'd sleep late and have a leisurely breakfast, then spend the day under a shady tree reading a book, while the other men were busy putting up fences or building the goat barn. Carlin's contribution to the work was in the form of suggestions: "Why don't you modernize? Get some generators in here! Get some electricity!" He also asked the kinds of questions that Mabel didn't appreciate, such as, "*Where does this outfit get its money?*"

Alice, on the other hand, had been raised on a farm and loved the work. "It was just what I needed! I'd been working in a department store for ten years, and my feet were broken down from standing on a cement floor—I was taking electric treatments on my feet every day. When I took my shoes off and went barefoot in the warm earth, my feet got better. I loved it there—it was like paradise!"

The Rudys were in Canada on a two-month visitors permit. When it expired, they had to leave. "Mabel knew I was unhappy with my husband," Alice recalls. "She took me aside before we left and said, 'Get rid of him! He's nothing but an anchor around your neck and that's all he'll ever be! I cannot tell you what to do or how to do it—just go and get rid of him!' She pinned some money in the cuff of my coat and said, 'You're welcome to come back!'"

In Seattle, the Rudys checked into the New Richmond Hotel. The next morning, as Alice recounts, "I said to him, 'Well, one of us has got to go to work, and I guess it's going to be me. I'm going downstairs to get a newspaper, so I can look for a job.' It was just like something took me by the shoulders and walked me over to the dock. I didn't look back! I caught the boat to Victoria; then took a bus to Nanaimo and a cab to Cedar, where I stayed the night with Mary Connally.

"The next morning, Bruce Crawford came over in the *Khuenaten* to pick up supplies, so I jumped on board and went back to the island with him. When Wilson saw me, he just raised his eyebrows—he didn't say a word!"

When Alice didn't return to the hotel, Carlin contacted the Seattle police and reported her missing. Realizing she'd probably gone back to the colony, he re-entered Canada, borrowed a rowboat in Chemainus and rowed the ten miles to DeCourcy Island.

Word quickly spread across the island that Rudy had landed and was looking for his wife. When Roger Painter notified Brother XII that Carlin had returned, he had a fit. "Throw him overboard!" he shouted. "Throw him off the cliff! Throw him in the ocean! Drown him!"

"We don't do that kind of thing here!" Painter roared. Rudy was seized, placed in an empty cabin and guarded all night. In the morning, Bruce Crawford and Bill Lowell put him in his rowboat and towed it out into Stuart Channel. Rudy was set adrift off Yellow Point and with some difficulty made it back to shore.

Carlin returned to Seattle, but kept bombarding Alice with letters. Most of them were intercepted by Madame Z, who screened all the mail. "She always put a hex on the mail to take away the outside vibrations," Alice recalls. "I saw her putting letters directly into the stove without even opening them, so I knew they were from him."

Alice admits she went through "an awful torment" leaving her husband, but says she's always been grateful for Mabel's advice. "She did me the greatest favour of my life when she told me to leave him, so I praise her!"

Alice remained at the colony, becoming one of the most hard-working members of the community. "I'd get up at two o'clock in the morning to get the washing out, so I could work in the garden," she recalls. "I baked thirty-five loaves of bread at a time—whole wheat, but I had to make white for Wilson. We canned a hundred quarts of vegetables a day. I planted sweet peas for the honey bees—and when those sweet peas bloomed, I was in heaven!"

Alice prepared most of Brother XII's meals. "I cooked a lot of custards, junket, and rice pudding for him," she recalls. "He'd had an operation in Italy and some of his digestive organs had been removed, so he had to eat real careful. I was the only one he'd let take his meal in to him. He liked me because I was impersonal. The others irritated him—they always had to be so perfect for 'The Brother.'"

Alice remembers that Brother XII spent a great deal of time writing. "He wouldn't allow kids at the Point because they were noisy. They'd disturb his concentration. One of them got hold of a tin pan one day and he was a-banging on it! Boy! Old XII come out of there like a lion! Any noise, any vibration would break his spell!

"He had a little water-spaniel named Topsy. She didn't bark—she didn't bother anyone. He loved Topsy. He kept chocolate candy for her—big boxes of chocolate drops. We didn't get any chocolate candy! I used to steal some once in a while and pass it around. And I used to steal his tobacco for the boys. I'd fluff it up so he wouldn't miss it. Here they were trusting me—the only one they trusted in the house—and I was swiping his tobacco!

"He asked me once, 'Do you know what this Work is about?' I said, 'No,' and he said, 'Well, thank God, *one*—just *one* is honest! If the people who came here would just admit they didn't know, they'd have a chance to learn!'

"What I couldn't understand was why they were all so afraid of him. One night, we were at the supper table and I said to everyone, 'You all act like a bunch of scared cats! What are you scared of? He's only a human being! He's only a man!'

"'*Well, if we fail here, we'll lose our souls!*'

"I said, 'Well, if I had a soul when I came here, I'm sure as hell going to have one when I leave! Anyway, *I am a soul,* so how can I lose my soul?'

"Afterwards, Mary Lowell dashed over to the Point and tattled on me. When Brother XII come down, I let him have it with both barrels! I talked back to him as if he were no more than—one of the goats there! They almost all fainted! '*Why, didn't you realize you were talking right into the power-house?*' It didn't bother me none. They were so afraid to talk back to him. They were like a bunch of puppets, like people you work on strings—marionettes!"

Alice admits, however, that Brother XII and Madame Z possessed powers beyond those of the ordinary person. "I remember once, Dion was racing up to the house to tell XII something—he was a little tattle-tale! Z didn't want him to tell XII whatever it was, so she put her mind on that kid and he stopped—just like that! He turned around and started walking back. That's how powerful she was.

"She told me once, 'You're the only one that's ever been able to work with me.' I liked her. I don't care what anyone else says, she was tops with me! I said to her once, 'If only I had your brains!' She laughed. 'You don't need my brains. I'll be the brains; you just do the work!' She wanted things done right. 'I may not always feel like it,' she said, 'but I'm always on the job!'

"I asked her once why she was at the colony. She told me she was there for what she could get out of it, for the knowledge XII had. 'He has something I want,' she said, 'and I'm going to get it—even if it kills me!'"

△ △ △

That summer, Brother XII did an unusual thing: he changed his name to Amiel de Valdes. On June 25, 1931, the following notice appeared in *The British Columbia Gazette*: "I, AMIEL DE VALDES, heretofore called and known by the name of Edward Arthur Wilson, of DeCourcy Island, British Columbia, hereby give public notice that on the 23rd day of March 1931, I formally and absolutely renounced, relinquished, and abandoned the use of my said name of Edward Arthur Wilson, and then assumed and adopted and determined thenceforward on all occasions whatsoever to use and subscribe to the name of Amiel de Valdes. . ."

Exactly six months later, on September 23, 1931, Madame Z changed her baptismal name of Edith Mabel Rowbotham to Zura de Valdes.

Brother XII and Madame Z took their new surnames from Valdes Island, but why did Wilson choose the name Amiel? The most likely explanation is that he identified, in some way, with the Swiss essayist Henri Frederic Amiel, author of the celebrated *Fragments d'un journal intime,* from which he'd quoted in *The Chalice.*

Did the name "de Valdes" symbolize Brother XII and Madame Z's new relationship as a couple? The name change indicates that they participated in some kind of marriage ceremony. For the disciples, however, life at the colony did not change: Amiel and Zura de Valdes continued to rule their subjects with an iron hand.

△ △ △

By now, Brother XII had accumulated a huge sum of money from the monthly donations he continued to receive, as well as from the life savings of families like the Sepulvedas, who had turned over everything to him. Most of the colony's banking was done by Bruce Crawford, who made weekly trips to Chemainus, Ladysmith, Duncan, and Nanaimo to cash cheques and convert funds into gold. American ten- and twenty-dollar gold Eagles, although not in common use, were still widely available at the time. Twice a month, Crawford visited banks in Victoria and Vancouver for the same purpose. According to Bruce McKelvie, Crawford later told him that he'd handled $100,000 in the Chemainus account alone—an enormous amount, considering, for example, that a sawmill worker in the early 1930s earned thirty-five cents an hour or less. On one occasion, Crawford accompanied Brother XII on the *Khuenaten* five hundred miles up the British Columbia coast to Prince Rupert, where the two men bought gold directly from the miners.

Brother XII continued to store his gold using the unique method he'd devised earlier. At night in the kitchen of his house at the Point, he and Madame Z melted wax in saucepans on the cast-iron stove, while stacks of gold coins glinted in the light of the kerosene lamp. Empty mason jars stood on the table. Like alchemists in a medieval workshop, the two bent to their task, filling the jars with gold coins, then pouring melted wax into each jar. The hot paraffin flowed into the spaces around the coins, dimming their lustre as it hardened around them. Like a priest and priestess presiding over an arcane ritual, the pair repeated the procedure many times as Brother XII amassed a fortune in gold.

Bruce Crawford constructed cedar boxes to hold the jars. The boxes were five inches square by nine inches deep, and a jar of gold fitted snugly inside each. Brass screws held down a wooden lid, and each box was equipped with rope handles, so that despite its weight it was easily portable. Crawford was repeatedly pressed into service, usually in the dead of night, carrying the boxes on and off the *Khuenaten* as Brother XII transferred his hoard of gold from one secret cache to another. "He would bury it in one part of the island, and then a few days later, he would dig it up again and take it to some other place," Crawford recalled. Like a pirate captain fearful of losing his booty, Brother XII kept his treasure on the move, hoping to outwit a possible thief. Crawford never knew the total value of the gold, since he wasn't permitted to handle it directly, but he estimated that the sum was a substantial one, judging by the number of boxes he made—forty-three in all.

The Barleys, meanwhile, had been transferred from Cedar to DeCourcy Island. Brother XII assured them that their residency there would be permanent and that, as Alfred put it, "further banging about from pillar to post (hitherto a regrettable necessity) had now become a thing of the past."

Both Alfred and Annie took part in the general work of the colony, although Alfred's tasks were considerably lighter than those of the other disciples, since he wasn't used to heavy labour. Most of the time, he worked as Roger Painter's assistant, cutting wood for the stoves. Barley didn't object to his own work, which wasn't demanding, but he often observed Madame Z zealously driving the other disciples, apparently taking delight in making their lot an unhappy one.

"In short," as he later summed up life at the colony, "there was the *exploitation* of willing service on the one hand, and on the other, the *diversion and sequestration of funds* from the purpose for which they were contributed. To put the whole matter in a phrase, E.A.W. pursued the methods and exhibited the spirit of the famous Mr. Squeers of Dotheboys Hall in his system of education: 'W-i-n-d-e-r, *Winder*. Now go and clean the winders. Then you'll know what winder is.'"

The disciples still weren't given any formal spiritual instruction, although there was a strong emphasis at the colony on the esoteric.

"They gave you what they called your 'inner name,'" Alice Rudy explains. "It was the name of your Higher Self—*Ramathiel*, or *Serathiel*, or whatever. My inner name was *Niadi*. Z told me, 'Never voice it out loud, but if you ever need help, call on this name!'

"They told me I was a young soul—only about a 3,500-year-old soul, which isn't very old. Alfred Barley was an old soul.

He told me he'd never left the earth at some deaths—he just came right back again into a new body. Roger Painter was Simon Peter in a past life, and XII was supposed to have been the Apostle Paul.

"He didn't want anyone reading. One time, he saw me reading something and he said to Z, 'What's she reading? *Take it away from her!* I don't want her reading *anything!*'"

There was one group ceremony that took place that summer on a small island not far from the Point. Dion Sepulveda helped to prepare the site. "We hauled some cement over to this unnamed island and built a square wooden form," he recalls. "Bruce Crawford and I mixed some concrete and poured it in to make this square cement block. Brother XII smoothed it off with a trowel and cut some mystical markings into it. A day or two later, when the cement had hardened, he painted it black and marked off the twelve signs of the zodiac in a circle around it."

Brother XII chose twelve disciples to participate in the ceremony. When he selected Alice Rudy, but not Isona Sepulveda, the former *prima donna* was so jealous she went berserk. She screamed and carried on so much that Roger Painter finally picked her up and tossed her into the ocean to cool her off. Dion waded out to his mother and put his arms around her until she calmed down.

Brother XII gave each of the disciples a short piece to memorize for the ceremony. "Mine was something about Babylon," Alice recalls. "I said to Bruce, 'What's mine about, anyway? Explain it to me!' 'Forget it!' he said, 'Just memorize it, that's all!' Roger said, 'To heck with it! I'm not memorizing mine! I'm going to read it!'"

The evening of the ceremony, the disciples donned hooded blue robes and rowed over to the island. Dion placed a small pile of dried moss and twigs on top of the cement block, while the others took up their positions around the circle. Holding a can of water underneath his robes, Dion then took his place beside Brother XII. The ceremony opened with Brother XII invoking the spirits from the four corners of the earth. At a certain point in his delivery, he raised his arms and cried, "*I now call fire down!*" This was Dion's signal. He threw water on the twigs and they burst into flame. As the fire leapt up, the disciples gazed into the flames and solemnly recited their pieces. At the end of the ceremony, they rowed silently back to DeCourcy Island.

The disciples were impressed by Brother XII's control of the elements. But in retrospect, Dion is sceptical. "It was an easy trick—he had white phosphorous in the damn stuff, I later theorized!"

As the year 1931 ended, the diligence and hard work of the disciples were impressively in evidence. They had cleared ten acres of land for vegetables, had planted an orchard—fruit trees alternating with nut trees—and had built a giant storehouse which they'd stocked with thousands of jars of home preserves. They had a dairy, greenhouses, a chicken house with brooders and incubators. They'd purchased modern farm equipment and had built a sawmill, so they could cut their own timber. Everywhere the disciples looked, they could see the fruits of their labour. They felt proud, knowing they'd reached their goal of making the colony self-sufficient—they had built their "City of Refuge."

In the outside world, the Depression worsened. There were eight million unemployed in the United States. In London, England, there were riots; and in Germany, Adolf Hitler was gaining power. As the world moved on its own timetable towards Armageddon, Brother XII continued to predict disaster: "In the East, I see plagues greater than any yet known to man. In South America, tremendous inundations. In Europe, in the Eastern parts of this continent, the sky is reddened with bloodshed. . ." In a secluded cove at the south end of DeCourcy Island, far removed from the political and social strife of the outer world, Brother XII stood in a rowboat and like an ancient Egyptian boatman used a single oar to propel himself across the calm waters of the lagoon. "First the overthrow—then the Silence—then THE RESTORATION. Think ye on these things."

△   △   △

Early in 1932, an incident occurred which threatened the security of the colony. In Seattle, Carlin Rudy talked to Alice's uncle, Sidney Brashears, and gave him the impression Alice had been kidnapped and was being held on DeCourcy Island against her will. Brashears called Alice's mother in Missouri who said she hadn't received a letter from her daughter for nearly a year; before that, she'd been a faithful correspondent. A burly six-footer, Brashears armed himself with a gun and crossed the border into Canada, determined to find out if Alice was alright.

Brashears arrived in Nanaimo in the last week of February and persuaded Sergeant Jack Russell and Customs Officer H.L. Good to accompany him to DeCourcy Island. As the police launch neared the Point, it was spotted by one of the colonists, who immediately ran to tell Brother XII. In a rage, he stormed out of his house and put a powerful curse against Attorney-General Harry Pooley and the other members of the cabinet, who he believed had sent the launch. He kept cursing so violently for such a long time that the boat had already entered the bay before he suddenly turned and rushed into the woods. Crashing through the underbrush, he flung himself face down in the salaal and lay motionless, swallowed up by the forest floor.

Alice scrambled up the ladder into the attic to hide, while Madame Z ran down the path to the beach. As the three men climbed out of the boat, she greeted them with a torrent of abuse and demanded to see their search warrant. Even the determined Brashears was stunned by Z's ferocious tirade. Since they didn't have a warrant, the police had no choice but to retreat. As soon as the boat was gone, Z went up to Mary Lowell and burst into tears. "I didn't know what I was doing," she sobbed. "I had to do something to take their attention away from Alice—they might put me in jail!"

When Brother XII returned from the woods, he and Madame Z put the ladder up and helped Alice down from the attic. "That's when they got thinking that maybe I'd better scoot," Alice recounts, "because otherwise they could get into a lot of trouble." Brother XII took Alice to Chemainus in the *Khuenaten.* "He told me when I left that he hoped I could come back," she recalls. "And he said, 'Keep yourself to yourself.' What he meant, I don't know. I think he meant stay away from Rudy."

Alice returned to Seattle, where she filed for a divorce from her husband. She says she has no regrets about the way things worked out, but nonetheless feels sorry for Carlin, who eventually lost his mind. "He wanted to go back there, but they didn't want him. He didn't realize that he didn't fit in. They wanted workers, not freeloaders! He was living on Whidbey Island, and he'd go down to the water when he saw a boat. '*It's them!*' he'd say. '*They're coming for me!*' And he'd wade out into the water and wave—that's how crazy he was!"

Alice claims that she never really understood the purpose of the group. "I asked Annie Barley afterwards, 'What was it all about? What were you trying to do?' She told me they were trying to bring in a child, through one of the families there, who would have the consciousness of a Jesus Christ, or something to that effect. My husband knew about it. When we first went there, he gave Mabel a present of a baby sweater, cap and booties. Boy! She blew her top! I guess he wasn't supposed to know that!

"What I didn't understand was why she and Wilson wouldn't be the ones to have this child; they were the ones with the knowledge and the power. But I don't know if Mabel could even have children—she hadn't had any. And if Wilson could have performed, why wouldn't he?

"And another thing—some of them had this crazy idea they were going to live forever. They didn't think they'd die in the physical body. You can't be too bright and think that! They were always going to explain it to me—they were going to write it down—they were going to put it in a book—they were going to put it on tape—but they never did."

Brother XII now seemed to develop an almost pathological fear of the authorities. He ordered all other construction work on DeCourcy Island halted and had the disciples build forts surrounding his headquarters at the Point. Made of rocks, logs and earth, they were cleverly camouflaged so as to be invisible from the water and showed a sophisticated grasp of military tactics and engineering with their intersecting lines of fire. The fortification below Brother XII's house was entered through a trapdoor in the ceiling. Once inside, the concealed occupant had a perfect view of the lagoon and could, as Roger Painter put it, "pop off" anyone coming into the harbour.

The colony's arsenal consisted of a British .303 and a case of twelve 6.5 mm Italian Mannlicher carbines, purchased by mail from the T. Eaton Company in Edmonton, plus a thousand rounds of ammunition. Brother XII kept six of the rifles in a gun rack mounted on the wall of his office and distributed the remaining weapons to those disciples he chose as guards to defend the colony.

"I was rather disappointed in his attitude towards everybody, especially the government," Bill Lowell said later. "I asked him why he was building forts and he said, 'None of your damned business! You are too inquisitive!' Afterwards, he came around and explained that it was for the protection of the people who were there and those who would come after, and that a time was coming when his enemies would come to the island to try to get him, and he didn't want to be taken by surprise."

As part of the defensive measures, Brother XII tried to block navigation between Link Island and DeCourcy Island by dynamiting a tree across the narrow channel that separated them. He told Bill Lowell to accompany him to the "Hole-in-the-Wall," as it was called, and put twenty-five sticks of dynamite in the tree's roots. When Lowell pointed out that the charge wouldn't topple the tree, but would only blow the dirt out into the water, Brother XII swore at him and asked him if he was going to obey. "I would like to have one man in this colony I can depend on!" he said. Lowell put the dynamite in the tree's roots and detonated it. As he'd predicted, the charge blew the dirt out into the water and the tree shuddered, but remained standing. After the blast, there was an explosion of another kind as Brother XII swore mightily because the tree didn't fall into the water.

Brother XII even issued written instructions to the disciples, "Details for Point Defence," which outlined the procedures to be followed in guarding the colony. Sentry duty was in four hour shifts, at 8:00 A.M., 12:00 noon, and 4:00 PM. The women walked from fort to fort, scanning the water for suspicious craft, particularly government vessels, while the men defended the forts, ready to repel any intruder. Most of the disciples didn't take Brother XII's militarism seriously, however. Roger Painter scoffed at it. "We all considered it a big joke," he said; while Annie Barley noted, "He had a mania about that sort of thing. I took it that he was a bit crazy on it and I did it to keep him quiet." But even so, the guards were conscientious in the discharge of their duties, warning off encroaching vessels and occasionally even firing upon curious or unwary boaters who strayed too close to the island's shores. The colony had become an armed camp.

"Brother XII seemed to be preparing for an invasion," Dion Sepulveda recalls. "He built gun emplacements and we did guard duty for him. But about this time of year, things started coming apart at the seams. Brother XII and Madame Z constantly quarrelled. Painter was called over to the Point more often—and, well. . . there was trouble!"

Dion thinks that part of the problem was Roger Painter.

"He was not the Skipper, but he was at least a Third Mate. He assumed a lot of power and he moved people around. Brother XII would give him orders, but he wouldn't obey them. Well, sometimes he would and sometimes he wouldn't. And it was a monument to Brother XII's own lack of captaincy that he didn't haul Painter before the mast and say, 'Dammit! You're fired!'"

The Sepulvedas decided to leave the colony while they could. Fermin talked to a local fisherman and arranged for him to take them off DeCourcy under cover of darkness. One night, at the appointed time, they all hurried down the path to the beach as a boat slipped quietly into the bay. The Sepulvedas clambered aboard and were soon chugging across Stuart Channel towards the lights of Chemainus—and freedom.

The next day, Fermin gathered Isona and the children around him. "We're going to stay in British Columbia," he said. "We're going to be a family again." With some financial help from Maurice Von Platen, the Sepulvedas bought a piece of land near Ladysmith, which they farmed for several years before eventually returning to California.

Dion Sepulveda looks back upon his days at the colony with mixed feelings. Although it was an idyllic time for him in many ways, he now views Brother XII in a much different light than he did then. His judgment of him today is a harsh one:

"My life with Brother XII was a normal, everyday life in which he was a normal, everyday individual. There was never any talk of the Master's work, or of the Master's teachings. I lived close enough to him to see that his demonstrating himself to his students was completely false. He was a false personality to them, which he dropped like a dirty shirt as soon as he was back at the Point. But he knew his teaching well, and he was all things to all persons within that teaching—he could masquerade to anyone. To the vegetarians on the island, he was a vegetarian. He was no vegetarian! Hell, he had the best cuts of meat money could buy! Every ten days, Bruce Crawford and I would go into town with a shopping list and spend hundreds of dollars on food items alone—caviar, gourmet items! No, they didn't talk about the teachings at the Point; they were more worried about their next trip to Nanaimo and getting a load of cigarettes—they were all chain-smokers! But if they got someone over to the Point who they wanted to impress, that was different. Then they would talk in the mystical languages. Very clever man, Wilson—he could represent himself as anything. But it was obvious he didn't believe in the teachings. How could he? He was gaining worldly goods from teachings which said you had to give up your worldly goods! There's a contradiction right there! A person who believed in the teachings would have put the cabin boy on some kind of regimen of learning. Never! It was never attempted! I know nothing about the teaching. Crawford knew nothing about it except how it was being used. Painter laughed at it! He and Bruce would drink beer in Nanaimo and laugh up a storm about how this was really the con of cons—the biggest con game of all time! And it is—in the hands of artists like E.A. Wilson!"

△   △   △

After the Sepulvedas left DeCourcy Island, life at the colony rapidly deteriorated as Brother XII and Madame Z placed even greater demands upon the disciples. "No slaves ever worked harder than the people at the farm," Annie Barley exclaimed. "And they couldn't work without being sworn at and cursed."

"Anybody that came into the harbour, there was some tirade caused," Roger Painter said. "He would order us to drive them out, threatening to ram them with the tug if they didn't get out of the harbour. We were sent out to order them off. He would stand on the shore cursing away, and I would row out in the boat and say, 'The Captain doesn't want you in the harbour—will you get out!'"

Madame Z's behaviour was also becoming increasingly irrational. "She came to me at Cedar once and accused me of doing things I had never done," Mary Connally recalled. "She said I had taken the car and had acted contrary to instructions, and that I should not be allowed to take the car and it was locked up. We never took the car out except on orders.

She gave the orders herself what was to be done. She would tell them to go to Chemainus to get material—and then she would run up and down the room like someone that was crazy. She would throw up her hands and shout, '*Fools! Fools! Damned fools! They have gone to Chemainus and I need the car!*' Well, they had gone to Chemainus entirely on her orders— and that was the first time I thought there must be something absolutely wrong."

Z was especially cruel to the women of the colony. Georgia Crawford worked in the fields from two o'clock in the morning until ten o'clock at night. When she fell down from sheer exhaustion, Z would rouse her to fresh efforts with her curses. One of Georgia's jobs was working in the potato warehouse, a shed nine feet by fifteen feet, where she had to sort and stack one-hundred-pound sacks of potatoes piled three tiers high to the ceiling. It was brutal work and after three days she couldn't go on. She was then given the job of goatherd. Following her charges over the steep terrain of DeCourcy Island, she fell and hurt her knee, which swelled up to twice its normal size and caused her excruciating pain. But Z refused to let her rest or minister to the injured limb, and when Georgia was an hour late getting the goats back into their pen, she was banished to Valdes Island.

"I had to gather my things together and walk over the bush trail with them on my back," she later explained. "It was agony. The pack was heavy and I had to sit down every few feet to rest my knee. The tug was going around in the afternoon, but I was refused permission to put my things on it. I fell every three or four steps. Then I had to row from the Point to Valdes."

Another time, Georgia was given the job of painting a shed that was built out over the edge of a cliff. She painted the three outer walls, but could only paint the wall facing the sea by hanging on precariously with one hand and reaching around with the other—risking serious injury should she fall to the rocks twenty feet below.

Why did Georgia submit to such treatment? "I had to do it,"

she explained. "I did not want to be parted from my husband. I had been parted from him for six weeks earlier—and I did not want my soul destroyed."

Brother XII's writings had described a colony of brotherly love, where members would live in an atmosphere of truth and honesty, and where only a voluntary discipline would prevail. But the conditions at the Brothers' Center were exactly the opposite.

"I wasn't there long until I found out I wasn't in a brotherhood of love," Bruce Crawford said later, "but in a brotherhood of hell. The only time I saw a live brotherhood was during the eleven months that he was away, because after they came back and set up their rule and government, there was nothing but blasphemy and cursing and contradictory orders. It seemed impossible to do anything to please them. I often wondered whether that long sea-trip didn't render them somewhat insane or something, because I never saw such actions."

Annie Barley also noticed that Brother XII appeared to be quite a different man from the charming gentleman she and her husband had first met in Southampton. "We often wondered if they didn't put on a show for us, especially at full moon," she recalled. "It was either that they were insane people or that they were taking drugs."

The hapless disciples who incurred the displeasure of either of the colony's leaders would receive the full force of their fury. Arms upraised, Madame Z would stamp up and down in front of the wretched offender, calling down "The Power" to smite the object of her wrath.

"I saw him stand and curse those people," Annie Barley recalled, "and when they got away from him, one by one, he was left there standing and cursing with his hand up, until he couldn't speak. He would go back trembling to the house with his voice gone—and that was the occurrence ten times a day, pretty nearly every day."

Why did the disciples stand for such abuse? "You stood for it for this reason," Crawford later explained. "Each one in turn was supposed to be loyal, and it was such a mental dominance for the sake of loyalty that if you raised your hand to protest any order, you might be separated from your wife or immediately deported from the island, and you would be destitute in a strange country."

The disciples were even subject to food rationing. A slice of brown bread with a spot of jam and one teaspoonful of tea to twenty gallons of water was the typical daily ration. When the disciples came over to Cedar to work, they were ravenous. Mary Connally took food out to them while they worked in the fields. "I thought it was the most terrible thing in the world to work people like that—without food," she recalled. "They were almost in the condition they would have stolen food, they were so hungry."

Mary was horrified by the stories the disciples told of conditions on DeCourcy Island: "They were told to kick men and throw them in the water, and if they didn't do absolutely as they were told, they were sent off the island without any money. These people had given everything that they had—and they were sent out stripped."

It was not until one after another of the disciples were cast out and those remaining realized, as Barley put it, "that this might go on indefinitely, until *all* had been made to run the plank in this way, and the Skipper left alone on the ship with his cronies and the booty, so to speak, that joint action became an imperative necessity."

The crisis came with the appalling treatment of Sarah Puckett. The seventy-eight-year-old retired San Francisco schoolteacher was told by Madame Z that she must drown herself by falling backwards out of a rowboat, so that her spirit could return to the colony and report on the afterlife. Sarah took this bizarre assignment seriously. For three consecutive evenings, she allowed herself to be rowed up and down in the deep waters off the Point. But each time she tried to throw herself backwards out of the rowboat, she was unable to do so because she failed to hear "the little voice" that she believed called every good Christian to heaven when it was his or her time to die. At the end of her third macabre cruise, Madame Z heaped such abuse upon Sarah for failing to do her duty for the cause that the despairing woman broke down and wept.

The conditions at the colony were now so dreadful that the disciples asked Barley to draft a letter for them to Brother XII. Alfred drew up what was in effect a "Declaration of Independence," which was signed by nine of the disciples and presented to Brother XII on May 15, 1932:

> To The Brother, XII:
> There has for some considerable time past been a growing sense of dissatisfaction and bewilderment at the conditions of life on this island—or rather, one should say, at the methods of administration pursued by the two responsible heads. This now growing to a climax, the possibility is foreseen of any one, or all of us, on some occasion which proves the "last straw" suddenly leaving self-restraint and taking action that later might be regretted. We therefore ask that a meeting be called at which all shall be present, and an explanation given which will render existing conditions tolerable, or, alternatively, an assurance that the state of things which we find unendurable shall come to an end.

Brother XII read the letter and was outraged that his actions should be questioned. He refused to hold the meeting. Instead, he interviewed each of the disciples separately and tried to create dissension within the group. Even now, some of the disciples were inclined to regard his refusal to meet with them as one more test of their earnestness.

Two weeks later, on the evening of June 1, Brother XII invited Mary Lowell and Edric Agate to his house since he'd drawn up a new will that he wanted them to witness. In the event of his death, everything would be left to Zura de Valdes. After he'd read the will aloud, the two signed it. Then Agate said goodnight and Mary went upstairs to sleep.

At two o'clock in the morning, Madame Z came into Mary Lowell's room and woke her up. "Mary," she said, "now that I've got everything in my name, I'm going to get rid of that outfit at Cedar and that outfit at the Point. I'm going to have things my way!"

Brother XII came in and sat next to the bed. He obviously wanted Mary's sympathy. "I'm going to run all these people off," he said. "They're no good!" He proceeded to denigrate the disciples, calling them vile names, and ended the conversation by saying, "There will be no one left except Agate and myself. He would like to have a woman here. I want you to promise to stay."

Mary was shocked by the request. "Why, I couldn't make such a promise," she replied. "I couldn't leave my husband."

The following day, Brother XII invited Annie Barley to his house for tea and during the visit told her he was concerned about her future. "If Alfred should die or become sick, have you any means of your own by which you would be able to live?" he asked. When she said she hadn't, he offered her the Cedar property, so that she'd have something that could be turned into money. Annie was suspicious of the offer, knowing how cunning Wilson could be, and said she'd have to think it over. "If you would accept it, my mind would be very much relieved," he said, before saying goodbye to her in a most friendly manner.

After discussing the offer with Alfred, Annie decided to accept it, even though the property was a financial liability since the taxes were heavy and hadn't been paid that year.

Annie reasoned that if the disciples were thrown off DeCourcy Island, they'd be destitute in a foreign country and would need a home—the property would provide one. The next morning, she informed Brother XII of her decision and he executed the papers giving her title to the land.

A few days later, Brother XII began taking the disciples to Cedar in the *Khuenaten*, two or three at a time. It would be the last they would ever see of him. Only a few loyalists, such as Agate and Harold Krause, remained on DeCourcy. The Barleys were the last to leave. "We were sent away a little more courteously than the others," Annie observed, "but still we were sent."

The colony on DeCourcy Island was now deserted—its houses vacant, its machinery idle. The sun beat down on the farm, with its abandoned buildings and desolate fields. The wind rustled the dry grass. At the Point, the waters lapped gently against the sandstone ledges of the lagoon as the *Lady Royal* rode at anchor, her sails hanging listless in the heat. Brother XII's dream had ended in the silence of a summer's afternoon and the solitude of a deserted community.

On the morning of June 5, 1932, the disciples gathered in the auditorium of the Center Building at Cedar. The atmosphere was charged with emotion as they openly discussed, for the first time, the extent of Brother XII's tyranny over them, and the fear and oppression that had ruled their lives. As they shared their experiences, they gained strength, and by the end of the meeting they had made a decision: they would stay together as a group and carry on the Work to which they'd dedicated their lives—but without Brother XII.

CHAPTER
XII
Rule Thou the Shadow

I n the law offices of Harrison and McIntyre on Bastion Street in Nanaimo, Victor B. Harrison was working at his desk when his secretary opened the frosted-glass door and announced that a delegation from the Aquarian Foundation was there to see him. Led by Roger Painter, the half-dozen members of the group crowded into Harrison's office, where they stood nervously for a moment before Painter announced that they wanted Harrison to represent them in a court action against Brother XII.

The disciples immediately launched into an account of how Brother XII had defrauded them. Mary Connally explained that she'd given him twenty-three thousand dollars after spending only a few hours with him in a Toronto hotel; Barley said he wished to sue for the return of the money he'd contributed, since he hadn't intended it for Wilson's personal benefit, but for the common welfare of the community. Harrison wrote everything down and assured the disciples he'd fight for them.

A few days later, Harrison drove out to Cedar to meet with the group again. As they'd instructed, he brought with him the young daughter of a mutual friend, since the disciples believed the presence of a child would somehow protect them from Brother XII's influence.

When Harrison and the girl arrived, they were hurriedly ushered into the Center Building through the back door. Painter explained that Brother XII had a spyglass and might be watching Cedar from DeCourcy. During the meeting, he kept going nervously to the window to see if a boat was coming over from DeCourcy Island.

"I was only about thirteen or fourteen years old at the time," remembers Roma Conroy. "It was quite an experience to see grown people terrified. I've never seen anything like it—the fear on the faces of these people. They were terrified of what he might do."

The disciples told Harrison about a mysterious house that Brother XII had built high up in a towering fir, so cleverly concealed no one would suspect it was there. He would retreat here for days at a time to meditate. Harrison wanted to see the house, so the group started out for the tree. As they approached it, Bill Lowell became so weak he could hardly walk.

"He couldn't keep on his feet," Harrison recalled. "He almost sat on the ground. And he kept looking back towards DeCourcy Island, which you could easily see from Cedar. I'm convinced he was under the influence of hypnosis—he must have been."

When the group arrived at the tree, the disciples drew back, overcome by fear.

"Come on, follow me up!" Harrison exhorted them. "Don't be afraid! We're in a lawsuit now; we have to show the court what this is all about!"

Harrison climbed up the wooden steps nailed to the trunk and disappeared into the branches of the tree. He climbed higher and higher until he finally reached the house. Opening the door, he stepped into a large wooden room that was empty except for a metal bedstead and mattress in one corner. On the wall, there hung a framed copy of "The Invocation of Light."

Bruce McKelvie, now the managing editor of *The Victoria Colonist*, was in Ottawa at the time, reporting on the Imperial Economic Conference. He received a letter from Harrison, telling him he'd been retained by two of the disciples to file suit against Brother XII. McKelvie returned to Victoria and waited eagerly for news that the cases had been officially filed. The weeks passed and he heard nothing further. He finally drove to Nanaimo to ask Harrison what was causing the delay.

As McKelvie recounts in his book *Magic, Murder, and Mystery*, the lawyer gloomily explained that he couldn't get the disciples to proceed with their cases.

"Why?" asked McKelvie.

"Do you remember that case in the police court in 1928, and how England's lawyer fainted?"

"Yes."

"That's it: they say that he was knocked over by the black magic of Egypt, and they're afraid that if they start action, they'll all be killed by similar dark powers. Then there was the disappearance immediately after of Bob England—and that has never been explained."

A few days later, McKelvie drove to Cedar-by-the-Sea with his twenty-year-old nephew, Neil McKelvie, to meet with the disciples. They were conducted into the auditorium, where two chairs were placed against a blank wall and twelve more arranged in a semi-circle around them. Everyone sat down and the disciples proceeded to tell McKelvie of the manner in which Brother XII had treated them.

"There is nothing wrong with the religion," they repeatedly stressed. "It is sound and true. It's Wilson; and the only thing we can believe is that he's not himself, that the powers of darkness have taken control of him."

Neil McKelvie was struck by the mental and emotional state of the group. "They seemed to be in a trance, or as if they had just awoken from a deep sleep," he recalls. "They looked like zombies with their haunted eyes. They were so fearful, they'd almost jump if you raised your voice. They were virtually appealing to my uncle to help them in some way."

"I understand you are afraid of Brother XII's magic?" McKelvie asked, looking around the half-circle of frightened faces.

"Yes," answered Painter.

Another member broke in: "Do you know he tried to kill Mary Connally with black magic last Tuesday, but we knew of it through occult means. She left her house and spent the night with Mrs. Barley. Bruce Crawford slept in her house and all night he had to wrestle with the black influence!"

"Yes," admitted Crawford. "In the morning, I was mentally and physically exhausted; I have hardly recovered yet."

McKelvie looked at the distressed disciples. He realized he'd have to come up with an ingenious solution to help them conquer their fear.

"This is Egyptian magic, isn't it?" he challenged them.

"Yes," answered Painter, "the most virulent kind."

"Pooh!" McKelvie snorted, snapping his fingers. "You've forgotten the first principle of magic!"

Painter and the others immediately sprang to their feet, demanding to know what he meant.

"I mean just what I say," McKelvie declared. "Don't you know that where there is magic native to the soil, no foreign magic has any potency?"

The disciples looked at him, speechless.

"And here you are," McKelvie continued, "living on one of the sacred grounds of the Cowichan Indians. Here, they made their magic. Here, they made their medicine. Here, the young men went through their warrior tests. Ye gods, the very ground is impregnated with magic! *As long as you are here, nothing in the world can harm you!"*

The disciples stared at McKelvie, stunned by this revelation; then a look of tremendous relief flooded across their faces and they all crowded around him, expressing their profound gratitude.

McKelvie and his nephew returned to the car. Roger Painter was the last one to say goodbye and he assured the reporter that the disciples would now proceed with the lawsuits. McKelvie drove away, delighted with the outcome, while Neil curled up in the back seat and fell into a deep sleep, exhausted by the experience.

On September 24, 1932, Mary Connally filed a claim against Brother XII, now legally known as Amiel de Valdes, in the Supreme Court of British Columbia for $42,100, plus $10,000 in personal damages. She named Zura de Valdes as a co-defendant in the suit. Mary charged that all of their representations to her were completely false and were part of a scheme "to deceive, ensnare, and delude the plaintiff of her money, property, and labour."

On November 7, 1932, Alfred Barley also filed suit against Amiel and Zura de Valdes, suing them for $14,232; he claimed he'd been the victim of a confidence game.

Three months later, on February 2, 1933, Wilson filed his defence. He denied the allegations made against him and asserted that the funds of the two plaintiffs had been given voluntarily and had only been used by him in the furtherance of the work upon which he was engaged. He stated that his books and other writings were "written under the overwhelming inspiration of spiritual forces, and were only intended for those whose consciousness of spiritual realities would permit them to read with understanding."

In the period immediately preceding the court cases, Brother XII initiated a new series of psychic attacks against the disciples. Kaye Kirchner, a Seattle mechanic and one of the twelve disciples banished from DeCourcy Island, was a victim.

"I was paralyzed by Brother XII for six weeks," he later told *Toronto Star* reporter Alexandrine Gibb, "and walked around like a drunken man for that time."

Gibb also talked to Arthur O'Sullivan, a brawny workman from Lethbridge, Alberta. "I was trying to follow the henchman of Brother XII around," he told her. "I thought if I tagged this 'Black Agate,' as they call him, I'd find his Master. I saw him get on the boat for Vancouver, and when I went to get into my car, I was suddenly stricken. It was just as if I'd been hit on the head. I couldn't drive: my arms were dead, my head felt the size of a balloon. I was paralyzed by the power of black magic. It didn't leave me for an hour, and for days I had a sore head."

On the morning of April 26, 1933, the disciples arrived at the court house in Nanaimo for Mary Connally's case against Brother XII. There in the front row of the courtroom they saw the "Black Dupe," Edric Douglas Agate.

In *Magic, Murder, and Mystery*, Bruce McKelvie described the role he played in helping the disciples overcome their fear. As he entered the court house to report on the day's proceedings, Victor B. Harrison came running up to him.

"Good Lord!" the lawyer exclaimed. "I can't get them into the witness box!"

"What's the matter?" asked McKelvie. "Brother XII hasn't turned up, has he?"

"No, but it's this damned Egyptian magic again! They say that Wilson has a satellite here who has thrown a spell around the witness box, and if anyone of them steps into it, he'll die!"

McKelvie thought for a moment, then realized his mistake: he'd localized the disciples' protection from Brother XII's magic to Cedar-by-the-Sea.

"Can you hold the Judge for ten minutes?" he asked.

"I think so," Harrison replied, starting for the magistrate's chambers, while McKelvie dashed across the street to the Malaspina Hotel. He remembered that in his luggage he had a double labret, or lip ornament, worn by the women of the Queen Charlotte Islands when the white man first came to the Pacific coast.

Grabbing the bit of stone, McKelvie puffed back to the courthouse. He met Roger Painter in the corridor, pulled him into an empty witness room and shut the door.

"See this, Roger?" he asked, cupping his hands around the labret.

"Yes, what is it?" Painter inquired, peering at the curiously-shaped ornament.

"It's the greatest charm on the coast," McKelvie assured him. "It used to belong to the most famous of Haida medicine women. As long as you are in association with that, no power under heaven can hurt you!"

Painter's face lit up. "Lend it to me," he begged.

"Lend it. Lend it? Why, man, I'd almost as soon lose my life as to lose that!"

"Oh, lend it to me!" Painter pleaded.

"How long?"

"Just for this case."

"Well, swear I'll get it back," McKelvie ordered.

Painter went down in a deep bow and solemnly pledged to return the labret at the end of the trial. McKelvie handed it over to him and he hurried away to inform the others.

Every witness, according to McKelvie, entered the witness box holding the labret, looked Agate straight in the eye and delivered their testimony.

The trial proceeded. On the stand, Mary Connally testified before Chief Justice Aulay M. Morrison that Brother XII had broken his trust and proved himself unfit for the Work he had set out to do for humanity:

"He did not fail until he came back from Europe, and when he came back, he started fooling us fast, until he smashed up everything that was capable of being smashed. It took him one year and six months to absolutely demolish everything and it was that demolishing, and the diabolical manner in which he did it—not only to me, but to others with me—that has made me come here and demand that those lands which were purchased for a certain purpose and a certain work be returned to us who are now living together at Cedar."

"What is his nationality?"

"He is an Englishman by birth. He doesn't look like an Englishman, though."

"How old a man is he?"

"He is fifty-four or fifty-five, I think. He is very swarthy, very dark. He is very much like the exhibited pictures of Mephistopheles."

When Harrison asked about Zura de Valdes, Mary explained that she lived with Wilson as his secretary and housekeeper.

"Doing general utility work?"

"Yes, bossing everything. He hid behind her skirts entirely. She did all the dirty work for him; and someone has said—was it Kipling or Bernard Shaw?—that the female of the species is more deadly than the male. Well, it certainly happened in that respect."

"Did Wilson ever tell you how you were to regard her?"

"He wrote to me once in a letter that she was his eyes, his ears, and his mouth; and she has told me with her own lips that what she said was absolutely the same as 'The Brother' said, and that her orders were his orders."

Mary explained that it was under Z's orders that she was moved to Valdes Island. She described the wretched conditions on the island and told of the brutal labour imposed upon her and the other colonists:

"I don't believe it is possible to conceive of any human being forcing people to work the way those people did us; and I cannot imagine people being such infernal fools as we all were; but that is the truth, and nothing but the truth."

Justice Morrison asked why the colonists didn't go to the authorities for help. Mary explained that they were under Wilson's mental domination and that he'd deliberately cultivated an atmosphere of mutual suspicion and mistrust:

"He has separated husband from wife. He vilified each friend to the other friend. He made me do the work I did without rhyme or reason. It is the most iniquitous and diabolical form and procedure that has ever taken place.

"I don't believe there has been a penal colony in the world, no penitentiary, no slave colony that was ever operated under more horrible conditions than this place over there was operated—and besides that, there was this thing hanging over people about their souls."

Mary explained to the Chief Justice that she was also claiming personal damages of $10,000, although "the damage to my physical body is something that cannot be paid for."

Harrison called witness after witness, who all corroborated Mary's testimony. Many said that she had understated, rather than exaggerated, her case.

"The story that she has told of the loads she carried and of the way in which she toiled has been minimized by her," Leona Painter declared. "She slaved!"

Frank Cunliffe, counsel for the defendants, astonished the magistrate by submitting no defence.

"There is no defence?"

"I have no witnesses," replied Cunliffe.

Justice Morrison awarded Mary her claim in full of $26,500, ownership of the DeCourcy group of islands, four hundred acres on Valdes Island, and special damages of $10,000.

The following day, Alfred Barley's case was heard, and even more secrets of the cult were aired before the curious spectators who packed the courtroom. Roger Painter, the long-haired former "poultry king" of Florida, gave the most sensational testimony of the trial when he described how Brother XII had tried to kill his enemies with black magic.

"It would be impossible to tell the story of such a hell on earth," Painter testified. "I was under terrific tension day and night. I didn't know what might happen, even into the possibility of losing my own life.

"The whole island, as I can look back through it all now, the whole scheme was to drive you into intense fear and confusion, so that you were glad to go and leave your money and goods behind, regardless of what it might cost you. That was the operation. . . We understood that we had to surrender everything. We believed in it. We did it."

Painter then related details of the occult procedure that Brother XII had used against his enemies:

"Now, in a particular case, the most tremendous mental domination that I have ever seen exhibited by any man, or any group of people, was by that man. He mentally endeavoured to control the mentality, the soul of everybody that came near him. If you raised one little finger, one thing in opposition, implacable hatred was given to you from that time on; and if need be, he would even put into operation what I call etheric work, working on the mind and body of a man. He even murdered him."

Mr. Harrison: "Have you any example that you can give of his trying to murder people by that mental process?"

"I certainly have."

"Can you mention the names?"

"I can mention plenty of names. I got a letter from him while he was in England, requesting me to go to work immediately on Mr. Pooley, the Attorney-General of British Columbia."

"In what way?" asked Mr. Harrison.

"To sever his etheric body from his physical body, that he might die."

"Any other persons?"

"E.A. Lucas, attorney in Vancouver, and Mr. Hinchliffe. Now, I don't know Mr. Hinchliffe's particular position in the government at Victoria, but I know that in this letter he said that he had opposed him in his request on the marriage relationship; and he was very bitter and said it was needful that he should be removed. And then there was Maurice Von Platen and Alice Von Platen, whom he instructed me to proceed against in an endeavour to sever them from their physical bodies."

"Would it be acceptable to construe it as physical force against these people?" asked Chief Justice Morrison.

"Not physical force; he didn't use that word."

"If I were to pick up that letter and read it, would it be a fantastic construction for me to say that I was to go and kill that person? Have you got any of those?"

Painter replied that he didn't have the letter: Brother XII had instructed him to return it, and Painter had mailed it back to him in Panama.

"You cannot recall the substance can you, or any of the phrases?" asked Harrison.

"No, not particularly. The letter as a general thing is clear in my mind, but I couldn't repeat the exact language; and he made this remark in the latter part of the letter: he said, 'Now, Abner, old scout, go to work and have me a scalp by the time I arrive home.'"

Painter then proceeded to describe an assassination attempt which he'd witnessed upon Brother XII's return:

"Now then in arcanum work, people sit in a circle, or a triangle, or in whatever shape they may elect to sit in. I found that all his work was towards, what we term in occult parlance, black magic of a most devilish kind. I side-tracked that work. He couldn't touch the one that he tried to injure because I side-tracked it. He even kept up this arcanum at twelve o'clock at night, and I have heard people say they did not believe in these things, but generally, if one will have a little intelligence and dig deeply, they will find that much wickedness has been committed by such things."

"Were you present at any of this?" Justice Morrison asked.

"Yes."

"Describe what you saw."

"You have an arcanum when there are three in the operation. There is the defendant sitting in one position, and Zura de Valdes sitting in another position, and myself sitting in another position. Now, we make certain statements to invoke certain powers—invisible, of course, your lordship—and the commission—whatever you want to establish, or work to be done in the etheric or mental realm—was done by the one that laid down the arca, and that was invariably Wilson. Oh, it would take months to relate all the things!"

"What did he say?"

"Well, for instance, he would stand a man up there in his imagination, someone that he hated, that he had this implacable hatred for. Like, I'm telling you that he stood up there one that is known locally in this town, and that is George Hobart, residing at the present time at Cedar-by-the-Sea."

"What did he say?"

"He would stand him up there in the center in his imagination, and he would then begin his tirade, cursing and damning that spirit, and then going down this way with his hand, and that way, cutting what they call the etheric, which is the finer body, from which the physical gets its life. The operation was supposed to—that is, the physical organism, as I understood it from him, the physical organism would gradually become depleted and die."

Painter accompanied his testimony with a vivid demonstration of this process of mental murder, slashing the air with vertical and horizontal strokes of his hands as he showed how Brother XII would quarter the torso of his intended victim.

At the end of the two hour hearing, Chief Justice Morrison awarded Alfred Barley his claim in full of $14,232; he later declared that the two cases he'd heard against Brother XII were "the strangest cases ever to come before a Canadian court of law."

$\triangle \quad \triangle \quad \triangle$

Mary Connally and Alfred Barley had won their court battle, but how they would realize their claims was a mystery. Brother XII and Madame Z had fled DeCourcy Island and their whereabouts were unknown. Shortly before the court cases, however, they'd vented their rage by making a raid on the colony and vandalizing the premises.

At the farm, houses had been pillaged and wrecked. Windows were broken, doors removed or torn from their hinges, and crockery smashed against the walls. The water-tanks had been punctured by bullet holes, fruit trees were uprooted, and the farm-equipment was either missing or damaged beyond repair. In the schoolhouse, desks had been hurled out through the windows with such force that their cast-iron fittings had broken on the ground. One of the cabins had even been crushed by a huge tree felled deliberately onto its roof.

At the Point, houses had been hacked and ripped, their doors, windows and cupboards removed or smashed. In one house, a kitchen cabinet had been torn off the wall and deliberately burnt in the yard outside. Brother XII's own house hadn't been spared. He'd gone through it with an axe in a destructive frenzy. His collection of model ships lay splintered on the floor, mingling with the shattered glass and broken frames of water-colours and etchings. In his study, books had been spilled from the shelves, papers were strewn everywhere, and the floor was littered with debris. There were huge gashes in the polished wood of his writing desk.

In the lagoon, the *Lady Royal* had been scuttled with a charge of dynamite. She lay on her side in the shallow waters, a hole blown in her hull just above the keel. Another explosion had shattered her mast, and her skylight and deck lights had been smashed with an axe. The beautiful sailboat Brother XII had loved was now a battered hulk abandoned on the beach.

Alfred Barley inspected the premises, making careful note of the damage. He discovered some evidence of Wilson's possible use of drugs. In a cabin formerly occupied by him, Barley found a metal box that contained needles for a hypodermic syringe. He also discovered some Trinitrin tablets, some medicine from Steadman's that Wilson took for his heart, and a small bottle of an unknown drug, labelled in Wilson's handwriting, "Ignatia, Z." Barley reasoned that the vandalism had been carried out only days earlier: a piece of Sunlight soap in a soap-tray, although dry on top, still had a few drops of water clinging to the underside.

Alexandrine Gibb of *The Toronto Star* was one of the reporters who talked to the disciples. She interviewed them in the Center Building, where she saw signs of Mary Connally's former life—a Persian carpet, a beautiful black and gold shawl, and a piano. The Asheville socialite was wearing a tweed skirt, torn stockings and muddy shoes when she spoke to Gibb. Her hands were roughened by hard work, her nails discoloured and broken.

"I cannot tell you what agony I suffered," she told the reporter. "I was abused, threatened, made to scrub floors, carry heavy loads, and I expected at any time to get shot in the back. Brother XII turned from a saint into a devil. He forced me to till the land, and he made the rest of the colony stand over me and make me work."

"Yes!" Painter broke in. "Her that used to have fifteen bathrooms in her own home!"

Painter had been plowing a muddy field when Gibb arrived. Rising up in all his filthy majesty, his eyes glittering with a weird light, he brandished his fist in the air and shouted, "He was the focal point of all evil! I am the focal point of good! I fought his evil powers!"

"You didn't have to stay with Brother XII," countered Gibb.

"We dared not leave. He would shoot us in the back. He drove the women into the fields and made them work from two o'clock in the morning until midnight. He made us believe that we must distrust each other. We were all warned to beware of the others. The entire colony seethed with fear, distrust, and black magic. Besides, he had the boats—we were marooned on the island."

"What do you mean by black magic?" asked Gibb.

"He would control our bodies. He forced us by his will power. The women were forced to carry big loads through the forests on the islands. They were taken from one island to another and left there alone at night. He drove us onwards with curses and foul language. We were slaves in reality."

"But why did you submit to his slave-driving methods?" asked Gibb.

"Just a test put on us by Satan himself. Those who survived it are here. The many who couldn't stand it have left. In the past four years, more than two hundred people have come and gone. They were not fitted to enter the Gateway of Truth."

△   △   △

In October 1932, six months before the court cases, Brother XII and Madame Z left DeCourcy Island. They travelled directly across the Strait of Georgia to Roberts Creek on the Sechelt Peninsula, about twenty-five miles north of Vancouver. Agate, who had been working as a real estate agent for the firm of Lowen, Morfitt and Harvey, bought property for them three miles north of the Union Steamship landing, registering it in the name of Harold Krause. Here, in a clearing in the bush several hundred yards from the waterfront, Brother XII and Madame Z went into hiding.

Agate and Harold Krause hauled supplies to the site in the *Khuenaten,* and Krause built a comfortable cabin on the property for the pair. He also built a secret room in the hollow stump of a giant cedar tree, where the couple could retreat if necessary. The room had wooden ledges for sleeping, and there was even a tiny compartment hidden behind a sliding panel in the rear wall, where they could further conceal themselves further. According to one account, Brother XII stored his gold at Roberts Creek under a sail taken from the *Lady Royal.*

An enormous quantity of supplies had been left behind at the colony when Brother XII and Madame Z decamped. These included vast reserves of flour, sugar, meat and feed that had been shipped by boxcar to the colonists at Chemainus, lumber and other building materials, coffee, tea, baby food, matches, blankets, four thousand jars of home preserves that the women of the colony had worked night and day to put up, and enough clothing to last for ten years.

Brother XII instructed Agate to sell everything to Bill Coats, who lived on nearby Gabriola Island. Coats bought the goods "for a song," as Roger Painter put it, and worked twenty hours a day for weeks transporting his haul to Gabriola. Coats's windfall included Brother XII's complete set of British Admiralty charts of the world—a stack that sat eighteen inches high and weighed over two hundred pounds—and the colony's arsenal of guns and ammunition. He later opened a store with his bonanza, making a comfortable living for years after selling off supplies that had been stockpiled for Armageddon.

Agate, who was wanted by the police as a suspect in the vandalism of the settlement, was now using the name "John Murray." He was Brother XII's link with the outside world, picking up his mail from P.O. Box 1177 in Vancouver and running errands for him in the *Khuenaten*. Agate occasionally visited his younger brother in Vancouver, Percy Mansfield Agate.

"Edric was a queer one," Percy recalls. "He had queer ideas, but he was a brain, alright. He didn't say much about this Brother XII business—just that he thought he was a brilliant man."

Agate dated his brother's sister-in-law, a girl named Ruth Johnstone. She recalls that they drank together in several West End hotels, took walks in Stanley Park, and occasionally toured the harbour in the tug. Agate was a fine pianist, liked to read *Weird Tales,* and joked that Ruth was born under a fire sign. "He was a loner," she says. "He never told you where he was going or what he was doing. He used to say, 'Don't be surprised, Ruth, if one of these days I'm gone.'"

Brother XII and Madame Z left Roberts Creek in April 1933, shortly before the court cases in Nanaimo. In Victoria, a bellhop at the Empress Hotel reported that the two were registered there during the trial and that they'd even had the latest editions of the newspaper delivered to their room, so they could follow the progress of the cases. By the time the police checked out the story, the pair had vanished.

After leaving Victoria, Brother XII and Z cruised north in the *Khuenaten,* hiding out in secluded coves and inlets as they worked their way up the coast. In Seymour Narrows, they picked up their mail at O'Brien Bay, then cruised north into Discovery Passage. At Sonora Island, thirty miles north of Campbell River, they encountered a British Columbia Provincial policeman, who wished the unlikely-looking tourists "good fishing" before moving on to more pressing duties. He apparently hadn't read the newspapers.

Leaving the northern tip of Vancouver Island behind, Brother XII and Madame Z followed the Inside Passage to Prince Rupert, western terminus of the Canadian National Railway. Here they either sold or scuttled the *Khuenaten* and boarded the train for Montreal. With the gold stashed in steamer trunks, one can imagine them settling into their berth for their journey east. It had been an easy, almost leisurely escape.

Edric Douglas Agate was waiting for them in Montreal. Like Agate, Brother XII was now travelling under a false name: he'd assumed the initials and surname of Mabel's first husband, John Coulson Skottowe, to become "Julian Churton Skottowe." From Montreal, the three fugitives booked passage for England.

△ △ △

Three months after the court cases in British Columbia, Brother XII was living quietly and anonymously in a small farmhouse called Cowley Lodge, near the village of Kentisbury in northern Devonshire. On July 31, 1933, he made a new will under his assumed name of Julian Churton Skottowe, leaving everything to Mabel Skottowe. The will was witnessed by a shoe retailer from Fremington named Charles Patterson, and by Agate, who signed as "James A. Murray, Gentleman."

Brother XII remained at Cowley Lodge for another year. On August 10, 1934, he was issued a new passport in London. He and Mabel left almost immediately for the continent. Their destination was Neuchâtel, Switzerland, and the trip was urgent—possibly a matter of life and death.

Swiss records show that Edward Arthur Wilson and Mabel Skottowe arrived in Neuchâtel on August 24, 1934. An elegant, prosperous town with a population of twenty-five thousand, Neuchâtel had a distinctly medieval charm, with fountains, picturesque streets and many fine patrician houses built of yellow sandstone. Alexandre Dumas once wrote that the town looked as if it were carved out of butter. Across the placid waters of Lake Neuchâtel, there was a breathtaking view of the entire middle range of the Alps, from Mont Blanc to the Bernese Oberland. The two new arrivals were met by Dr. Roger Auguste Schmidt. Born in nearby Thielle-Wavre and a graduate of the University of Geneva, Schmidt and his family had spent a year at the colony in British Columbia before returning to Neuchâtel on June 15, 1933. Since Schmidt had been Wilson's personal physician, it seems likely that Wilson had come to Neuchâtel to seek medical aid.

Dr. Schmidt was working at the Clinique du Chanet, a private medical clinic located at 1 Route de la Chanet, on a hill overlooking Neuchâtel. The clinic specialized in the treatment of tuberculosis and its patients came from all over Europe. The four-storey building had tall windows which opened onto balconies, so that patients could be wheeled outside to inhale the invigorating mountain air. For at least part of his sojourn in Neuchâtel, Wilson was a patient here, although not for tuberculosis, under the care of Dr. Schmidt.

During the same period, Wilson rented an apartment at 19, Rue des Beaux-Arts, a handsome building in the center of Neuchâtel, close to the lake and to the University of Neuchâtel. Only two blocks away was the Musée des Beaux-Arts, with its famous eighteenth-century clockwork dolls of Pierre Jaquet-

Droz, which had fascinated European royalty. Nearby in the Museum of Ethnology, Wilson probably took the opportunity to examine its fine collection of Egyptian antiquities. Or perhaps, from the Quai Osterwald, he contemplated the tranquil waters of the lake and the majestic panorama of mountains in the distance.

Wilson's enjoyment of the pleasures of Neuchâtel lasted only a few short months. With the setting sun crowning the summit of the Alps with gold, he died in his apartment in the Rue des Beaux-Arts at nine o'clock on the evening of November 7, 1934. The death certificate, which was signed by Dr. Schmidt, provides few clues to his last days. Schmidt indicated the cause of death according to the International Classification of Causes of Death as: "XIV. 148 a," which means *sclerosis of the coronary arteries = angina pectoris*. Wilson was fifty-six years old. The death certificate lists him as *celibataire*—single.

On November 11, Wilson's body was cremated at the Cimetière de Beauregard, and his ashes sent to his family in England—probably to his mother in Bournemouth, who died three months later on February 14, 1935 (Wilson's father had died six years earlier). The Swiss authorities have no record today of the identity of the individual to whom the ashes were sent.

On November 14, a one-line notice of Wilson's death appeared in *Feuille d'avis de Neuchâtel*. His Swiss identity card was stamped "DÉCÉDÉ." Mabel Skottowe apparently left Neuchâtel soon afterwards, since her identity card reads, "The certificate of nationality was returned to the D.P.N. [Departement de Police de Neuchâtel] on March 2, 1935, because she left in November, 1934." Of Brother XII's treasure, forty-three boxes of gold coins weighing an estimated half a ton, there was no trace.

The lack of detailed information about Wilson's death has led to a great deal of speculation about the circumstances surrounding it. Some writers have portrayed Mabel Skottowe as keeping a stone-faced vigil by the bed, waiting for the sallow, sunken figure of Wilson to die. They have even suggested that she may have helped him on his way with a discreetly administered dose of poison. Did Mabel have access to a certain numbered Swiss bank account? Upon his death, did she quietly take possession of the $400,000 that he had accumulated during his seven-year reign as Brother XII? And did she then step out into the streets of Neuchâtel, ending her liaison with the man with whom she had shared so much?

Edric Douglas Agate, who may have been able to provide the answers to such questions, arrived at his parents' home in Wallington, North London, shortly after Wilson's death. He told his family that he thought that war with Germany was inevitable, and that he didn't want to be involved in it because he didn't wish to take life in any way. He then packed up a large quantity of his mother's china, saucepans, blankets and other household goods. Agate loaded everything into several large steamer trunks, plastered labels all over them and set off for America.

Months passed and his parents heard nothing more from him. Finally a letter arrived from southern Oregon. Edric wrote that he was living in a remote area, high up in a pine forest. He'd built himself a log cabin, and was growing vegetables and keeping some chickens. When he needed money, he cut down a tree and sold it in the town below. Edric's father was angry at his son for the kind of life he'd chosen, and tore up the letter. That was the last that was ever heard of Edric Douglas Agate.

Mabel Skottowe was seen on only a few occasions over the years. Sometime in the late 1930s, she was recognized in the lobby of a luxury hotel in Zurich by a woman from Nanaimo, then living in Europe. She was also seen on the street in Montreal one time. Alice Rudy reports that Mabel lived in Seattle for awhile, where she tried without success to start a group of her own, based upon Brother XII's teachings.

Mabel was seen for the last time in Nanaimo in the 1940s. A

former workman at the colony was walking along Front Street when he noticed a late model black sedan pull up to the curb. A haughty-looking woman in furs stepped out. He was amazed to recognize Madame Z. He went up to her and asked what had brought her back to Nanaimo. *"Morbid curiosity,"* she replied; she then stepped back into the car and was driven away.

△　△　△

The news of Brother XII's death in Switzerland did not reach the disciples at Cedar until several years later. On September 3, 1938, Mary Connally wrote to Alfred Barley that she had received information that Wilson had died some time ago, and that it might be possible to recover something from his estate on the basis of the judgments which were given against him in their favour.

Barley was initially dubious. "We have heard many rumours about E.A.W. from time to time," he replied, "that he is here, there, or somewhere else, and hitherto I must say I have not been inclined to consider seriously any of them. You do not say what the source of your information is, but can you be certain it is not just another of these rumours?"

Mary wrote back that Wilson's death had been confirmed, and that Frank Cunliffe, in conjunction with the London firm of Craigen, Hicks and Company, was making a claim for her against his estate, which consisted of an unclaimed inheritance from his parents of 2,156 pounds, 3 shillings, and 11 pence. Barley agreed to join forces with Mary in order to finance a claim against the estate.

Wilson's creditors included Mary Connally, who filed a claim for £8,250; Alfred Barley, who filed for £1,600; Dr. Roger Schmidt, who filed for £140 for medical services rendered; and Margery Wilson, his first wife, who filed a claim from Auckland, New Zealand, for £720, arrears of payment under a separation deed. Since Wilson's estate was insufficient to pay his debts, his creditors only expected to receive payments proportional to their respective claims.

The hearing opened in London at the Royal Courts of Justice in the Strand on October 13, 1939. It was delayed by the outbreak of World War II, and eventually adjourned *sine die*. In the spring of 1943, it was re-opened. After dragging on for another three years, the claims were finally settled by the Chancery Court on October 2, 1946. By that time, legal costs had consumed most of the value of the estate and the payments to the claimants were nominal.

Brother XII was dead, yet several people close to the story, besides Alfred Barley, had difficulty believing it. Bruce McKelvie, for one, held that "a man who was so false in life could not be depended upon in death." In a talk he gave in 1953, McKelvie stated: "The death report may be true, but it is quite possible that he is still alive." Even Victor B. Harrison, the lawyer who acted for Barley in making his claim against the estate, declared: "It is just expedient for him to be considered dead."

Could Wilson have faked his death in collusion with Dr. Schmidt? In many courts of law, a death certificate is not considered *prima facie* evidence of death. Death must still be proved by corroborative means. If Schmidt were devoted to Wilson, he could easily have signed the death certificate, while the body that was cremated could have been the corpse of a patient in the Clinique du Chanet who had died at the same time.

There are a number of reports of Wilson being sighted after November 7, 1934, the official date of his death. The most persuasive and intriguing is that of the late Donald M. Cunliffe, the son of Frank Cunliffe and himself a lawyer. The events he witnessed took place when he was a boy of twelve, but always remained vividly in his memory. He writes:

> In the latter part of June 1936, as our family was preparing to move to our summer home at Qualicum Beach, my father received a telephone call, as a result of which he told us that

our departure would be delayed for two or three hours. Our car was partially packed, and he invited me to accompany him to the home in Cedar of "Lady Mary" Connally.

I was given a jigsaw puzzle to work on, while my father and "Lady Mary" discussed their business with some degree of urgency. I remember hearing reference to "The Brother," discussion of boat schedules, and references to San Francisco. Near the end of this discussion, which lasted for about one hour, my father stood up, and in closing his briefcase, said words to the effect that, "There seems to be nothing left but for me to try to meet him in San Francisco, and it might be better if I took my family along." At this point, I was most attentive and heard "Lady Mary" say, "I am not sure that he would be willing to see you there," whereupon my father replied, "We will just have to take our chances." In the car on the way home, my father told me that I was not to mention anything of this to my mother or to my sister until he said so.

About a week later, Frank Cunliffe announced to the family that they would be driving to San Francisco for a two week holiday. Donald Cunliffe resumes his account:

When we arrived in San Francisco, we checked in at either the St. Francis or the Sir Francis Drake Hotel. My father made a number of telephone calls to attorneys in San Francisco and to one shipping line, inquiring as to the whereabouts of a ship, the name of which I have forgotten. The following day, I was given the option of going shopping with my mother and sister, or accompanying my father on certain business calls. There was no question that I would have nothing to do with the shopping trip, so I went with my father to a bank building and sat in a waiting room for about half an hour, while he talked to a lawyer in the bank building. Following that, we went to another bank with the lawyer and withdrew what to me appeared to be a sizeable amount of cash. This was placed in a bag and then placed in the other lawyer's brief case. Following that, my father made another telephone call which I could not hear, and we went to lunch together. Following lunch, we went to the docks and boarded a liner. I was put in the charge of a seaman or officer, and was shown around the ship, while my father vanished into the bowels of the same ship. My tour having been completed, I waited at the head of the gang-way and eventually my father re-appeared, without the brief case, with a man I can best describe as being quite pale, who was dressed in white and had a white wide-brimmed hat. I was particularly struck by his eyes, although I cannot recall why. There was no shaking of hands as my father and the man parted. He spoke only once, which was, "I shan't see you again, Cunliffe, but I may be in touch." My father said nothing, but looked extremely grim.

I was naturally very curious about this transaction, and asked my father who the man was, whether he was Brother XII, and my father said that he was not permitted to say, but that he hoped he never had to deal with a man like him again.

That appeared to be the end of the incident, for I took it more or less instinctively that my father wanted no further discussion of the matter.

When asked to describe the man on board the ship in more detail, Donald Cunliffe recalled: "There was an impression of whiteness about him. His hat was white—his clothes were white—his shoes were white. Everything about him was white. And these gleaming eyes! This man *lived!* He was vibrant! I met Churchill once—a totally dissimilar person—but the same kind of electric energy seemed to flow through him."

A year later, the same man made contact with Frank Cunliffe again. Donald Cunliffe relates:

In July of 1937, I was at home on a Saturday morning,

preparing for a trip to Smithers, B.C., for a visit to my uncle and cousins. My father was not yet home from the office, and my mother and sister and the maid were at Qualicum Beach at the summer home. The telephone rang, and it was a long distance call for my father. I informed the operator that he was not yet home, but was expected shortly. The operator, while the line was still open, addressed the calling party as a "Mr. Wilson," and wished to know whether he would call again, or whether my father should place the call on his arrival at the house. After some humming and hawing, the male voice instructed the operator to have my father call the Trans-Atlantic operator in Gibraltar. About five minutes later, my father arrived home and I passed on the message to him. He appeared to be quite surprised, but sent me from the room and as I left, I heard him calling long distance. Shortly thereafter, I returned to the room and found my father sitting in his chair with a perplexed look on his face. I asked if that was the same man I had seen the year before at San Francisco, and my father said, "Yes," and (something which was most unusual for him to say), "I hope he goes to hell!"

Later on that afternoon, I went back to my father's office with him and he showed me the corporate seal of the Aquarian Foundation, and said when he died to keep this, because some day it would become a matter of history.

Donald Cunliffe's fascinating account certainly suggests that Brother XII may have fabricated his death in Switzerland in 1934. If so, he wouldn't have been the first person to successfully accomplish this subterfuge. In the absence of further information, his death remains another elusive piece in the mysterious puzzle of his life.

△   △   △

In spite of their intention to continue the Work, the former disciples of Brother XII didn't remain together at Cedar. Over time, the group dispersed. The Crawfords were the first to go, returning to Florida soon after the court cases. "Hereafter, I'm not taking orders from no one," Bruce Crawford declared. "I'm just gonna listen to my Higher Self."

Bill and Mary Lowell were the next to leave. In September 1935, they loaded up a trailer and drove to Oceano, California, accompanied by Sarah Puckett. In a farewell note to friends at Cedar, Sarah wrote: "We kept the faith, we did our duty, we finished our task. We have been released from 'old obligations' and are now free to bid farewell."

In the fall of 1937, Roger Painter, the Barleys, and Kaye Kirchner moved to Marysville, Washington, north of Seattle, where they started a berry farm. During a long walk through the berry canes, Painter tried to persuade a newlywed couple who were visiting the farm to join the community, telling them that by using the knowledge he possessed they could have a child who would become the next Christ.

Alfred Barley strained his heart in the hot springs outside Portland, Oregon, and died on May 14, 1940, at the age of sixty-eight. He was cremated and his ashes were scattered in his favourite grove of trees, which his friends always referred to afterwards as "Alfred's grove."

Roger Painter died on August 13, 1950, at the age of seventy, also from a heart attack. After his death, his wife Rachel went to the police and told them Painter had hypnotized her before he died and was controlling her from beyond the grave. She was committed to a mental hospital in Sedro Wooley, Washington.

Annie Barley moved to Halcyon, California, where she lived like a pauper, alone in a single room. Her books provided solace, but there were times, she said, when she was so lonely she even welcomed visits from people she didn't like. Annie collapsed and died on May 22, 1955, at the age of eighty-five, while baking bread.

Mary Connally remained in British Columbia after the

others left, moving to DeCourcy Island, where she lived with her secretary, Margaret Whyte. When Margaret left, Mary stayed alone on the island, hoisting a white tablecloth up a flagpole every morning so that her friends across the channel would know she was all right. She never found it in her heart to condemn Brother XII, and before she returned to North Carolina, she told Victor B. Harrison: "For the old Brother, I'd give that much money again, if I had it to give." Mary died on October 20, 1947, at the age of seventy-six, in the Blue Gables nursing home in Asheville, North Carolina.

Spurred on by persistent rumours that Brother XII's gold still remained on the islands, treasure seekers over the years ransacked and dismantled the colonists' cabins, dynamited the wells, and dug all over Valdes and DeCourcy Islands. But to this day, no one has yet announced the discovery of Brother XII's treasure.

One unusual find was made quite by accident. Sam Greenall, Mary Connally's caretaker on DeCourcy Island, was keeping chickens in one of the colony's outbuildings. Every time he went inside the chicken house, he bumped his head—for some reason, the floor was built too high. He decided to lower it. When he ripped it up, he discovered a trapdoor. Certain he'd stumbled on the gold's hiding place, he excitedly pried up the door and peered into the gloom. Seeing a bundle, he eagerly reached down to examine it more closely. It was a loose roll of tarpaper. Lifting it out of the vault, Greenall unfurled it and read the inscription. Scrawled in chalk on the dark surface was a final message from Brother XII, an angry shout from the past: *"For fools and traitors—nothing!"*

△   △   △

What became of the original seven Governors of the Aquarian Foundation? Although they were each affected in different ways by Brother XII, there's little doubt he left his mark on the lives of all of them.

Will Levington Comfort felt responsible for leading so many astray with his initial endorsement of Brother XII. His last two novels, *Apache* and *The Pilot Comes Aboard,* were praised by critics, but failed to achieve the commercial success for which he'd hoped. Comfort died in Los Angeles on November 2, 1932, at the age of fifty-four, of complications arising from acute alcoholism—a death, it was said, hastened by his disillusionment over his experience with Brother XII.

Coulson Turnbull's association with Brother XII damaged his reputation as an astrologer. He never went back to Santa Cruz, but remained in Vancouver, where he continued to practise astrology. The strain of his involvement with Brother XII, including his collapse in court in 1928, left him, in many respects, a broken man. He died in Vancouver on July 30, 1935, at the age of seventy.

Maurice Von Platen returned to Pasadena, but continued to spend summers at Cedar. He rarely discussed Brother XII, but in a small booklet he published in 1934, *A Modern Pilgrim's Progress,* he makes a veiled reference to him in the chapter "Vampires I have Known," in which he warns readers that "the most dangerous of all vampires is that person who knows the occult side of the Universal Law. Through his knowledge, he deliberately draws upon the life force of the persons who do not know how to protect themselves against his attempts. The result of this may even be DEATH." Von Platen died in Pasadena on January 17, 1938, at the age of seventy-eight.

Joseph Benner started his own organization after breaking away from Brother XII. In 1932, he published the monthly lessons he wrote for his students as a book, *The Way to the Kingdom.* Despite financial hardships, Benner struggled on for many years, believing there was a real need for his teachings. He died in Akron, Ohio, on September 24, 1938, at the age of sixty-six. In a strange sequel to his death, Benner's metaphysical classic *The Impersonal Life* was discovered in the 1960s by Elvis Presley, who eagerly embraced its philosophy and gave away hundreds of copies to people he met—an unexpected connection between Brother XII's disciple and the King of Rock 'n' Roll.

Edward Lucas continued to practise law in Vancouver. He often joked about his time with Brother XII, remembering him with affection. Lucas remained a Theosophist, but one with his own unique interpretation of the philosophy. He believed, for instance, that the Masters of Wisdom would never allow the atom to be split. Lucas sold a screenplay to Twentieth Century-Fox for a Janet Gaynor film, but the movie was never made. An expert on the Civil War, he appeared in 1957 on the television quiz program "The $64,000 Question." He won his round, but the show was cancelled before he could return. Lucas died in Vancouver on December 14, 1961, at the age of seventy-eight.

Phillip Fisher, who had a nervous breakdown in 1928, never fully recovered his mental health, continuing to suffer from paranoia and delusions of grandeur. He became obsessed with the idea of conspiracies to the extent that he believed the cartoon figures on the cover of the British magazine *Punch* contained clues to the existence of an international plot to take over the world. Fisher formed a society to research the conspiracy and renamed his house at Boat Harbour "The Punch Bowl." In 1954, he tried to found a "City of Light," modelled after the Aquarian Foundation, in the hills behind Chemainus. In his latter years, Fisher would become extremely agitated whenever he talked about Brother XII and had to be hospitalized several times as a result. Fearing that a further disturbance would kill him, his doctor refused to ever let him be interviewed on the subject. Fisher died in Nanaimo on March 10, 1979, at the age of eighty-four.

△   △   △

Conventional methods of research have yielded a great deal of information about Brother XII. But what insights into his life could an experienced and reputable psychic provide?

The author thought it would be interesting to find out. He therefore decided to consult James H. P. Wilkie, a psychic of international renown.

A dark, heavyset man in his late sixties, Wilkie first became aware of his psychic powers as a boy growing up in the Scottish highlands. He would often see a large brown hand beckoning him to follow it across the moors. Hours later, he would awaken from an overshadowed state, sitting on some desolate rock miles from home, brooding on half-remembered glimpses into an unseen world. The hand, he later learned, belonged to his spirit guide, a four-thousand-year-old Egyptian priest named Rama, whom he soon began to channel. Trained by the famous Scottish medium Jean Thomson, of Kircaldy, Fife, Wilkie has lectured widely in North America, spoken at universities and foundations, and been consulted by businessmen and celebrities. On September 13, 1962, on a Toronto radio program, he predicted the Cuban missile crisis six weeks before it occurred. He has also consulted with U.S. astronaut Edgar Mitchell, following Mitchell's ESP experiments in space. Wilkie's feats have been chronicled in Allen Spraggett's book *The Unexplained* and in his own book *The Gift Within*.

Wilkie receives visitors in a drawing room richly decorated with his collection of art. Paintings cover the walls, and religious icons, woodcarvings, Japanese silkscreens, and marble and bronze statuettes crowd together in a bizarre display of his eclectic taste. A statue of an Oriental mandarin stares inscrutably across the room towards the bust of an Egyptian pharaoh. Wilkie, who had no prior knowledge of Brother XII, sat on a Victorian settee surrounded by scarlet cushions. Given a photograph of Brother XII, he concentrated for a few moments, then began to speak rapidly as he received impressions about him from his spirit guide, Rama:

"His name was given to him from the spirit world by his guide. It was more his connection with Christ than it was astrological. I feel as if he knew Christ at one time—or thought he did. He looked upon himself as a previous disciple who'd become exalted.

"In his youth, he was a restless soul. He had terrible depressions. He was in contact with forces he had to obey; he knew he couldn't lead a normal life. There was a time when he lived alone, completely isolated—he wanted no contact with a human being. I feel that when he was younger, he was more pure, more ordained psychically and spiritually.

"I see him writing in trance-like states. If you could watch him in those moments alone, you'd see his face change completely as his guide came through. He had visions of the past and the future—he received information about Egypt. I am given the word *Luxor*. That particular site in Egypt was important to him.

"He was what we would call insane many times. He was definitely possessed. He worked with angels—spirits of all kinds, sometimes of the lower order. He drew radical, earthbound souls to him. He drew powers of darkness—he was drawing evil around him at different times. When you write about him, you are writing about many different personalities in one lifetime.

"Did he ever give himself another name? If he did, I'm not surprised—he changed his name as he evolved. This man had the power to take a person's life and change it totally. It wouldn't take him long to get followers. Those who believed in him still believe in him—the effect he had on them is something they will never forget.

"He wasn't a normal man: he was a unique, almost freakish individual. Yet he had a great spiritual gift. He was meant to be a leader and to have a group. That was his destiny. His background didn't really shape him—he was born to be a messianic figure of some kind."

Wilkie was asked to describe Brother XII's female companion, Madame Z:

"She was an eccentric person, a mystical type. She was fascinated by ritual magic. She had a flair for the theatrical. She was the kind of person to whom witchcraft and black magic appeal deeply.

"She saw the powers he had, and was attracted to him—he appealed to her animal and mystical nature. She saw forces in him she could blend with and use. She was more fanatical than evil—she was both good and evil, clever and mixed-up."

Asked about Brother XII's death, Wilkie answered: "His death came at the right time, karmically. But it wasn't a normal death. It was planned. It was as if someone finally cornered him, and then—through either poisoning or physical attack—murdered him. I know that someone was doing something to him physically. Someone planned his death."

"Could it have been Madame Z?"

"She may have instigated his death through her knowledge of either drugs or magic. He might have had a massive heart attack, but it wouldn't appear to be murder. I see her as if she were possessed. She could be an evil person, but he was never an evil person."

"Is Madame Z still alive?"

"I am not psychically aware of her death. I'm picking up a hot country—somewhere that's cheap to live, where it's easy to survive. I'm picking up heat—tremendous heat—and a foreign language. South America, possibly. She planned to go there. This woman had terrific powers—she could live a long time. But I have the feeling her life is over. She's in some place where people look after her—a home or a hospital. She's mentally confused—she may be crippled or insane. It meant so much to her to have the power; then she felt empty. Guilt—she felt tremendous guilt."

"Did she take Brother XII's money?"

"She lost the money—she never had the luxury it could have brought her."

"Do any of Brother XII's papers survive?"

"She took all of his papers with her after his death. They're in a suitcase somewhere. She keeps it locked. She guards it constantly—she won't let it out of her sight. It contains all his writings—his journals, his mystical diaries, all of his secrets. If someone goes near it, or tries to take it from her, she becomes terribly upset—she becomes frantic. It may be that her death alone will reveal its contents. Again, I'm picking up that she's confused. She could be just another alcoholic."

"What was the message that Brother XII wanted to bring to the world?"

"He wanted to be a prophet, a martyr, a messiah. He believed that thousands would follow him, that he would play an important role in history. But his vision became corrupted; he couldn't live the laws he taught—he wasn't spiritual enough to uphold a true humility. He wanted to control, instead of lead. He became a spiritual megalomaniac.

"It could have been a wonderful mission, but the ego killed him—the selfishness, the greed, the fanaticism—the passion to believe that he could become a god on earth. He was self-destructive. He killed himself."

Wilkie paused, then said something surprising:

"I feel his presence in the room now. He's telling me he's advanced, he's evolved in the spirit world. He apologizes to his followers and he tries to help the ones he hurt. He thanks those who still believe in him and those who've forgiven him. Each time someone forgives him, he can go further spiritually because that soul has helped him.

"He wants people to know he's not dead. He may have died physically, but he's not dead. *There is no death*: that would be his message now. He wants people to know that—*there is no death*.

"He's already emerging spiritually—he's advancing in the spirit world, preparing for the day when he'll come back with complete humility to serve in whatever manner he chooses."

Brother XII was certain that he would be remembered. "My work will live," he declared. His books and his writings constitute his legacy and deserve to be recognized as a significant contribution to the literature of the occult. Had he lived up to his ideals, his work might be better known today. Still, he added his own revelation of truth to that of the mystics and prophets who came before him—and those who will follow.

The events of Brother XII's life reflect many of the meanings of the twelfth house of astrology, traditionally the house of karma and mystery. It is the house of self-undoing, imprisonment, bondage, secret enemies, sacrificial service and mystical inspiration. Representing the assimilation of all experience, it signifies completion, fulfillment, transformation—and ultimately, the transfiguration of the individual, nation and race. As the house governing reincarnation, the twelfth house is said to be the one from which the future saviours of mankind will spring. Brother XII's life can be interpreted in the context of these various meanings.

The story of Brother XII is a dramatic example of the dangers inherent in following teachers who claim divine authority, and is a reminder of the vital need to distinguish between the true and the false prophet—and the often tragic consequences of a mistaken devotion to a religious leader. Ironically, Brother XII repeatedly warned in his own writings against such a danger, teaching that man is his own Master and Saviour, and that the disciple's allegiance must be to the Higher Self.

Brother XII was certainly one of the most remarkable religious figures in recent history to exploit his knowledge of the occult to amass a personal fortune. Yet he was more than just a fraud and an imposter. In spite of his personal failure, he gave eloquent expression to the spiritual truths upon which he believed the foundations of the New Age would be built. The message he proclaimed stands as a truth beyond his life, an ideal towards which people today can still aspire:

"'Give up thy life if thou would'st live,' saith Wisdom. Surrender self. Thus shalt thou come to know thy true Self, which knows not birth nor death, but is eternal. Rule thou the shadow—thine outer form; subdue its will to thine, the lower to the Higher. This is the way of Life."

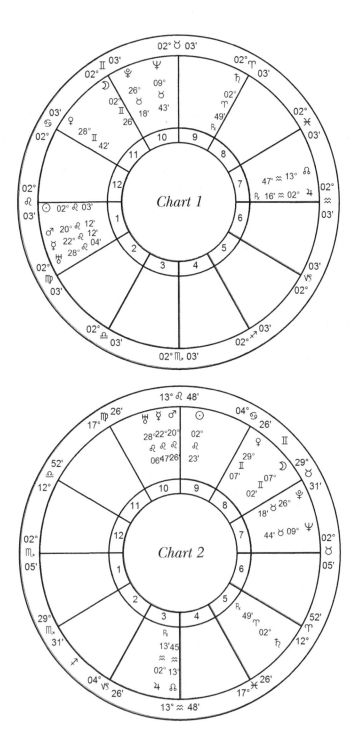

358

The Birthchart of Brother XII

Edward Arthur Wilson
born July 25, 1878
Birmingham, England

Commentary by Zachary Casper

No time is recorded for the birth of Brother XII. Therefore, the technique of the Solar Chart, cast for sunrise on July 25, 1878, is here employed (Chart 1). The main feature of this horoscope is the stellium or cluster of four planets, including the Sun, in the sign Leo. This is a fixed fire sign, giving self-assurance, dignity, leadership, and often spiritual aspiration. It is also a sign of self-indulgence and pleasure. The aspects or angles which the Sun makes to other planets is considered very important in any horoscope. Here, the Sun is opposing Jupiter in Aquarius and squaring Neptune in Taurus; both of these aspects are considered difficult for the expression of the higher side of the planetary energies involved. The Sun-Jupiter opposition gives enthusiasm and a fascination with religion, as well as an affinity for travel. It also denotes recklessness and physical appetites which are difficult to control. According to *Alan Oken's Complete Astrology*, the Sun-Neptune square "usually becomes manifest as a liking for the mystic, occult, and illusionary, but with a strong tendency to get lost along the path. More often, it represents a deceptive individual, one who presents the most advantageous side of himself, while hiding his true nature and motivations." It is interesting to note that both Jupiter and Neptune are particularly connected with religion, Jupiter in a formal way through churches and spiritual hierarchies; Neptune in a more formless or mystic sense. These three planets form a configuration known as a "T-square," which indicates mutual difficulty.

Another outstanding feature of this chart is the conjunction of three planets, Mars, Mercury, and Uranus in Leo. This aspect gives incredible energy and drive, particularly in the mental sphere. Mercury, the planet of intelligence and the mind, receives the raw energy of Mars and is uplifted to a higher plane of thinking by Uranus, the planet of the higher or superconscious mind. Alan Oken writes: "The individual is inventive, original, and very quick to arrive at a correct conclusion without necessarily having to analyze all the data. There is a tendency, however, to be quite opinionated, and one is always eager to express oneself in new and unusually unconventional ways." Uranus is said to rule occult studies and utopian ideals, including communal living.

Two planets were found in Gemini, the Moon and Venus. Gemini is an air sign governing education, communication, and travel. The Moon here gives a personal liking for such activities, particularly discussion and debate in which the individual is pleased to prove the correctness of his viewpoint and convert the listener to his way of thinking. Thus, the power and self-assurance indicated by the Sun in Leo found a perfect outlet through the Gemini Moon for Brother XII to communicate and persuade others to follow his particular views on life. Venus in Gemini tends to give a desire for change and variety in the love-life, which often manifests as short-lived relationships.

The second chart (Chart 2) is cast for 1:00 PM., a time

chosen through intuition and experience as likely the most correct. Here, we find Scorpio rising, a sign said to rule the experiences of sex, death, and regeneration, as well as giving a strong interest in occult or mystic activities. Scorpio is a water sign, befitting an individual who was a sea-captain. In this chart, the Sun is found in the ninth house, which rules religion, philosophy, and journeys to foreign lands. The other Leo planets fall in the tenth house, the house of career, profession, and public image. It is easy to understand why Brother XII became a leader. His ideas, Mercury, were expressed with great energy, Mars, and appealed to others through the higher mind, Uranus. No wonder his message found some public response.

The Moon and Venus in this chart are found in the eighth house, a house associated with Scorpio in astrological tradition. Besides expression of Scorpionic traits, the eighth house gives a talent for the management of other peoples' resources, apparently a specialty of Brother XII. We find in the seventh house the two outermost planets, Neptune and Pluto. The seventh house governs partnerships and marriage, and the presence of two of the most unusual planets here shows that his romantic liaisons were certainly of a different order than is the norm. Such planets, if well aspected, would indicate a partner of remarkable spiritual and evolutionary potential. However, as they are afflicted here, just the reverse is indicated. The squares formed by the Sun and Jupiter to Neptune have already been mentioned; Pluto as well is horribly afflicted, receiving squares from Mars, Mercury, and Uranus. Thus, the power side of Pluto—sadism, revenge, and black magic—would become manifest in his life through his partner.

Saturn, the planet of self-discipline, restraint, and duty, is found here below the horizon, in the fifth house, where it is relatively weak. Saturn in the sign Aries is said to be in its fall; thus the potential good qualities of patience, perseverance, and forbearance would not manifest easily. However, Saturn forms some extremely good aspects to other planets, such as a trine to the Sun and sextiles to the Moon and Jupiter, which indicate the possibility of discipline and simplicity manifesting in the life. Seen in a more occult sense, the good aspects of Saturn represent rewards reaped from previous lifetimes of decent living. Unfortunately, the weak position of Saturn was ultimately not able to overcome the Leonian traits of self-aggrandizement and indulgence in pleasure. Also, the Moon's South Node, indicator of activities performed in past lifetimes, is here found in Leo in the midheaven. This shows that Leo tendencies were brought over from the past in a strong manner and would prove difficult to control. The power of a Leo personality often proves overbearing unless there are planets in Virgo to give discrimination or Libra to give balance, which are absent in this chart.

The problem in this horoscope is that there are too many planets in fixed signs: Leo, Taurus, Scorpio, and Aquarius. These signs give strength, determination, and perseverance, but they need to be balanced by planets in mutable signs, which give intelligence, introspection, and analysis. There are only two mutable-sign planets found here. Cardinal or active signs give the necessary activity for the release of energy in a constructive way, but only one is found here. This horoscope is somewhat reminiscent of that of Benito Mussolini. Like the Italian dictator, Brother XII too came to an inglorious end, with many heavy karmic debts to be repaid in future lifetimes.

Postscript

The waves slapped against the sides of the boat as we drifted alongside the eerily eroded cliffs on the south side of DeCourcy Island. Scrambling ashore, we climbed up a sandstone path to the deserted farm where little had changed in the decades since Brother XII's disciples had plowed the fields and tended their vegetable gardens in the hot summer sun. It was the fall of 2000 and I was accompanied by James A. Santucci, Professor of Comparative Religion at California State University in Fullerton, and a camera crew headed by award-winning filmmaker David Cherniack, who was shooting an hour-long television documentary about Brother XII. Over the next several days, we explored the former haunts of the colony's leader at DeCourcy, Valdes Island and Cedar-by-the-Sea, revisiting the legend of Brother XII and mulling over the implications of his story for our time. Santucci had written the first detailed account of Edward Arthur Wilson's activities in his article, "The Aquarian Foundation," published in 1989 in the academic journal, *Communal Societies*, having been intrigued by newspaper clippings about Brother XII that he'd discovered in the files of Henry N. Stokes, editor of the *Oriental & Esoteric Library Critic*. One of the foremost scholars studying the Theosophical movement and the rise of new religions, Santucci was eminently qualified to place Brother XII in the proper historical context and to provide insight into his character and behaviour in relation to other cult figures he had studied. As we inspected the forlorn shell of the House of Mystery, rummaged through the tumbledown remains of the colony's dilapidated structures, and examined the remnants of a stone fort that had once protected Brother XII's house at DeCourcy, we reflected on what, in the words of former adherent Edward Lucas, this "little brown leaf of a man with a large heart and a rare spirit" had accomplished, what had gone wrong and why.

There are conflicting views about Brother XII. Some people consider him to have been a charlatan from the outset, a devious mountebank intent on duping his gullible followers; others cut him considerably more slack, holding the view that he was a genuine prophet and mystic who was derailed in his mission, someone more to be pitied than condemned. In his review in *BC BookWorld* of the original edition of this book, the respected man of letters George Woodcock observed that at the heart of the story there was "a malign core shining as darkly as a poison-filled Borgia jewel," while Alexander Blair-Ewart, the editor and publisher of the magazine *Dimensions*, was more sympathetic, regarding Brother XII as an initiate who had succumbed to the perils of messianic delusion, his work subverted by negative forces of a greater magnitude than he could transform: "There will come a time when all of these failed messiahs will be seen for what they really are—the frontiersmen and women at the boundary of the New Age, overwhelmed and tragic martyrs who dared great things in a time of troubles, all of them doomed to become the opposite of themselves and afterwards live with the shame and pain of having failed themselves, their vision and their followers."

As I discussed such issues with Santucci, he pointed out that Brother XII possessed all the characteristics of the *magus* or civilized shaman; his ecstatic experiences appeared legitimate, as evidenced in *Foundation Letters and Teachings*, and his purported contact with supernatural beings was an age-old phenomenon and didn't discredit him. Scientific studies of channeling have shown actual physiological changes taking place in the brains of mediums, he added, which made me wonder: was some part of Brother XII's brain overshadowing his personality when he was in trance or was a separate discarnate entity indeed speaking through him?

On Valdes Island, James and I walked up the hill to the former site of the Mandieh Settlement, where Brother XII's soul mate Myrtle Baumgartner had lived in the fall of 1928. We paused to admire the idyllic views of the Strait of Georgia framed by pine trees and to savor the beauty of the spot that she found so comforting during her sojourn on the Island. Myrtle is undoubtedly the most tragic individual in the Brother XII story; she suffered two miscarriages and nearly lost her mind in the process, yet she becomes an even more poignant figure when one reads the letters she wrote to her estranged husband, and realizes how deeply she loved Brother XII. The letters, which were only discovered after the initial publication of this book, were included as exhibits in the divorce proceedings that her husband brought against her, as she'd made no attempt to conceal the fact that she'd committed adultery; rather, the letters were her attempt to explain why she'd been impelled to do so. She wrote that as early as 1920, she saw the man whom she would later recognize as Brother XII in her dreams. In one particularly memorable dream, she was crossing a long and exposed bridge and battling cold and cruel winds as she attempted to reach a figure waiting for her on the other side: "I made little progress, but in the face of almost insuperable odds, I kept right on because *he* was waiting and I must reach him."

I awoke with the firm conviction that somewhere the true one was awaiting me, and in my mind's eye, I had a very clear picture of his appearance. At intervals, I dreamed of him again. Then in 1922 came my long and wonderful Egyptian dream—and this same man again figured prominently in the dream. I knew that I never really loved anyone but *him*—but it never occurred to me that he was on earth in physical embodiment. From 1922 onward, the contact in night consciousness was almost constant. My dream life became my real life, and while I had my outer life and my outer love and outer duties, they truly seemed a means to an end—a ladder upon which I must climb to stand on the mountain top with *him*.

Myrtle added that she knew that the man she met nightly was her "Beloved" because "there was between us a rhythmic electric bliss when in each other's presence that simply left one spellbound, and which when once experienced left absolutely no room for doubt. When you have come into the presence of that one—once—you will never again wonder—you will *know*."

Myrtle claimed that Brother XII was "the one true mate created with me, the only one in all the universe to whom I am truly married," and said that the two of them had used their energy to help her husband overcome his illness, rejoicing when he'd done so. She reiterated that she still loved him, but it wasn't "the great love," adding, "And while I love you very dearly, Eddie, and my heart yearns over you daily, I know and have known for years that my love for you was maternal. That is why it did not satisfy you."

Myrtle went on to describe her initial meeting with Brother XII as follows:

Then in 1926 came a great dedication to the service of humanity, taken also in my night consciousness. This great service was a joint service which I undertook with this Beloved One, with whom I had been in contact for years. Even yet, though, I did not know he was in physical embodiment. Now for the great experience. Upon my arrival at the A.F. Headquarters, I was met at the boat by Coulson Turnbull, and an hour or so later ushered into an office where—well, I can hardly speak of it—I saw walking to meet me this One. I gasped and the expression on his face was of as intense a surprise. It was reunion, and no power on earth, no personality, no principality, no consideration can sever us twain. I *know*. I know and he knows—our experiences have been identical. We both know of the service of dedication to a joint work; we took it together, are fully conscious of all that it entails, and that work is going forward regardless of who individually suffers.

At the time, Myrtle never dreamed of the heartache she would subsequently suffer. To what degree she was mistreated or spurned by Brother XII remains unknown, yet three months after writing these words, she wired her husband: "If you will have me back, may I come? Heartsore and weary."

Myrtle's attempt at reconciliation was cruelly rebuffed; her embittered husband ripped the telegram in half before replying, "Absolutely no!"

Myrtle's letters reveal that Brother XII was evidently telling the truth when he said that he met Myrtle for the first time when she visited the Foundation headquarters, although Robert England testified in court that he'd told him he'd met Myrtle on the train between Seattle and Chicago, a meeting immortalized in *The Vancouver Province* headline: "OSIRIS AND ISIS MET ON TRAIN BETWEEN SEATTLE AND CHICAGO." That encounter, which is such an integral part of the Brother XII story, was reiterated in England's damning letter to Wilson and in affidavits filed by the dissenting Governors, seeking to have the Foundation dissolved, so there seemed no reason to doubt it, despite Wilson's denial, until the discovery of Myrtle's letters. Did England simply get it wrong, making a mistake that became enshrined as fact over time? Apparently so, though it also seems unlikely, as he was an acute observer, a detail-oriented person by nature and by virtue of his professional training. One possibility is that Brother XII lied to England about the circumstances of the couple's meeting, making it appear to be a far more glamorous liaison than it really was in order to justify the controversial affair. Or could Myrtle have intentionally deceived her husband in a key detail in the letter? The divorce papers confirm that Brother XII and Myrtle were together in Chicago, subsequently returning to Cedar, which is why the disciples dubbed her, "The Magdalene from Chicago."

The most likely explanation for the historical confusion is that England was indeed mistaken; Myrtle initially met Brother XII at Cedar, subsequently traveling with him to Chicago to attend the Third Party convention, and later returning with him to the settlement, where her presence was kept a secret.

In this second edition of the book, I have chosen to leave the scene on the train as it stands, since so many of the individuals in the narrative were operating under this assumption concerning the meeting of Brother XII and Myrtle, while pointing out in this postscript that the event likely differed from that described. Though the pair's romantic liaison during a transcontinental train journey was part of the Brother XII legend for years, the discovery of Myrtle's letters illustrates how easily an inadvertent error can lead to a version of history that may be significantly different from the reality of actual events.

Brother XII's abandonment of Myrtle in the aftermath of her failure to produce the next World Teacher undoubtedly contributed to her emotional collapse, yet his actions in the situation foreshadowed his later mistreatment of Mary Connally and the other disciples who had placed their trust in him. How could the same man who had written, "Thoughts, if they are to reach the hearts of men, must be borne upon the wings of Love," end up conducting midnight rituals in the cabin of the *Lady Royal* in an attempt to assassinate his enemies?

Yet as Jim Santucci and I discussed such matters with David Cherniack during the making of the documentary, I found myself asking: did he *really* change? Or was he always a short-tempered, volatile individual who could twist off at the slightest provocation? The earliest example of Wilson's erratic behaviour was in England in 1926 when his application to join the Buddhist Lodge of London under the name "Brother XII," rather than his ordinary name, was refused. According to Buddhist scholar Christmas Humphreys, "He replied like a small school-boy in a huff," while Harry J. Strutton, editor of *The Occult Review*, writing of Brother XII's exploits in hindsight, said that he'd detected in Wilson "a latent wildness and instability, which, to say the least, were disconcerting."

Strutton added that prior to Brother XII's departure for Canada, persons he declined to name had made efforts to have him certified insane. The insanity issue continued to shadow Wilson, for the workmen employed to construct the settlement wondered at times if he was mentally unbalanced, since he would give contradictory orders and erupt into a rage over the smallest thing. And at one point, the dissenting Governors considered trying to have him committed, though Edward Lucas later apologized in a letter, using his affectionate term for his former friend, "If I have thought the Old Man was loony and finally up and said so—well, I suppose that is a way mates have."

Following Brother XII's return to the colony from England in 1930, his episodes of bizarre behaviour, rages and paranoia increased in frequency and intensity, culminating in the frightening image invoked by Annie Barley at the 1933 court proceedings of a demented leader standing with his fist in the air cursing his cringing disciples until he couldn't speak anymore: "He would go back trembling to the house with his voice gone and that was the occurrence ten times a day, pretty nearly every day."

How does one explain such behaviour? Was it caused by drugs or by an incipient insanity? Could there be a darker, unsuspected reason for these debilitating attacks?

In June of 2005, I discovered a fascinating book by Deborah Hayden, *Pox: Genius, Madness and the Mysteries of Syphilis.* It describes how this terrifying disease had afflicted people such as Ludwig van Beethoven, Franz Schubert, Charles Baudelaire, Gustav Flaubert, Vincent van Gogh, Friedrich Nietzsche, Oscar Wilde, James Joyce, Adolf Hitler, and other notable figures of the nineteenth and twentieth centuries. Looking at Brother XII's life through the lens of retrospective diagnosis, the classic signs of syphilis appear. For a start, Wilson's years as a mariner would have provided numerous opportunities for infection. It's a matter of record that he fell sick in the South Seas, thereafter enduring a lifetime of relapsing ill-health, a characteristic sign of syphilis. In addition to his cardiovascular problems, which are frequent indicators of syphilis, he exhibited the classic symptoms of neurosyphilis, especially during the colony's latter days, including irrational behaviour, violent rages, paranoia, megalomania, delusions of grandeur, and an identification with religious, mythic or royal figures. A sense of impending doom is a sign of tertiary syphilis; such fears in Brother XII's case may have been expressed through his visions of war, destruction and death. An obsession with money can be another indicator; Brother XII accused his followers of withholding money from him and obsessively guarded his hoard of gold. Syphilis ravages the physical body, but as Hayden points out, myriads of pale and twisted spirochetes can stimulate the brains of persons infected with the disease to transcendent heights of genius and euphoria.

I returned to my Brother XII research files and rummaged through dozens of cardboard boxes looking for the tapes and transcripts of three telephone calls I had made years earlier. Eventually, I found the call to Nanaimo historian and author Lynne Bowen, who told me the surprising news that when she'd been writing a university paper on Brother XII, she'd spoken to a young doctor who worked in the same clinic as Dr. Alan B. Hall, who Wilson had once seen as a patient. The doctor disclosed to her that it was relatively common knowledge among the tightly-knit medical community that Dr. Hall had treated Brother XII for syphilis.

Bowen told me, "Dr. Hall treated him once a week for a year, and on a couple of occasions, he was taken over to DeCourcy Island to make a house call." When she called Dr. Hall herself to check out the story, he confirmed that Brother XII had visited him once a week for approximately a year for the treatment of a medical condition. When she asked what the condition was, he replied that he couldn't tell her, that it was privileged information.

"And you're sure it was syphilis?" I asked.

"I certainly think it's very likely that he did have it. That was the general view whenever Brother XII's name came up; when the doctors were talking, they would say, 'Oh yes, we treated him for syphilis.'"

In the 1930s, an organic compound of arsenic known as Salvarsan was used to treat syphilis. It was typically injected once a week, so Bowen's description squared on that count. The drug was effective to a degree, though it's tragic to think that individuals such as Brother XII, as well as so many of history's cultural giants, were tormented by a disease that can be cured today, for the most part, by a shot of penicillin.

Following my conversation with Bowen, I called her informant, Dr. Michael Scott-Kerr, who confirmed the syphilis diagnosis. "Yes, that was the case," he told me. "I remember that it was mentioned a number of times, though Dr. Hall kept that information private."

I also called Dr. Hall, who was well on in years at the time, though his voice was still strong on the phone. It was one of the shortest research calls I have ever made, for when the elderly physician realized that I wished to inquire about his controversial patient, he abruptly terminated the conversation.

Wilson's medical records appear to have been destroyed, so it seems unlikely that the documented evidence of his condition will be found, yet reviewing the symptoms, the diagnosis certainly seems to fit. Syphilis attacks the vocal cords, causing hoarseness, a condition that may have manifested in Wilson's rasping voice. It also damages the gastrointestinal tract, its victims typically enduring innumerable abdominal surgeries in a fruitless effort to find relief; this appears to also have been the case with Wilson; according to his housekeeper Alice Rudy, he underwent surgery in Italy on his digestive system and subsisted on a special diet of soft foods. He also suffered from angina pectoris, a condition that can be syphilitic in origin. Wilson's fear that he might die at any time is a typical concern of individuals afflicted with aortic syphilis. He was also susceptible to the cold, another feature of syphilis. Did he withdraw from his followers in the fall of 1929 because he was having an outbreak of symptoms that he didn't wish them to see? Could the impulsivity associated with neurosyphilis have triggered his trip to England? And was his electric energy and messianic fervor caused by the disease's progression? The exalted states he describes in his writings are reminiscent of the mystical excitements of a Nietzsche or a van Gogh, individuals possessed with a sublime vision of life and a genius for expressing their insights into the nature of human existence. In Brother XII's case, his visionary sensibilities may well have been fueled by the disease, its symptoms superimposed upon a personality already in the grip of megalomania.

If Brother XII indeed had syphilis, it makes him a more sympathetic figure. Syphilis was a disease that Carl Jung called "the poison of the darkness" when he described its manifestation in Nietzsche, a phrase that eerily echoed the words that the anguished disciples used when informing Bruce McKelvie that Brother XII had changed. There was nothing wrong with the teachings, they stressed; it was the teacher himself who was impaired: "The only thing we can believe is that he's not himself, that the powers of darkness have taken control of him." Perhaps this malevolent influence was merely their unwitting metaphor for the disease itself.

For those individuals who have left a legacy of intellectual and artistic accomplishment, both in spite of syphilis and perhaps in part because of it, the disease is not necessarily the master key to unlocking the mystery of their lives. It did not give them their genius; they possessed it already, though it may have intensified or extended their gifts, making their drive to create that much more urgent. The convictions that Brother XII held about his mission in this life and the zeal with which he worked to implement his vision were part of his character, regardless of the disease that infected his body, though it may have amplified his innate mystical tendencies and oracular genius; to what extent syphilis both inspired him and insidiously destroyed him will probably never be known.

What to make of his life and work? James Santucci regards Brother XII as a man of extremes, a contradictory, volatile and sometimes cruel individual who expected too much of his followers and was bitterly disappointed when his work never achieved the success or recognition that he anticipated. Brother XII placed certain demands upon his disciples in order that they might experience a breakthrough in consciousness. Though they were harshly mistreated, the disciples accepted these demands as a necessary prerequisite to attaining enlightenment, no matter how abusive their ordeals might seem to an outsider. While not condoning Brother XII's actions, Santucci points out that when one is dealing with spiritual teachers, one is not necessarily dealing with ethical beings: "I don't necessarily find a correlation between ethics and religion. We're dealing with power. And Wilson was involved with the development of power, however he interprets it. He called it enlightenment. This is what he promised. This power is much like fire. It can either cook your food or it can burn you."

Santucci is one of the few observers who has attempted to view the situation from Brother XII's point of view, to understand how he may have felt frustrated by the disciples and why, given his nature and pathology, he reacted so violently: "Think of this as a reaction on the part of a totally committed individual who believed that he was betrayed by his followers, and,

as a result, they deserved nothing. So he gave them nothing—
and disappeared."

Brother XII's disciples were surprisingly forgiving of their
leader. Mary Connally mourned the change in Wilson, declaring, "If the Brother would only come back and be his old
self, we would be only too glad to join with him again, and
forget the past," while Alfred Barley observed in a letter to
The Occult Review that Brother XII's "fatal course of action in
direct contravention of everything he had written shall result
in having educated us into a realization of those truths which
before had been but words on paper."

If one reads Brother XII's works in their entirety, one is
struck by the authority with which he writes and by the clarity
and precision of his prose. The disciples who accepted him as
their teacher believed that he possessed the knowledge and
wisdom that he so eloquently expressed; though disillusioned,
many continued to regard him as having the spiritual power
and insight that he claimed. Truth itself did not change, he
wrote in one of his monthly Instructions, only the forms into
which it was poured, and through which it was imperfectly expressed from age to age:

Only the Wise may know the mystery of the Cycle: birth,
growth, maturity, decay, death—which is but birth into another section of the Cycle—so turns the wheel. He who
imagines the last word spoken, the final revelation made, is
yet far from *the beginning* of Wisdom. It is only with these or
similar thoughts in mind that we may hope to approach the
Mysteries. Such thoughts must flow into the mind unconsciously and without effort; their Source is in That which
is above mind and below it, and from Which mind itself
is born—the worlds of reality, the Gateway to the Temple
of the Mysteries. Man is born of woman, lives out the fret
of life and passes on. Nations rise and fall, creeds blossom
and decay, Teachers and Messengers arise, serve and pass
to further service. Men are left with three things—the tra-

dition of the past, the hope of the future, and the work of today. The last is the sum and substance of the other two. Only Eternal Truth endures. Creeds and religions are but the man-projected shadows of Its light. From It all comes, to It all returns—It is at once the Source, the Sustenance, the Goal.

Brother XII's story is a cautionary tale that foreshadows the various cult tragedies that have occurred in recent decades. He was not just a parlour mystic or armchair theoretician, but someone who possessed real occult and mystical power. He was a maverick and rebel, a man of action who fearlessly tackled contentious social issues and waded into politics with a vengeance. His intensely dramatic life proved once again that truth is stranger than fiction. Yet as he himself observed, initiation is a quaking path to travel and failure is the rule, rather than the exception. Like so many others who followed him, his utopia crashed on the rock of personality, though the best of his writings still shine with a light uniquely their own and will no doubt find an audience again.

Like the restless wanderer of Tennyson's poem "Ulysses," Brother XII sought new worlds, voyaging to the farthest shores of consciousness, his gods, the ancient deities, his disembodied Master, his guide. It is a curious tale, admittedly, but the figure at the center of it can now be more fully understood by a new generation of readers and by all those who find themselves drawn to the power of that strange and singular individual the world knows as Brother XII.

Index

ABBOTT, FORREST, 201
Abbott, Frank, 201
Abbott, Marie Belle, 200-1
Agate, Edric Douglas, 268, 274,
321-23, 329, 330, 338, 339, 340,
343; a.k.a. "James A. Murray,"
341; a.k.a. "John Murray," 339
Agate, Percy Mansfield, 339
Amiel, Henri Frederic, 307;
Fragments d'un journal intime,
307
Aquarian Foundation, 30, 39-
69; appointment of advisory
council, 277-78; *The Aquarian
Foundation: A Movement for
the Unification of All Men of
Good Will*, 62, 159; dissolution
of, 113-26, 127-48, 179, 219-
23, 227-28, 229, 258-59; first
Annual General Meeting, 66-
69, 70, 82-83, 97; fund-raising
for, 56-59, 82, 83-85, 107-9, 307-
8; hierarchy of settlements,
283, 291; membership,

62, 155, 222; objects and
constitution of, 45-46, 117;
political philosophy of, 71-74;
recruitment for, 39-53; second
Annual General Meeting, 81,
97-100; tenets of, 31-32, 279
Astrology, 28, 30, 46, 47, 50, 53,
89, 90, 110, 121, 134, 200, 214,
237, 244, 263, 279, 351, 357;
and reincarnation, 53, 113,
134
Austin, Sir Herbert, 20

BAILEY, ALICE, 52
Barker, Judge, 213, 217
Barley, Alfred Henry, 30-34, 53,
122, 133, 138, 139, 140, 244,
260, 266, 269-72, 275, 277, 278,
279, 281-83, 284, 285, 291, 292,
309, 320, 321, 322, 324, 332,
335, 336, 344, 345, 349; case
against Wilson, 332-35; *The
Drayson Problem*, 30
Barley, Annie, 30-34, 54, 122, 138,

377

Made in United States
North Haven, CT
13 November 2022

26666093R00245